29:

D0678717

From pre-school to post-grad, girls get a different education from boys. They play with dolls more than blocks, they learn to be passive and docile in elementary school, they're channeled into traditional "feminine" occupations in high school and college, and they are often passed over when it comes to graduate fellowships. On the other side of the desk, women teachers are paid less, they advance less, and they're often stereotyped as authoritarian and unfeminine.

Schools reflect the larger society's attitudes toward sex roles, and they are a strong force in perpetuating them. But schools can also be an important laboratory for testing the status quo. This comprehensive collection gathers the best available pieces to show how sexism operates at all levels of education. It also suggests how schools can be reformed to allow both girls *and* boys to pursue their individual interests and fulfill their true potential.

JUDITH STACEY has taught courses on women in education at Richmond College. She is a doctoral student in sociology at Brandeis University. SUSAN BÉREAUD taught one of the first courses on women in education, at Cornell in 1970. She has done research on sex stereotypes in French children's literature. JOAN DANIELS is educational director of Building Blocks, a Montessori school on Staten Island. She is working on development of a non-sexist curriculum for young children.

# And Jill Came Tumbling After

*SEXISM IN AMERICAN EDUCATION*

*Edited by*
**JUDITH STACEY,**
**SUSAN BÉREAUD,**
**AND JOAN DANIELS**

*A LAUREL ORIGINAL*

Published by
Dell Publishing Co., Inc.
1 Dag Hammarskjold Plaza
New York, New York 10017

Copyright © 1974 by Judith Stacey, Susan Béreaud,
and Joan Daniels
All rights reserved. No part of this book may
be reproduced in any form or by any means without
the prior written permission of the Publisher,
excepting brief quotes used in connection with
reviews written specifically for inclusion in
a magazine or newspaper.
Laurel ® TM 674623, Dell Publishing Co., Inc.

ISBN: 0-440-32111-5

Printed in the United States of America
First printing—February 1974
Fifth printing—February 1978

## ACKNOWLEDGMENTS

"Why Are There No Woman Geniuses?" by Anna Garlin
Spencer. From the book *Woman's Share in Social Culture*
by Anna Garlin Spencer. Second Edition. Copyright 1925
by J. P. Lippincott Company. Reprinted by permission of
the publisher.

"Are Women Prejudiced Against Women?" by Philip Goldberg.
Copyright © May 1968 by Transaction, Inc., New Bruns-
wick, N. J. Reprinted by permission of the author and
*Transaction*.

"Toward an Understanding of Achievement-Related Conflicts
in Women" by Matina S. Horner. From *The Journal of Social Issues*, Volume 28, No. 2. Reprinted by permission of
the publisher.

"The Education of Women" by Florence Howe. Copyright ©
1969 by Florence Howe. Originally appeared in *Liberation*
magazine. Reprinted by permission of the author.

"Male and Female" by Evelyn Goodenough Pitcher. Copyright
© 1963 by The Atlantic Monthly Company, Boston, Mass.
Reprinted by permission of the author and *The Atlantic
Monthly*.

"As the Twig Is Bent" by Carole Joffe. From *Journal of Marriage and the Family*, August 1971. Reprinted by permission
of the author and the National Council on Family Relations.

"Are Little Girls Being Harmed by 'Sesame Street'?" by Jane

Bergman. Copyright © 1972 by The New York Times Company. Reprinted by permission of the publisher.

"Children's Books: The Second Sex, Junior Division" by Elizabeth Fisher. Copyright © 1970 by The New York Times Company. Reprinted by permission of the publisher.

"A Report on Children's Toys." Reprinted with permission from *Ms.* Magazine

"The Impact of the Women's Liberation Movement on Child Development Texts" by Zelda Klapper. From *American Journal of Orthopsychiatry*, Vol. 41, No. 5, October 1971. Copyright © 1971 by the American Orthopsychiatric Association, Inc. Reprinted by permission of the author and the publisher.

"Two Lives" by Carolyn Karkosza. Reprinted by permission of the publisher, *Up from Under.*

"Schools are Emasculating Our Boys" by Patricia Sexton. Reprinted by permission of the author. First appeared in *The Saturday Review of Education.*

"Do Schools Sell Girls Short?" by Betty Levy. From *Today's Education: Journal of the National Education Association*, December 1972. Copyright © 1972. Reprinted by permission of the author and the publisher.

"Teacher Interactions with Boys and with Girls" by Pauline Sears and David H. Feldman. Copyright © 1966 by National Association of Elementary School Principals. All rights reserved. Reprinted by permission of the publisher.

"Look Jane Look. See Sex Stereotypes." Reprinted by permission of Women on Words and Images, P.O. Box 2163, Princeton, New Jersey 08540. A complete report of sex stereotyping contained in children's school readers by thirteen of the top publishers. Available for $1.50.

"Sex-Role Pressures and the Socialization of the Male Child" by Ruth Hartley. From *Psychological Reports*, 1959, 5. Reprinted by permission of the author and the publisher.

"High-School Women: Oppression and Liberation" by Jenny Bull. Copyright © 1970 by *Women: A Journal of Liberation*, 3028 Greenmount Avenue, Baltimore, Maryland 21218. Reprinted by permission of the publisher.

"Down the Up Staircase" by Richard Rothstein (excerpted). Copyright © 1971 New University Conference. Originally published in *This Magazine Is About Schools*, Summer 1971. Reprinted by permission of the author.

"Realistic Counseling for High-School Girls" by Iris Tiedt.

From *School Counselor*, Volume 19, Number 5. Reprinted by permission of the author and the American Personnel and Guidance Association.

"Women in U.S. History High-School Textbooks" by Janice Law Trecker. From *Social Education*, March 1971. Reprinted by permission of the author and the National Council for the Social Studies.

"High-School Sex(ist) Education" by Janice Albert. Reprinted by permission of the publisher, *Up from Under*.

"Our Failures Only Marry: Bryn Mawr and the Failure of Feminism" by Liz Schneider. From *Woman in Sexist Society: Studies in Power and Powerlessness* edited by Vivian Gornick and Barbara K. Moran. Copyright © 1971 by Basic Books, Inc., Publishers, New York. Reprinted by permission of the publisher.

"The Second Sex in Academe" by Ann Sutherland Harris. From the *AAUP Bulletin*, Vol. 56, No. 3, September 1970. Reprinted by permission of the publisher.

"Women and the Literary Curriculum" by Elaine Showalter. From *College English*, May 1971. Copyright © 1971 by the National Council of Teachers of English. Reprinted by permission of the author and the publisher.

"Sexism in History" by Ruth Rosen. From *Journal of Marriage and the Family*, August 1971. Reprinted by permission of the author and the National Council on Family Relations.

"Teaching is a Good Profession . . . for a Woman" by Adria Reich. From *The Red Pencil*, Vol. 3, No. 2. Reprinted by permission of the author.

"The Harvard Ed School" by Betsey Useem. From *How Harvard Rules Women*. Reprinted by permission of the How Harvard Rules Women Collective.

"Women and the PDKs" by John Askins. From the *Detroit Free Press*, Thursday, September 21, 1972. Reprinted by permission of the publisher.

"Para-Professional" by Cleo Silvers. Reprinted by permission of the publisher, *Up from Under*.

"Portrait of a Teacher" by Frances Gray Patten. From *Good Morning, Miss Dove* by Frances Gray Patten. Reprinted by permission of the publisher, Dodd, Mead & Company.

"Academic Women" by Mary Ellmann. Copyright © 1965 by the American Jewish Committee. Originally published in *Commentary*. Reprinted by permission of the author and the publisher.

"Discrimination and Demography Restrict Opportunities for Academic Women" by Alice Rossi. Copyright © 1970 by McGraw-Hill, Inc. Originally published in *College and University Business*, February 1970. Reprinted by permission of the publisher.

"Feminist Experiment in Education" by Barbara Harrison. Copyright © 1972 by Harrison-Blaine of New Jersey, Inc. Originally published in *The New Republic*, March 11, 1972. Reprinted by permission of the publisher.

"Twelve and Turned-On" by Sharon Wolfson. Copyright © 1970 by *Women: A Journal of Liberation*, 3028 Greenmount Avenue, Baltimore, Maryland 21218. Reprinted by permission of the publisher.

"Jumping the Track" by Alice Leland di Rivera. Copyright © 1969 by Alice di Rivera. Originally published as "On Desegregating Stuyvesant High" in *Sisterhood Is Powerful*. Reprinted by permission of the author.

"It's Time for Equal Education" by Ann Scott. Reprinted by permission of *Ms.* Magazine.

# CONTENTS

## III: Down with Dick and Jane

## IV: Sexism in High School

## V: Are Colleges Fit for Women?

## VI: View from the Desk

## VII: The Feminist Response

*Appendix*

# INTRODUCTION

*No gown worse becomes a woman than the desire to be wise.*

—MARTIN LUTHER

"Let me imagine," suggests Virginia Woolf in *A Room of One's Own*, "since facts are so hard to come by, what would have happened had Shakespeare had a wonderfully gifted sister, called Judith, let us say." What follows is not a very appealing fantasy. With much the same talents and whims as her brother, Judith meets only scorn and derision. She is not sent to school and is discouraged from reading. Betrothed against her will, she runs off to London. When she hangs around stage doors, she is abused rather than casted by an actor manager. She becomes pregnant and kills herself to lie "buried at some crossroads where the omnibuses now stop outside the Elephant and Castle."

Not very pleasant. But on second thought, Virginia Woolf points out, no woman in Shakespeare's time could have had his genius, "for genius like Shakespeare's is not born among laboring, uneducated, servile people." And the women of sixteenth-century England were laboring, uneducated, or servile.

The time and setting are changed for us. We live in a newer continent in a later century where women are not all laboring, uneducated, or servile. If there are still no Judith Shakespeares, we cannot blame that on schools. For in twentieth-century U.S.A., education is a compulsory commodity that girls receive as freely and fully as boys.

Or do they?

Because American public schools have been coeducational for more than 100 years, it has been assumed that they treat boys and girls alike. And although the universities remained a male stronghold into the present century, by 1970 few doubted that the battle for equal rights for women in higher education had long been won. Yet as the new feminism directs its energies to a reexamination of our social institutions, the myth of equal schooling is giving way.

It shouldn't be a surprise. As society's official socializing agent, schools both reflect and perpetuate the prevailing social norms. Indeed they can inhibit social change as well. Certainly the literate public is by now well aware of the school's role in oppressing blacks and the poor. Yet it has just begun to notice that along with the new math and ancient history, schools have been teaching sex roles too. And good students that they are, girls have been learning gradually, but thoroughly, that intellectual and creative fulfillment are not for them. While preschool girls outshine boys on tests of general intelligence, they fall behind by the time they reach high school, and the gap widens during late adolescence and adulthood. Strange it took so long to notice that females are our largest class of "underachievers"!

Women's consciousness has come a long way in the past several years. Bit by bit women have been decoding the hidden curriculum which teaches females their second-class status. Feminist analyses have uncovered the discrimination and sex-role stereotyping in school textbooks, classes, guidance counseling, extracurricular activities, and personnel policies. Nor have we stopped with muckraking. Analysis has led to action. Women's Studies and affirmative action plans are campus commonplaces; Dick and Jane face new competition from the outpourings of feminist presses; and intrepid young women force the gates of prestigious all-male high schools.

Of course, all this assumes that schools can overcome their conservative origins and become agents of social change. Just this issue lies at the crux of an educational debate that has raged for two decades. Volumes of educational criticism have documented the obvious and subtle ways in which schools undermine the dignity of youth and sabotage the development of mature, autonomous individuals. But as it turns out, the critics' concerns were limited to male individuals only.

When Paul Goodman wrote his now classic *Growing Up*

*Absurd,* he specified that his concern was for "young men and boys" rather than "young people" because the problems discussed "belong primarily, in our society, to the boys: how to be useful and make something of oneself." Girls, he felt, had an important but only indirect stake in these issues, "for if the boys do not grow up to be men, where shall the women find men?" And Edgar Friedenberg, in *The Vanishing Adolescent,* justified his preoccupation with male students by explaining that in the process of self-definition and the establishment of self-esteem "boys have a tougher time."

Such bold-faced chauvinism is not in style these days, but the general public has yet to be convinced that our schools and our society make self-realization doubly difficult for young women.

At the core of feminism is an attack on the restrictive nature of sex roles. The imposition of arbitrary cultural standards of femininity and masculinity inhibits the natural development of young people. The timeworn debate over whether nature or nurture, heredity or environment, is the more important developmental influence has been revived. We stand far to the nurture side of the controversy; we believe that sex-role identity is primarily learned and that schools play an integral role in the process. Certainly there are biological differences between women and men. But the extent to which they are responsible for differences in behavior and personality has yet to be determined.

There is impressive evidence that social conditioning is the crucial factor in the development of sex-role identity. Anthropologists like Margaret Mead have documented the enormous cultural variability in sex-role norms. In an early work, *Sex and Temperament,* Mead described three strikingly different South Pacific cultures. Neither the Arapesh nor the Mundugumor differentiated ideal personality traits by sex. The Arapesh cultivated affectionate, generous, gentle dispositions in all their children, while the Mundugumor socialized girls and boys alike to be competitive, aggressive, independent. But the neighboring Tchambuli did stylize behavior by sex. Their women earned the tribe's sustenance while the men adorned themselves and their sacred objects. On the basis of these findings, Mead concluded that "many, if not all, of the personality traits which we have called masculine or feminine are as lightly linked to sex as are the clothing, the manners, and the form of headdress that a society at a given period assigns to either sex." If neighboring cultures can develop sex-role norms with such apparent arbitrariness, then the biological roots of such norms are neither universal nor transcendent.

Further evidence for the primacy of social influences on sex-role identity can be found in John Money's work with pseudohermaphrodites.[1] When physicians discover that a child has been assigned incorrect gender at birth, many initiate hormone therapy and attempt to reassign the child's gender. Money has found that after a child is beyond the age of three or four it is impossible to reverse its sex-role identity without severe psychological repercussions. Even by that early age the child has developed a powerful sense of His and Hers. If a child's sex-role identity can defy biological gender, cultural influences must be strong indeed.

Sex differences do appear early, however, and biological determinists see the verbal precocity of little girls and the higher-activity level of male infants as evidence of innate differences in cognitive style. One eminent investigator of psychological sex differences, Jerome Kagan, finds it useful "to assume that the earlier a particular behavioral difference appears in the life cycle, the more likely it is influenced by biological factors."[2] Although Kagan takes great pains to underplay the social implications of biologically determined psychological differences, his strategy leads him to some dangerous interpretations, for example, his conjecture that the alleged dearth of female musicians and painters is "the price women pay for their initial *left-hemispheric* advantage." Given this, a teacher might come to the absurd and damaging conclusion that there is no sense bucking nature by encouraging girls to develop artistically. Although the early appearance of sex-related

[1] John Money, "Psychological Approach to Psychosexual Misidentity with Elective Mutism: Sex Reassignment in Two Cases of Hyperadrenocortical Hermaphroditism," *Clinical Pediatrics*, 1968, pp. 331–339.

[2] Jerome Kagan, "The Early Emergence of Sex Differences," *School Review*, February 1972.

differences in verbal ability and muscular activity has been demonstrated, they seem small indeed compared with the tremendous social and cultural influences that bombard children from birth. A bias in favor of sex differences tends to exaggerate their relative significance. By focusing on the difference, we tend to forget that in most traits and abilities, the overlap between the sexes is enormous.

Although the sexes have traditionally been assigned different roles and personalities, we cannot accept the cry *"Vive la différence!"* We believe that the time-honored complementarity of the sexes masks their fundamental social inequality. Whenever there is a difference in caste, there is oppression. Historically, the socially defined difference between the sexes has meant the oppression of women by men. It has also meant that women have seldom realized their creative and intellectual potential.

This collection is concerned with the role of education in maintaining these unjust and wasteful sex roles. It brings together writings that document the extent to which sexism pervades our educational system from romper rooms to postdoctoral "fellow"ships. It shows that women in our culture are educated less seriously, less expensively, and even less often than men. The barriers to their education come in three basic styles—institutional, cultural, and psychological.

Institutionally, schools often segregate girls from boys for all or parts of the curriculum. They exclude girls from various activities and spend more money on those reserved for boys. They pay men more and advance women less. Cultural norms take over where institutional restrictions leave off. They subtly but relentlessly undermine female aspirations. Patriarchal prejudices pervade the curriculum. Primer after primer teaches children that men work and women mother, that boys climb and girls fall. The division of classroom labor mimics adult mores: "I need three strong boys to carry these books," and "Which of the girls would like to dust?" And well-intentioned guidance counselors make the message more explicit. They help boys to elect auto mechanics and girls home economics; they push successful boys toward professions while discouraging such unrealistic and undesirable ambitions in girls.

If institutionalized discrimination and cultural prejudice proscribe women's intellectual sphere, psychological barriers help keep women from challenging the boundaries. Both women and men have internalized the notion that women are intellectually inferior and should be subordinated to men. Many women do not believe they can be successful and even willfully deny the possibility. Researchers find that whereas boys reliably predict and take credit for their own academic performance, girls predict they will fail, and they attribute their unexpected success to luck. Self-doubt and prejudice keep the stereotypes alive and well. When women gracefully, even gratefully, accept their second-class options, they reinforce the cultural bias that these are natural and good. These biases in turn reinforce institutional discrimination. And so the sexist circle is complete, and another generation is educated to believe in woman's inferiority.

Our book is concerned with all three types of discrimination. It documents and analyzes institutional, cultural, and psychological varieties of sexism in education. The selection of material here reflects a feminist viewpoint. Our first concern throughout has been to show how sexist school practices harm girls and women. We have also included evidence that sex-role pressures are limiting and injurious to males as well.

There is an unfortunate second bias in this collection. Although we attempted to have it otherwise, this is mainly a white, middle-class book. Minorities and the poor are certainly affected by sexism, and they suffer from many of the same problems this book details. In fact, women in these groups get the worst treatment of all in education and employment. But the seldom-admitted reality is that feminism is primarily a white, middle-class movement that has tended to focus on problems of white, middle-class women. Minority and poor women have been understandably more concerned with problems of race and class. Though theoretical efforts abound, there is not yet an organizational framework that unites the efforts of sex, race, and class struggles. We hope, and believe, that this book will be useful to poor and minority sisters, but we recognize that they are inadequately represented in its selections.

We have organized the material developmentally from early childhood to higher education. A separate chapter is given to the problem of sex bias in the education profession. The good news is saved for last. Attempts by feminists to revise curriculum and combat discrimination in education have met with much resistance, but with some success. The success stories dominate our final chapter.

The obstacles to self-realization are set forth in the introductory chapter, "No Woman Geniuses?" Assumptions regarding the differing natures of women and men and their appropriate social spheres influence the way women have been and continue to be educated. They affect too the way women respond to the education they do receive. Writing sixty years ago, Anna Garlin Spencer responded aptly to a question that still plagues women today: where are your geniuses of first rank? Her still-valid response focuses on the institutional and cultural restrictions that have proscribed the intellectual ventures of the protected sex. The rest of the chapter illustrates the ways in which women and men have internalized the belief in women's intellectual inferiority.

Philip Goldberg demonstrates that college women devalue scholarship when the authors are believed to be female. Matina Horner's research on women's motive to avoid success has become a classic in feminist psychology. In the present article she reports a recent replication of her initial study that substantially confirms her earlier findings, albeit with an interesting new twist. She shows that educated women still find themselves in the double-bind of trying to be both successful and "feminine."[3] What is new in this study is the increasing disaffection her male subjects displayed toward the American success ethic. Florence Howe concludes the chapter by reminding us of the philosophical antecedents to present-day prejudices. She takes us back to the classics for a feminist review of male philosophies of women's education. With mentors like Aristotle and Milton, small wonder her students lacked great expectations.

[3] This is one phenomenon that appears to be particularly race and class specific. There is evidence that minority and working-class women do not experience the same conflict. See: Peter J. Weston and Martha T. Mednick, "Race, Social Class, and the Motive to Avoid Success in Women," and also p. 63 of Matina Horner, "The Motive to Avoid Success and Changing Aspirations of College Women," both in Judith Bardwick (ed.), *Readings on the Psychology of Women.* New York: Harper and Row, 1972.

This limitation of aspirations begins quite early. Chapter Two deals with early childhood education. Infants and toddlers face little institutional discrimination. They learn quickly, however, that blue is for boys and pink is for girls. Modeling themselves after the grownups around them, they absorb cultural norms with astonishing rapidity. The articles in this chapter, therefore, focus on the early influence of cultural sex-role norms. The first three articles describe sex-role stereotypes in young children. Evelyn Pitcher focuses on parental influence, while Carole Joffe observes children in a "progressive" nursery school setting. Although the school she observed was attempting to challenge traditional attitudes, it encountered remarkable resistance from the youngsters. Even at age three, sex-role stereotypes are firmly entrenched.

The exact process of sex-role development is not fully understood. One explanation for the tenacity of these youthful stereotypes is their convenient relationship to early cognitive stages. Lawrence Kohlberg has suggested that sex-role development closely parallels cognitive development. Children may latch onto sex distinctions as a handy conceptual tool.[4] But stereotypes are also actively promoted by the sexist milieu in which children grow up. Jane Bergman invites you to tune in to "Sesame Street," America's most popular babysitter, to see part of the problem. Or join Elizabeth Fisher as she thumbs through any child's favorite picture books to find sex stereotypes run rampant. Or think about the doll/truck dichotomy of children's toys. And just to make certain that parents do their job, child-rearing manuals make the message explicit. For more than a quarter of a century, Dr. Benjamin Spock has been the Confucius of American child care. In his bible for mothers, *Baby and Child Care*, and in regular *Redbook* advice columns he effectively counseled millions of mothers to stay home and nurture the sex-role identities

---

[4] Lawrence Kohlberg, "A Cognitive-Developmental Analysis of Children's Sex-Role Concepts and Attitudes," in Eleanor Maccoby (ed.), *The Development of Sex Differences*. Stanford: Stanford University Press, 1966. For a comprehensive review of contemporary theories of sex-role development (although the author's sexist bias occasionally intrudes) see Paul Mussen, "Early Sex-Role Development," in Nancy Reeves (ed.), *Womankind*. Chicago: Aldine Atherton, 1971.

of their preschool children.[5] Even in his 1970 book, *Decent and Indecent*, he spoke positively of women's "inborn aptitudes" and "feminine drives" as he intoned the conventional wisdom on sex roles:

> In bringing up our children—boys as well as girls— I think we should be enthusiastic about their maleness or femaleness as attributes to be proud of, enjoyed, emphasized, rather than taken for granted or even denied as they so often are today. A boy should know that his father enjoys his company in a special way because they can talk about cars or carpentry or sports. Even a small boy should feel that his mother appreciates his manly help in carrying things for her, opening doors, running errands, fixing things.
>
> A girl needs from her father compliments on the attractiveness of her appearance, on her skill in feminine occupations, and particularly on her thoughtfulness and helpfulness.
>
> Most of all a girl needs a mother who shows warm affection for her and who shows enthusiasm for playing the role of woman herself—with verve and style. It is in these matters that many American women depreciate womanhood, depreciate themselves, depreciate their daughters. They fail to inspire in them any conviction that the role of woman and mother can be as fascinating and creative as any other, whether or not there is an outside career.[6]

Heavy attacks from the women's movement have begun to raise Dr. Spock's consciousness. In a rather fashionable apologetic in the Sunday magazine of the *New York Times* Dr. Spock wistfully renounced his earlier prejudices.[7] But child psychologist Zelda Klapper finds that the women's

[5] For a provocative discussion of Dr. Spock's impact on post-World War II women and children, see "Women and Children First," in Philip Slater's *The Pursuit of Loneliness*. Boston: Beacon Press, 1970.

[6] New York: McCall's Publishing Co., 1970, pp. 57–58.

[7] Benjamin Spock, "Male Chauvinist Spock Recants—Well, Almost," *New York Times Sunday Magazine* (September 12, 1972), pp. 98–100.

movement has had little or no impact on the professional literature of child development; sex roles continue to go unchallenged.

Cultural sex-role norms receive institutional reinforcement when children enter elementary schools. Although most elementary schools are coeducational, they begin to introduce subtle sex-tracking into the curriculum. Classroom housekeeping chores are sex-typed. Playground activities are often segregated. And in many classrooms boys are encouraged in scientific and mechanical projects while girls are constantly reminded to act like "little ladies." And so, grade-school children begin to exhibit the same psychological conflicts about sex roles we have already encountered. "Down with Dick and Jane" our third chapter, explores the sexism of elementary schools and school children. Interest in sex differences at this level predates the new feminism. In the mid-fifties and early sixties, educators worried about the plight of young boys in the so-called "feminine" environment of schools. As late as 1970, a female sociologist, Patricia Sexton, published a book attacking the schools for producing *The Feminized Male*.

In this chapter she presents the core of her position, which we have dubbed the "poor-boy fallacy." According to this argument, boys are penalized in schools for their inability to conform to female standards of decorum. True, on the average, boys receive poorer grades and more detentions than girls. But as feminists like Betty Levy point out, the conformity for which girls are rewarded may well be more harmful in the long run. It may be that schools are more guilty of "feminizing" girls. The poor-boy tradition is rooted in a firm commitment to traditional sex roles; it looks to segregated classrooms and boy-oriented curricula to protect the interests of boys. Equally firm is the commitment of feminists to do away with rigid sex distinctions and to make the school experience livelier and more rewarding for all children.

The article by Sears and Feldman reviews research that explodes the myth that schools treat boys and girls alike. Boys demand and receive more attention of every sort from teachers. They are criticized, instructed, and rewarded more than the girls. In addition to family influences and social roles in school, curriculum materials have their effect: be it readers or math books or Newbery award winners, elementary children's books continue where the picture books left off. Boys have more fun.

The final studies in this chapter confirm that by the time they reach fifth grade, children have learned the lesson well. Boys worry about their masculinity. Girls begin to fear success. Ruth Hartley interviewed preadolescent boys and found them to be quite anxious about their ability to conform to their stylized conceptions of maleness. Grace Baruch is currently applying Matina Horner's "motive to avoid success" concept to her research on the sex-role stereotypes of elementary- and secondary-school youngsters. The article included here is an early report from that project which documents the emergence of the "femininity" vs. achievement conflict in fifth-grade girls.

If elementary schools maintain the illusion of identical treatment of the sexes, the high schools begin to segregate quite openly. Girls learn to sew while boys learn to saw; girls keypunch, boys compute; girls cheer as boys score. Here we find the institutionalization of sexist cultural norms. The formal segregation of schools is buttressed by the de facto segregation of adolescent social groupings. Chapter Four begins with young feminist Jenny Bull's analysis of the oppressive nature of the high-school woman's experience, in which she links sexism to racism and capitalism. A major institutional way the society perpetuates race, class, and sex distinctions is through an elaborate tracking system, and "Down the Up Staircase" methodically details the subtle mechanisms at work.

Handmaidens to the tracking system are standardized vocational tests and guidance programs. Elective courses give young people the illusion of choice as trained personnel direct them into class-, race-, and sex-appropriate slots. Sex bias is built into the preference tests and young women are consistently misguided in career planning.

The same sex bias pervades the curriculum for coeducational classes, where the achievements of women are largely overlooked. High-school history texts prefer Betsy Ross to Sojourner Truth and the flapper to the feminist. Janice Trecker relates this denigration of women's struggles to the low aspirations of high-school women. Even sex education, a supposedly radical innovation, often teaches sex roles, not sex. The virtues of motherhood are extolled while the blackout on birth control information insures tragic accidents. The heterosexual bias of these courses is rivaled only by their more generalized aversion to human sexuality.

Women have even less to cheer about in higher education. By the time they reach college, they find the institutionalization of sexism in bold relief. In admissions, rewards, facilities, and curriculum their second-class status is hammered home. Chapter Five, "Are Colleges Fit for Women?" opens with a selection by M. Carey Thomas, president of Bryn Mawr for nearly thirty years. In 1908 when Thomas reflected on her hard-fought struggles to provide higher education for women, she thought the war had been won. But as in so many of the nineteenth-century feminist campaigns, victory was far from complete. Now four out of ten entering college students are women, and a few have even invaded the ranks of the Yale men. But of those top-ranking high-school seniors who do not go on to college, three quarters are female. And in the universities, as elsewhere, a general principle for women applies: the higher, the fewer. In fact the proportion of doctoral degrees awarded to women slipped from 16 percent in the early 1930s down to 11 percent in the 1960s.

The problem is not strictly numerical. Even more than in high schools, the curricula of the universities segregate women from men. Classrooms for future engineers, executives, and city planners are filled with men. Women study to become teachers, nurses, and social workers. Furthermore, the curriculum stubbornly ignores the accomplishments of women. It refuses to take seriously the historical nature of our oppression. For this reason our chapter title reverses the query which infuriated nineteenth-century feminists like M. Carey Thomas: "Are women fit for college?" Thomas responded to that challenge by making Bryn Mawr a citadel of intellectual rigor. Her success accounts for the elation she expresses in the speech we have excerpted. The succeeding article, by Liz Schneider, analyzes the gradual erosion of Bryn Mawr's feminist heritage.

Ann Sutherland Harris, in "The Second Sex in Academe," presents an overview of sex discrimination in higher education today. The next two articles document sexism in the teaching of literature and history. How, asks Elaine Showalter, can young women be expected to identify with *The Portrait of the Artist as a Young Man*? Ruth Rosen reminds us that not even books on women's history are immune to sexist historiography.

The shortage of female academic role models must be viewed in the context of the broad social pattern of sex discrimination in work. Chapter Six, "View from the Desk," surveys the status of women at all levels of the education profession. Institutional, cultural, and psychological barriers confront women here. Teaching is characterized as a female occupation. And certainly women are drawn to this field above all other professions. But when examined closely, educational institutions reveal the same hierarchy as the larger society: power lies mainly in the hands of men. Women teach toddlers, men chair school boards; women are adjunct lecturers, men are college presidents. This familiar differential forms part of the hidden curriculum of sex-role learning that we have seen before. It teaches the teachers as well as their charges the subordinate position of women.

Historically popular stereotypes of teachers, particularly female teachers, have been less than flattering. The female teacher was generally caricatured as a humorless spinster who couldn't make it as a woman. As with all stereotypes, this one contained a germ of truth. The following teacher's contract, actually in use well into the twentieth century, suggests a way in which many communities imposed a moral straitjacket on their female teachers:

I promise to take a vital interest in all phases of Sunday-school work, donating of my time, service, and money without stint for the uplift and benefit of the community.

I promise to abstain from all dancing, immodest dressing, and any other conduct unbecoming a teacher and a lady.

I promise not to go out with any young men except in so far as it may be necessary to stimulate Sunday-school work.

I promise not to fall in love, to become engaged, or secretly married.

I promise not to encourage or tolerate the least familiarity on the part of any of my boy pupils.

I promise to sleep at least eight hours a night, to eat

carefully, and to take every precaution to keep in the best of health and spirits, in order that I may be better able to render efficient service to my pupils . . .[8]

The fictional portrait of the teacher from *Good Morning, Miss Dove,* while austere, does reflect the admiration and respect a devoted teacher could inspire. The price for this respect, however, was high. One could be a teacher or a woman, not both.

Mary Ellmann gives an account of recent fictional portrayals of academic women, where there is no such respect and admiration as Miss Dove inspired. The academic women who spring from the pens of our major male novelists today are either physically deformed or morally dissolute. Clearly, women of accomplishment disturb the ivory-tower serenity of their male colleagues. Reality bears this out. Women at all levels of the educational profession are excluded from the smoker and club-room gatherings where policies are set, information is shared, and the relationships strategic to advancement are formed. Sociologist Alice Rossi documents the actual patterns of discrimination that confront faculty women on American campuses.

Women—students, teachers, and parents—are challenging these patterns from day care to graduate school. Our final chapter brings together examples of their efforts to combat sexism in schools. The campaign proceeds on three major fronts: consciousness-raising, legal action, and curriculum reform. In-service classes, parent groups and educational conferences have been formed to sensitize participants to the many varieties of sex bias in education. They also help members to become aware of their own psychological barriers to nonsexist education. Barbara Harrison describes the resistance feminist parents and teachers met when they tried to raise consciousness in a progressive private school.

Discrimination is the target of legal action. Women are initiating legislation and court cases to attack the institutional forms of sex discrimination. A. L. di Rivera relates her successful court battle to desegregate Stuyvesant High, a prestigious science high school. Since then Congress has passed a law making sex discrimination in education illegal. Title IX of the Higher Education Act of 1972 declares, "No person in the U.S. shall on the basis of sex be excluded from participation in, be denied the benefits of, or be subjected to discrimination under any education program or activity receiving federal financial assistance." Ann Scott provides teachers and students with a guide to this and other relevant legislation as well as with a blueprint for legal action against educational discrimination.

Feminist presses, publications, and courses have poured forth to overhaul, replace, or invigorate school curricula. High-school and elementary-school teachers have begun to introduce units on women into the standard curriculum, but most of the energy has been released on the campuses. Despite considerable academic opposition and condescension, Women's Studies is now a campus fact-of-life. Individual women's courses continue to proliferate (close to 1000 in the fall of 1972), and several colleges confer masters' degrees in the field. But now that Women's Studies has got a foot in the door, it has raised its own political and educational issues. Central to these is the relationship between the academic and political arms of the women's movement. Is the mission of Women's Studies to direct scholarship to the study of women? Or must it become a conscious political force for women's rights? Are the established disciplines appropriate models for feminist scholarship? Or must Women's Studies develop structures and traditions of its own? Who should control its curriculum, and who should receive it? And who should decide?

Answers to these questions vary with the individual and the institution. Local conditions—funding, constituency, departmental structure, age—largely determine how a particular women's program will reconcile issues of ideology and governance. Many are struggling to establish the academic legitimacy of the new discipline. Marilyn Webb, who teaches at experimental Goddard College, believes feminist studies must break with patriarchal academic tradition if it is to develop the collective strength of women.

Our book concludes with Florence Howe's lecture to the New York State education department on the topic of equal education for women. In describing her own experience teaching women's studies, she suggests the inevitable relationship between liberal education and social change.

Although schools cannot be expected to solve social problems, they can and should release the energy that will tackle them. We share Florence Howe's conviction that teacher education is the crucial link in the chain. If teachers can be educated to the sexism in schools (and they can), then they can circumvent the most chauvinist curricula.

And so this book is dedicated especially to teachers and teachers-of-teachers and teachers-to-be. We have selected and arranged its contents with their needs and interests in mind, and the appendix provides ready access to available resources for feminist education projects. We hope that teachers and students will join our commitment to struggle on all fronts for a liberating education for women.

It will not be easy, and it will not come soon. The sexism which permeates our educational system must be uprooted in all its guises. We have institutional, cultural, and psychological obstacles to contend with. There is discrimination, de jure and de facto. There are cultural shibboleths emblazoned in every textbook, in every toothpaste advertisement. More personally, there is the prejudice and self-doubt—the internalization of the myth of male superiority.

It is a difficult task, but there are tools available to us. We can form consciousness-raising groups to increase our own awareness and our own self-esteem. We can teach courses about women to students and parents and teachers and school boards. We can lobby and caucus in unions and conferences, in legislatures and Congress. We can fight discrimination in the courts. We can "girlcott" the media and the manufacturers until their insidious sexist creations are no longer profitable. And we can write textbooks and fairytales and classics of our own. Create new forms of culture. Even build our own schools. We can do all these things, and we have already begun.

There is a long way to go, but it is worth the struggle. For we are all prisoners of gender, not sex. Urged to be masculine or feminine, we conform or rebel, but we do not grow free. To serve the god Masculinity we commit sins of aggression. To appease Femininity we commit sins of passivity. One is more vicious, but both destroy lives. The alternative is a world in which gender loses its power to decree human options. The goal is to allow each individual to freely choose roles and personal styles. Only then can whatever is genuinely natural about sex differences come out.

Schools cannot create a nonsexist world. They can join in the struggle or continue to thwart it. They can either continue to perpetuate the old roles and relationships between women and men, or they can begin to free girls and boys from the rigid and stunting identities that have been imposed by our culture. We hope this collection will help them choose wisely.

# I.
# No Woman Geniuses?

# WHY ARE THERE NO WOMAN GENIUSES?

*ANNA GARLIN SPENCER*

*Society places many artificial obstacles in the way of women's achievement. In a book published in 1912, Anna Garlin Spencer discusses these barriers which she, as a professional woman, knew first hand. Sixty years later, despite significant progress in women's education, her analysis is still relevant.*

The failure of women to produce genius of the first rank in most of the supreme forms of human effort has been used to block the way of all women of talent and ambition for intellectual achievement in a manner that would be amusingly absurd were it not so monstrously unjust and socially harmful. A few ambitious girls in the middle of the nineteenth century in Boston, the Athens of America, want to go to high school. The board of education answers them, in effect: Produce a Michelangelo or a Plato and you shall have a chance to learn a bit of mathematics, history, and literature. A few women of marked inclination toward the healing art want a chance to study in a medical school and learn facts and methods in a hospital. Go to! the managing officials in substance reply: Where is your great surgeon, what supreme contribution has any woman ever made to our science? A group of earnest students beg admission to college and show good preparation gained by hard struggle with adverse conditions. You can't come in, the trustees respond, until you produce a Shakespeare or a Milton. The demand that women shall show the highest fruit of specialized talent and widest range of learning before they have had the general opportunity for a common-school education is hardly worthy of the sex that prides itself upon its logic. In point of fact no one, neither the man who denies woman a proper human soul nor the woman who claims "superiority" for her sex, can have any actual basis for accurate answer to the question, Can a woman become a genius of the first class? Nobody can know unless women in general shall have equal opportunity with men in education, in vocational choice, and in social welcome of their best intellectual work for a number of generations. So far women have suffered so many disabilities in the circumstances of their lives, in their lack of training in what Buckle calls "that preposterous system called their education," in their segregation from all the higher intellectual comradeship, in the personal and family and social hindrances to their mental growth and expression, that not even women themselves, still less men, can have an adequate idea of their possibilities of achievement. Nothing therefore is more foolish than to try to decide a priori the limits of a woman's capacity. What we do know is this, that there have been women of talent, and even of genius reaching near to the upper circles of the elect; and we know also that these women of marked talent have appeared whenever and wherever women have had opportunities of higher education and have been held in esteem by men as intellectual companions as well as wives and manual workers. The connection between these two facts is obvious. . . .

Anyone can see that to write *Uncle Tom's Cabin* on the knee in the kitchen, with constant calls to cooking and other details of housework to punctuate the paragraphs, was a more difficult achievement than to write it at leisure in a quiet room. And when her biographer says of an Italian woman poet, "during some years her Muse was intermitted," we do not wonder at the fact when he casually mentions her ten children. No record, however, can even name the women of talent who were so submerged by childbearing and its duties, and by "general housework," that they had to leave their poems and stories all unwritten. Moreover, the obstacles to intellectual development and achievement which marriage and

maternity interpose (and which are so important that
they demand a separate study) are not the only ones that
must be noted. It is not alone the fact that women have
generally had to spend most of their strength in caring
for others that has handicapped them in individual effort;
but also that they have almost universally had to care
wholly for themselves. Women even now have the burden
of the care of their belongings, their dress, their home life
of whatever sort it may be, and the social duties of the
smaller world, even if doing great things in individual
work. A successful woman preacher was once asked
"what special obstacles have you met as a woman in the
ministry?" "Not one," she answered, "except the lack of a
minister's wife." When we read of Charles Darwin's wife
not only relieving him from financial cares but seeing that
he had his breakfast in his room, with "nothing to disturb
the freshness of his morning," we do not find the explanation of Darwin's genius, but we do see how he was
helped to express it. Men geniuses, even of second grade,
have usually had at least one woman to smooth their
way, and often several women to make sure that little
things, often even self-support itself, did not interfere with
the development and expression of their talent. On the
other hand, the obligation of all the earlier women writers
to prepare a useful cookbook in order to buy their way
into literature, is a fitting symbol of the compulsion laid
upon women, however gifted, to do all the things that
women in general accomplish before entering upon their
special task. That brave woman who wanted to study
medicine so much that not even the heaviest family burdens could deter her from entering the medical school
first opened to her sex, but who "first sewed steadily until
her entire family was fitted with clothes to last six
months," is a not unusual type.[1]

Added to all this, the woman of talent and of special
gifts has had until very lately, and in most countries has
still, to go against the massed social pressure of her time
in order to devote herself to any particular intellectual
task. The expectation of society has long pushed men to-

[1] Mrs. Thomas, graduated in first class of Women's Medical College
of Philadelphia; served as City Physician at Fort Wayne, Ind., eight
years.

ward some special work; the expectation of society has until recently been wholly against women's choosing any vocation beside their functional service in the family. This is a far more intense and all-pervading influence in deterring women from success in intellectual work than is usually understood. . . . The mildest approach on the part of a wife and mother, or even of a daughter or sister, to that intense interest in self-expression which has always characterized genius has been met with social disapproval and until very recent times with ostracism fit only for the criminal. Hence her inner impulsion has needed to be strong indeed to make any woman devote herself to ideas.

# ARE WOMEN PREJUDICED AGAINST WOMEN?

*PHILIP GOLDBERG*

"Woman," advised Aristotle, "may be said to be an inferior man."

Because he was a man, Aristotle was probably biased. But what do women themselves think? Do they, consciously or unconsciously, consider their own sex inferior? And if so, does this belief prejudice them against other women—that is, make them view women, simply because they *are* women, as less competent than men?

According to a study conducted by myself and my associates, the answer to both questions is Yes. Women *do* consider their own sex inferior. And even when the facts give no support to this belief, they will persist in downgrading the competence—in particular, the intellectual and professional competence—of their fellow females.

Over the years, psychologists and psychiatrists have shown that both sexes consistently value men more highly than women. Characteristics considered male are usually praised; those considered female are usually criticized. In 1957 A. C. Sheriffs and J. P. McKee noted that "women are regarded as guilty of snobbery and irrational and unpleasant emotionality." Consistent with this report, E. G. French and G. S. Lesser found in 1964 that "women who

*PHILIP GOLDBERG is Associate Professor of Psychology at Connecticut College in New London. His research has centered on the social-clinical areas of psychology. He is presently conducting research on the cognitive and personality variables associated with voting behavior.*

value intellectual attainment feel they must reject the woman's role"—intellectual accomplishment apparently being considered, even among intellectual women, a masculine preserve. In addition, ardent feminists like Simone de Beauvoir and Betty Friedan believe that men, in important ways, are superior to women.

Now, is this belief simply prejudice, or are the characteristics and achievements of women really inferior to those of men? In answering this question, we need to draw some careful distinctions.

Most important, we need to recognize that there are two distinct dimensions to the issue of sex differences. The first question is whether sex differences exist at all, apart from the obvious physical ones. The answer to this question seems to be a unanimous Yes—men, women, and social scientists agree that, psychologically and emotionally as well as physically, women *are* different from men.

But is being different the same as being inferior? It is quite possible to perceive a difference accurately but to value it inaccurately. Do women automatically view their differences from men as *deficiencies?* The evidence is that they do, and that this value judgment opens the door to anti-female prejudice. For if someone (male or female) concludes that women are inferior, his perceptions of women—their personalities, behavior, abilities, and accomplishments—will tend to be colored by his low expectations of women.

As Gordon W. Allport has pointed out in *The Nature of Prejudice*, whatever the facts about sex differences, anti-feminism—like any other prejudice—*distorts perception and experience*. What defines antifeminism is not so much believing that women are inferior, as allowing that belief to distort one's perceptions of women. More generally, it is not the partiality itself, but the distortion born of that partiality, that defines prejudice.

Thus, an anti-Semite watching a Jew may see devious or sneaky behavior. But, in a Christian, he would regard such behavior only as quiet, reserved, or perhaps even shy. Prejudice is self-sustaining: It continually distorts the "evidence" on which the prejudiced person claims to base his beliefs. Allport makes it clear that antifeminism, like anti-Semitism or any other prejudice, consistently twists the "evidence" of experience. We see not what is there, but what we *expect* to see.

The purpose of our study was to investigate whether there is real prejudice by women against women—whether perception itself is distorted unfavorably. Specifically, will women evaluate a professional article with a jaundiced eye when they think it is the work of a woman, but praise the same article when they think its author is a man? Our hypotheses were:

Even when the work is identical, women value the professional work of men more highly than that of women.

But when the professional field happens to be one traditionally reserved for women (nursing, dietetics), this tendency will be reversed, or at least greatly diminished.

Some 140 college girls, selected at random, were our subjects. One hundred were used for the preliminary work; 40 participated in the experiment proper.

To test the second hypothesis, we gave the 100 girls a list of 50 occupations and asked them to rate "the degree to which you associate the field with men or with women." We found that law and city planning were fields strongly associated with men, elementary-school teaching and dietetics were fields strongly associated with women, and two fields—linguistics and art history—were chosen as neutrals, not strongly associated with either sex.

Now we were ready for the main experiment. From the professional literature of each of these six fields, we took one article. The articles were edited and abridged to about 1500 words, then combined into two equal sets of booklets. The crucial manipulation had to do with the authors' names—the same article bore a male name in one set of booklets, a female name in the other set. An example: If, in set one, the first article bore the name John T. McKay, in set two the same article would appear under the name Joan T. McKay. Each booklet contained three articles by "men" and three articles by "women."

The girls, seated together in a large lecture hall, were told to read the articles in their booklets and given these instructions:

In this booklet you will find excerpts of six articles, written by six different authors in six different professional fields. At the end of each article you will

find several questions. . . . You are not presumed to
be sophisticated or knowledgeable in all the fields.
We are interested in the ability of college students
to make critical evaluations. . . .

Note that no mention at all was made of the authors'
sexes. That information was contained—apparently only
by coincidence—in the authors' names. The girls could
not know, therefore, what we were really looking for.

At the end of each article were nine questions asking
the girls to rate the articles for value, persuasiveness, and
profundity—and to rate the authors for writing style, professional competence, professional status, and ability to
sway the reader. On each item, the girls gave a rating of
from 1 (highly favorable) to 5 (highly unfavorable).

Generally, the results were in line with our expectations
—but not completely. In analyzing these results, we used
three different methods: We compared the amount of
antifemale bias in the different occupational fields (would
men be rated as better city planners, but women as better dieticians?); we compared the amount of bias shown
on the nine questions that followed each article (would
men be rated as more competent, but women as more
persuasive?); and we ran an overall comparison, including both fields and rating questions.

Starting with the analysis of bias by occupational field,
we immediately ran into a major surprise. (See box following.) That there is a general bias by women against
women, and that it is strongest in traditionally masculine
fields, was clearly borne out. But in other fields the situation seemed rather confused. We had expected the anti-
female trend to be reversed in traditionally feminine
fields. But it appears that, even here, women consider
themselves inferior to men. Women seem to think that
men are better at *everything*—including elementary-
school teaching and dietetics!

Scrutiny of the nine rating questions yielded similar
results. On all nine questions, regardless of the author's
occupational field, the girls consistently found an article
more valuable—and its author more competent—when
the article bore a male name. Though the articles themselves were exactly the same, the girls felt that those
written by the John T. McKays were definitely more

These are the total scores the college girls gave to the six pairs of articles they read. The lowest possible score—9—would be the most favorable; the highest possible score—54—the most critical. While male authors received more favorable ratings in *all* occupational fields, the differences were statistically significant only in city planning, linguistics, and—especially—law.

| | Mean | |
| *Field of Article* | MALE | FEMALE |
| Art History | 23.10 | 23.35 |
| Dietetics | 22.05 | 23.45 |
| Education | 20.20 | 21.75 |
| City Planning | 23.10 | 27.30 |
| Linguistics | 26.95 | 30.70 |
| Law | 21.20 | 25.60 |

impressive, and reflected more glory on their authors, than did the mediocre offerings of the Joan T. McKays. Perhaps because the world has accepted female authors for a long time, the girls were willing to concede that the female professionals' writing styles were not *far* inferior to those of the men. But such a concession to female competence was rare indeed.

Statistical analysis confirms these impressions and makes them more definite. With a total of six articles, and with nine questions after each one, there were 54 points at which comparisons could be drawn between the male authors and the female authors. Out of these 54 comparisons, three were tied, seven favored the female authors—and the number favoring the male authors was 44!

Clearly, there is a tendency among women to downgrade the work of professionals of their own sex. But the hypothesis that this tendency would decrease as the "femaleness" of the professional field increased was not supported. Even in traditionally female fields, antifeminism holds sway.

Since the articles supposedly written by men were exactly the same as those supposedly written by women, the perception that the men's articles were superior was obviously a distortion. For reasons of their own, the female subjects were sensitive to the sex of the author, and this apparently irrelevant information biased their judgments. Both the distortion and the sensitivity that precedes it are characteristic of prejudice. Women—at least these young college women—are prejudiced against female professionals and, regardless of the actual accomplishments of these professionals, will firmly refuse to recognize them as the equals of their male colleagues.

Is the intellectual double-standard really dead? Not at all—and if the college girls in this study are typical of the educated and presumably progressive segments of the population, it may not even be dying. Whatever lip service these girls pay to modern ideas of equality between men and women, their beliefs are staunchly traditional. Their real coach in the battle of the sexes is not Simone de Beauvoir or Betty Friedan. Their coach is Aristotle.

# TOWARD AN UNDERSTANDING OF ACHIEVEMENT-RELATED CONFLICTS IN WOMEN

*MATINA S. HORNER*

*A woman should be good for everything at home, but abroad good for nothing.*

—EURIPIDES

*A woman who is guided by the head and not the heart is a social pestilence: she has all the defects of a passionate and affectionate woman, with none of her compensations: she is without pity, without love, without virtue, without sex.*

HONORÉ DE BALZAC

*And it is highly probable that the undoubted superiority of the male sex in intellectual and creative achievement is related to their greater endowment of aggression . . . The hypothesis that women, if only given the opportunity and encouragement, would equal or surpass the creative achievements of men is hardly defensible.*

ANTHONY STORR

*Their (women's) physical and psychological disabilities render them unfit to make important decisions or hold positions of power.*

DR. EDGAR BERMAN

DR. MATINA HORNER received her Ph.D. from the University of Michigan and taught at Harvard before becoming President of Radcliffe College.

The prevalent attitudes and perspectives found throughout history, amidst both scholarly and popular circles, on
the nature of women, their special qualities, potential,
abilities, and roles, seem, with few exceptions, to have
converged on the idea that femininity and individual competitive achievement are two desirable but mutually
exclusive goals. This is especially true of achievements
reflecting intellectual competence and leadership potential. The aggressive, and hence masculine, overtones
inherent in a capacity for mastering intellectual problems,
attacking difficulties, and penetrating to the heart of the
matter are considered obvious. Almost by definition,
therefore, competence in intellectual matters or decision-
making prowess have been equated with qualities antag-
onistic to or incompatible with those defined as feminine.
Femininity has, since the time of Freud's treatise on the
"Psychology of Women" (1933), been equated with the
absence or repression of aggressiveness:

> The repression of their aggressiveness, which is im-
> posed upon women by their constitutions and by
> society, favors the development of strong masochistic
> impulses . . . Masochism is then, as they say, truly
> feminine.

In a recent book on human aggression Storr (1970)
argues, for instance, that:

> It is highly probable that the undoubted superiority
> of the male sex in intellectual and creative achieve-
> ment is related to their greater endowment of aggres-
> sion . . .

Thus, our attitudes have not advanced very far beyond
Aristotle's notion that women never suffered from bald-
ness because they never used the contents of their heads.
Society has instead remained faithful to a stereotype of
women which has evolved over the centuries and which is
characterized by a general inability to reconcile competence, ambition, intellectual accomplishment, and success with femininity. When, for instance, women stray
from the image and do use their heads and develop their
minds, they are praised for having *masculine minds.* As

Marya Mannes has indicated, only a superwoman in the traditional sphere is granted the privilege of exploring her potential in the outer world without being totally rejected:

> Nobody objects to a woman's being a good writer, sculptor, or geneticist, if at the same time she manages to be a good wife, a good mother, good-looking, good tempered, well-dressed, well-groomed, and unaggressive.

It is indeed a tribute to the tenacity of this image that even today most people continue to connect sex with certain characteristics and occupations. They do this despite the fact that fundamentally there is nothing intrinsically feminine about typing or teaching nor intrinsically masculine about medicine, surgery, physics, law, investment counseling, preaching, or just plain thinking. One might in fact just as easily or rationally argue that women are constitutionally better suited for surgery than are men by virtue of the smaller size of their hands and their greater finger dexterity that makes them so "competent" at embroidery. The impact of this age-old stereotype is especially striking if we consider the fact that women as well as men in this country are equally exposed to and immersed in a culture that, until very recently at least, rewarded and placed a high value on achievement and stressed individual freedom, self-realization, and the full development of one's individual resources, including their intellectual potential. Nevertheless, a peculiar paradox exists: we have a culture and an educational system that ostensibly encourage and prepare men and women identically for careers which our data indicate other social and, even more importantly, internal psychological pressures really limit to men, especially in the postadolescent years.

It has taken us a long time to become aware of the extent to which we have incorporated or internalized this image of women and how much of an influence it therefore exerts on our attitudes and behavior. It is very clear in our data that most of the young men and women in the samples we have tested over the past seven years still continue to evaluate themselves in terms of the dominant societal stereotype which says that competition, independence, success, competence, and intellectual achievement reflect positively on mental health and masculinity but are basically inconsistent with femininity. These young people have apparently learned, accepted, or taken it for granted that the right to master Erikson's "outer world space" belongs to the men and the only appropriate domain for a feminine woman is "inner world space," which includes the domain of "affective or expressive competence."

The information received from both internal and external sources reinforces these ideas and makes it especially difficult for a capable, achievement-oriented young woman whose sense of self-esteem includes feelings of competence or a desire for success in nontraditional areas to maintain any stable sense of identity or self-regard as a *feminine* woman. If we assume that a confident belief in one's own masculinity and femininity is a very fundamental part of one's identity, the potential roots for self-doubt, for conflict and for anxiety about achievement, leadership, or power in women becomes apparent. It may well be that a comparable kind of anxiety exists for men in the domain of "affective competence," for instance, being a particularly warm or sensitive young man may raise doubts about one's masculinity. This is a relevant issue which is currently being investigated but takes us beyond the scope of the present paper concerned with achievement-related conflict in women.

### A Psychological Barrier to Achievement in Women

Mead argued in 1949 that "each step forward as a successful American regardless of sex means a step back as a woman." Maccoby has pointed out, the "girl who maintains qualities of independence and active striving (achievement orientation) necessary for intellectual mastery defies the conventions of sex appropriate behavior and must pay a price, a price in anxiety." Both of these ideas are encompassed in my conceptualization of the Motive to Avoid Success ($M_{-s}$) which was developed almost seven years ago in an attempt to understand or explain the major unresolved sex differences detected in previous research on achievement motivation (Atkinson, 1958; McClelland et al., 1953) as well as to identify an internal psychological representative of the kinds of conflict that have been described. When the Motive to Avoid Success was first introduced as a psychological barrier to achievement in women, it was conceptualized within the framework of an expectancy-value theory of motivation as a latent, stable personality disposition acquired early in life in conjunction with standards of sex-role identity. In expectancy-value theories of motivation, the most important factors determining the arousal of these dispositions or motives and thereby the ultimate strength of motivation and direction of one's behavior are (1) the expectations or beliefs the individual has about the nature and likelihood of the consequences of his/her actions, and (2) the value of these consequences to the individual in light of his/her particular motives. Anxiety is aroused according to the theory when one expects that the consequences of their action will be negative. The anxiety then functions to inhibit the action expected to have the negative consequences; it does not, however, determine which action will then be undertaken. In other words, within this framework avoidance motives inhibit actions expected to have unattractive consequences. They can tell us what someone *will not* do, but not what they *will* do. This is the function of approach motives (Atkinson and Feather, 1966; Horner, 1970).

With this in mind, I argued that most women have a motive to avoid success, that is, a disposition to become anxious about achieving success because they expect negative consequences such as social rejection and/or feelings of being unfeminine as a result of succeeding. Note that this is *not* to say that most women "want to fail" or have a "motive to approach failure." The presence of a "will to fail" would, in accordance with the theory, imply that they actively seek out failure because they anticipate or expect positive consequences from failing. The presence of a motive to avoid success, on the other hand, implies that the achievement-directed tendencies of most otherwise positively motivated young women are inhibited by the arousal of a thwarting disposition to be anxious about the negative consequences they expect will follow the desired success. While such a motive as the "motive to approach failure" may exist, it is clearly not conceptually the same variable which I have

described as the "motive to avoid success." The two ideas
are as independent of each other, both theoretically and
with regard to their behavioral implications, as are the
positive "motive to achieve success" $(M_s)$ and the
inhibitory "motive to avoid failure" $(M_{-f})$ in Atkinson's
theory of achievement motivation (Atkinson and Feather,
1966).

Our data indicate that the emphasis on the new freedom for women has thus far not been any more effective
in doing away with this tendency than were previously the
vote, trousers, cigarettes, and even changing standards of
sexual behavior. If anything, our more recent data indicate somewhat of a backlash phenomenon since the mid
60s. The negative attitudes we find expressed toward
successful women have increased and intensified to a dis-
proportionately greater extent than have the positive ones
and this is true of both male and female subjects. In a
medical article G. M. Carstairs makes a similar point
when he argues that in the professions, in academic life,
and in businesses in which women have won acceptance
on supposedly equal terms, strain, concealed embarrass-
ment and self-consciousness remain. In other words, while
legally opening its doors to women, society has at the
same time been "teaching" them to be anxious about succeeding. They are led to expect negative consequences for
undertaking and doing well at competitive nontraditional
endeavors which defy the conventions of role-appropriate
behavior.

A quick review of the results of several of the studies
we have done over the past few years on the nature and
development of this anxiety and its functional significance
or impact on the achievement strivings and performance
of women will substantiate this idea.

*Individual Differences in the Strength of the*
*Motive to Avoid Success: Its Assessment and*
*Functional Significance*

In the initial study (Horner, 1968), it was hypothesized
that the motive to avoid success would be significantly
more characteristic of women than of men, and also more
characteristic of high-achievement oriented–high-ability
women who aspire to and/or are capable of achieving

success than of low-achievement oriented–low-ability women who neither aspire to nor can achieve success. After all, if you neither want nor can achieve success, the expectancy of negative consequences because of success would be rather meaningless. It was assumed that individual differences in the strength of the motive to avoid success would be aroused by the negative incentive value of success and the expectancy of negative consequences because of success which are present in any competitive achievement situation in which performance reflecting intellectual and leadership ability is to be evaluated against a standard of excellence and *also* against a competitor's performance. Once aroused, the tendency or motivation to avoid success would inhibit the expression of all positive motivation or tendencies to do well and thus should have an adverse effect on performance in these situations. It was assumed, furthermore, that the negative incentive value of success should be greater for women in interpersonal competitive than in noncompetitive achievement situations, especially against male competitors, particularly if they are "important" males.

In order to test our hypotheses about the presence and impact of the motive to avoid success, it was necessary to develop a measure of individual differences in the motive. Inasmuch as content analysis of fantasy material has over the years since Freud and Murray proven to be a useful and valid way to measure human motives, this method was adopted. At the end of the Standard Thematic Apperceptive Test (TAT) for measuring the Achievement motive in which verbal leads rather than pictures were used, an additional verbal lead connoting a high level of accomplishment in a mixed-sex-competitive achievement situation was included. For the ninety females in the initial study, the lead used was "After first-term finals, Anne finds herself at the top of her medical-school class." For the 88 males in the sample, the lead was "After first-term finals, John finds himself at the top of his medical-school class." The subjects were predominantly freshmen and sophomore undergraduate students at a large midwestern university.

A very simple present-absent system was adopted for scoring fear of success imagery, as an indication of the motive to avoid success. The specific criteria used were developed in accordance with Scott's (1956) results which showed what happens in a Thematic Apperception Test when a person is confronted with a cue or situation that represents a threat rather than a goal or simultaneously represents a goal and a threat. These can be found in Horner, 1968, and Horner, 1970. Very briefly, the Motive to Avoid Success is scored as present if the subjects in response to a thematic lead about a successful figure *of their own sex* made statements in their stories showing conflict about the success, the presence or anticipation of negative consequences because of the success, denial of effort or responsibility for attaining the success, denial of the cue itself, or some other bizarre or inappropriate response to the cue. In accordance with our hypothesis in the first study, fear of success imagery dominated the female responses and was relatively absent in the male responses.

In response to the successful male cue, more than 90 percent of the men in the study showed strong positive feelings, indicated increased striving, confidence in the future, and a belief that this success would be instrumental to fulfilling other goals, such as providing a secure and happy home for some girl, for example:

> . . . (John) is thinking about his girl Cheri whom he will marry at the end of med school. He realizes he can give her all the things she desires after he becomes established. . . . He is pleased with himself. . . . He is thinking that he must not let up now, but must work even harder than he did before. . . . He may even consider going into research now.

Fewer than 10 percent of the men responded at all negatively and these focused primarily on the young man's rather dull personality.

On the other hand, in response to the successful female cue, 65 percent of the girls were disconcerted, troubled, or confused by the cue. Unusual excellence in women was clearly associated for them with the loss of femininity, social rejection, personal or societal destruction, or some combination of the above. Their responses were filled with negative consequences and affect, righteous indignation, withdrawal rather than enhanced striving, concern, or even an inability to accept the information presented in the cue, for example:

> Anne will deliberately lower her academic standing the next term, while she does all she subtly can to help Carl. . . . His grades come up and Anne soon drops out of med-school. They marry and he goes on in school while she raises their family.

> Anne is unhappy and either terribly rich or so ambitious that family, husband, et al., and friends are tools to be used in the advancement of her career.

> Anne is a code name for a nonexistent person created by a group of med students. They take turns taking exams and writing papers for Anne . . .

> . . . Aggressive, unmarried, wearing oxford shoes and hair pulled back in a bun, wears glasses and is terribly bright.

In other words, women showed significantly more evidence of the motive to avoid success than did the men, with 59 of the 90 women scoring high and only 8 of the 88 men doing so ($p < .0005$).

The pattern of sex differences in presence of fear of success imagery found in the first study have, by and large, been maintained in the subsequent samples of white men and women tested since that time. The major difference has been an increase noted over the past two years (from 10 to 18 percent) in the extent to which fear of success imagery or negative consequences are expressed by male subjects in response to cues about successful male figures who have come to be viewed increasingly as lacking a social consciousness and having Waspish or selfish personalities.

> . . . John will finish med school with very high honors—marry the fattest woman in town and become an extremely rich and self-centered doctor.

The fact that college students of both sexes, but especially the men, are currently taking an increasingly negative view of success as it has been traditionally defined is reflected in our most recent data collected in the winter of 1970 (Prescott, 1971). Forty-seven percent of the male freshmen undergraduates in this sample showed negative imagery in response to the cue, a significant increase with respect to previous male samples. Even in this sample, however, significant sex differences in the presence of fear of success imagery were maintained. The content of the stories, however, did differ between the sexes. Most of the men who showed fear of success were not concerned about their masculinity but were instead likely to have expressed broad existential concerns about finding a "nonmaterialistic happiness and satisfaction in life." These concerns played a minor part in the female stories. Most of the women high in fear of success imagery continued to be concerned about the discrepancy between success in the situation described and feminine identity. In the past two years, this concern has been manifested in several new themes not evident in previous work, for example:

Anne is coming back from hearing the good news in class. She knows she can be as good as any male doctor. She only regrets that they treat her as so unfeminine. She feels out of place and has *a fear of becoming a lesbian . . . Maybe she shouldn't have cheated* on the exam, then the other men would have felt better about her being stupid. She pushes this out of her mind, enters her apartment, and takes a nap. She is tired and *unhappy and really has no tangible reason to be sad. She probably won't be a doctor anyway.*

Anne runs home happily to tell her husband about her status. He is not so thrilled, being a business-school graduate who is not happy in his job. Anne wanted to marry William but wanted to pursue her career. Everyone warned her it would never work and that a girl didn't belong in law school anyway. Her husband kept silent on the subject, not wishing to lose her. She is pleased at her success and knows she can continue to do well. She wants to go on to a career in law and doesn't particularly want children. He wants to do as well as she is, but feels unable to.

She will go on in law school. *He will substitute sugar for her pills so she gets knocked up.* She has the baby—in between lectures—and an hour later is back at the books. He hits his head against the wall.

One of the objectives of several studies done was simply to observe the incidence of Fear of Success imagery in female subjects at different ages and at different educational, occupational, and ability levels. The specific content of the verbal lead used in each sample was altered so as to make the situation described more consistent and meaningful with respect to the age, educational level, and occupation of the subjects being tested. For instance, in the junior-high and high-school levels the cue used was "Sue has just found out that she has been made valedictorian of her class." The results summarized in Table 1 show that the incidence of $M_{-s}$ in the samples we've tested has ranged from a low of 47 percent in a seventh-grade junior-high-school sample to a high of 88 percent in a sample of high-ability current undergraduate students at a high-ranking eastern school. The incidence of fear of success found in a sample of administrative secretaries in a large corporation, all of whom were able high-school graduates, was also high (86.6 percent). In each of the female *college* samples tested so far, fear of success imagery has ranged from 60–88 percent.

## Empirical Evidence with Respect to the Impact of the $M_{-s}$ on Levels of Aspiration and Performance in Achievement-Oriented Situations

In light of the vast sex differences found in the presence of Fear of Success imagery, it seemed very important to study the differential impact of individual differences in the motive to avoid success on performance and levels of aspiration in achievement-oriented situations, and, furthermore, to understand what personal and situational factors are most effective in arousing the motive or in keeping it in check.

In accordance with the theory, the motive to avoid success affects performance only in situations in which it is aroused. The assumption that fear of success is aroused in situations in which there is concern over or anxiety about

## Table I
### INCIDENCE OF "FEAR OF SUCCESS IMAGERY" FOUND IN VARIOUS SAMPLES TESTED BETWEEN 1964 AND 1970

| Study | Year Data Gathered | Nature of the Sample | N | Number and Percent of the Subjects Showing "Fear of Success Imagery" in Response to the Cue Used | | | |
| --- | --- | --- | --- | --- | --- | --- | --- |
| | | | | TAT Format Standard Verbal Cue | | Questionnaire Format | |
| | | | | N | % | N | % |
| Horner, 1968 | 1964 | *Freshman and Sophomore College Undergraduates* | (178) | | | | |
| | | Males | (88) | 8 | (9.1) | | |
| | | Females | (90) | 59 | (65.5) | | |
| Horner and Rhoem, 1968 | 1967 | *All Female* | | | | | |
| | | Junior High (7th grade) | (19) | 9 | (47.0) | | |
| | | Senior High (11th grade) | (15) | 9 | (60.0) | | |
| | | College Undergraduates | (27) | 22 | (81.0) | | |
| | | Secretaries | (15) | 13 | (86.6) | | |

| | | Students at an outstanding Eastern University | | | | | |
|---|---|---|---|---|---|---|---|
| Schwenn, 1970 | 1969 | Female Juniors (Pilot Study) | (16) | | | 12 | (75.0) |
| Horner, 1970 | 1969 | Female Juniors/Seniors | (45) | 38 | (84.4) | 34 | (75.5) |
| Watson, 1970 | 1970 | Female Summer-School Students | (37) | 24 | (65.0) | | |
| Prescott, 1971 | 1970 | Male Freshmen | (36) | 17 | (47.2) | | |
| | | Female Freshmen | (34) | 30 | (88.2) | | |
| | | Same Females 3 months later | (34) | 29 | (85.3) | | |
| Horner, 1970 | 1969 | Female Law-School Students | (15) | 13 | (86.6) | | |

| | | Graduates from the Harvard Law School 1953–1969 | Questionnaire Form—Fear of Success | | |
|---|---|---|---|---|---|
| | | | High | Blank | Low |
| Horner and Glancy | 1970 | (1) Males (400) | 22 (5.5%) | 175 (43.75%) | 203 (50.75%) |

(Less than 10% of the 225 men who answered the questions scored high in fear of success.)

| | | (2) Females | High | Blank | Low |
|---|---|---|---|---|---|
| | | 1950s (39) | 15 | 14 | 10 |
| | | 1960–1964 (30) | 14 | 10 | 6 |
| | | 1965–1969 (88) | 45 | 26 | 17 |
| | | (157) | 74 (47.0%) | 50 (32.0%) | 33 (21.0%) |

(69% of the 107 Ss who actually answer the questions scored high in fear of success.)

competitiveness and its aggressive overtones was tested in the first study (Horner, 1968). The level of performance of the subjects on a number of achievement tasks in a large mixed sex competitive situation was compared with their own subsequent performance (thus controlling for ability affects) in a strictly noncompetitive but achievement-oriented situation in which the only competition involved was with the task and one's internal standards of excellence. The girls high in the $M_{-s}$ performed at a significantly lower level in the mixed sex competitive condition than in the noncompetitive condition. The girls low in fear of success, on the other hand, did better under the competitive condition as did most of the men (2/3) in the study (Horner, 1968).

Table 2

The Motive to Avoid Success and Performance in Competitive and Noncompetitive Achievement Situations

|  | Perform Better in Noncompetitive Condition | Perform Better in Competitive Condition |
|---|---|---|
| $M_{-s}$ | | |
| High | 13 | 4 |
| Low | 1 | 12 |

$$X^2 = 11.374 \qquad p\ .005$$

SOURCE: Horner, 1968.

Anxiety about success was the only one of the four psychological variables for which individual differences were assessed in the study that predicted female performance. It is important to note that the motive to avoid success showed no relationship with the affiliation motive which was also assessed, nor did the latter predict to the performance of the female subjects. The results of the study clearly indicated that young women, especially those high in the motive to avoid success, would be *least* likely to develop their interests and explore their intellectual potential when competing against others, especially against men.[1]

[1] These conclusions were supported by the responses of the subjects to a questionnaire following their performance in each of the three experimental achievement-oriented conditions. The subjects were asked to indicate on a scale "How important was it for you to do

Our more recent work, much of which is still in progress, has been concerned primarily with an intense and critical analysis of the factors which are particularly prone to arouse anxiety about success and those most effective in minimizing its influence.

## Consequences of the Motive to Avoid Success

It is clear from all we have said thus far that unfortunately femininity and competitive achievement in American society continue even today to be viewed as two desirable but mutually exclusive ends. As a result, despite the recent emphasis on the new freedom for women, there remains a psychological barrier in many otherwise achievement-motivated and able young women that prevents them from actively seeking success or making obvious their abilities and potential. There is mounting evidence in our data suggesting that many achievement-oriented American women, especially those high in the motive to avoid success, when faced with the conflict between their feminine image and developing their abilities and interests, tend to disguise their ability and abdicate from competition in the outside world—just like Sally in the "Peanuts" cartoon who at the tender age of five says:

> I never said I wanted to *be* someone. All I want to do when I grow up is be a good wife and mother. So . . . why should I have to go to kindergarten.

When success is likely or possible, threatened by the negative consequences they expect to follow-success, young women become anxious and their positive achievement

---

well in this situation?" In both competitive conditions the mean level of importance reported by subjects high in anxiety about success was significantly lower than for subjects low in anxiety about success (p .05). In the noncompetitive condition the difference was in the same direction but fell short of the conventionally accepted level of significance (p .10). For subjects high in motive to avoid success differences in mean level of importance between the noncompetitive condition and each of the competitive conditions were significant (p .05), but no significant differences were found between the conditions for the subjects low in motive to avoid success. (Horner, 1968)

strivings become thwarted. In this way, their abilities, interests, and intellectual potential remain inhibited and unfulfilled.

A recent analysis of the data in the initial study together with that of our most recent studies show however that this does not occur without a price, a price paid in feelings of frustration, hostility, aggression, bitterness, and confusion which are clearly manifested in the fantasy productions of these young women. A comparison of the thematic apperceptive imagery of those high and low in the motive to avoid success in response to the cue "Anne is sitting in a chair with a smile on her face" made this quite clear. Whereas more than 90 percent of those low in fear of success imagery in response to the "smile cue" wrote positive, primarily affiliative stories centering on such things as dates, engagements, and forthcoming marriages as well as a few on successful achievements, less than 20 percent of those high in fear of success were of this type. The rest of the responses, if not bizarre, were replete with negative imagery centering on hostility toward or manipulation of others.

The following stories are characteristic of those written by the girls low in fear of success.

(1) Her boyfriend has just called her . . . Oh boy. I'm so excited; what shall I wear? I wonder if I should buy something new to wear. Will he like me? I am so excited. Anne is very happy. Anne will have a marvelous time . . .

(2) Anne is happy—she's happy with the world because it is so beautiful. It's snowing, and nice outside— she's happy to be alive and this gives her a good warm feeling. Well, Anne did well on one of her tests . . .

(3) Anne is alone in her room. It's a beautiful day . . . Her two closest friends have just met marvelous people and believe they are in love. Other nice things have happened to them . . . the beautiful day and her friends' happiness create an aura of happiness about her. She is happy to know that they at least have the things they want . . .

(4) Jane has just received a letter from the biological society of America. She is alone in the room. She did a wonderful experiment with a mutant mouse and broke through in biological science . . .

In comparison with the above, the stories written by the girls high in fear of success were dramatically different and distressing; for example:

(1) Anne is recollecting her conquest of the day. She has just stolen her ex-friend's boyfriend away, right before the High School Senior Prom. Anne was jealous of her friend's popularity, and when they decided not to associate with each other Anne decided to do something to really get back at her friend—take her boyfriend . . . She wanted to hurt her and succeeded by taking the boyfriend away underhandedly . . .

(2) Anne is newly married and she and her husband are visiting friends who have toddlers. The children have been shy with the strangers, but eventually seemed to warm up. The little girl will approach Anne's husband, but not Anne . . .

(3) Anne is at her father's funeral. There are over 200 people there . . . Her mother, two brothers, and several relatives are there. Anne's father committed suicide . . . She knows it is unseemly to smile but cannot help it . . . Her brother Ralph pokes her in fury but she is uncontrollable . . . Anne rises dramatically and leaves the room, stopping first to pluck a carnation from the blanket of flowers on the coffin.

Until now one could only speculate about how much of what was expressed in the fantasy productions of these girls was a true reflection of their actual behavior or intents and secondly, if it was, what repercussions there might be. There is some evidence in Prescott's recent data that some of what is fantasied actually does materialize in behavior.

In his study Prescott was attempting to study the relationship between efficacy imagery on the TAT and certain attitudes and behaviors in education and politics. Efficacy was defined as the subjective experience of one's ability to be competent or to effect desired changes on his environment. It is assumed to be highly related to feelings of self-esteem and is assessed by the presence of efficacy-related imagery on the TAT.

For the thirty-six men in the study, the predicted theoretically consistent relationship between the presence of this type of imagery and specific types of behavior in education and activism in politics was found. For the women, however, the pattern of relationships was confused.

In an attempt to resolve some of the confusion in the female data, Prescott turned to the motive to avoid success and duplicated the previously observed relationship between fear of success and negative-aggressive imagery in response to the smile cue, as well as the significant sex differences in presence of the Motive to Avoid Success.

Prescott went on to observe that 72 percent of the women high in fear of success compared with only 44 percent of those low in fear of success tended to contradict the teacher (p .10) on bases other than those of educational interest. For the men, and low-fear-of-success women, such challenges to the teacher were associated with other efficacious educational behavior, such as staying after class, doing extra work, and hating to have the bell ring at the end.

Prescott speculates that the tendency for high-fear-of-success women to contradict their teachers is a behavioral manifestation of their tendency to write aggressive or hostile stories in response to the smile cue. His argument that this is potentially an example of the frustration-aggression hypothesis receives some support in the data which show that for women, presence of the motive to avoid success and considerations of how consistent one's behavior is with the traditionally accepted female sex role mediates the relationship between efficacy imagery and efficacious behavior in education and politics. For instance, when the behaviors discussed involved direct competition, women usually saw themselves in a supportive, subordinate role, being nurturant and helping someone else. Only the low-fear-of-success women were, like the men, likely to be involved with political actions in which they themselves were competing for office.

A strong negative relationship between efficacy score and motive to avoid success was found ($r = -.40$). For the high-fear-of-success group the mean efficacy score was $-2.11$, for the low-fear-of-success group it was $+2.75$, while the overall mean efficacy score for women was 0.

The results from some new data gathered by Watson as

part of a larger study which show a significant relationship between the motive to avoid success and reported drug-taking are also of interest at this point. The drug-taking measure involved a self-report questionnaire. Reports were taken on categories of pot, speed, LSD, and others. Fre-

### Table 3
#### Fear of Success and Reported Drug-Taking
#### Subjects All Female

|  | Never | Moderate | Heavy |
|---|---|---|---|
| Fear of Success | 5 | 6 | 13 |
| No Fear of Success | 7 | 5 | 1 |

$$X^2 = 8.12 \qquad df = 2$$
$$p\ .02$$

quency of use was measured on a six-point scale ranging from "Never" to "4 or more times a week." All drugs were totaled and split into three major groups: Never $= 4$; Moderate $= 5-7$; Heavy $= 8$ or more.

The causal direction of this observed relationship can only be a matter of speculation until further analyses are completed. Just what the functional significance of heavy drug use is for high-fear-of-success women remains a question that must be considered along with the rest of the data showing that for women the expression of the achievement needs or efficacious behavior is blocked by the presence of the motive to avoid success. In light of the high and if anything increasing incidence of this motive the predominant message from our data continues to be that most otherwise achievement-motivated young women, when faced with a conflict between their feminine image and expressing their competences or developing their abilities and interests, adjust their behaviors to their internalized sex-role stereotypes. In order to feel or appear more feminine they disguise their abilities and withdraw from the mainstream of thought, activism, and achievement in our society. As the data indicate, however, this does not occur without a high price, a price paid by the individual in negative emotional and interpersonal consciences and by the society in a loss of valuable human and economic resources.

## REFERENCES

ATKINSON, J. W. (ed.), *Motives in Fantasy, Action, and Society*. Princeton, New Jersey: Van Nostrand, 1958.

ATKINSON, J. W., and N. T. FEATHER, *A Theory of Achievement Motivation*. New York: Wiley, 1966.

ERIKSON, E. H., "Sex Differences in the Play Configuration of Preadolescents." *Am. J. of Orthopsychiatry*, 1951, *21*, 667–692.

ERIKSON, K., *Wayward Puritans*. New York: Wiley, 1966.

FREUD, S., "The Psychology of Women." In Freud, *New Introductory Lectures on Psychoanalysis*. New York: Norton, 1965.

HORNER, M., "Sex Differences in Achievement Motivation and Performance in Competitive and Noncompetitive Situations." Unpublished doctoral dissertation, Universtiy of Michigan, 1968.

HORNER, M., "Femininity and Successful Achievement: A Basic Inconsistency." Chapter 3 in Bardwick, Douvan, Horner, and Gutman, *Feminine Personality and Conflict*. Belmont, California: Brooks-Cole, 1970.

HORNER, M., "The Motive to Avoid Success and Changing Aspirations of College Women." (Unpublished, preliminary draft, 1970.)

HORNER, M., and W. RHOEM, "The Motive to Avoid Success as a Function of Age, Occupation and Progress at School." (Unpublished research report, 1968.)

KOMAROVSKY, M., "Functional Analysis of Sex Roles." *Amer. Soc. Rev.*, 1959, *15*, 508–516.

LIPINSKI, B. G., "Sex-Role Conflict and Achievement Motivation in College Women." Unpublished doctoral dissertation, University of Cincinnati, 1965.

MCCLELLAND, D. C., J. W. ATKINSON, R. A. CLARK, and E. L. LOWELL, *The Achievement Motive*. New York: Appleton-Century-Crofts, 1953.

MEAD, M., *Male and Female*. New York: Morrow, 1949; also New York: Dell (Laurel Edition), 1968.

PRESCOTT, D., "Efficacy-Related Imagery, Education, and Politics." Unpublished honors thesis, Harvard, 1971.

SCHWENN, M., "Arousal of the Motive to Avoid Success." Unpublished junior honors thesis, Harvard, 1971.

SCOTT, W. A., "The Avoidance of Threatening Material in Imaginative Behavior." In J. W. Atkinson, (ed.), *Mo-*

*tives in Fantasy, Action, and Society.* Princeton, New Jersey: Van Nostrand, 1958.

STORR, A., *Human Aggression.* New York: Bantam, 1970.

TANGRI, S., "Role Innovation in Occupational Choice." Unpublished doctoral dissertation, University of Michigan, 1969.

WATSON, R., "Female and Male Responses to the Succeeding Female Cue." Unpublished paper, Harvard, 1970.

# THE EDUCATION OF WOMEN
*FLORENCE HOWE*

Recently, on a train, a Goucher College student met the editor of a relatively new magazine. "Why don't we get your magazine?" she queried.

"Isn't Goucher a girls' school?"

"Sure, but what's that got to do with it?"

"Well, we didn't think you'd be interested—it's about careers."

This is a perfectly commonplace attitude. Even in 1969, it is assumed that women who go to college are generally sitting out four years of their lives before becoming wives and mothers. During my nine years at Goucher, I have found little encouragement for any other view. Unfortunately, statistics bear me out only too well. Though more women than ever before go to college, and even receive degrees, fewer proportionately go on to graduate school. The faculties of colleges and universities naturally reflect this condition: there are fewer women on the faculties of women's colleges than there were in the 30s; the percentage of women on the faculty of the University of Chicago has dropped from 8 percent at the end of the nineteenth century to a recent low of 2 percent; and a number of

*DR. FLORENCE HOWE taught at Goucher for nine years and now is Professor of English and Women's Studies at the State University of New York, Old Westbury, New York. She is a founder of the Feminist Press, author of numerous articles and a frequent speaker on women's issues. She is president of the Modern Language Association.*

university departments are searching currently for their token female. And as studies continue to show, when men and women of comparable education and experience are employed, women's salaries and rates of promotion are significantly inferior to men's. In spite of a century of sporadic hue and cry about women's rights, and in spite of our rhetoric about the equality of women, even in spite of the pill and the recent outburst of women's liberation groups, women remain a passive majority of second-class citizens.

Our education is chiefly to blame, but of course after one has said that, one must add at once that education reflects the values of our society and is to a major extent controlled by those values. That is to say that we do not think of our girl students as we do our boys—and this is true from the beginning of their school years as well as on to graduate school where women are openly discriminated against for reasons which I do not here need to list. What would happen to men if women were, indeed, allowed to compete in a system equally open to them? This is, of course, a rhetorical question, since it is not likely to happen. We do know that white men, in our culture, are by and large loath to compete with black men, and our friends tell us that women will have to wait until those male racial and economic problems are solved.

Economic and political problems cannot, obviously, be solved by educational institutions. But colleges can educate their students quite deliberately to those problems, and even, if they will, to work toward their solution. Generally speaking, the purpose of those responsible for the education of women has been to perpetuate their subordinate status. There is a hoary story still being told about the difference between educating men and women. It goes like this: "When you educate a man, you educate an individual, but when you educate a woman, you educate a family." Obviously, the story is meant to compliment women as traditional carriers of culture. But more to the point is the role that woman is channeled into by her culture. The question of purpose in education is dependent upon a prior notion of hierarchy. Put another way, education is prophecy fulfilled: imagine women educated for a push-button household and a consumer's life and you create institutions

to effect that. To illustrate, I want to look at the views of
five men—I choose men because for the most part they
have been responsible for our history and our education.

First, Plato and Aristotle, who illustrate two poles: the
revolutionary believer in equality between the sexes and the
conservative believer in the inferiority of women. Plato, as
revolutionary, writes in the *Republic* that, "There is no
occupation concerned with the management of social affairs which belongs either to woman or to man, as such.
Natural gifts are to be found here and there in both creatures alike; and every occupation is open to both, so far as
their natures are concerned." He concludes, therefore, that
"we shall not have one education for men and another for
women, precisely because the nature to be taken in hand is
the same." When he describes roles for women, he allows
them "their full share with men" in all areas of life,
"whether they stay at home or go out to war." He continues, "Such conduct will not be unwomanly, but all for
the best and in accordance with the natural partnership of
the sexes." Obviously, Plato's notions have not only not
prevailed; they are hardly known today.

To read Aristotle on the same subject is to learn how
little a student may learn from a teacher. For to the question "why educate women?" Aristotle would have answered, "Certainly not." This is his key statement, from the
*Politics*: "We may thus conclude that it is a general law
that there should be naturally ruling elements and elements
naturally ruled. . . . The rule of the freeman over the slave
is one kind of rule; that of the male over the female
another. . . . The slave is entirely without the faculty of
deliberation; the female indeed possesses it, but in a form
which remains inconclusive. . . . It is thus clear that while
moral goodness is a quality of all the persons mentioned,
the fact still remains that temperance—and similarly forti-
tude and justice—are not, as Socrates held, the same in a
woman as they are in a man." Aristotle thus offers no
education to women. Or if we think of her in a category
close to the slave's, only such education as will make her
more useful to man, her master. The defining of capability
—or "role definition"—controls education. And Aristotle's
voice has prevailed. He and the early Church fathers settled
the noneducation of women for nearly two thousand years.

Milton's is a useful voice to illustrate the perpetuation of woman's subordinate status in a form somewhat more subtle than Aristotle's. In fact, Milton is my favorite example of such a view, one that I find still dominant today. To Goucher students, I usually say, study him closely: he is the enemy. You must understand your enemy if you are to defeat him. Women are teachable, Milton says, though just barely and only under careful conditions. Certainly, they need to be observed and looked after constantly or trouble may follow, as it did for Eve in the garden. But the order is plain enough: God teaches man and man teaches woman, just a bit of this or that, enough to keep her in her place. Milton's main idea is hierarchy: woman is subordinate in status, inferior in intellect, and even less reliable than man in matters of the heart.

In matters of the heart, Jonathan Swift has argued, either sex might claim distinction—for foolishness and corruption. "I am ignorant of any one quality," he writes in "A Letter to a Young Lady on her Marriage," "that is amiable in a Man, which is not equally so in a Woman; I do not except Modesty and Gentleness of Nature. Nor do I know one Vice or Folly which is not equally detestable in both." If women are more full of "nonsense and frippery" than men, their parents are to blame for failing "to cultivate" their minds. "It is a little hard," Swift continues, "that not one Gentleman's daughter in a thousand should be brought to read or understand her own natural Tongue, or be judge of the easiest Books that are written in it. . . ." Swift's remedy is to offer himself as tutor for the young lady in question; in *Gulliver's Travels*, he recommends education for both sexes.

When I asked my students what they thought of Swift— expecting at least some delight or surprise at his modernity —one sophomore said, "Why, he's insulting. I didn't like him at all." She added that his attitude was patronizing and demeaning: "He doesn't care anything about the girl. All he cares about is that she please her husband. That's why he wants her to be able to read. So that she can carry on a conversation with him."

Marianne's sharp disgust surprised me and some of the other students present, one of whom commented gently

and slightly in wonderment: "But that's just why I'm going
to college and taking English courses. My boy friend is at
college and I think that I should be able to keep up to his
interests and his friends. You know, I want to know what
he's talking and thinking about."

Both students had in mind a passage in which Swift
offers his young lady a rationale for the education of her
intellect: "to acquire or preserve the Friendship and
Esteem of a Wise Man, who soon grows weary of acting the
Lover and treating his Wife like a Mistress, but wants a
reasonable Companion, and a true Friend through every
Stage of his Life. It must be therefore your Business to
qualify yourself for those Offices." That is, to function
interestingly for one's husband—or children. The question
of self or vocation is entirely absent, as it is from the concerns of the majority of women in college today.

About a hundred years after Swift wrote his essay,
Harriet Taylor and John Stuart Mill began a long and complex intellectual relationship, one of the results of which
was a book that Mill published in 1869 called *The Subjection of Women*. Like Swift, Mill believed that sexual
differences do not entirely, if at all, control the intellect.
Women are not a separate and lesser species but, as Mill
put it, they are a separate class or caste, created and controlled by men through a process of socialization that includes depriving women of education.

I want to quote from Mill's book at some length because
I think it is still the best single piece of analysis and because
it is his only significant work not available in paperback.
First, his argument about the alleged inferiority of woman's
"nature":

> Standing on the ground of common sense and the
> constitution of the human mind, I deny that anyone
> knows, or can know, the nature of the two sexes, as
> long as they have only been seen in their present rela-
> tion to one another. If man had ever been found in
> society without women, or women without men, or if
> there had been a society of men and women in which
> the women were not under the control of the men,
> something might have been positively known about the
> mental and moral differences which may be inherent

in the nature of each. What is now called the nature of women is an eminently artificial thing—the result of forced repression in some directions, unnatural stimulation in others. It may be asserted without scruple, that no other class of dependents have had their character so entirely distorted from its natural proportions by their relation with their masters. . . .

Women's relations with their "masters," according to Mill, are unique for an "enslaved class," for two reasons; their universality in time and space, their perpetuation seemingly without "force." "The subjection of women to men being a universal custom," Mill begins urbanely, "any departure from it quite naturally appears unnatural." On the other hand, most women accept their state. In fact, "All causes, social and natural, combine to make it unlikely that women should be collectively rebellious to the power of men." Thence follows an analysis by a "master" of the master's point of view: "Women," Mill begins,

are so far in a position different from all other subject classes, that their masters require something more from them than actual service. Men do not want solely the obedience of women, they want their sentiments. All men, except the most brutish, desire to have, in the women most nearly connected with them, not a forced slave but a willing one, not a slave merely, but a favorite. They have therefore put everything in practice to enslave their minds. The masters of all other slaves rely, for maintaining obedience, on fear—either fear of themselves, or religious fears. The masters of women wanted more than simple obedience, and they turned the whole force of education to effect their purpose. All women are brought up from the very earliest years in the belief that their ideal of character is the very opposite to that of men; not self-will and government by self-control, but submission and yielding to the control of others. All the moralities tell them that it is the duty of women, and all the current sentimentalities that it is their nature, to live for others, to make complete abnegation of themselves, and to have no life but in their affections. And by their affections are meant the only ones that they are allowed to have—those to the men with whom they are connected, or to the children who constitute an additional and indefeasible tie between them and a man. When we put together three things—first, the natural attraction between opposite sexes; secondly, the wife's entire dependence on the husband, every privilege or pleasure she has being either his gift, or depending entirely on his will; and lastly, that the principal object of human pursuit, consideration, and all objects of social ambition, can in general be sought or obtained by her only through him, it would be a miracle if the object of being attractive to men had not become the polar star of feminine education and formation of character. And this great means of influence over the minds of women having been acquired, and instinct of selfishness made men avail themselves of it to the utmost as a means of holding women in subjection, by representing to them meekness, submissiveness, and resignation of all individual will into the hands of a man, as an essential part of sexual attractiveness.

Mill concludes this section of his book by summarizing:

In no instance except this, which comprehends half the human race, are the higher social functions closed against anyone by a fatality of birth which no exertions, and no change of circumstances can overcome; for even religious disabilities . . . do not close any career to the disqualified person in case of conversion.

The remedies Mill proposes are changes in law and the opening of educational and vocational opportunities to women. His ideal is "freedom of individual choice" regardless of sex:

If the principle is true, we ought to act as if we believed it, and not to ordain that to be born a girl instead of a boy, any more than to be born black instead of white, or a commoner instead of a nobleman, shall decide the person's position through all life —shall interdict people from all the more elevated social positions, and from all, except a few, respectable occupations.

It is a pity to spoil Mill's peroration with a sour note, but he makes, in the end, a nineteenth-century distinction between married and unmarried women. Whatever her talents and inclinations, the married woman ought to stay at home—for practical reasons at least. No housekeeper can replace her with economy and efficiency both. When he pleads for woman's presence in the university and at the bar, Mill is pleading for the unmarried woman alone.

Obviously, in 1969 we do not officially hold to Mill's distinction between married and unmarried women. And yet our suburban style of life institutionalizes Mill's notion of economy: by the time a woman pays for a babysitter and a commuter's ticket, she might just as well stay at home. In fact, though our forms may look different, essentials have not been altered for the majority of women since Mill's day. And some beliefs about us harken back to Aristotle and Milton, though now they are part of the unconscious of college-educated females. For example, the basic assumption about women's biological inferiority, dealt what one might have expected to be a death-blow in the 1940s by Simone de Beauvoir, comes to college annually in the heads and hearts of freshmen women.

Four years ago, I began to use as a theme in a freshman writing course, "the identity of woman." Some of the corollary reading assigned has included D. H. Lawrence's *Sons and Lovers*, Elizabeth Bowen's *The Death of the Heart*, Doris Lessing's *The Golden Notebook*, Mary McCarthy's *The Group*, Kate Chopin's *The Awakening*, Simone de Beauvoir's *The Second Sex*, a collection of essays entitled *Women in America*, and Ralph Ellison's *Invisible Man*. In every class I have taught, someone has asked, "Why are our books only by women?" or "Why do we have to read mostly women writers—they're always inferior to men." Even in something as simple as athletics, girls have been eager to point out that female swimmers are inevitably inferior to male swimmers. Only once in all the classes I have taught did a student point out that males of some cultures, say Vietnam, may be physically "weaker" than females of another culture, say the Soviet Union or the U.S. And I have typically received lengthy essays "proving" that women must be inferior since in the whole length of recorded history so few have been truly great. At the same time, I should point out that a questionnaire I used did not verify the impressions I gained from class discussion and student themes. It was as though the students answered the questionnaire in terms of what was "supposed to be."

The same split occurred with regard to the question of women's social equality. On paper, the students indicated a belief in its existence. In class and on themes, they gave evidence that they lived their lives in the chains Mill described and analyzed. Their dependence on male approval came out particularly in discussions of coeducation, though with varying degrees of openness and consciousness. Close to the surface and freely aired was the question of dressing for boys. It was a relief, students said, to be able to live whole days at Goucher in jeans and no make-up. And they joked about looking very different—sometimes unrecognizably so—when they left the campus for a date or a weekend. Very few students said that they dressed in a particular way to please themselves. Much more difficult to get at was the deeper question of sexual role in the classroom's intellectual life. I have had only a few students able to say, as one did this year, at the beginning of an essay, "Men distract me." In fact, that was why she had come to Goucher. In high school classes, Virginia became aware of her unwillingness to be herself: either she was silly or silent. Here at Goucher, she said, she was able to say what she thought without worry about what boys would think of her. Moreover, she was going to be a lawyer because that was the most "male" occupation she could think of. She wanted to show that she could do what any man could. If she could manage that, then she could be "independent," and that, she said, was a meaningful goal.

Virginia is an exception. Obviously women go to college today in numbers that would boggle Mill's brain. But most come without genuine purpose, or, when they discover purpose, it is in Mill's or Swift's terms. About halfway through one term, my freshmen were talking about the motivation of a character in a story by Doris Lessing. Joan tried to make a point about the complexities of motivation by saying that she had come to Goucher only because her parents had wanted her to go to college and this was as good a place as any and that for nearly a whole term she had been wondering what she was doing here, but now she understood what her purpose might be, not only here but for the rest of her life. The class hung on her words, but she grew suddenly shy of naming her discovery. Finally she said, "Enjoyment. I think that I am here to enjoy not myself but life—and also later on, after I get out of college." Joan was immediately chastized for "selfishness": "The purpose of life," another student said, "is to help other people." Most of the twenty students sitting in the circle proceeded to take sides; a few tried to reconcile the two positions: "helping other people" might itself be enjoyable." "If you enjoyed tutoring in Baltimore slums," one girl retorted, "then you weren't doing your job properly." The discussion raged as few classroom discussions do. I said nothing, except at the end when we had to stop for supper. Then I commented that no one had mentioned, in more than an hour, earning money or having an ambition or vocation; no one had talked about the fulfillment of her identity in terms of satisfying and useful work. The girls were not particularly astonished; my terms meant very little to them, at least at that time. The girls who were most numerous and most vocal were those who thought that "service" or "helping people" should be performed for its own sake, because that was morally right, not as an enjoyable act for the individual to perform or for any other reason. This is the woman-slave mentality that Mill was describing a hundred years ago.

It is clear that a social order sends girls to college who are generally unconscious of their position in that society. And on the whole, colleges do very little to sort out the conflicts girls feel. How can they please themselves and please their (future) husbands and/or satisfy the demands of class and society? Their conflicts have grown sharper, more fierce and destructive, since Mill's day. For women a hundred years ago, the problem was to fight for the right to an education or to be allowed to vote. Women have these rights. But in fact a woman is—unless she closes her eyes completely—pulled terrifically in two opposing directions. They are not parallel lines: marriage and career.

On the one hand, she is still playing with dolls, dressing

to suit boys, and pretending to be dumb in a co-ed high school class. She is still a continual disappointment to her mama if she returns from college each term without an engagement ring. She wants—and naturally so—to get married and have children. To assume that a career would not conflict with marriage and child-rearing, at least as our present society is arranged, is an error.

On the other hand, her college education assumes that even if she is not going on to a career or graduate school, she should specialize for two years in some particular area of knowledge. The curriculum, moreover, doesn't help her to work out the dual roles she may have to assume, that is, if she is not simply a housewife. It assumes, largely, that the problem doesn't exist. The curriculum is geared to vocation, however narrowly conceived. An English major will send you to graduate schools, for example. But nothing I can think of at Goucher prepared women for marriage or motherhood.

Why do we educate women? Cynically, I might answer, to keep them off the streets. Certainly, we are not thinking of them even as we do think of men—as the future engineers and administrators of a complex bureaucracy. Then why design curricula for women that are remarkably similar to those for men? Why, especially when they and their teachers assume a lesser degree of serious intellectual commitment from female than from male students, even from those avoiding the draft. I have heard a few male professors at women's colleges candidly admit either the "ease" with which it is possible to teach women or the "bore" it is. And women like me fret about the "passivity" of our students. But mostly we do little to promote a reawakening or an altering of students' or faculty's consciousness. "There, there," one professor was overheard saying to a weeping freshman, "don't cry about that paper. In a few years, you'll be washing dishes and you won't even remember this course."

I have spent a lot of time on the purpose of education because I think that we must be conscious of our motives. Are we, as one student put it recently, educating girls to become "critical housewives?" I for one am not, not at least any more than Hopkins' professors are educating "critical husbands." We can do better than that for our students and I think we should. Women and men both need work lives and private relationships. Women need to be educated for consciousness about themselves as members of a society they can learn to change. Even if women are to spend some years of their lives at home with small children part or all of the day, these are few years when compared to a lifetime. Without what I call a "work-identity," moreover, women, their families, and society generally lose a great deal.

# II.
# Pink and Blue:
# The Color Line

# MALE AND FEMALE

*EVELYN GOODENOUGH PITCHER*

*The controversy over the origin of sex differences—whether innate or learned—has raged for centuries and the last word is still to be said. Evelyn Goodenough Pitcher does not take a stand on the issue, though her studies of preschool children indicate that psychological sex differences exist from a very early age and that parents unconsciously encourage them. This essay was first published a decade ago before the present rebirth of feminism, explaining perhaps the author's complacent view of women's status. Commenting on the mother's role, Pitcher remarks, "she knows that the worlds of both sexes are hers"!*

How early do young children play a distinctive sex role, and how do parents accent sex differences in young children? Evidence from a recent study of mine suggests that by two and through ages three and four, boys and girls have strikingly different interests and attitudes, which their parents steadily influence and strengthen.

The influence is inescapable. In my study, fathers and mothers who were questioned agreed that women are more indirect, illogical, circuitous in their thinking than

*EVELYN GOODENOUGH PITCHER is chairwoman of Eliot-Pearson Department of Tufts University. Her books include* Children Tell Stories: An Analysis of Fantasy *and* Helping Young Children Learn.

men. Men's thinking was considered to be more analytical, definite, precise, abstract, direct. "Men have a quantitative, analytical, objective interest in things," was a typical remark. The woman's mental approach was described to me as "cunning and deceptive, intuitive, subjective." Be a listener at a women's luncheon and note the subjects of conversation; do the same with a group of men. Eavesdrop on a woman's telephone conversation; listen to a man's. It has long been a byword that men like to talk about business, politics, and the mechanisms of their cars, while women commonly talk about their friends, their hats, and their children. Is this true?

If men and women are really thus different in their thinking, or if they are believed to be, how would this influence the development of young children? How can we find out? I devised a simple experiment which allowed me to take boys or girls, one at a time, into a room to play with a box of brightly colored plastic chips the child had never before seen. During a ten-minute period I recorded everything said, and thus had some tangible record of the way the child was thinking.

The forms and problems the game presented seemed to fascinate the boys, so that they kept talking about the chips, wondering about their use, how they could be arranged, where they had come from. If the boys' remarks left the immediate situation, they rarely went far away.

The whole business intrigued the girls much less. Like women bored by men's conversations, after a few minutes they would look up and say, "I'm going to a party tomorrow," or, "We have blue wastebaskets at our cottage at the beach." Their digressions included comments about planting seeds, birthday parties, Christmas, friends, gifts, clothing, visits to doctors, pictures on the wall, quarrels with brothers, conversations with mothers. The tendency of the female to jaywalk in conversation was amply illustrated by the little girls.

Had the parents themselves presented different models of thinking to their children and thereby influenced the way the children thought? And what about different kinds of interests in boys and girls? Did parents expect the girl to be more "intuitive, subjective," and the boy to be more "analytical," with an "objective" interest in things?

To find out about this, I questioned parents about what they thought made their little girls feminine and what characterized masculinity in the little boys.

Both fathers and mothers clearly regarded it as feminine to be interested in pretty clothes, domestic habits, families, or babies, or for a girl to identify herself with women. They expected a girl to be more social, more interested in herself and in other people than a boy would be. They reported of their girls, "She looks at people's faces and observes their expressions. She observes relationships," or, "She wins by guile; she has bright playful ideas calculated to win and attract attention." In addition, the girl—never the boy—is marked as especially feminine because of her coquetry, in such remarks as "seductive, persuasive," and "She cuddles and flatters in subtle ways." It would seem that by noticing such social awareness and coquetry in the little girls, parents encourage the development of precisely these traits.

In contrast, parents regarded it as masculine to be interested in objects or ideas, not persons. Parents commented often on the boys' preoccupation with bulldozers, trucks, cement mixers. The boy, as the parents reported him, was not only interested in objects but in making them work.

Would young boys and girls actually show such a difference in interest in people or objects as parents seemed to expect? To answer this question, I again devised a simple test. I gave a child a paper and pencil and asked him to make something. Any parent will know that with a child from two to four I got usually meaningless scribbles, often slightly formed but still hardly recognizable as drawings. Clearly, nothing could be learned from the marks themselves; the point was to ask the children what they had drawn and then to record their intentions.

The result was significant and fascinating. Over 50 percent of the girls drew, or said they had drawn, persons, while only 15 percent of the boys did so. In just as great disproportion boys were drawing things, such as a car, a park, a bench, an egg, a train, a tree. The girls' drawings also showed a marked interest in the family, in babies, in clothing, in domestic activities, which was not apparent in the boys' drawings. When asked what they had drawn, girls made such remarks as, "Susie on roller skates, sleeping"; "Just a girl, with snaps instead of buttons"; "A man with an orange shirt, white hair, like Grandpa. He's barefoot in the grass, because it's summer." Usually boys would only name the object.

The impression that the greater interest of women in persons and the greater interest of men in things and processes begin at an early age was confirmed also by the stories children made up in response to the simple request, "Tell me a story." Here are some typical examples:

### TWO-YEAR-OLD GIRL

Once there was a little kitty cat, and he scratched. Then the Mommy spanks the kitty. Then the kitty doesn't cry. He scratches the Mommy. The Mommy puts him in jail, but he has friends and he can peek at them. More friends come, but they're going to be naughty friends and spank the kitty. He scratches them and cries because he doesn't like naughty people.

### TWO-YEAR-OLD BOY

A camel, and he went down the mountain, and he fell down. Then he fell down in a hole. Then a bear came and saw, but he shoot the bear. Then he jumps on the bear. Then he ride on the horse and go, "Giddyup, giddyup," up the mountain.

### THREE-YEAR-OLD GIRL

A little girl, gone to a party. Her got dressed up. Her came back home and got spanked 'cause her been a naughty boy 'cause she got into Mommy's ink. And she spilled it all over the floor, over the rug, and over the floor. Then she went to bed.

### THREE-YEAR-OLD BOY

A broken train was going down a hill. And it splashed right in the water. The engine driver got wet. A big wolf came along. And the Indians came too, and ran into the water. A big Indian was very mad and chased the engine driver, and they fight. The Indian wins, and the engine driver is dead.

Analysis of some 360 stories collected from children of from two to five years revealed that girls tend to present people more vividly and realistically and to identify themselves with the personalities and experiences of others. Direct conversations are often quoted in the girls' stories, and people are more individually conceived and characterized by their names. The boy, on the other hand, speaks with significantly greater frequency of things. He seems especially fascinated by vehicles of transportation and machines, and talks about rockets, boats, cars, trucks, ambulances, fire engines, covered wagons, parachutes. He is interested in mechanical gadgets, too, such as the cement mixer and typewriter, and in such elements of nature as sun, ice, rain, snow, and hurricane. The girl's interest in objects is more likely to be in personal or household equipment, or in productive nature—leaf, tree, flower. She mentions relatively few vehicles of motion.

Among the people most prominent in the girls' stories are parent figures, and the girl is much more likely than the boy to express emotions about the parental figure, particularly the mother.

If the boy is experiencing intense reactions to his mother and father, he rarely expresses them directly. From the stories, it would seem that the girl's personal awareness and personal identity are sharpened by seeing the mother doing things all day with which she can identify. The boy, on the contrary, especially one whose father goes away to a business or profession all day, sees little he can copy or take to himself. Under the circumstances, it is not surprising that he is less aware of himself as a person than the girl. The girl usually knows in great detail what it is to be a mother. The boy more often discovers masculinity and identifies himself with it in a general way —in the policeman, fireman, soldier, Indian. These are the masculine roles he can comprehend and play at imitating as he cannot do with his father's role as factory worker, executive, lawyer, or scholar.

It also seems that the girl's early identification with her mother may influence her ideas about morality, for she is over and again more personally and maternally involved in her judgment of what is good or bad than is the boy. The girl seems not to be the more moral of the sexes, but the more personally concerned with morality. Even at an early age she moves in her traditional role of guardian of domestic morality. She can be emotionally and personally involved as she identifies both with the mother who must punish naughtiness and with the child who is naughty. The badness the girl reports is usually minor and spiteful—tearing dresses, ripping trousers, snatching candies, spilling milk or ink, cracking things, scattering crumbs. The girl is skilled in planning punishment at once devastating, personally rejecting, and humiliating.

Considering the amount of aggression and destruction in the three-year-old boys' stories, relatively little is labeled naughty. For the most part, the gamut of physical aggression is described, atrocity is piled on atrocity, and there seems no particular reason why it should start or stop. For all this aggression, the boy most often mentions two forms of punishment—spanking and jailing. Clearly, the expression of aggression is more common than the consideration that aggression should be punished.

It is the boy rather than the girl who seems to move into a concern for the larger social aspects of goodness and badness. He sees the possibility of good and evil in the same person and specifies that standardized kinds of good and bad characters, such as witches or police, might have other qualities. For boys the arena of evil is more often out of the house. It is the boy who matches forces of good and evil in organized warfare, who sees a responsibility for saving people or fighting from a sense of duty.

All these data from children would be consistent with the observation that questions of social or personal morality among adults are largely regulated by women, while men generally formulate the problems of law, labor, or diplomacy. Children in this study suggest that such differences are already identifiable in the years two through five.

Although almost as many girls as boys speak of aggression, it tends to be much more violent with the boys than with the girls. One almost feels and hears the reverberation of crashing, shooting, and pounding as general catastrophe reigns. Boys have much more shooting in their stories, and often use the word "fight," suggesting an adversary and a definite concern as to who will win. They biff and butt, roll on the ground, punish with their hands, puke and whiz, lasso and tie up, poison and hook with rope ladders. They use oral aggression freely, in addition to swords, knives, bows and arrows.

Girls show in their stories a relatively more prosocial, adultlike aggression. Among the girls, even shooting is not so likely to be synonymous with violence or death. The girl seems, indeed, more sensitive to the personal implications of death, and more likely to see death as a reversible process, with persons disappearing and returning. The boy seems more likely to deny the reversibility of death. His greater expansiveness in ideas, on the other hand, may lead him to be more receptive to abstract considerations of the finality of life or of a life hereafter, as the following story shows:

> Once there was a terrible crocodile with sharp teeth. He saw a person, ate him up, and he got fatter, fatter, and fatter. He threw up and died. He was underground. He couldn't get up, 'cause he was dead. He went back to seed; he has a little seed like you have a baby in your stomach. And he grew up to be a crocodile again, because he was planted in the ground and up came a crocodile again. And that's the end.

In considering such a theme as food, or eating, which includes the providing, preparing, or partaking of food and drink, data from the stories show that it is obviously the girl who markedly identifies with the female role of cook and hostess. The girl mentions specific meals and is interested in the eating of food as a social occasion, and in the preparation of food. The boy is not so likely to mention specific foods; breakfast, lunch, and dinner are likely to be just in the routine of the day.

The girl's interest in food again suggests the female's loving concern with details, her tendency to utilize experience in the enhancement of self. Similarly, mention of clothes or apparel is not only more popular with the girls, but among them is treated with more attention to detail, to color, to suitable costume. The boy is not much interested in the details of dress except when he mentions a cowboy suit or an Indian costume. The girl is also likely to comment on general appearance, to perceive greater subtleties of emotional tone in characters—"a nice smile," "a stern voice," whereas the boy tends to a more generalized description of persons or references to being "mad" or "glad."

A concern with friendship and pleasure from interpersonal relationships, a mention of friend or friendship are more frequent among the girls. It is the girl, not the boy, who refers to love, courtship, and marriage. Already, in the early years, the female is attentive to the predatory task of ensnaring a husband. A memorable example is the story from a four-year-old girl which seems to express the association of feminine sexuality and the sea, which appears so often in myths:

Once there was a fish named Flower. She went down in the water and said, "Oh, my gosh, where's my lover?" She went down in the cellar where my house is. She saw a big father fish which had a sword in his nose. She ran away from the house and hid in another house. She ran up the water and flapped out. She ran away. She went to another house in a deep, deep river. She saw her own home which had her lover in it. They kissed each other. That's the end.

These stories from children bring out the different emphases expressed by boys and girls in fantasy themes. Such differences must in part have arisen from the different ways in which society makes demands or presents opportunities to children of different sexes.

I have already made reference to the parent interviews as providing evidence of cultural demands and expectations; a closer scrutiny of the material comparing the father's interviews with those of the mother reveals a curious differential in parents' sex-typing.

Both fathers and mothers allow what appears to be tomboyishness in girls during the early years, while they try to discourage what might be feminine behavior in their sons. Their attitude seems to reflect the general pattern in America, where our culture tends to grant the female the privileges of two sexes: with impunity she can dress like a man; she can at will interchange the "little boy look" with cloying femininity. She can use any name—her own or her husband's—enter any job, any area of education, or she can make a career of motherhood. She can be independent or dependent, or both, as and when she pleases.

The male has no corresponding freedom. He is increasingly expected to help in the home, but this is largely because the woman without servants demands such help. Deviations in dress, appearance, or job that reflect the feminine are immediately suspect. If a man is actually feminine in his instincts, even homosexual, he must never appear to be so.

It was impressive to observe to what extent the father more than the mother was responsible for sharpening such differences. There were clear indications that fathers especially tended to emphasize what seemed to be an exclusive masculinity in their sons. "He gets mad if I tease him about his interest in anything girlish and therefore babyish," said one father about his two-year-old son. "His father was furious when I painted his nails red," said a mother about her husband's reaction to fingernail polish on his son. And another mother remarked, "On Halloween a boy can't wear anything feminine. The idea of lipstick horrifies a father."

A direct question followed such observations as those I have just mentioned, and brought out the same contrast between father and mother. A father, when asked if he would be disturbed by aspects of femininity in his son, said, "Yes, I would be, very, very much. Terrifically disturbed—couldn't tell you the extent of my disturbance. I can't bear female characteristics in a man. I abhor them." But a mother said, "Jimmy is not as masculine. But he'll grow up to be considerate and kind. Gentlemanly, rather than masculine." Another father was distressed and scornful at signs of his son's femininity. "He's always interested in flexing his muscles. Perhaps he has to prove that he's masculine—that's why I call him feminine." The same boy's mother admitted that at one time she was very much concerned about her son's femininity, but reasoned thus, "I am aware these people make splendid contributions to the world. I'd try to help. I would turn all my energies to producing a good environment for him."

A father was also more likely to appreciate femininity in his daughter. One mother reported her husband's pleasure when she put their six-month-old daughter into a dress for the first time. "That's much nicer than these old pajamas," said the father. Another mother reported that her husband blanched when he found she had cut her daughter's long hair. "Promise me that you will never, never cut it again," he said.

Still another father taught his son how to react to femininity in his baby sister. "His attitude toward his sister is masculine, very big-brotherly. I've impressed him with this—to be careful, treat her nice, 'oogle-google' with her." The same boy's mother remarked, "My husband talks in a high voice to the little girl, in a deep bass voice to Jimmy." Other remarks show that there is a tendency for the father to grant his daughter a special, privileged place: "It is so inevitable to spoil a first child, I'm glad my first child was a girl," and, "I'd be stricter with a boy than with a girl, perhaps because my own father was stricter with me. Mary [daughter] once asked me [the father] which of my 'girls' I liked best—her or her mother. One is always conscious that there is a little sex factor between a little female child and her father."

Indeed, half of the little girls' fathers pointed out their daughters' coquetry in a way to show that they were themselves personally intrigued. Ten different fathers made the following remarks, describing their daughters:

"Very coquettish. Gallantry and consideration work with her."

"Seductive, persuasive, knows how to get me to do things she can't get her mother to let her do."

"Inclined to be coy and a little seductive."

"A bit of a flirt, arch and playful with people, a pretended coyness. Sometimes she seems like a Southern girl—may be a little flirt when she gets older."

"Soft and cuddly and loving. She cuddles and flatters in subtle ways."

"Engages in outward display of affection."

"Her coyness and flirting, 'come up and see me sometime' approach. Loves to cuddle. She's going to be sexy—I get my wife annoyed when I say this."

"Certain amount of flirtatiousness to most everyone, especially strangers. Occasionally with me too. Little shy looks and smiles—attention-getting devices. I am probably completely taken in by her."

"She is extremely loving, always coming around hugging and kissing. She loves to play with me at night. I always heard that girls look more to their fathers than to their mothers."

"A soft person, lovable, affectionate."

Such statements suggest that there may be some general truth about father-daughter relationships in the remark of one father: "Femininity cannot be divorced in my mind from a certain amount of sexuality." Such an attitude of the fathers must be presumed to be conditioning their little daughters in this aspect of femininity.

Again, in contrast, only half of the mothers mentioned the flirtatious character of their daughters at all, but when they did so, showed no such personal involvement. Where the father said, "She flirts with me," the mother, in one way or another, said, "She flirts with her father or with other people."

Only sparse examples could be gathered from the interviews to indicate that the mother was playing an active part in encouraging her son to a more masculine role insofar as interaction between the sexes, or the cultivation of manly custom, is concerned. Mothers are as likely to take their sons to a tea party as to visit a railroad yard, and are as likely to give their daughters overalls as dresses. The fathers appeared more likely to view the boy as a male trapped in a world of women and needing to guard his uncontaminated masculinity from association with the female sex.

Of course, the impact of this expectancy of the child appears in his everyday behavior. In children's drawings, we noticed that if a boy drew a person, he would almost invariably draw a boy, whereas girls would draw either girls or boys, almost indifferently.

Thus, it would appear that the father has much greater interest, and hence influence, than the mother in accentuating differences between boys and girls. He likes the little girl to be a little girl and enjoys her femininity, but expresses himself with intolerance about any show of femininity in his son. The mother, however, seems more like a mother animal, treating the babies in her litter with little distinction. Perhaps the mother can afford to be relaxed, since she knows that the worlds of both sexes are hers. She has no real need to promote the purity of either, except insofar as she wishes to please her husband and go along with general cultural mores.

It seems from the evidence I have here presented that boys and girls are from early age subjected to influences that would develop different characteristics. However, the parents interviewed were apparently unaware that they were doing or saying anything directly to foster in their children interest or lack of interest in people. They were probably influencing their children in two ways. First of all, by subtle rewards and punishments, if only those of tone of voice, they perhaps registered approval or disapproval as situations arose. Second, we assume that the girl tends to imitate the mother and the boy the father by reproducing their kinds and sources of interests.

The question arises whether parents really create such distinctions as I have described in otherwise undistinguished personalities. Or do parents—and all our cultural influences—just develop and accentuate tendencies that children are born with? Of course, it is impossible to come to any firm conclusions about whether or to what extent psychological sex differences are innate or learned or both. But however the differences arise, it is clear that they exist from a very early age in children in our society, and that we might do well to consider such differences in planning children's education.

# AS THE TWIG IS BENT*

*CAROLE JOFFE*

A problem within the field of socialization that has recently been raised with new urgency is that of sex roles. This renewed attention is coming about in large part as a result of issues currently being raised in the women's movement; a central theme of the analysis emanating from this movement is that American society demands the socialization of both men and women into fixed sex roles, at great cost to the individual needs of members of both sexes.[1] This socialization is said to be omnipresent, literally starting at birth with the proverbial blue or pink blanket that is given to the newborn infant. But although the women's movement has caused a new focus of attention on this phenomenon of early socialization into sex roles, certain social scientists have long given attention to the same topic. Kagan, for example, has noted the signifi-

* I am grateful to Shelden Messinger and to Norman Denzin for help with an earlier draft of this paper.

[1] For example, Millet's statement: "Because of our social circumstances, male and female are really two cultures and their life experiences are utterly different . . . Implicit in all the gender identity development which takes place through childhood is the sum total of the parent's, the peers', and the culture's notions of what is appropriate to each gender by way of temperament, character, interests, status, worth, gesture, and expression. Every moment of the child's life is a clue as to how he or she must think and behave to attain or satisfy the demands which gender places upon one." Millet, p. 31.

*CAROLE JOFFE is a doctoral candidate in sociology at the University of California, Berkeley.*

cance of the differential treatment accorded male and female infants and the effects this has for the child's subsequent sexual identity (Kagan, 1964). But although it is generally agreed—both by those who adopt a critical stance and those who seemingly are interested only in description—that sex-role socialization is everywhere, certain institutions are of course more crucial in the cultural transmission of these expectations than others. Two of the most centrally involved agencies in the sex-role socialization of the young (and hence two that are currently undergoing severe criticism) are the family and the schools. In this paper, I will discuss experiences of children with respect to socialization in one of these institutions, the nursery school. For many children, it must be remembered, their attendance at nursery school marks their first institutional contact outside of the home and thus this kind of school can justifiably be seen as performing critical socialization functions. In my analysis. I will attempt to demonstrate both what the school seemed to be demanding from the children in terms of sex-appropriate behavior and how the children themselves conceived of their sex-role obligations. It is hoped that a close look at the quality of sex-role socialization received by persons in their first institutional setting will not only enlighten us further as to the meaning of sex roles in American society, but also, for those of us committed to some form of change in the institutions "serving" our children, such a study might suggest some policy implications.

Before proceeding to my own findings, I will briefly comment on work done to date on nursery schools and socialization into sex roles. Although no major work appears to have been done specifically on nursery schools as *facilitators* of sex roles,[2] there has recently been some attention paid to other educational institutions as they relate to sex roles. Several writers have noted the significance of the fact that at the elementary-school level most teachers are women and the effects this has on children of both sexes in terms of classroom behavior (Clausen, 1968; Sexton, 1969; and Silberman, 1970:153). Because elementary schools are geared, in Silberman's term, toward "docility,"

[2] Although there has of course been a huge amount of work done on nursery-school age children in the area of "sex differences."

this reinforces cultural messages about appropriate behavior little girls are already receiving elsewhere; in the case of little boys, this sets up a conflict in view of their masculine-oriented socialization, with the result being that some claim the only boys who do well academically at the elementary level are those who become "feminized" (Sexton, 1969). But other than noting these two quite important facts—that most primary-school teachers are female and that the school situation puts forth an ideal of docility among students—there does not yet seem to be accounts of the *specific* ways in which schools foster socialization into sex roles. Certainly there remains a gap in studies of the nursery school in this respect. In this paper I will attempt to pinpoint various structural and ideological features of the preschool and discuss their relationship to this kind of socialization.

A final digression before I begin will be to make clear my own bias about the issues under discussion, "sex roles." The teatment of sex roles in this paper will be substantially different from that it receives in much of the socialization literature. A common feature of the huge number of studies of preschool children and sex roles is that, for the most part, what constitutes appropriate "sex roles" is not made problematic (Oetzel, 1966). The researchers had a preconceived idea of what the content was of proper masculine and feminine roles and tested the children to see how well they conformed to these already existing measures.[3] Thus, for the majority of the researchers in this field there is a seeming acceptance of prevailing ideas about maleness and femaleness: children who don't comply with these concepts become listed as deviants. I will be taking the position that the idea of sex roles, particularly for children of preschool age,[4] is a very problematic matter and should be approached with great

---

[3] A pleasant exception to this genre is the work of Hartley (esp. 1959) who tested *conceptions* of sex roles among children, and found, among other things, that children of working mothers sextyped fewer items than those of nonworking mothers.

[4] Even for those who take the fact of physiological differences between the sexes as a legitimate basis for the establishment of fixed sex roles, it is generally agreed that the physiological differences that exist between children of pre-school age are of minimal significance. See Hamburg, 1966.

skepticism. The reader should understand that what I will
be discussing is how the school fosters contemporary
*notions* of sex roles and what use of these notions the
children make; I will not be speaking to the issue of what
the "real" differences between the sexes are and therefore
what would constitute legitimate sex-role socialization. An
additional bias that will occur is that in spite of the lack
of discussion about what sex-role socialization *should* be,
I nevertheless will take a position against what I feel are
the most blatantly damaging forms of sex-role socialization
that are the norm now, e.g. channeling members of each
sex into restrictive roles that limit the life options and
behavioral choices of each. Accordingly, in this paper the
"good" school will be one in which these attempts at imposing such damaging sex roles are minimized while the
"bad" school is one that encourages them.

## A Case Study of One School

In this section I will report on two separate periods of
participant observation at a nursery school. Although at
the time of the observations, I was also concerned with
other factors, I will deal here exclusively with the findings
on sex-role socialization and how the children themselves
conceived sex roles. I will first briefly describe the research
situation.

The first series of observations were made over a period
of two months in the spring of 1970 at a parent-nursery
school in the San Francisco Bay area, California. (A
parent-nursery is one in which in addition to two full-time
teachers, each of the participating parents takes a weekly
shift at the school). The school I observed was affiliated
with the Unified School District, although some of the parents paid tuition. There were regular teacher-parent meetings and parents were encouraged to help formulate school
policy.

The children observed in the first series consisted of 22
students, 9 male and 13 female, ranging in age from three
and one half to four and one half. The school was racially
mixed, consisting of about an equal number of children of
white professionals and graduate students, and black children from lower-income families. The second set of ob-

servations, carried out in January–February 1971, were of the afternoon session of the same parent-nursery and thus a certain proportion of children who had been seen in 1970 were seen again almost a year later. Twelve of the children observed during the afternoon session had initially been seen earlier and nine had not been seen before. In this second group, there were fourteen females and nine males, with the percentage of black children being somewhat higher than it had been in the previous group. The age of the children in this group covered a span from four and one half to five.

Each of the classes had two full-time female teachers (one black and one white in each case) and each day from three to five mothers would also work. (The school claimed to be eager to have fathers of the children participate as well, but except on a very sporadic basis e.g., emergencies, fathers did not participate during the periods of my observation). As an observer, I essentially took the role of a participating mother (*albeit* without a child), e.g., watching children in the yard, reading stories, etc. Additionally I attended parent-teacher meetings and had opportunities for extended conversations with both teachers and parents.

I will start my discussion by offering in broadest terms an analysis of the school's overall "attitude" toward sex roles and the type of behavior that seemed to be expected from the children in this respect. In each of the sessions I observed, there was an extremely positive (in terms of the value bias mentioned earlier) orientation toward sex roles: there was no active move to impose any notion of correct sex-typed behavior and most impressive, there was a very relaxed response toward those children who violated normal expectations about members of their sex group. Clearly then, the school I happened to study represents a negative case in terms of any attempt to show dramatically how damaging socialization takes place in nursery schools. I do believe, however, that such a school is useful to us in spite of its atypical quality. First, in examining such a "good" school, it is possible to draw out policy implications for other less liberated institutions; second, as we shall see, even in a school committed to avoiding imposition of these notions of sex stereotypes, inadvertent sex-role socialization does take place.

Starting a discussion of sexism in the schools in reverse, therefore, I will list the features of this particular school that are indicative of its policy of not stressing sex roles. Most generally, there was no structural indication of two separate categories of persons: bathrooms, for example, were not segregated and often children of both sexes would use them together; all activities in the school program were officially open to both sexes and the participation of all children in some of the more traditionally sex-typed activities, e.g., cooking, washing dishes, was consistently sought. Most striking, as I already indicated, was the tolerance shown those children whose behavior showed varying degree of sex identity "confusion", e.g., those children who with regularity would dress as members of the opposite sex and assume the "wrong" sexual identity in games of "house." The school's most notable example of what elsewhere might be termed as "deviation" is K., a Polynesian male who frequently dresses in women's clothes, occasionally wears his hair in "feminine" fashion, and in games with the other children, often assumes female identities, e.g., "sister." As I will discuss later, there is a certain variation among the children as to how K's behavior is received. In terms of his teachers, however, I was struck by the firm commitment on their part to noninterference. Both felt it would be unnecessarily upsetting, both to K. and to the other children, to in any way make an issue out of this behavior. Rather, in discussion with the observer, one of the teachers stressed she viewed such behavior as very creative and emotionally beneficial—"it's good for him to have all kinds of experiences." Both of the teachers referred to K.'s foreign background as a factor which although not entirely understood by them, might conceivably explain some of his actions, particularly his mode of dancing. In sum, then, the vocabulary of motive which seemed to be in operation among the teachers with regard to sex identity "switching" was that it was common to many children; it was in many aspects a "creative" exercise; it would only be to all the children's detriment to have such action questioned by adults.

What I have described above is the school's official position toward socialization into sex roles; I believe that this represents a type of institution, on an imaginary continuum of "bad" to "good" schools, that is in ideological terms, impressively free from sexism. However, special attention must be paid to the variety of ways in which inadvertently sex-typing nonetheless does take place in this school. The first point to make is that while it is easy to gain a sense of the teacher's policies, one cannot as readily presume to summarize all the parents' attitudes. As mentioned, this school is one in which parents work a weekly shift, and thus each child was exposed regularly to approximately 18–20 different women. To understand all the subtle influences playing on the children, ideally one would have to determine systematically each of these women's own attitudes about sex roles. While observations suggest that most of the mothers shared the teachers' assumptions in this regard,[5] there nevertheless occurred a series of small events in the interactions between children and mothers (and teachers to a certain degree as well) that in a cumulative sense could well serve to convey to the children messages about sex-role expectations. One of these seemingly trivial events, which occurred fairly often, was the acknowledgment of the girls' clothing:

> M. walks in wearing a dress she has not worn before. One of the mothers says to her, "M., what a pretty little lady you are today."

One might argue of course that admiring a child is not the same thing as sex-typing her. Nor will I suggest that admiring a child is "wrong" and should not be done. I have to point out however that in some cases this unavoidably has consequences for the child's self-conception in terms of gender identity. Not surprisingly, the pattern I noted of compliment giving was that *girls were more frequently admired than boys, and moreover, girls received more compliments on days they wore dresses rather than pants.* It is outside the context of this paper to consider how ultimately damaging it is for little girls to be responded to in this way. I use this example simply as an illustration of one of the variety of subtle ways in which girls (and boys) get cues as to differing social images of femininity and masculinity.

[5] One teacher told me of having at one point had some difficulty persuading some parents to accept the idea of nonsegregated bathrooms.

An event which I observed far less frequently and which conceivably served the same function of transmitting cues as to appropriate sex-linked behavior as was the occasional positive reinforcement a boy would get when he ably defended himself against a physical attack, as in the following:

> L. and N. have been arguing over the use of a spade. N. pushes L. and L. responds by delivering a solid punch to N.'s chest. A mother who has witnessed the scene says to the observer (within hearing of L.), "Did you see the punch L. gave N.? He really can take care of himself like a man."

Because there is such strong prohibition against fighting in the school, in fact incidents like the above do not occur very often, i.e., the fights occur, but most mothers would not give this kind of approval; but whether in this context or in others, e.g., physical strength contests in games, there no doubt occurs a differential amount of reinforcement accorded to boys' physical exploits than to girls, with the obvious implications for self-concept of each sex.

A far more clear-cut example of damaging sex-role socialization offered to the children can be found in the quality of the media in use at the nursery school. There is clearly a lag—perhaps somewhat unavoidable—between the school's own attitudes toward sex-typing and quality of materials in use at the school. The storybooks read to the children, the songs taught them at music time, the traditional children's games they play[6]—all contain to a great extent vestiges of dominant social attitudes toward sex roles. For example, a mother leading the children in singing, sings a form of the typical children's song in which each character performs a different task:

> And the daddy went spank-spank, and the mommy went "shh-shhh." (The song concerned a child who had made noise on a bus.)

[6] To gain a sense of the extent to which sex-typing occurs in traditional children's games, see Iona and Peter Opie, *The Lore and Language of Children.* Oxford: Clarendon Press, 1959.

The lag, as I stated, is at least in part unavoidable. There simply do not yet exist adequate nursery-school materials, especially storybooks, that are free from sex-typing.[7] An accommodation made by some teachers who work in the nursery school is simply to alter the stories as they read them to the children (Denzin, 1970:20). But until the same serious effort is made to prepare materials that are free from sexism that recently appears to have at least been started in the preparation of nonracist material the quality of children's objects in the school (here I am including both literature and toys) will remain a major source of traditional sex role.

Another factor in the school that I see as inadvertently contributing to an unfortunate notion of sex specialization is the fact that all the adults working there are female. Again, this is something that the school itself does not prefer, but rather it is a reflection both of the structure of the individual families participating in the school program and the job arrangements that presumably most of the children's fathers have. We can speculate about several possible consequences the all-female population of the school might have on the children's conceptions of sex roles. I would suspect that for these children the main consequence of this situation is the realization that in our society child care is exclusively a female function. For these children, their school life is essentially a continuation of their family life, in that they predominately spend time with their mothers (and other females) and rarely see adult males. In a situation such as this, one can readily understand the source of the pattern noted by many—that children make clear distinctions between expectations from father and mother (Henry, 1963:127-146).[8] For those

---

[7] One might argue though that the situation is better in nursery schools than in elementary schools because so much of nursery school literature is concerned with animals and fantastic adventures, etc. It is in the elementary school textbooks that the worst offenses take place, with the very stereotyped notions of sex roles presented in the family scenes. A movement is currently starting in California to take legislative action against these textbooks.

[8] One of Henry's most revealing findings was that although children made these sharp differentiations between role of mother and father,

working toward a future in which there is meaningful sharing of child-care responsibilities between parents, the lack of men at institutions such as these makes the attainment of such a goal more difficult. We can see how the unfortunate cycle of American family life as it now exists is maintained in these and similar situations: fathers due both to their own lifelong socialization which has stressed extensive interest in nurturant functions as "unmasculine" and to their actual job situations, don't participate in this type of school; mothers even with cooperative schools such as these, don't have careers and spend far more time with the child than the father does. The father takes on a somewhat formal role, seen largely as the final authority in disciplinary matters (Henry, 1963)—thus it ultimately becomes somewhat a bizarre deal to all concerned (father, mother, child) to have men take an active role in childcare.

### Awareness of Sex Roles among Children

In this section I will discuss how the children seemed to respond to the school's efforts to minimize sex-role imperatives and to the inadvertent socialization that nonetheless took place. The reader should bear in mind that how children perceived sex roles is of course not simply a function of what transpired in the school; their own families as well as numerous other influences in their lives (e.g., television)[9] also contributed to this awareness.

On the basis of my observations, I conclude that while all the children in the school had correct knowledge about their gender identity,[10] there did not exist among these children any patterned recognition of appropriate sex roles; the children as a group did not perceive certain activities or modes of behavior as being the exclusive property of

---

they in fact were very unhappy about them! "But many expressions of traditional masculinity and femininity are now felt by children to be intolerable." Henry, p. 137.

[9] With regard to television, it must be mentioned that the favorite program of nearly all the children in the school I studied, "Sesame Street"—although in other respects excellent—does very little, if anything, to challenge traditional conceptions of sex roles.

[10] It is generally believed that children gain a sense of gender at approximately eighteen months. See Hamburg, 1966.

one sex. Although there were no systematic efforts to articulate the rights of males and females, on a more sporadic basis the simple fact of sex difference itself would occasionally be invoked as an attempt at behavior control. Under the appropriate conditions, e.g., an encounter between persons of both sexes, one of the parties would sometimes point to the fact of sex difference as an attempt to justify his actions. The following is an example of this use of sex categories as an "ideology of control."

> C. and two other girls are playing on top of a large structure in the yard. A. (male) comes over and C. screams, "girls only!" to which A. screams back, "No, boys only!"

I think the above example is especially useful because it emphasizes the reciprocal (and thus in a sense, meaningless) character of these exchanges. "Girls only" is immediately countered with "boys only" and thus one can reasonably conclude that to neither of the contestants is there any serious belief in an essential "male" or "female" aspect of the structure under dispute. Rather sex differences are called forth as a seeming last-ditch effort to impose one's will when the other means of behavior control typically in use have not been effective.

Further evidence that this use of sex categories is quite unrelated to the child's actual perception of sex-appropriate behavior can be found in the behavior of K., the boy who was mentioned earlier as often assuming the identity of a female. K., who elsewhere tampered with quite fundamental assumptions about proper "male" conduct, nonetheless used sex categories in the same way as mentioned in the previous case.

> S. (female) is playing the guitar. K. comes over and asks her to let him play it. When she refuses, S. says, "that's for boys, not girls."

In general then the pattern is that the children will make reference to sex categories when there is a reason to do so (which usually means when a piece of property is under dispute). It should also be pointed out that this ideology was consistently quite unsuccessful; I never in fact saw a

child yield to his or her opponent, simply because sex
categories were cited, although other ideologies, e.g., the
value of sharing, in similar situations sometimes do work.
In sum, we might look at the use of sex as an ideology
of control in childhood as a revealing caricature of the
adult world and its usage of sex categories. Like these
children, adults also invoke sex as a means of behavior
control; the crucial differences are that among adults, the
two categories are utilized in a patterned way (some would
call it male supremacy) and both male and female adults
—unlike these children—actually behave in accordance
with this ideology.

The only other regular mention of sexual categories that
I observed on the part of the children came in the reactions of some to the sex identity "switching" of K. and
several others (in addition to K., I noted about five others
—one male and four females—who also periodically assumed roles of the opposite sex).[11] For example, upon
seeing K. dressed in feminine apparel, a typical comment
would be, "Hey, that's for *girls*". However, neither K.'s nor
any of the other children's violations of behavioral expectations in this matter ever became a major issue in the
school for the remainder of the children (in large part, I
believe, because of the low-keyed reaction of the adults in
the school). Thus, for example, although in games of
"house," the clear majority of the children chose identities
consistent with their sex, there was minimal or no questioning of the fact that some of their playmates acted in the
opposite way. So it might be concluded, therefore, that on a
daily basis, a conscious awareness of different sexual categories were not a dominant theme in the life of this nursery
school—although comparative studies suggest that the situation can be very different in other preschools (Greenwald,
1970).

## Male and Female Subcultures

Although the children themselves did not articulate sex
categories as a major factor in their school lives, I, as an

---

[11] An additional tribute to the strength of sex-role socialization in
our society can be seen in the fact that in a nonthreatening environment such as this, only 5–6 children regularly experimented with
assuming opposite sexual roles.

observer, did nonetheless see very intriguing patterns of "sex differences" in terms of friendship networks and play preferences. A small percentage of the school population (4–5 girls and 3–4 boys) assumed on a fairly consistent basis elements of what might be called traditional sex roles. The boys in question established a form of "masculine subculture," playing mainly with each other out of doors, and while the girls I refer to did not establish as exclusive a social grouping, they did spend a great deal of time in an all-female society, and for the purposes of discussion, we can analyze their activities in terms of a female subculture. In this section, I will further describe each of these so-called subcultures, explore the possible relationships to male and female groupings found later in the life cycle, and finally ask what these subcultures reveal about the school itself as a facilitator of sex roles.

The group I have designated as the "male subculture" consisted of a friendship circle of three boys, L., P., and G., all black with the occasional participation of W., also black (the four made up the entire black male population of the school; thus, as will be discussed later, race is obviously a central factor here also). It is on the following grounds that I have chosen to see this group in this particular light: they, of all the other individuals or informal groups in the school, spend the greatest amount of time outdoors, mainly playing at very active games, e.g., racing tricycles; they are the most "aggressive" persons in the school, judged simply on the number of physical fights they have with one another and with outsiders; their speech, finally, contains frequent use of phrases of "toughness" that one does not as often hear from the other children, e.g., "don't mess with me," "I'm gonna take care of you," etc.

This group neither exclusively plays with each other nor only plays at active outdoor games. It is interesting to note though that in their intersections both with other children and with other activities, they typically bring their "masculine" mode of behaving to the new situation. In other words, when they play with other children, they immediately attempt to assert dominance; when at cooking sessions, they will demand to be first, take the other children's materials as they are needed, etc. Finally, perhaps most interesting—although least susceptible to generalization—is the quality of the friendship I noted between one

member of this group, L., and a black female, V. I noted
that on those occasions that L. breaks away from his
friends and plays separately with V., they both refer to
themselves as the "L. Brothers." In other words, this seems
to suggest that V. is accepted as long as she literally becomes one of the boys. In general, then, I am arguing that
both in terms of the large amount of time this group
chooses to spend solely with each other and in view of their
prevailing interpersonal style, it is useful for us to consider
them as a masculine subculture within this school. (It
should be stressed that this decision is partially reached by
comparing them with the other males in the school who
show a far greater range of behavior.)

The group I consider as the female subculture participated to a far greater extent in a variety of activities and
associated with persons of both sexes outside of their immediate circle than did the males mentioned above. The
reason I am treating them in this light is because of the
very definite group identity that existed among them, and
more particularly, because of the daily recurring rituals
that took place within the group. These rituals included,
for each member, the scheduling of individual actions in
relation to the group and also the constant location of oneself in the groups' very powerful social hierarchy. Although
they often made forays to persons and events outside of
the group, members seemed to return periodically to a
"quorum" (e.g., at least two out of the five) both to report
on themselves and to reaffirm their group ties. In the following example, we can see a case of the most simple
function performed by this group, e.g., members' use of one
another to orient themselves to school life:

M. arrives at school and immediately goes up to J. and
H. (both also part of this circle) and says, "Hi, J., I'm
playing with you today, right?" J. answers, "No, I'm
playing with H. now."

It should thus be noted that although the group is looked
to as a primary source of companionship, it is also the
constant source of rejections, as persons trying to maintain
places in the social hierarchy of the group drop low-status
friends for higher ones. In the next example, there is a
more dramatic case of a group member rejecting her com-

panion of the moment (who actually is only a marginal member of the group), but then attempting some accommodation:

> H. and A. (marginal member) are playing together in the yard. J. and a group of others call out to H. to join them at the swing. Although A. hasn't been invited, she goes along also and hangs around on the fringes of the group. H. looks at A. sheepishly and then says to the observer standing nearby, "Carole, would you play with A. for a while?"

The reader might very well question at this point my labeling as "female" this tendency toward exclusion and social ranking. As I have reported elsewhere (Joffe, 1970), in fact, nearly all the children engaged in it on occasion; the point is that it appeared to be only within this group that this behavior was so regularly tied to the same persons and hence had meaning in a *social group*.

Our next task is to see the resemblances that exist between the male and female subcultures I have described and those that occur elsewhere in the life cycle. In fact there does seem to be a quite uncanny resemblance between the behavior noted in the nursery school and that observed by Henry in his study of adolescent culture in a high school. Speaking of the differing nature of male and female friendship groups, Henry said:

> Boys flock; girls seldom get together in groups above four . . . Boys are dependent on masculine solidarity . . . the emphasis is on masculine unity; in girls' cliques the purpose is to shut out other girls (Henry, 1963: 150).

In the behavior of these nursery-school children we appear, then, to have a case of what might be seen as anticipatory socialization; the male and female subcultures noted in the nursery can almost be considered embryonic forms of those that occur in adolescence. What do these recurring patterns tell us about the "nature" of males and females, and more specifically, about the role of the varying institutions providing behavior settings for the children and the adolescents? The first point to be stressed is that for Henry, the

difference in male and female culture he saw were directly
traceable to the different social circumstances of each of
the groups. The tendency of the boys to "flock" was attribut-
able to the fact that the most significant activity in their
lives was team sports; the girls' competitive behavior was
basically due to a variety of circumstances which all converged to make the chief task of their lives an overwhelming necessity to be "popular," i.e., compete for boyfriends
and other affirmations of their "femininity." Obviously in
such a developed form, these same circumstances do not
have meaning at the nursery school level: the boys do not
play team sports and the girls are not involved with courtship. To understand why therefore such similar patterns
were observed at the nursery, we have to first consider the
possible salience of some factors not directly related to sex
itself, but mainly we have to take fresh account of the
strength of the sex-role socialization that has already imposed itself by the age of five.

In explaining the particular cases of male and female
subcultures that were observed in this school, we have also
to consider the relevance of race as a contributing factor
in the former and conceivably "idiosyncrasy" in the case of
the latter. As mentioned, all participants in the male subculture were black, and counting the fourth occasional
member, this group included the entire black male population of the school. While the question of the situation of
black children in a nursery school such as this one deserves
far more extended consideration, initial observations suggest that it is very likely that the group in question, in its
impetus to establish a separate identity, was at the very
least attempting to assert a mixture of both maleness *and*
blackness. As for the idiosyncratic nature of the female
subculture, it should be remembered that in a nursery
school of a fairly small and stable population, one child
can establish a tone that is picked up by others and becomes a part of school ritual. In the case of the exclusion-
ary behavior that I mentioned as being a central aspect of
the female society, I noted in the first set of observations
that it appeared to be J., a member of this group, who
initially introduced the particular vocabulary of exclusion-
ary categories to the entire school. Thus, in its particular
forms in this school, it might be reasonably said that this
behavior was partially due to one or two children.

To the extent that the behavior I noted goes beyond the limits imposed by race and idiosyncrasy (and certainly in the case of the girls, I am convinced it does), and can be validly related to sex, I think that what we have is eloquent testimony not to the "differences" between the sexes, but to the degree to which these children have somehow picked up notions of how their society both expects and encourages separate cultures of male and female. Going beyond this initial fact of separateness, the differing characters of each of the societies suggests evidence of the very early age at which at least some children perceive the existence of differing assumptions of correct male and female behavior. Somehow, the little boys I observed "knew" that a comfortable[12] sense of self, in relation to masculine identity, was achieved by at least partial isolation from female things and by disproportionate aggressive behavior. Similarly the notion had somehow been conveyed to the little girls in question that one defines oneself by one's friends and if necessary, betrays one's friends. Seen in a certain way, the lack of female solidarity—which has both been put forward as a central theme of the analysis of many in Women's Liberation and which also has started to yield as a result of the exposure of many women to the Movement —can be seen to have taken root among some females at an astonishingly early age.

To end the discussion with an attempt to link these arguments to the nursery school, specifically to determine the extent to which the school itself is accountable for this situation—on the surface, the findings are puzzling. I have shown a "good" school—one that in no way appeared to consciously foster notions of sex stereotypes—and yet some of the children acted in traditional ways. This leads to two quite obvious conclusions: The first is that the nursery school does not exist in a vacuum; teachers, parents, and children all bring to the school experiences from outside settings, e.g., the family, which often have drastically different conceptions about sex roles. The second conclusion is simply that this study has actually learned very little about the *mechanisms* by which sex-role expec-

---

12 I use this word "comfortable" of course in a very tentative way. I am trying to convey the idea that acting in such ways as they did clearly fulfilled some notion they had of "what made sense."

tations are transmitted. We have seen very clear-cut policies adopted in this school to minimize children's awareness of sexual differentiation, but we have seen their limitations. In terms of research strategy, it would seem that to understand completely how sex-role socialization takes place, especially in such a good setting, participant observation is only the first of several necessary lines of action. A final comment pertinent to further research is to reiterate that the present paper represents a task only half-completed. It is imperative next to study a "bad" traditional school and examine its structural and ideological aspects as well as its students' responses. It is only by such a comparative approach that we will be able to gain a fuller sense of the role actually played by the school itself in the transmission of sexual stereotypes.

## REFERENCES

CLAUSEN, J., *Socialization and Society*. Boston: Little, Brown, 1968.

DENZIN, N. K., "Children and Their Caretakers." Paper prepared for Social Science Research Council, Self-Concept Work Group of the "Learning and the Educational Process Subcommittee on Compensatory Education."

GREENWALD, S., "A Study of Sex Identity, Self-Imposed Sex Segregation and the Peer Group in Preschool Children." Unpublished paper, 1970.

HAMBURG, D., and D. T. LUNDE, "Sex Hormones in the Development of Sex Differences in Human Behavior." In Eleanor Maccoby (ed.), *The Development of Sex Differences*. Stanford: Stanford University Press, 1966.

HARTLEY, R., "Sex-Role Concepts Among Elementary School Age Girls." *Marriage and Family Living* 21: 59–64, 1959.

HENRY, J., *Culture Against Man*. New York: Vintage, 1963.

JOFFE, C., "Taking Young Children Seriously." Paper Presented to the 1970 American Sociological Association Meeting, 1970.

KAGAN, J., "The Acquisition and Significance of Sex-Typing." In M. Hoffman (ed.), *Review of Child Development Research*. New York: Russell Sage, 1964.

MILLET, K., *Sexual Politics.* New York: Doubleday, 1970.

OETZEL, R., "Annotated Bibliography of Research on Sex Differences." In Eleanor Maccoby (ed.), *Development of Sex Differences.* Stanford: Stanford University Press, 1966.

SEWARD, G., and R. E. WILLIAMSON, *Sex Roles in Changing Society.* New York: Random House, 1970.

SEXTON, P., *The Feminized Male.* New York: Vintage, 1969.

SILBERMAN, C., *Crisis in the Classroom.* New York: Random House, 1970.

# ARE LITTLE GIRLS BEING HARMED BY 'SESAME STREET'?

*JANE BERGMAN*

Tokenism has come to "Sesame Street." Since its inception, the much-publicized vanguard heavy of educational programs has educated children in part by its consistent presentation of a world virtually without female people. For a little girl engaged in her own passionate struggle for self-definition, watching "Sesame Street" last year—and even this fall—was like taking lessons in invisibility. Each appearance of a female character in her constricted, stereotyped role was doubly damaging because female characters actually appeared so very rarely.

Partially in response to protest about the program's relentless sexism, "Sesame Street" has added two female characters to the cast—one of them a "mail-lady." What else has changed? Is sexism gone from the "new" "Sesame Street"? Tune in:

Puppets play an important role. In the puppet universe last season, when a female appeared—which was seldom—she was almost invariably a strident mother, a hapless, hopelessly vague mother, or a simpering, querulous little girl with pigtails and a squeaky voice.

This season, there have been additions to the heavily male puppet cast, mainly in the group scenes: a lady in an incredible rococo hat waiting for a bus; a pony-tailed cheerleader; a monster-woman named Arlene Frantic who sits with two male monsters on a TV game-show panel, and Sally Screamer, a trembly hysterical game-show contestant who wears—right, an incredible rococo hat.

When my young son heard me mention that there are

still almost no female puppet-people on "Sesame Street," he disagreed: "There's that mother, you know."

"Roosevelt Franklin's mother?" I asked. Roosevelt Franklin is an amiably rebellious black boy who, last season, was continuously being chased and cornered by his overbearing mother and forced to say his alphabet. Lately Mom seems to have mellowed—read, become more "feminine"; her new image involves greater cooperation with her son in his triumphs. (She still apparently lives in an apron.)

My son said there was also "that other mother in the other family."

"Oh. Any others?"

"No."

The subtle shift in Ms. Franklin's attitude does nothing to improve the pervasive momism of the puppet world, and so we have Grover, a wonderfully helpful monster, recently telling a little man who keeps throwing tangerines away over his shoulder to create beautiful offstage smashing noises: "Is your *mommy* going to be *mad* at *you!*"

The cartoon world is as bad, or worse; it's simply overwhelmingly male. Interspersed throughout each program are often more than ten cartoons, most of them designed to teach reading or number skills. Typically, last season, all were narrated by males and almost all were about males. Sometimes, these days, one or two cartoons on a given day will be introduced or narrated by females or will show a female character; these are brief, and very few have been shown so far. On December 8, a randomly selected day of the "new" season, cartoons were shown fourteen times, and *all* were by and about males. How does a little girl conceptualize the idea of woman's absolute nonexistence?

What about the new films? Many deal with such topics as animals or farming or how things are made. The ones about human beings invariably show boys and men as active, competent people who do things, girls and women as placid domestic workers, spectators, or passive objects—often, as human backdrops for stories which are really about such things as the lives of vegetables.

A film repeated often on the "new" "Sesame Street" shows James, a New Mexico Indian boy. He narrates while we see him walking to the school bus with his two sisters following him. (If one weren't aware of the imperatives of "Sesame Street's" pervasive anti-feminism, the question might logically arise: Why isn't it at least half *their* story?) We see kids running outside after school—boys in the foreground, girls somewhere behind them. In James's home, not surprisingly, sex-role stereotypes are the rule: Mother makes tortillas and serves them to the seated family, and mother and grandmother make necklaces out of corn.

Another recent film shows men fishing from a boat with nets. Again, a little boy narrates: "My brother steers the boat; it's hard work."

Still another: A man in a kayak navigates rapids and performs stuntman tricks with impressive skill and a confident mastery of the environment which is really exhilarating to see.

In contrast are these two very typical portrayals of females:

A little girl is shown passively watching a fishbowl. Her voice is heard: "My goldfish has two eyes like me, but I wonder if *he* sees things like I do." The camera hustles to a fish's-eye view, and the rest of the film shows how the fish—the only "he" in the film—perceives the world.

Or two girls are seen playing with a doll house, as a voice sings a tinkly, sugary song whose organizing idea seems to be this: "One, two, two little dolls, two little chairs, two little girls had a little doll house." In addition to the fact that the girls are shown doing only the most inactive stereotypically "feminine" play, there is the suggestion that they themselves can be seen as little objects suitable simply for inclusion in a rather boring musical list.

Watching such films, I find myself longing to see a woman or girl doing *anything* I can relate to, and painfully aware of what it must be like for my four-year-old daughter to try to find a picture of herself anywhere in the images she sees here. "Sesame Street" shows her not possibilities, but walls.

In addition to puppets, cartoons, and films, there are ongoing scenes showing the real people who live on Sesame Street. In typical events involving children, girls have been and still are much more visible than in any of the puppet, cartoon, or film sections: at least half are girls. It seems clear that the generally greater prominence of girls here is directly related to the curious *deadness* of "Sesame Street" children. Basically, what they do is line up and listen, take orders, follow directions, pay attention, and strive, with beautifully programed success, to produce the worshiped *right answer*. In accordance with our cultural stereotypes, such roles must be heavily filled by girls. (There has been criticism of this aspect of the program, and my impression is that lately the kids are just slightly less catatonic. Either they've started breathing by executive fiat or I'm getting used to the docile simpering that passes for "life" on "Sesame Street.")

Even while occasionally getting more active girls into the live sections, "Sesame Street" frequently blows it. For example, Gordon is seen assembling a team of kids for a basketball game. A few boys run up—none of them exactly Willis Reed, but most of them competent-looking—and, finally, they're joined by one daring smallish girl. Gordon's response is, "Hey! How'd *you* get in here?"

The addition of the two new women to the live adult cast is an apparent attempt to correct last season's objectionable ratio of three men to one woman. Molly the "mail-lady" was the showpiece, very visible on the first new program, not very visible now. (A recent scene in which Bob delivers a package has him mentioning that he is acting *for* Molly, but she never appears.)

Maria, the other newcomer, is much better integrated into the life of the program: it's good to have her there. But it must be emphasized that the change is largely undercut by the addition to the cast of at least *four* new men, actually setting the balance at seven men to three women, and by the appearance, on any given program, of several men but only one woman. The result: Females are, consistently, heavily underrepresented in terms of actual air time—just as they were on the "old" "Sesame Street."

At least as significant, the old sexist stereotypes are alive and well. A recent sequence shows the charming monster Grover falling in love with Maria at his first meeting with her. She arrives, and he is transfixed, after the manner of swains through the centuries; his mouth falls open, he sighs wildly, he becomes entirely hysterical trying to anticipate and fill all her requests. Breathless, feverish Grover is practicing chivalry, a behavior which reduces the adored female to an object; she is, in effect, told, "Your wish is my command—so sit still." Grover is ingenuously explicit about the cause of his passion: "OHHHH, she is so *pret-ty*." So much for Maria, the ex-person.

Then there's Susan, the one woman who "integrated" last season's male cast, a determinedly cheerful home-maker notable for her impeccable posture. Susan is still the quintessential housewife, spending her days in mindless domestic service: shopping for oranges (she counts them with the kids), endlessly icing homemade cakes and serv-ing juices and hanging balloons for kids' parties, or just posing with a laundry basket or in front of her dishtowel and refrigerator—and always with this highly inappropri-ate smile on her face. (It has been mentioned on the program that Susan once did have a vocation. She was a nurse—what else, a surgeon? Now she simply looks neat, devotes herself to others, stays home, needs nothing—and never, never *does* anything.)

All in all, "Sesame Street" *has* changed, from being in-credibly sexist to being slightly less sexist. And *that's* what we used to call tokenism.

I have the impression that originally the program was put together in part with an eye toward upgrading the image of men for the benefit of black children who have had small opportunity to see brothers or fathers function-ing in the world with autonomy and self-respect. Even if this be true, there can be no justification for the creation of a program for black *and* white boys *and* girls full of such vicious, relentless sexism.

With exquisite verisimilitude, the program shows little girls that, in our culture, being female is being nobody. It is also a fact that black people were once literal slaves. Would black parents object if "Sesame Street's" blacks—not all, just almost all—were fat, kerchiefed mammies and cotton-picking, shuffling Uncle Toms?

As a feminist, I am engaged in an effort to make our home a place where sexist stereotypes will not be perpetu-ated, where our children can feel free to learn about be-coming not aggressively "masculine" or passively "femi-nine," as defined by a hideous cultural stereotype, but hu-man. For my husband and me, it is very much an ongoing struggle with our own conditioning, and we are trying, al-ways, to make whole people out of the male and female puppets we once felt ourselves to be. For our daughter, we want a life truly full of the joy of knowing herself to be *real*. We want her to have a continuing sense of the options involved in self-definition.

Watching "Sesame Street" this season—last week, in fact —I had too many moments when the only appropriate response seemed to be to turn off the set.

Hey! "Sesame Street"! Is *that* the right answer?

# CHILDREN'S BOOKS:
# THE SECOND SEX,
# JUNIOR DIVISION

*ELIZABETH FISHER*

We live in a sexist society. Almost from birth we are in-doctrinated with the notion of male superiority and female inferiority, male rights and female duties. It is in the earliest years that children form images of their worth, their future roles, the conscious and unconscious expec-tations placed upon them. Investigating books for young children in book stores and libraries I found an almost incredible conspiracy of conditioning. Boys' achievement drive is encouraged; girls' is cut off. Boys are brought up to express themselves; girls to please. The general image of the female ranges from dull to degrading to invisible.

Since females comprise 51 percent of the population of the United States, one would expect them to be equally represented in the world of picture books. On the contrary they vary between 20 and 30 percent. There were five times as many males in the titles as there were females, four times as many boys, men, or male animals pictured as there were females. In special displays the situation was even worse. The fantasy worlds of Maurice Sendak and Dr. Seuss are almost entirely male. The three major prize-winners for this year, displayed together on a table at Brentano's, were all about males: *Sounder* about a black boy by William Armstrong, *A Day of Pleasure* by I. B. Singer, and *Sylvester and the Magic Pebble*, by William Steig. Where are all the missing females? Have they been

*ELIZABETH FISHER is a writer and the editor of* Aphra, *a feminist magazine.*

exposed to the elements, as with primitive tribes? Or are they sequestered behind walls, as in Southern Italy or the Near East?

This preponderance of males is not limited to humans. Animals in books are male for the most part. Elephants, bears, lions, tigers are males or, as in the Babar books, isolated females are shown in the company of a majority of males. In the veld it is the female lion who does all the work; in the picture-book world she doesn't exist. There are some books about female animals, and an occasional reference to the female of the species. Cows, obviously, are female. Hens. too. In "Rosie's Walk" by Pat Hutchins, a hen walks unscathed and unnoticing through all kinds of dangers—reenforcing the stereotype that nothing ever happens to she's. Sylvia the Sloth is the heroine of a not unpleasing book. Somehow the female animals tend to be those whose names are synonyms of derogation. Petunia the Goose, Frances the Badger—I suspect the choice of these animals reflects the low esteem in which women are held. A rhinoceros is male, a hippopotamus female. Leo Lionni's snail in *The Biggest House in the World* is a he who has a father but no mother, in clear controversion of biology.

Only in Noah's Ark does Biblical authority enforce equal representation for males and females. Except for Random House's *Pop-up Noah*, which has eliminated Mrs. Noah and does not show the animals in equal distribution on the cover—males have a slight edge of course. The wives of Ham, Shem, and Japheth, present in the Old Testament, were missing from all three children's versions I examined. Things have come to a pretty pass when one has to go to the Old Testament for an upgrading of the female.

It should be mentioned that folktales tend to treat women somewhat better than do books with contemporary settings. Possibly this is because the former are often based on themes of comeuppance and vindication of the underdog, spontaneous products of wish-fulfillment and the unconscious, while the latter are written to please or to sell. After all, although Hansel comes up with the device of dropping pebbles so that he and Gretel can find their way home, it is Gretel who disposes of the witch by pushing her into the oven. Wives are smarter than their husbands, and women make fools of the powerful. The folktales reflect a preindustrial culture where, though women may not have had equality, they did play vital functioning roles. They were not consuming or sexual objects, justified only by motherhood, as today's world all too often defines them. They were producers who functioned in agriculture and home industries such as spinning and weaving, who worked side by side with their men. Evidently the folktales survive because they have certain psychological validities.

In the more modern downgrading of the female, not only are animals generally male, but personifications of the inanimate—machines, boats, engines, tractors, trains, automobiles—are almost invariably so. In life, ships are she's; in picture books—"Little Toot," Max's boat Max in *Where the Wild Things Are*—I have yet to come across one that was not a he. Automobiles, at least in France where the Citroen D.S. 19 (*déesse*—goddess) is highly admired, are often thought of as feminine, but not by picture-book authors and illustrators. One exception to the masculinity of machines was written back in 1939 when Virginia Lee Burton created Mike Mulligan and his steam shovel Mary Anne.

This marked absence of the female applies even more strongly to books about blacks. Analogies between racism and sexism date back before the nineteenth century: both Mary Wollstonecraft and Thomas Paine compare black slavery to female slavery. In this country the woman's rights movement of the nineteenth century grew out of the Abolitionist movement, as today's Women's Liberation Movement relates to the Civil Rights Movement. History repeats itself. Just as black men achieved enfranchisement long before black or white women, so in the picture-book world have blacks achieved integration with whites and representation for themselves without a corresponding integration for the female, black or white. One of the earliest efforts in this direction was Jerrold Beim's *Swimming Hole* about black and white boys swimming together, and since then there have been a spate of books about blacks and whites and about blacks alone. But the only picture book I found about a black girl was Jacob Lawrence's *Harriet and the Promised Land* based on Harriet Tubman's life. Ezra Jack Keats has done several pic-

ture books about small boys, and a recent one of his, *A
Letter to Amy*, does bring in a girl, but in a token and
not altogether flattering way. Peter is bringing Amy a letter to invite her, the only girl, to his birthday party, when
he bumps into her accidentally. Amy runs away in tears.
Later, the other boys say, "Ugh! A girl at the party!" but
she comes anyway. One little girl can make it in a group
of boys, from Robin Hood's Maid Marian on down through
the centuries, but she'd better know her place.

Virginia Woolf pointed out that throughout literature
women were generally shown only in relation to men, and
this is still true in the picture-book world. Friendship between boys is much touted; friendship between boys and
girls is frequent; but friendship between girls gets less
attention, though surely this is a norm in life. The frequent
depiction of one girl in a group of boys would seem to
represent wish fulfillment for girls as well as boys. A boy
is considered unmanly in a group of females, but a girl
who achieves acceptance in a group of boys has evidently
raised herself, the exception that proves the rule of general
female inferiority.

Since there are so few females in the picture-book
world, one would think they'd be very busy, but such is
not the case. What they do is highly limited; more to the
point is the sheer unreality of what they do not do. They
do not drive cars. Though children see their mothers
driving all the time, not a single description or picture of a
woman driver could I find. In the world today women are
executives, jockeys, stockbrokers, taxidrivers, steelworkers,
in picture books these are nonexistent.

Little girls in picture books tend to be passive, though
sometimes manipulative. They walk, read, or dream. They
seldom ride bicycles; if they do, it is seated behind a boy
as in Dr. Seuss's *One Fish, Two Fish, Red Fish, Blue Fish*.
When I came across a little girl sailing paper boats in a
book by Uri Shulevitz, I was overwhelmed with grateful-
ness. And the same might be said for my responses to
Suzuki Beane and Eloise, both of whom are presented as
highly exceptional.

Though there have been women doctors in this country
for over a hundred years, and pediatrics is one of their
preferred specialties, there is not a single woman doctor
to be found. Women are nurses, librarians, teachers—but

the principal is always male. They have emotions; they get angry; they disagree; they smile; they approve or disapprove; they want to please. What they do not do is act. Boys do; girls are—a highly artificial and unsatisfactory dichotomy.

In a country where over forty percent of the women work, I know of only one picture-book about working mothers, Eve Merriam's *Mommies at Work*. But it wasn't in stock in any of the bookstores I visited. However, while commendable—there are Mommies who split atoms, build bridges, direct TV shows, who are dancers, teachers, writers and doctors—it is also highly apologetic. The end, "all Mommies loving *the best of all* to be your very own Mommy and coming home to you," (my italics) gives it away. We don't feel the need to say about Daddy that he loves his children more than his work. Couldn't Mommy matter-of-factly like working and baby, too, as I'm sure many do?

No boys and girls must get the message—it's all right to work, but only if your work is subordinated to your role as mother. What does it matter that that will last twenty years and the rest of your life may well be spent as supernumerary, doing some kind of busy work? Or semitrained and at the bottom of the labor heap? This is the kind of contradiction that produces guilt and neurotic conflicts in mothers, fathers, and children, instead of the simple sharing we could achieve if men and women were taught to expand their roles.

A few other books, selected not entirely at random, will show some of the methods by which children are indoctrinated at an early age with stereotypes about male activity and female passivity, male involvement with things, women's with emotions, male dominance and female subordination. *A Tree Is Nice* by Janice Udry, illustrated by Marc Simont, seemingly innocent, is actually devastating when analyzed with an aware eye: a boy is high up in a tree balancing while a girl is on the ground watching. Successive pages show a boy fishing, a boy rolling in leaves, and another holding a rake, while a big girl leading a small boy walks by. Then a double-page spread with a huge tree in the center pictures seven boys and three girls. One of the latter is on the ground helping a little boy up into the tree; the other two are on low limbs close in to the main trunk. The boys are shown adventuring, one hanging from a rope, the other five climbing way out or high up. Other pictures show a boy drawing in the sand, a boy in a tree, and boys planting trees. Note that there are nineteen boys pictured to eight girls.

Another seemingly innocent book is William Steig's *CDB*, a clever pun-puzzle book with pictures captioned by dialogue in letters. This is a funny book but implicit attitudes about girls and women are revealed. There are twice as many pictures of boys as girls in the book, and the girls tend to be passive or helpers. When they do anything, they do it badly or are discomfited. A boy is shown on skates; the girl has fallen down. A girl turns a somersault, but it doesn't agree with her, she is dizzy. A girl dancing in a field of flowers is an exception and, giddy from the unusual activity, she is in ecstasy. There are angry females, several of them, but no angry males. Male work is respected; a boy tells a man writing at a desk, "If you're busy, I'll run away." Women are never shown in this context; they are at everybody's service. A woman tells fortunes—the supernatural has offered one of the few exciting outlets for women down through the ages, and witches and still making it, in and out of the Women's Liberation Movement.

One of the worst offenders in this brainwashing about roles and expectations has, perhaps, the most influence— Richard Scarry. His *Best Word Book Ever* is a big illustrated dictionary with the Scarry trademark, humanized animals, demonstrating meanings and activities. Scarry's male-female divisions are scarifying: many more males, naturally, but they *really* do get to do everything. Toys, for example, are defined by showing thirteen male animals playing with exciting toys—a tricycle, blocks, castle, scooter, and rocking horse, as well as the traditional toy soldiers and electric trains. Two female animals play with a tea set and a doll! In the Scarry orchestra, out of twenty-eight animals playing instruments, the two females were assigned those drawing-room clichés, the piano and the harp. The percentage in the New York Philharmonic is no better, but at least there the women play cello and bass viola. Many pages had only males as protagonists, but the one page which showed only women was . . . what else? *In the Kitchen*. The most infuriating page was entitled "Things We Do." Males in Scarry's book world dig, build, break, push, pull, and do fifteen other active things, including eat. The only two things females do are watch and sit.

What kind of world will a little girl educated on Scarry expect to grow into? It's a meager, thankless, and unrewarding prospect. No wonder both boys and girls identify with the boy's role in life.

Particularly sad is the realization that these books are perpetrated by women as well as men—women authors, illustrators and children's book editors. There are very good reasons why women so often "fawn like the spaniel"— the phrase is Mary Wollstonecraft's—but isn't it about time we stopped? It's true that till now men have had all the power, and in a world steeped in patriarchy, women internalize the notion of female inferiority and transmit it to the next generation, perpetuating the cycle. But awareness is upon us. The task of bringing women up to full human status is not going to be easy. To start here, however, at the earliest years, should bring results.

Protests about the retrograde situation have already risen in the Women's Liberation Movement, including an article in the first issue of *Women: A Journal of Liberation.* Women active in the movement are writing new children's books. A conference is planned to educate children's book editors. Several groups have protested primary-school textbooks and "Sesame Street" to some effect. The quarterly, *Aphra,* dedicates part of each issue to feminist criticism of various aspects of our culture, with articles on child-care books and children's television in prospect. As the movement grows, so will the protests. Editors and authors take note. Better meet change now, head on, than be forced into it or bypassed later on.

# A REPORT ON CHILDREN'S TOYS

from *Ms.* Magazine

Intensive analyses of toy catalogs, observation in toy stores, interviews with toy executives, and questionnaires probing adult and child attitudes toward certain toys reveal three major findings: (1) "Masculine" toys are more varied and expensive, and are viewed as relatively complex, active, and social. (2) "Neutral" toys are viewed as most creative and educational, with boys receiving the most intricate items. (3) "Feminine" toys are seen as most simple, passive, and solitary.

These conclusions and the following items are excerpted from a 1972 study conducted by Louis Wolf Goodman and Janet Lever, Yale University sociologists whose exploration of sex-typing of children's toys has yielded considerable evidence of a double standard in children's play.

In thirty hours of Christmastime observation in a toy department no field worker reported a single scientific toy bought for a girl.

Adults seem to follow three rules in purchasing children's toys: (1) Up to the age of two years, children of both sexes can receive many of the same toys (for example, stuffed animals, blocks or educational toys to learn colors and numbers). The older the child the greater the need to differentiate between male and female sex-appropriate toys. (2) Most adult toy buyers defined a set of "traditional boys' toys" and a set of "traditional girls' toys" according to social norms for each sex. (3) While some adults stuck rigidly to the above guidelines, others constructed a secondary rule to allow a child they knew well to request and receive a specific toy, regardless of the toy's "sex-appropriateness."

While children are encouraged to share toys with their siblings, this encouragement is directed primarily to sex-appropriate toys. Playtime with cross-sex siblings is spent in "neutral" (not sex-specific) games like hide-and-seek and tag and kickball, or if the play is indoors, the time is spent watching television, playing cards, or with a board game.

When 42 boys and 42 girls were surveyed as part of the study, they reported an almost identical number of gift items. However, 73 percent of the boys' gifts were toys, while only 57 percent of the girls' gifts were toys. (Girls receive clothes, jewelry, money, and furniture more often than boys.) Boys receive not only more toys but a wider range of toys than do girls.

The observers found that adults spent more time choosing toys for boys than they did choosing toys for girls. This may be due to differences in attitudes about boys' and girls' toys, and also to the fact that a greater variety of boys' toys were on the shelves.

Male sales personnel sold the more expensive items such as gas-powered planes, microscopes, bicycles, and speedways, while saleswomen handled the less expensive items (thus reinforcing the relationship between the toy price and sex-type of toy reported below).

Three out of every four chemistry sets the researchers saw advertised pictured only boys on the boxtop. The remaining 25 percent pictured boys and girls; none pictured girls alone.

Doll sales represented 18 percent of 1971's $3.7 billion business, making dolls the single most valuable item in the trade. And within the category "dolls," it is the fashion doll that is far and away the leader.

A study of the Christmas toy catalogs of nine major department stores yielded 102 distinct categories of items illustrated exclusively with pictures of boys, compared to 73 showing only girls.

Craft kits and art supplies are advertised with pictures of children of both sexes or with girls only, but rarely with boys alone (with the exception of a few items like metal-craft sets).

Building blocks that are simple wooden cubes and

wedges and the old standard "Tinkertoys" are shown with both sexes pictured on the package. On the other hand, complex Erector-set toys, which "teach a wide range of engineering principles," are exclusively marketed to boys.

When marketing costumes for children, one catalog casts boys in a number of different prestigious or exciting roles—Indian chief, astronaut, highway trooper, race-car driver, marine, and Superman. The girls' projected roles seem less authoritative in comparison—drum majorette, nurse, bride, ballerina, Indian princess, and fairy princess.

A doctor kit marketed for boys had "stethoscope with amplifying diaphragm . . . miniature microscope . . . blood-pressure tester . . . prescription blanks, and more." The nurse kit, on the other hand, came equipped with "nurse apron, cap, plastic silverware, plate, sick tray with play food"—seemingly closer to the role of waitress than that of medical practitioner.

In catalog pictures illustrating the use of toys and games, the father is often seen in the role of "instructor" or "play companion," while the mother is placed in the role of "spectator," or, on two occasions, is shown "cleaning up."

In a parallel study this year on sex-type depictions of males and females on toy boxes, Sarah Wernick Lockeretz, Susan L. Kannenberg, and Karen Drew found that, of 860 toy boxes in a large toy store, 50 percent of the toys costing under \$2 were aimed at girls, with only 31 percent of the toys in that price range aimed exclusively at boys, and the remaining 19 percent "neutral." However, in the "\$5 and over" category, 18 percent were girl-oriented, but 34 percent were directed to boys.

# THE IMPACT OF THE WOMEN'S LIBERATION MOVEMENT ON CHILD DEVELOPMENT TEXTS

*ZELDA S. KLAPPER*

> *The important thing*
> *is to pull yourself up by your own hair*
> *to turn yourself inside out*
> *and see the whole world with fresh eyes*
>
> PETER WEISS, *Marat/Sade*

Regardless of the nature of its origins and independent of its destiny, the Women's Liberation Movement has released a cascade of challenges at some of our most cherished notions in child development. One has only to scan one of their monthly schedules of seminars and workshops to appreciate the source of a growing body of new doctrine and dissent: "A Woman's Place—the Changing Image;" "The Nuclear Family;" "New Approaches to Child Rearing;" "Towards a New Feminism: Social and Political Aspects" (May, 1971 Newsletter, Westchester Women's Liberation Coalition).

There are five identifiable Women's Liberation Movement propositions that are specifically relevant to the field of child care: (1) the nuclear family is an arbitrary development that may obstruct a child's optimum development; (2) early growth processes are not critically dependent upon the biological mother; (3) traditional gender-roles are artificially imposed upon children by the

DR. KLAPPER *is an Associate Professor of Psychology at the Rose Kennedy Center of Albert Einstein College of Medicine.*

culture; (4) the assumption of gender-roles by children is counterproductive to their developmental health; and (5) mental health may be better ensured by the early transfer of responsibility for child rearing from the mother to the community.

Public attention has not been directed toward these five issues solely by the writings and speeches of members of the Women's Liberation Movement. Various research and action projects have been initiated to monitor television commercials and stores in order to discourage the production of stereotyped gender-based toys such as fashion dolls and homemaking sets, pink for girls and blue for boys, etc.; a list has been compiled of children's "nonsexist" books by a collective of mothers, high-school students, librarians, editors, and other professionals; collectively run infant-care centers have been established; male homosexual couples have petitioned to adopt children; the Erie County Family Court has approved the adoption of an eight-year-old girl by an unmarried, unrelated schoolteacher.

But what about the books and texts in the field of child care and development? These provide an authoritative source of information for nonprofessionals as well as for child care specialists. To what extent are the authors and editors responding to the five Women's Liberation Movement propositions?

## The Effect of the Nuclear Family on Child-Rearing Patterns

It is the Women's Liberation Movement position that "the heart of woman's oppression is her child bearing and child rearing roles . . . the power hierarchies in the biological family, and the sexual repressions necessary to maintain it—especially intense in the patriarchal nuclear family—are destructive and costly to the individual psyche."[1] Further, the purpose of replacing the nuclear family with the extended or "organic" family is "to release the children from the disadvantages of being extensions of their parents so that they can belong primarily to them-

[1] Shulamith Firestone, *The Dialectic of Sex.* New York: Bantam, 1970.

selves."[2] The core of women's distress is attributed by a psychiatrist to the change from the dyadic family—mother and child—to the nuclear family.

In the texts reviewed (aside from an occasional speculative thought that it may not be necessary to have both father and mother to rear children), the traditional view is preponderantly upheld:

> The child properly requires two parents: a parent of the same sex with whom to identify and who provides a model to follow into adulthood, and a parent of the opposite sex who becomes a love object and whose love and approval the child seeks in return by identifying with the parent of the same sex.

Some would keep the family, but strongly recommend that a pet be added to the core group. Even more direct support is given to the function of the nuclear family by those texts concerned with psychopathology and therapy in childhood with the thesis that "the child's basic attachment is to his parents and . . . no one can really replace them," and that the "parent-child relationship [represents the] most important single category of variables imping-ing on the personality development and socialization of the child."

In no scholarly text is the view that parenthood is "a viciously competitive sport, ostensibly for the sake of children" brought up. But neither is serious consideration given to Margaret Mead's well-known prediction that the family and marriage patterns as they now exist will and should disappear by the year 2000. Professional journals, periodicals, and newspapers cite her criticisms of the nuclear family and its tradition of exclusive upbringing of a child by a close inseparable mother with the negative consequence, among others, of the fear of stranger and strangeness in the modern child. The reviewed books and texts tend to disregard the existence of this point of view. What does appear is concern for the strains imposed by the isolated nuclear family, particularly in middle-class families deprived of institutionalized substitutes for ex-

[2] Germaine Greer, *The Female Eunuch.* New York: McGraw-Hill, 1971.

tended kin, and the possibility that marriage is a condition of risk for many women: one group of women identified as the freest of mental illness was made up of middle-aged, unmarried women who have careers.

In an examination of family variation and mental health the depiction of some rather disastrous consequences in Senegal of the transition from communal to nuclear family is presented without reference to the possibly broader issues, although what is expressed echoes women's liberation movement concern about the nuclear family:

> The family nucleus becomes the standard model. The father and the mother are the proprietors of the child as object, bearer of hopes and new values. . . . The notion of plural "fathers and mothers" has no longer any connection with reality: the child no longer belongs to the group. He must rapidly confront competition and solitude and be responsible for himself and his freedom. Relationship to the group has lost its strength and has been replaced by other narrower and more narcissistic investments: "to do" and "to have" fill the void left by the loss of being or personality.

Although an occasional suggestion is made that it is a myth that the middle-class nuclear family is the only possible kind of family, and that perhaps child-rearing is too complex for the individual small family unit to deal with, proposals of alternatives apparently evoke the same kind of dread of tampering with the forces of nature that has been captured in tales such as Howard Fast's, in which "man-plus," the superchild, is reared by placing children on 8000 acres of national forest with thirty or forty parents to guide their growth. By the end of the tenth year, success was so complete and the children's cognitive growth so vast that teachers, parents, the outside world, and even spoken language systems were dispensed with.

It is in this context that the books reviewed consider such collective arrangements as the kibbutz, the age-mate camp, and the commune. Although Bronfenbrenner has many positive thoughts about the USSR children's collective—with one upbringer for four children and peers for models—he questions the personal outcome. The Israèli kibbutz, in which children are brought up by professional *metapalets* or foster mothers, and with peer models, has also been questioned. Diffusely evaluated accounts of community-based group foster homes, peer groups in general, and one-parent homes reflect some interest in the interactive processes, but, overall, the level of interest in the dynamics of peer interaction as a replacement for nuclear-family models has been literary not scientific, grossly comparable to the science-fiction account of Fast.

## The Biological Mother as Primary Upbringer

Betty Friedan has repeatedly claimed "It is the child who supports life in the mother . . . and he is virtually destroyed in the process." According to Edward Zigler's recent statement as Director of the Federal Office of Child Development, "a fair mother is better than a good center."

Although current books acknowledge that in particular instances a particular mother may damage a child's psychological health, not one author questions the availability of any evidence that the biological mother is, in fact, crucial in early development. The issue is simply not raised. Only indirectly, in studies of temperament differences in infancy, is the traditional view that a child's early behavior directly and exclusively emerges from maternal practices challenged by research evidence. "Temperament must be given the same systematic attention that is now devoted to maternal and other environmental factors" appears to be a cry in the wind.

Rather, the current books reviewed adhere closely to the traditional position that "the primary object relationship that ensures development [is] the child's need for the mother and the mother's readiness to fullfill this need." Although some consider "the importance of mother's motivation for caretaking functions [and the] variations in the sensitivity of most, the liturgy is repeated that "motherly love is by its very nature unconditional. . . . nature, soil, the ocean."

To the extent that serious consideration is currently

given in these books to evidence related to the role of the mother in early life, the stress is likely to be equally placed on "the" mother and "mothering adults," and the nature of the infant's experience with the mothering adults, with stress on the necessity of mothers loving their infants, and on "attachment." Research has been caught up with the entire question of early experiences and their positive effect on cognitive growth. The benefits of early stimulation are generally automatically tied in with the presence of the mother, even though there are no systematic studies of the importance of maternal attachment for healthy development. (In fact, there has been a suggestion that "detachment" from the mother should be investigated as a class of behavior related to cognitive growth.) The tie-in prevails:

> The whole trend of recent work on the effects of separating the young child from his mother has been to show the vital importance for the individual's social development both of adequate stimulation during early infancy and also of the establishment during infancy of a stable relationship with a single mother-figure.

## The Origin of Gender Role in Children

According to Germaine Greer, "The 'normal' sex roles that we learn to play from our infancy are no more natural than the antics of a transvestite."

In general, the current books in child development do address themselves to the issue of "masculine" and "feminine" behavior traits as products of socialization rather than the expression of innate sexual differences. The presence of sex stereotypes in toys and books is acknowledged, and the processes of selective praise and punishment for sex differences in behavior and differential imitation of appropriate sex models are identified. "Children learn that girls play with dolls and boys with trains. They are not born with this information . . . they are culturally conditioned." However, the discussion of environmental influences on gender role is generally isolated from the recitative accounts of boy-girl differences in attitude, in temperament, in interests ("Boys appear to cheat more than girls on what are regarded as 'masculine' tasks," etc.)

There are also expressions of convictions that "Sex differences appear not because we expect them but we expect them because they emerge early," and that "genetic factors tend to be fundamental to the behavior patterns that emerge. Males are more active, aggressive, adventurous and object oriented. Females are more passive, accepting, nurturant and people-oriented." In his recent book addressed to teenagers, Spock has proclaimed, "Biologically and temperamentally, I believe women are made to be concerned first and foremost with child care, husband care, and home care. Regretfully they have been 'confused' by their education." In most instances, these accounts merely imply what others have expressed, namely the belief that not only are these differences innate, but that they should be socially reinforced.

## The Psychological Effect of Gender-Role Development

Independent of the issue of the origin of gender-role is the question of the psychological significance of developing an identity based largely upon gender-specific attitudes and behavior. The position of Women's Liberation Movement is centered on the deep concern about the lack of self-worth and the prevalent self-hatred that becomes part of the young girl's conscious and unconscious expectations of her future role and the process of being forced to accept an inferior role, learning to believe in her own inferiority. Although not as central, concern about the damaging effect on boys of gender-specific expectations, of having to be "manly," has been expressed by the women and by men who are sympathetic to the Women's Liberation Movement.

Aside from an occasional suggestion that "it may be that sex roles in terms of what is the masculine and what is the feminine thing to do are much less important than we thought them to be" and that a more systematic study of sex differences in child-rearing is needed, no critical evaluation of gender role appears in the books reviewed. On the contrary, there are voiced complaints about the diffuseness of gender roles in primary reading textbooks, and neutral, non sex-linked male and female behavior, expression of the need for fostering sex-role identity (as in Spock's cry that "mothers and fathers don't accentuate the differences in sex roles enough") and vigilance about a society that is about to rob the father of his power and status.

Many traditional attitudes toward sex differences persist. Some texts still provide growth charts of unclothed children with the sexual parts blocked out, and the eyes masked. Though the membership of NAMH has just adopted a position paper on homosexuality in which deviate sexual behavior is not regarded as a specific mental or emotional illness or as a danger either to individuals or to society, the treatment in current child development books of the issue of homosexuality is as it always was—disregarded. If mentioned, it is as if in passing, with one study comparing pupillary reactions of heterosexual and homosexual men to pictures of nude women. Female homosexuality is never mentioned.

### Transfer of Infant Rearing Responsibility to the Community

In Sweden, the Women's Liberation Movement, Group 8, plans to include children from six months of age in day-care centers. French law requires every community with a population of more than 2000 to provide an *école maternelle* for children up to age six, and almost every community or urban center has its *crèche* for infants as young as two months. In the crèche, or infant nursery, trained baby nurses give infants their meals, fresh air and exercise, and are on duty from 7 A.M. to 7 P.M., including weekends and vacation periods.

In the face of claims from all over by infant-care-center advocates that the children do well, have less thumb-sucking, better verbal ability, and precocious coordination in these settings, there are no reports of, or projected designs for systematic studies of communal infant rearing. There is a widely expressed interest in the overall aspects of psychological development occurring before the child enters school, but as yet the fundamental issue of full-time infant-care centers for women, across social class, is not being examined by child-care specialists. What is indirectly expressed is resistance in the form of traditional assumptions, without evidence, that

> from the age of about three months to three years, ego growth is in the symbiotic phase; this is a critical period of development . . . anything that disrupts the mother-child relationship during this time will have a deleterious effect on the development of the youngster.[3]

Margaret Mead comments in her recent review of Elizabeth Janeway's *Man's World, Woman's Place*, "the myth that woman's place is in the home . . . though patently untrue in many ways, forms the basis of most private attitudes and public discussions." And, one can add, of most of the books in the field of child care and development. This lack of responsiveness is possibly because the issues are too recent for current consideration, and probably because cultural attitudes are so firmly implanted. It is widely recognized that "the focus on childhood in American culture is unique. We have set a new record. No other people seems ever to have been so preoccupied with children, so anxious about them, or so uncertain of how to deal with them."

It is distressing that the implications for child care and development that are part of women's reexamination and new consciousness of their lives and life styles have not been more directly confronted by those who are considered specialists in human development.

[3] S. Finch and R. McDermott, *Psychiatry for the Pediatrician.* New York: W. W. Norton, 1970.

# III.
# Down with Dick and Jane

# TWO LIVES

*CAROLYN KARKOSZA*

I wish all girls in school were like me. If you ask them what they want to be when they grow up they will say a model, movie star, or nurse. Boys would say ugh you're a girl, and girls would say ugh you're a boy. When I go to school I don't like to be left out from others, so I act like them even though I hate it. It's like I'm living two different lives a liberated one at home, and a nonliberated at school. Our principal says we can't wear pants to school. Every other school around can wear pants but we can't. I keep waiting for somebody to start wearing pants, but I keep thinking you do it, you make the first step. Yet something keeps stopping me. I wish I had the nerve to do it. On our playground they have some seperation the girls are on one side and boys on the other. I am at the age of nine, and I'm trying to make my way through life, trying to live one life but I can't. It's hard for me. I want to be free, but I guess if I stay like this living two lives I don't know what will happen to me or what I'll be.

# SCHOOLS ARE EMASCULATING OUR BOYS

*PATRICIA CAYO SEXTON*

*The problem of sex discrimination in schools was not invented by today's feminists. It was a subject of much concern to educators in the 1950s and early '60s, but they identified the victims as boys, not girls. Since under-achievement and misbehavior were principally boys' problems, it followed that elementary schools must be guilty of anti-male bias. In her recent book, The Feminized Male, sociologist Patricia Sexton carries this position to the extreme. The editorial reprinted here presents the core of her argument, to which Betty Levy responds in the following selection. Curiously enough, Sexton calls herself a feminist, though she makes her priorities perfectly clear: where the sexes are concerned, girls take a back seat.*

Boys and the schools seem locked in a deadly and ancient conflict that may eventually inflict mortal wounds on both. In vastly disproportionate numbers, boys are the malad-justed, the low achievers, the truants, the delinquents, the inattentive, the rebellious. If teachers had only girls in their classes, they would find it easy, though dull, going, and we probably could double class size and still keep high standards of achievement and decorum. National delin-quency rates are five times higher among boys than girls; in New York City 63 percent of all dropouts are boys; more

*PATRICIA SEXTON is Professor of Educational Sociology at New York University and author of* The Feminized Male.

than twice as many boys as girls under fifteen are currently first admissions to public mental hospitals.

While we know many things about the boy-school conflict, our factual understanding is still too primitive to permit us to go far beyond conjecture. Boys are often raised by strong and assertive women at home (the "modern woman") and then turned over to strong and assertive women at school. Seventy-two percent of all teachers, remember, are women. Yet a boy, if he wants to be a real boy, must free himself from the domination of these women and operate under his own power; hence, there is inevitable conflict for those who take on the painful job of struggling out of the maternal cocoon to become men, and partial or sometimes total emasculation for those who don't.

The problem is not just that teachers are too often women. It is that the school is too much a woman's world, governed by women's rules and standards. The school code is that of propriety, obedience, decorum, cleanliness, silence, physical, and, too often, mental passivity. Some of this, perhaps a lot, may be good and necessary. The military establishment is able to enforce some of this code—obedience and discipline—on men without making sissies of them. But when it is not alloyed with the stronger masculine virtues, as it often is in the military but seldom is in the schools, trouble is brewed.

Unfortunately, the masculine virtues are usually diametrically opposite to the school's female ones. The masculine stress is on aggressiveness in all things, rather than passivity. It is on action and movement rather than sitting still, independence rather than obedience, speaking out rather than keeping quiet, strong group loyalty and group competition rather than individual competition—fearlessness, courage, and daring rather than timidity and surrender—conflict, struggle, and a good fight rather than perpetual peace. The female code is to make as much effort as possible in studies, the male to make the least. Basic to the problem is that boys have more energy and muscle for action and trouble; they take in more food and their output of carbon dioxide may be as much as 40 percent more than that of girls.

Though the boy must learn to be his own authority, the school insists that he obey its authority, however arbitrary and irrational it may be. This may be reasonably good preparation for the lower rungs of a large white-collar organization or military service, but not for real manhood or free citizenship.

But the young lad's woes do not end there. Besides the school's style, there is also its content. Again, alas, this subject matter seems all too frilly and feminized. English and literature especially, the inescapable subjects, seem typically so overcast by feminine tastes as to repeatedly suggest to boys that the provinces of written language, books, imaginative expression, art are the exclusive property of women and the strange men who take interest in such flights of fancy.

If we are to stuff boys every term with English courses, surely we can find ways to convince them that "good" literature can be tough, masculine, simple, perceptive, and expressive of their own feelings and experience. Why, for example, in teaching Shakespeare, sacrifice the blood and bawdiness and the action plots, as wild as Goldfinger, to the lyricism of the language—that tends more often to be stressed?

All of this leads us back to something about which we have intermittently talked but done nothing—education that is active, exploratory, problem solving, adventurous, aggressive. Because boys want to conquer their world (and universe) rather than nest in it, they are often fascinated by machinery, technology, and the absorbing secrets of the natural world, secrets that man has, by mind, mouth, and hand, wrested from nature for use in its exploitation. These male interests are almost too apparent to mention. Yet the schools go on in their lumbering way, as though science and technology were an upstart fortune-seeker, invading the realm of the liberal arts with gadgetry and "things." The situation is often so bad and so ridiculous that a boy can come to manhood without picking up, in school, even elementary knowledge about the inner workings of standard parts of his intriguing environment—cars, radios, TV, space vehicles, building construction, etc.

I do not suggest that boys and girls should be segregated for instruction. The scanty evidence we have suggests that this is not preferable to coeducation. Besides, such segregation always works a hardship on someone—in this case it would be, as it used to be, the girls. But limited separation, for certain ages or subjects, might work better. We don't know. I am inclined to think, however, that the education that would best suit boys would also suit girls, at least better than what they now get, and I think we have to worry less about girls becoming more masculine than about boys becoming more feminine.

As a feminist I must admit to some selfish and ulterior motives. Only as men become at once stronger and more intellectual will it be permissible or advisable for women to do so. And, whatever improvements are made in the curriculum for the sake of boys will also profit girls.

# DO SCHOOLS SELL
# GIRLS SHORT?

*BETTY LEVY*

Recent critics of the schools have explored the contradiction between what schools *say* they do and what they
*actually* do. The ostensible purpose of schools is to educate
everyone and to equalize opportunity for all. Liberal reformers who accept this purpose at face value bemoan the
fact that schools are "failing" (i.e., not educating), whereas
more sophisticated analysts move beyond the stated purpose of schools and reveal that schools are "succeeding" in
differentially socializing pupils by race, class, and sex.
These socializing functions are all the more powerful when
one considers that they occur despite efforts of many well-
intentioned educators to achieve the schools' stated aims.

Illich, Friedenberg, Holt, and others have described how
the institutional demands of schools (passively "being
taught," acquiescing to imposed rules and routines, and so
on) conflict with learning and individual development
goals. Wasserman, Reimer, Freire, Rothstein, Jencks, and
others have discussed the role schools play in perpetuating
existing social and economic inequalities. Schools may not
"make a difference" in the sense that they do not dramatically improve the life chances of the poor, of minority
groups, or of women, but they do "make a difference" in
that they remain an effective instrument of social control.
Schools, after all, were not created to change society, but to

*BETTY LEVY is a doctoral candidate in Development and Learn-
ing, Teachers College, Columbia University.*

maintain it and thus help keep existing dominant groups dominant.

What most critics have failed to examine is how traditional demands of schools function to perpetuate traditional sex roles. For girls, the schools' expectations and the traditional sex-role expectations are congruent and provide a strong double-barreled message reinforcing girls' obedience, docility, and dependence. For boys, the schools' expectations often conflict with traditional sex-role expectations, resulting in a confusing double message: Be aggressive, active, achieving, and independent (be masculine), but also be passive, quiet, and conforming (be a *good* pupil).

As a result, boys tend to be more acting-out in school and more noticeable, whereas girls tend to be more completely socialized into "goodness" and thus more easily ignored. The long-lasting result is potentially more positive for boys, since the "masculine" characteristics are related to intellectual development and self-actualization, whereas the strong, consistent pressures on girls to be "feminine" and "good pupils" promote characteristics that inhibit achievement and suppress females' full development.

Recent discussion of sex-role socialization in schools has been dominated by concern for boys who, it is contended, are forced to meet feminine standards of behavior and thinking by the overwhelmingly feminine atmosphere of the elementary school. Because the emphasis has been on boys' problems, the situation of girls has been overlooked. As a result, the schools' "feminization" or "domestication" training is seen, by implication, as good preparation for "real womanhood." The fact that girls are being doubly trained—at home and at school—to be docile and conforming is not of concern. What is of concern is that boys might be treated badly in school, that is, "like girls." The fact that the school as an institution demands conformity and obedience for most children is not noted. Rather, female teachers are labeled "the enemy" in the destruction of male minds!

An incredibly large number of studies have been addressed to the question, "Do female teachers discriminate against boys?" The results of these indicate that boys, far from being discriminated against, provide more intense stimuli for teachers and receive more positive as well as more negative attention from teachers than do girls. Teachers may yell at boys more, but teachers also give them more praise, more instruction, and more encouragement to be creative than they give girls. Girls are either ignored or rewarded merely for following directions and for doing assigned work.

Many studies have demonstrated that boys make up the majority of teachers' behavioral problems and that teachers tend to discipline boys more harshly than girls. In *Psychology of Women: A Study of Bio-Cultural Conflicts,* Judith M. Bardwick speculates that a boy learns in school that he can get attention and respect from his teacher and his peers for nonconforming behavior. Thus, teacher criticism, a seemingly negative response, may actually lead boys toward greater independence, autonomy, and activity.

A boy whom the teacher harshly reprimands may temporarily feel put down but may also learn to defend and assert himself more as an independent being. The girl who is softly told she "did something bad" while the teacher gives her a reassuring (patronizing?) pat is less likely to develop self-assertive behavior that carries the risk of disapproval.

Moreover, research done by R. L. Spaulding indicates that a disproportionate number of teachers' negative remarks to girls concerned incorrect answers ("You're wrong, Sally"), a pattern that could only reinforce girls' sense of inferiority.

Other evidence indicates that even by the pre-school years, boys tend to be more realistic about their achievements than do girls. Perhaps the criticism boys receive tends to be more task-oriented, helping them to better evaluate their skills. Girls may be receiving more general and more personal criticism leading to an oversensitivity to criticism and a tendency to do tasks to gain social approval rather than to meet one's own standards.

In my opinion, we need more unbiased research to determine differences in how teachers discipline and criticize boys as opposed to girls and how these differences affect their development. Also, teachers need to become increasingly self-aware of how they may be subtly shaping boys more toward independent achievement and girls more toward dependence and nonsustained achievement.

Also we need to discover if teachers are held more firmly

accountable for maintaining order than for facilitating learning. If this is so, it is no wonder that they desire passive, conforming behavior from boys and gratefully receive it from girls.

Schools reinforce traditional sex roles in many ways. One way is through the authority structure of the school itself. Eighty-five percent of all elementary school teachers are women; 79 percent of all elementary school principals are men. Schoolchildren do not need to be taught the differential status of men and women—they learn it simply by attending school.

Another mechanism of sex-role reinforcement is segregated classes and activities. A number of grade schools have been "experimenting" with sex-segregated classes. The all-boy classes emphasize large-muscle physical activity, team games, building, repairing, and other tasks "ordinarily performed by fathers." In one school, the all-girl classes include such activities as "dressing up like mother and playing house."

Even with classes that are not sex-segregated, certain activities, such as cooking and sewing, are encouraged primarily for girls, and other activities, such as woodworking, are encouraged primarily for boys. Physical education and playground activities frequently are sex-segregated. As children move through elementary school, certain subjects, such as English, come to be regarded as "girls' subjects" while other subjects, such as math and science, are perceived as "boys' subjects."

Even in free schools where there is no conscious attempt to sex-type, the policy of allowing children to follow their own interests usually results in condoning the pervasive sex-typed activities the children have learned outside the school. Effective open classrooms, while basically noninterventionist, still require children to master basic skills. But intervening to require choices and activities that are free of sex-typing has apparently not yet become an important concern of the open classroom.

The separation of boys and girls for seating, hanging up coats, and so on, and the choice of class helpers calls attention to sex distinctions and sex roles. So does sex-typing in elementary-school reading materials.

What can educators do to challenge and correct the

detrimental effects of sex-role socialization in schools?

First, they must realize that schools mirror the elitism, racism, and sexism of our society. Thus, efforts to challenge sexism in schools must be perceived as part of a larger and long-range struggle to change the inequalities which schools maintain and perpetuate.

Issues which will benefit all men and women, not merely a privileged few, should have the highest priority. For example, attempts to open up the school authority and decision-making structure to all those groups affected by it are more basic than attempts to get a few more female principals. Efforts to rid schools of sexist attitudes and practices must be linked with broader efforts if all are to be successful.

Second, since sex-role stereotypes are so pervasive, an individual teacher may find it helpful to work with other teachers in consciousness-raising groups and sex-role committees to better understand and struggle with the ways we are oppressed by (and oppress our students with) sexist ideas and behavior. In addition to collective efforts to change classroom practices, teachers should form schoolwide committees to focus on curricular programs and materials; challenge sex-segregated classes and activities; and gather data on hiring and promotion practices, salaries, and so on.

# TEACHER INTERACTIONS WITH BOYS AND WITH GIRLS

*PAULINE S. SEARS*
*AND DAVID H. FELDMAN*

*According to the dictums of educational psychology, sex-role learning is a basic developmental task for elementary-school children and should therefore be encouraged. In 1966, Pauline Sears and David Feldman investigated the teacher's role in this process. Their perspective is non-feminist, but their review of the educational literature lends support to the feminist view that, in fact, sex-typing impedes children's development in other areas. In response to their findings, the authors ask: when should the elementary teacher take "an active, interventionist, reconstructive role rather than reflecting the mores of the child's surrounding culture?"*

One of the important developmental tasks facing children of elementary school age is the adoption and maintenance of a sex role which will help them eventually to reach a sense of real identity. Many factors affect the way a child works at—and works out—this developmental task, but we are particularly concerned here with the teacher's part in this task. In our elementary schools, which have long been coeducational, teachers work with boys and girls. Do the teachers react differently to boys than they do to girls? If they do, what effect does this have on the intel-

*PAULINE S. SEARS is Professor of Education; DAVID F. FELDMAN is Research Assistant; both at the Stanford Center for Research and Development in Teaching, Stanford, California.*

lectual and social development of the individual boy and girl?

We began exploring these questions by preparing a short questionnaire in which we asked for teachers' opinions about their own behavior in relation to boys and to girls. We wanted to know whether teachers think they do, or should, behave differently toward boys than they do toward girls. In about half of our sample, both the men and the women teachers said that they do make some differentiation in their behavior. However, a majority of the teachers in the sample did not think that the aims of their teaching are different for boys than they are for girls, nor did they think that specific techniques of approval and disapproval are more effective with one sex than with the other.

A logical next question is: Do teachers actually behave in the classroom as they think they behave? The next section of this article presents information from studies that involved classroom observation of various samples of elementary school teachers.

What we actually know about teacher behavior in regard to the sex of children is not really very much. The monumental *Handbook of Research on Teaching*[1] lists seventy-three references reporting measurement of teacher classroom behavior by systematic observation. But not one of these studies, it appears, indicates to whom—boy or girl—the teacher behavior was directed.

There are several studies testing the hypothesis that boys receive a larger number of disapproval contacts from their teachers than girls do. The earliest of these, by Meyer and Thompson,[2] was carried out by time sample observation spread over an entire school year. Three sixth-grade classes, all taught by women, were used. In each classroom the boys received significantly more disapproval or blame than the girls did. And, interestingly enough, boys also received more praise or approval than

---

[1] N. L. Gage, *Handbook of Research on Teaching*. Chicago: Rand McNally, 1963.

[2] William J. Meyer and George G. Thompson, "Teacher Interactions with Boys as Contrasted with Girls," in Raymond G. Kuhlens and George G. Thompson (eds.), *Psychological Studies of Human Development*. New York: Appleton-Century-Crofts, 1963.

the girls did, although this difference was significant in only one classroom.

Why the greater disapproval and blame for the boys? The boys may have been more outwardly aggressive in the classroom than the girls were, and we suggest that the teachers may have been responding by counteraggression. And why the greater praise and approval for boys, as shown in one classroom particularly? Perhaps the teachers were trying to reduce the aggressive and reinforce the positive behavior of the boys by praising any positive behavior they exhibited. Or perhaps the praise reflected guilt on the teachers' part over their own overtly critical reactions to the boys' behavior.

A larger study by Spaulding,[3] using twenty-one fourth- and sixth-grade classes (thirteen men teachers and eight women teachers), produced similar results on disapproval. But these teachers interacted more with boys than with girls on every one of the four major categories of teaching behavior: approval, instruction, listening to the child, and disapproval. Thus it appears that boys receive more of the teacher's active attention than girls do. Is this because they demand more attention from the teacher than do the more passive, dependent girls? Informal observations in elementary classrooms have suggested that boys in upper-elementary grades participate more than girls do in classroom discussion, making more statements and asking more questions. Perhaps in some sense their independent talk pushes the teacher to respond to them.

Further light on the disapproval question is shed by Spaulding's breakdown as to how, and for what, the disapproval was conveyed. Seven categories were devised for the aspect of behavior disapproved: violation of rules, personal qualities of child, thoughtlessness, task mechanics, lack of knowledge or skill, lack of attention, poor housekeeping. Lack of attention was the most frequent cause for disapproval: around 40 percent for both boys and girls. But another 40 percent of the total disapproval received by the girls was for lack of knowledge or skill

[3] Robert L. Spaulding, *Achievement, Creativity, and Self-Concept Correlates of Teacher-Pupil Transactions in Elementary Schools,* Cooperative Research Project No. 1352, U.S. Department of Health, Education, and Welfare, Office of Education, Washington, D.C., 1963.

("No, Mary, not 24!"), whereas when the boys were disapproved, only 26 percent of the time was it for this
reason. As expected, boys considerably exceeded girls in
the frequency of disapproval received for violation of
rules: boys, 17 percent; girls, 9 percent. These differences were significant.

Another difference appeared in the tone of voice used
for disapproval. Teachers criticizing a boy were more
likely to use a harsh or angry tone; criticism of girls was
more likely to be conveyed in a normal voice. Jackson's
recent work (personal communication[4]) divides teacher
interaction with children into three categories: instructional, managerial, and control or prohibitory. Sixth-grade
boys, according to these results, get into at least eight
times more trouble than girls do on the last two categories. Probably they have a more difficult time than
girls have in adjusting to the institutional aspects of the
classroom. Alternatively, it is possible that much of the
"trouble" teaches at least some of the boys that they can
create some interesting effects in the classroom by being
independent of the teacher.

If these results are typical for elementary classrooms
generally, what should we expect the social learnings of
boys and girls to be as they go through many hours of
interaction with teachers during their elementary school
years? One consequence might be a cumulative increase in
independent, autonomous behavior by boys as they are
disapproved, praised, listened to, and taught more actively
by the teacher. Another might be a lowering of self-
esteem generally for girls as they receive less attention
and are criticized more for their lack of knowledge and
skill. In fact, the Sears study[5] found bright fifth- and
sixth-grade girls to be significantly lower than boys of the
same intelligence in their own self-concepts of mental
ability. Of course, a number of rival explanations are
possible for this finding.

[4] Philip W. Jackson, Personal communication, 1966.

[5] Pauline Snedden Sears, *The Effect of Classroom Conditions on the
Strength of Achievement Motive and Work Output of Elementary
School Children.* Cooperative Research Project No. OE-873, U.S.
Department of Health, Education, and Welfare, Office of Educa-
tion, Washington, D.C., 1963.

A fourth study of teacher interaction with boys and girls was done by Lippitt and Gold.[6] Generally, teachers made more supportive remarks to girls and more critical remarks to boys. However, when the children were divided as to whether they were judged high or low on social power (the ability to get other children to follow), striking sex differences emerged in the low social power groups. Teachers were much more supportive (and less critical) of low-power girls than of low-power boys.

Direct observation of teacher behavior is obviously the clearest indication of what is actually going on in the way of teacher-pupil interaction. However, we can make some inferences about behavior from indirect measures: teachers' reports of students' behavior, their ideas on the kind of child who gives them the most satisfaction, grading practices, and perceptions by the students themselves of teacher behavior.

Torrance[7] asked a large number of teachers to describe incidents in which they believed they had rewarded creative behavior in the classroom. Rewards were thought to consist of such behavior as being respectful of the unusual questions and ideas of children, providing for periods of nonevaluated practice, and helping children to see the consequences of their ideas. Of 224 incidents reported, 172 mentioned the sex of the child—74 percent involving boys and 26 percent, girls. Torrance concludes that this ratio is only fair since other evidence suggests that girls receive more rewards than boys do for conforming school behavior. One wonders if girls receive the implicit message that creative thinking is for boys and conformity is for girls.

Torrance also reports two separate but identical studies in which boys and girls were observed as they experimented with science toys and suggested how they might be used. The first study showed that boys have many more good ideas than girls have. This finding startled Torrance who discussed with the teachers and parents the possibil-

[6] R. Lippitt and M. Gold, "Classroom Social Structures as a Mental Health Problem," *Journal of Social Issues* 15: 40–50; 1st quarter 1959.

[7] E. P. Torrance, *Guiding Creative Talent*. Englewood Cliffs, New Jersey: Prentice-Hall, 1962.

ity of misplaced emphasis on sex roles during the early years, with consequent interference in the development of potentialities.

The following year the project was repeated with a new group of students. This time the girls came up rather strikingly, demonstrating and explaining as many ideas as the boys, according to the observer recording. But when the students were asked who contributed the better ideas, they said—and they said it both years—that the contributions of boys were better than those of girls. It is possible that this occurred because the subject matter was science, which may be thought to be a "masculine" field. It would be interesting to see how contributions would be evaluated if the task were composing poems.

Although the evidence is by no means conclusive, there seems to be a trend toward differences in grading and evaluation in favor of girls, even though there is a contrasting trend indicating that boys achieve at least as well as girls. Most of the research in the area of grading practices has been focused on the secondary school, so we are not free to assert that the same trends would be found at the elementary level. However, many of the same classroom conditions exist at both levels and what small data there are point in the same directions as those of the secondary school studies.

There are six possible combinations of teachers and students which could be studied for sex differences in grading and achievement: single-sex classes with male or female teachers and mixed classes with male or female teachers. Of these six possibilities, only mixed classes are commonly found in the United States. However, a comparative study of twelve countries[8] shows differences in interest and achievement in mathematics between boys and girls taught in single-sex, as opposed to coeducational, schools. This study finds that boys do better than girls in mathematics in both kinds of schools, but especially in countries with a large proportion of single-sex schools (Belgium and France).

At least two things must be kept in mind with regard to the above study: it is a study of *achievement* on a

8 Thorsten, Husén, *et al.*, *A Comparative Study of Outcomes of Mathematics Instruction in Twelve Countries*. New York: Wiley, 1966.

standardized test, not grades; and it is a study of mathematics achievement among junior-high school and high-school children. We would first have to compare achievement with grades and then run the entire study for elementary school children in order to speak with authority about sex differences at this level. This study does, however, include all six possible combinations of teachers and pupils; other studies are less complete.

Two such less complete studies, cited by Waetjen and Grambs,[9] corroborate Husén's findings and, to an extent, expand them. Carter[10] tested achievement versus grades in beginning algebra, holding IQ constant. Although the differences in achievement slightly favored boys, their grades were significantly lower. As in Husén's study, the sex of the teacher was not as important as the sex of the child. All of the classes in this sample were mixed classes with male or female teachers. It would be interesting to see if the discrepancy between grades and achievement would hold true for Husén's cross-cultural data as well.

Hanson's study[11] included students at both primary and secondary levels, but it was done twenty years ago. He found that a much larger percentage of the boys in his sample (N-3000) received A or B grades on an achievement test than received A or B grades from their teachers (48 percent versus 29 percent).

Coleman's data for adolescents[12] agree with the above findings. Coleman also shows that girls' grades vary less than boys', presumably because social pressures affect the sexes differently.

Thus, from the limited evidence we have, it seems that girls are given higher grades than boys despite the fact that boys achieve at least as well as girls and, in some cases, better.

9 Walter B. Waetjen and Jean D. Grambs, "Sex Differences: A Case of Educational Evasion?" *Teachers College Record* 65: 261–271, December 1963.

10 E. S. Carter, "How Invalid Are Marks Assigned by Teachers?" *Journal of Educational Psychology* 43: 218–228, April 1952.

11 Earl H. Hanson, "Do Boys Get a Square Deal in School?" *Education* 79: 597–598; May 1959.

12 James Coleman, *The Adolescent Society*. New York: The Free Press, 161, pp. 252–253.

It seems likely that the children the teacher likes best are those whose talents and behavior facilitate the teacher's own satisfactions in his teaching. With this in mind, Sears[13] asked a group of elementary teachers to rate the children in their classes in terms of how much the teacher enjoyed having each one in the group. Since a number of personality and ability measures on the children were available, it was possible to obtain a composite picture of the kind of child these teachers like to teach. For data analysis, the children were divided into ability groups by sex, so results appear for the bright and less bright (average ability) boys and the same for girls.

Bright boys are liked by the teacher if they are friendly and self-sufficient. Quite different correlates appear in the boys of average ability whom the teacher likes. Here the teacher welcomes affiliative, dependent motivation; good feelings of confidence; and solid work habits. If the boy has only average ability, these characteristics may permit the maximum influence by the teacher. Independence is not so much desired for these boys. For girls, teachers' values appear to be met if girls show good student behavior and are friendly. Work habits should be good in the girl of average ability, but are not so important for the bright girl. Emphasis is on friendly, agreeable qualities for both groups of girls.

Making systematic observations of teacher-child interaction requires hours of time in the classroom by outside observers. Several studies have avoided this by using the children, who are present in the classroom anyhow, as the "observers."

For example, in Meyer and Thompson's study,[14] children were asked to nominate four fellow class members for a number of situations in which children receive approval or disapproval from their teacher for some behavior. The responses given by boys and girls were analyzed separately. Highly significant differences appeared. Both boys and girls believed that boys received more disapproval than girls. There were no sex differences in their beliefs about the teacher's distribution of praise.

13 Sears, P., *op. cit.*

14 William J. Meyer and George G. Thompson, *op. cit.*

NcNeil[15] obtained first-grade children's ratings on teacher behavior toward boys and girls in reading groups. The children's perceptions were that boys had fewer opportunities to respond than girls and received more negative comments on their performances.

Davidson and Lang[16] had boys and girls respond to an adjective checklist containing favorable (for example, "generous") and unfavorable (for example, "a sloppy worker") traits. The children did this by completing the following statements: "My teacher thinks I am . . ." and "I think I am . . ." More girls than boys believed the teacher thought of them favorably. However, for all the children there was a strong positive relation between how favorably they believed the teacher saw them and how favorably they viewed themselves. This may indicate a response set toward optimism or pessimism as the children filled out both forms, or it may show that at the elementary level, children's self-concepts are considerably influenced by their ideas of how that "significant other," the teacher, feels about them. According to Coleman,[17] the teacher does not have a very significant influence, apart from his instructional role, at the high-school level. But it seems likely that for younger children, perhaps particularly for young girls, the influence is more profound.

There have been periodic complaints that the elementary school is a feminized organization in which young boys lack masculine models for good academic achievement. Thus Kagan,[18] in an ingenious experiment, found that second-grade children view common objects in the classroom (blackboard, book, page of arithmetic, school desk) as more clearly associated with femininity than with masculinity.

[15] John D. McNeil, "Programed Instruction Versus Usual Classroom Procedures in Teaching Boys to Read." *American Educational Research Journal* 1: 113–120; March 1964.

[16] H. H. Davidson and G. Lang, "Children's Perceptions of Their Teachers' Feelings Toward Them Related to Self-Perception, School Achievement, and Behavior." *Journal of Experimental Education* 29: 107–118; December 1960.

[17] James Coleman, *op. cit.*

[18] Jerome Kagan, "The Child's Sex Role Classification of School Objects." *Child Development* 35: 1051–56; December 1964.

But Clapp[19] found no differences in fall-spring achievement gains of fifth-grade boys studying with men or with women teachers. This was a large study: over 600 boys with 28 women and 17 men teachers. Husén, working with the international sample of thirteen-year-olds previously mentioned, found mathematics performance superior among students taught by men, but this difference disappeared when related variables were taken into account.

Ryans' study[20] of teacher characteristics involved a national sample of over 1400 elementary teachers, of whom 86 percent were women. Differences between the sexes in personal-social characteristics were as follows: men were less responsible and businesslike in classroom behavior, more favorable toward democratic classroom practices, more inclined toward permissive, child-centered educational viewpoints, and more emotionally stable than women.

One suspects that the last word on this subject has not been said. It is likely that selection of men teachers at the elementary level proceeds according to somewhat different rules than selection of women, resulting in samples which are not really comparable on dimensions other than that of sex. Still to be carried out is the crucial experiment of having equal numbers of enthusiastic and talented men and women to teach primary children.

Other articles in this issue have presented evidence on sex differences in children, some of which may be innate. The authors of this article suggest that social learning of sex roles is also important. It is likely that parents, mainly unconsciously, start the process of teaching "sex roles," and that teachers, also without being fully aware of what they are doing, continue the process. Artistic production is not expected of boys; excellent problem solving is not expected of girls. But society might benefit by having all children develop both these skills to the fullest. A chapter

[19] Rufus C. Clapp, "The Relationship of Teacher Sex to Fifth Grade Boys' Achievement Gains and Attitudes Toward School." (Unpublished doctoral dissertation, Stanford University, 1966.)

[20] David G. Ryans, *Characteristics of Teachers*. Washington, D.C.: American Council on Education, 1960.

by Maccoby[21] provides thorough documentation of temperamental differences (not known to be innate or a product of social learning) between boys and girls—differences which are associated with intellectual, rather than social or emotional, performance. Here we clearly get into the teacher's chief function—the development of children's ability to think reasonably, independently, and creatively.

Maccoby proposes that optimal intellectual performance comes about in children when boys are less bold and impulsive than the "real" boy and when girls are less timid and inhibited than the "real" girl. This hypothesis suggests a reduction and modification of maximum differential treatment of the sexes. If we are interested in maximizing *intellectual* functioning, we may have to revise our ideas about what constitutes a "proper" sex role and what experiences best contribute to its function.

A complication is that we are not sure of the effects on children of specific teacher behaviors. Spaulding, as we mentioned previously, found that teachers criticizing boys were more likely to use a harsh or angry tone, while their criticisms of girls were more often conveyed in a normal tone. We do not know the effects of these behaviors. Quite possibly the harsh tones, intended to cause boys to conform, actually foster a defiant, independent attitude which reinforces the very behavior the teacher wished to subdue. Associated with this may be the boldness and impulsiveness which Maccoby has found to be detrimental to good thinking in boys.

Our goal, then, will be to specify the kinds of teacher behaviors that will focus boys' and girls' interest on intellectual tasks. The behaviors may or may not be quite different for each sex. McNeil[22] has found, for example, that first-grade boys made more progress in learning reading under programed instruction while girls did better in the usual reading groups under teacher direction.

In similar vein, Kagan[23] has the following to say:

[21] Eleanor Maccoby, *The Development of Sex Differences.* Stanford, California: Stanford University Press, 1966.

[22] John D. McNeil, *op. cit.*

[23] Jerome Kagan, "Personality and the Learning Process." *Daedalus* 94: 558; Summer 1965.

"There are strong semantic associations between the dimensions of 'masculinity' and 'femininity' and specific areas of knowledge for most adult members of western culture. This is an unfortunate marriage for one would hope that knowledge would retain some neutrality amidst the warring factions of the mind. It may be possible, however, to alter this associational link between domain of knowledge and the sex roles through modifications in the procedures and atmosphere in the elementary schools."

In some degree, certainly, teachers must support the values current in the culture in which they teach. Probably in most instances the teachers themselves wish to do this because their own values are similar to those of parents and the culture in general. Such agreement leads to harmony. Now in what circumstances does the elementary teacher have a unique role in that he may or should consciously deviate, for a planned useful purpose, from the mores he sees around him?

A current example is the excitement about the so-called "culturally deprived" child. His teacher is regarded as needing to provide compensatory stimulation for the kinds of stimulation the child receives in his own home environment. This is for the ultimate good of the child and of society. The teacher here is taking an active, interventionist, reconstructive role rather than reflecting the mores of the child's surrounding culture. In a more general sense, what changes would we suggest in the desired outcome of the educational process?

We begin here by suggesting that society needs men who carry some of the "feminine" characteristics of sensitivity to other people and responsiveness to emotion, as well as tougher "masculine" characteristics. Society also needs women who are somewhat tougher in their thinking processes than they now are, more confident of their own ability to solve problems, less conforming to social pressures. As teachers can contribute by their own attitudes and behaviors to the development of these abilities and attitudes, so will society profit.

Or, should we say, "*Vive la différence*"?

# LOOK JANE LOOK.
# SEE SEX STEREOTYPES.

*WOMEN ON WORDS AND IMAGES*

Johnny says girls aren't fun.

Janey says she wants to be a doctor when she grows up, but she knows girls cannot be doctors, so she will be a nurse instead. Dick says he will be an engineer. Sally says she will be a Mommy.

Dick says girls are stupid. Janey says she might be only a girl, but she isn't stupid at all.

Where does this all come from? Some station is transmitting a clear message to our children about their place in life. They have been tuned in from birth to a frequency that directs everything they attempt, from skipping rope to getting a Ph.D. Something insures that any deviation from the usual norm will be fraught with personal hazards and traumas.

If Janey does become a doctor, she will feel guilty at not being a Mommy, or as good a Mommy as she "ought" to be. Johnny will not feel at all guilty about being a doctor, whether he is a Daddy or not.

Dick will say girls are stupid and most girls will agree with him, except for Janey, who is thereby on the way to becoming an "aggressive" woman. Sally, however, would

*Women on Words and Images is a 25-member task force of the Central New Jersey NOW organization. This article is based on its study, "Dick and Jane as Victims; Sex Stereotyping in Children's Readers." For details on obtaining complete copies of the report—including information on specific readers—write: Women on Words and Images, Box 2163, Princeton, New Jersey 08540. A program based on the study, with slide presentation, is also available to professional and community groups.*

feel very bad indeed if she called Dick stupid, for it might wound his self-esteem, which, even at the age of nine, Sally knows is a very serious thing.

Johnny will spend much of his working and playing life with boys, who he expects, will be much more fun than girls, and his wife, locked into domesticity, will be even less fun as a result of her confinement.

Sally, being a complete Mommy, will drive her children from one achievement to another, imprison them in a spotless home, and project her own ambitions onto them in a classic smotherlove pattern until they finally break for freedom. Then Sally will find herself out of a job, frustrated, and "growing old," often before her chronological time.

Where does it all begin? One early source of the messages children receive is their elementary-school readers. These readers abound in stereotypes. Typical girl in any reader is a frilly thing with a smile on her pretty face and a passive attitude toward life.

What is at issue is the way in which girls are portrayed in these stories—the activities in which they engage, the attitudes they display, the way in which people treat them, the generalizations which are made about them, and the directions for future life and work which are offered to them—as contrasted with the treatment of boys, whether contemporary or historical—their activities, their ambitions, their hopes and dreams, and their ultimate objectives. The degree to which the treatment of boys and girls differs obviously offers a perspective on current social expectations for each sex.

This study of elementary-school readers was made from 134 books published by 14 major publishing companies in the United States used currently in three suburban New Jersey towns. From 2760 stories read, some startling ratios were derived:

| | |
|---|---|
| Boy-centered to girl-centered stories | 5:2 |
| Adult male to adult female main characters | 3:1 |
| Male to female biographies | 6:1 |
| Male to female animal stories | 2:1 |
| Male to female folk or fantasy stories | 4:1 |

Ingenuity, Creativity, Bravery, Perseverance, Achievement, Adventurousness, Curiosity, Sportsmanship, Generativity, Autonomy, Self-Respect. The development and display of these traits is the major theme of the great majority of reader stories. These are the traits universally regarded in our society as positive and desirable. They spring from a solid sense of self and are considered not merely socially useful but necessary for survival as well. Those who possess such traits can be said to have power over themselves, their surroundings, and their circumstances. They "have it made." Who are the chosen ones who virtually monopolize the leading roles in these tales? Males—young and old. The odds against females making it are *four* to *one*.

Let's look at the evidence.

Ingenuity, Cleverness, Creativity, Resourcefulness. The male protagonists of the stories in this category meet situations with intelligence. They try unusual, thoughtful, or daring approaches to their problems. They make things, build things like walkie-talkies and soapbox racers, create things like ice sculptures, silver pitchers, even television commercials. They use their "wits" in promotional schemes, capturing hijackers or dealing with a genie. Girls are conspicuously absent from most of these tales.

The discrepancy is so large that the girl who figures out how to earn bus fare when she finds herself stranded seems like a visitor to these pages. Another girl who discovers silk when a cocoon falls into her tea is far more typical, since her discovery is fortuitous, a "happening," not a product of her cleverness.

Perseverance, Industry, Initiative. In this area, the favorite story line shows the protagonist overcoming all sorts of obstacles, like the young man who clings to his bug collection over the family's strenuous objections which they withdraw (one assumes) as soon as he is hailed for the discovery of a rare specimen.

Persevering boys are a dime a dozen. Persistent girls are, like that bug, a rare specimen. One girl is a tennis player who overcomes pain, hunger, depression, and *a dirty tennis dress* to win her match. (The dress keeps the feminine stereotype alive and well.) Another girl who had the initiative to vote for herself in a class election is

defeated eighteen to 1 for her bad manners, i.e., unfeminine, aggressive deportment.

Boys show industry and initiative in overcoming obstacles as they shear sheep, study guppies, track down
the pilferings of a raccoon. One boy overcomes sensitivity to cold water through a grueling training in order to
become a life guard, and a crippled boy earns enough
money through fishing to buy a brace and special shoes
for himself. Even the handicapped, if male, show more
autonomy, initiative, and perseverance in overcoming
obstacles than two-footed females who listlessly droop
through the pages of the readers.

Strength, Bravery, Heroism. Since most people think
that strength, endurance and coping with danger are male
prerogatives, it will come as no surprise that boys are in
great demand where these themes appear. It's a boy who
skates all day after eluding capture by Indians to warn a
distant village of an impending attack. Boys rescue adults,
girls and other boys from fires, cattle stampedes, drown-
ings, storms, angry bulls and buffalo, and save planes and
spaceships.

From time to time, girls act bravely too. They carry
warnings by horseback, for instance, or go to the rescue
of a wrecked ship. But, far more often they are only seen
saving little, *younger* siblings or small animals, or working
as sidekicks to clever boys outwitting hi-jackers or jewel
thieves.

It is through achievement that a boy in the readers
seeks approval. As he learns the necessary operations to
go forward, he gains confidence and as he gains confidence, he looks less to others and more to his own mastery. His female counterpart seeks approval by being
pleasing, docile and defaulting—i.e., living vicariously,
like the girl whose brother becomes a great artist because
she encourages him to shape up and stop dreaming. One
wonders what advice *he* gave *her*?

Routine Helpfulness, Elective Generativity. Generativity is something one *elects* to express as a representative
of the culture whereas routine helpfulness (making beds,
washing dishes) is service work with servant overtones.
Throughout the series, both boys and girls perform rou-

tine drudge work but with such different basic assumptions.

Girls are expected to be helpful in this way. Boys often acquire moral points for their helpfulness. When girls in the readers attempt to be helpful, it is usually through imitation of a stereotyped motherly role. They cheer up and wash younger boys and even mend their clothes. But the restrictive, unfriendly aspects of motherliness are all too often stressed, when, for example, a girl angrily makes her little brother clean up a wall he has dirtied, or scolds the boys for not eating their dinner.

Adult women are mainly generative as *mothers*—teaching cookie baking and dirt-chasing. It is men—fathers, grandfathers, school masters, older brothers, and just plain boys—who, three to one, encourage others to learn the things they have mastered.

Boys elect to be generative, not only toward animals, plants, and younger children, but also toward adults. Girls tend to *feed* growing things, rather than experiment with and guide them. When boys choose to help sister with *her* dishes (à la papa), it is noteworthy that girls are being helped to accomplish tedious, dead-end jobs. There is nothing generative in this exchange.

Thus it would appear that the creative and compassionate aspects of parenting, those called generatively (and its close relative, nurturing) are removed from the mothering stereotype and assigned to men. Later this interest in fostering the growth of the young can be transferred to interest in important professions such as pediatrician, professor, or civil rights leader—mothers need not apply.

Apprenticeship, Acquisition of Skills, Coming of Age. Another popular story line concerns coming of age—a child who masters an adult skill or fills a grown-up's shoes. Time and again, the child is a boy and the shoes are a man's, as when a boy becomes a real member of a submarine crew after passing a crucial training test, or a son manages the ranch when his father has to leave. "Pa had left him to be the man of the house. Here was the dead grizzly to prove that he had been worthy of the trust."

Boys are stimulated to feel pride and self-worth at the prospect of becoming an adult. The highest praise any of the girls in this category receives is to be told explicitly or by implication that she behaved as competently as a boy.

When a girl masters a grown-up skill, it is usually a domestic one—she makes a cowboy scarf for her brother or overcomes schoolmates' hostility by baking cookies for the fair. Her skills lead through a revolving door back to the pots, the pans, and the sewing box.

Earning, Trading, Acquisition. When it comes to earning money or acquiring possessions, boys are predictably the central actors in a hall but a few of the stories. The enterprising males trade, earn money and obtain benefits for themselves by doing everything from working in roundups to teaching Spanish.

The readers convey to boys that getting rich (downright greed and avarice) is a highly desirable goal for them. But what can a poor girl do? Marry well. Marrying a rich man of high position is shown as a desirable goal for girls. In the fantasy tales, they are willing to be given by their fathers to this type of stranger without a murmur. There is practically no mention of the fact that girls need to learn how to earn a living too, or, that they might *like* to.

Competitiveness. Use of Power. Most competitive stories deal with sports such as football or racing and a few with intellectual competition or 4H projects. Girls are allowed to compete about half as often as boys. But, when it comes to winning, the ball game goes to the boys. If one were to handle winning in general as a broader category, then boys in the readers are the overwhelming winners at life, reasoning, swimming, football, baseball or anything else you can name.

Although girls win at least half as often in sports as do boys, in the readers, it's often the result of a fluke, or after the boys have painstakingly taught the girls to play in the first place.

In all the stories, males both large and small are in the position of power. They bestow financial rewards, prestige, personal validation, jobs, and incentives.

Exploration, Mobility, Imaginative Play, Adventure. In the process of growing up, children come to grips with future possibilities and situations, using role-playing and fantasy as a dress rehearsal.

In story after story, adventure after adventure, the reader boy finds out about the world he lives in and his relationship to it. His adventures take him exploring in China, panning for gold, meeting bears in Yellowstone National Park, weathering a tornado, accompanying Amudsen to the North Pole and catching cattle rustlers. No one is clocking miles for boys as they go adventuring.

As you might expect, adventures for girls are severely limited in quantity and constricted in space. A girl watches her first snowstorm, but from the safety and comfort of a house. By the third and fourth grades, adventure stories fill the readers, and female characters are increasingly phased out. When females do investigate the wider world, there is a "Catch 22." They must be led there by males and be shown what to do. The girl who discovers some old paintings in a cave is accompanied by her father.

And what about dressing up and pretending to be the someone you might become someday? Boys fantasize about becoming a cowboy, an astronaut, a wild-animal trainer, a housebuilder, a king. They're scientists conducting experiments, or adventurers on an imaginary trip with some little green men.

What are our female Walter Mittys doing? They discover a box and play "house in it all day." For every girl in the readers who dreams of becoming a tightrope walker, there are hundreds whose minds are mired in domestic arrangements, and who never stir out of the compound of their own backyards.

Autonomy, Normal Assertiveness, Selfhood. Active Mastery is the composite of all the qualities that lead to growth of the self. Boys are advised to be autonomous, separate individuals, to reason, plan, and execute activities which promote their independence. This is partly accomplished by boys going about alone so frequently and acting as surrogate adults. They rarely hold back or doubt their prowess for long—success is all but assured because they *are* boys.

Girls need not apply for personhood. Stories about girls behaving as complete and independent persons are so rare that they seem odd. But the type of selfhood and achievement extolled for boys in the readers and coming together in all the active mastery traits is a conforming one, the type prized in our society.

The readers shy away from stories about living up to one's convictions, though we do have the story of the boy who finally succeeds in hatching a dinosaur egg despite ridicule from his sister and (what is this?) the girl who takes her leaf collection to school and, facing down a male detractor, instructs the class.

There is some vague hint at a struggle for identity in what are called "tomboy" stories in the trade. The "sissy" stories are never categorized as such but they turn up now and then too. A girl who has a knack for baseball helps win the game and makes a deal for the boys to do the dishes so that she can practice. In a girl's world, dishes must always have primacy. If a boy acquires a doll at the risk of derision, it is in order to trade with a girl for her printing press. (A girl is apparently not expected to be interested in a printing press when a doll looms.)

In one story, an Indian boy succeeds in becoming a brave despite the fact he liked to make baskets and blankets. Usually the outcome for the girl who wants to assert herself as a human being is less felicitous. An Indian girl wants to be tall, brave and strong like the males of the tribe. But, she is teased and told, in a prediction that comes true, that if she does not stop following braves, the laughing waters will turn her into a shadow.

Girls are subjected to contemptuous remarks for their supposed ineptitude at skills boys acquire "naturally," "except Rachel," who has to play ball *better* than boys to win their praise.

Friendship. A real friend, as defined by the readers, is usually of the same sex, and males are better at friendship too. Boys are considered to be demeaned by association with girls, though girls may associate with boys, when permitted, without losing caste. There are a few brother-sister friendships. A diluted form of friendship, really "pairings," are shown in the illustrations from time to time, and these "pairings" may cross race, age, and sex boundaries. But rarely does the text reinforce these messages.

The rigid separation of the sexes that occurs among preteens is foretold and perhaps even helped along by the reader's sex-segregation policy.

Dependency and pseudodependency. Passivity. Incompetence. Fearfulness. People who have these traits— people who are docile, fearful, dependent—cannot conceive of themselves becoming responsible for their own lives or taking the active role in a situation. They are denied the dignity of solving their own problems. They see themselves as the Other, one who supports those who act, or one who provides the background against which the action takes place.

The goals are painfully limited. If they do act, it is usually stupidly. Naturally, they have mishaps. Inevitably, they turn away from the frightening, punishing, overwhelming outside world and focus on the friendly, familiar terrain of the home. Naturally they are victims and targets for ridicule.

Could anyone seriously hold up such narrow, unenviable, life-denying traits for our children to model themselves on?

More subtle indoctrination, which is unhealthy for little girls, is the insistence on self-abnegation and the womanly "virtues" of domesticity. The message clearly written between the lines for even the slowest reader to read is for girls to be obedient and comply uncomplainingly—even happily—with the wishes of others. What happens to a girl who is told repeatedly to minister to others needs and comforts and to put others first? She gets in the habit of putting herself last—behind the stove where she thinks she belongs.

Passivity, Docility, Dependency (Pseudo- and Real). Always it is the female of the species who exhibits this mild, soft, spiritless behavior within the readers. Mothers move through these pages like so much ectoplasm. Little girls endlessly play with dolls, cry over dolls, give tea parties, look on helplessly or passively or admiringly while boys take action. Tommy, on the other hand, doesn't play house—he builds one. Sally's role in the same

sorry tale is clear—she puts on her bonnet and admires
the results.

In story after story, girls like Sally are shown as spectators of life. They are given things, told things, provide a
ready-made audience and instant admiration for whatever's going on. In illustration after illustration, as well as
in the stories themselves, girls look on. They look on while
boys play cowboy, look on while boys make carts, look on
while boys rescue animals, look on while boys save the
day.

Girls often depend on boys when they are quite capable of handling the situation themselves. One finds she
does a lily skate when she has Mark to lean on. Another can
out of reach a jar if a boy brings a stepladder. Almost without exception females in the readers are subordinates to
others. Girls, small and large, are helped out of one difficulty after another by their brothers, older or younger.
On a trip to the store, the two boys, symbolically enough,
walk in front. The two girls follow meekly behind.

Gender terminology is often used as a means of indicating or underlining characteristics in animals or inanimate things. Soft, delicate fluffy kittens are usually female.
So is the lazy magpie. Boisterous, playful dogs are male.
Old people who are mean and ugly are female. (Possibly
an unconscious carryover of the wicked old witch syndrome, but where is the equally infamous bogey man?)
Wise old people are without exception male, and a human
being of any stature is male by definition. Thus, heirogly-
phologists are "men" who study Egyptian writings, and
elsewhere we meet "sayings of Wise Men."

We don't want to be unreasonable and hold the readers
responsible for the sexism built into the English language,
which symbolically has handed over the entire world to
the men, with pronouns like the bisexual "he" for he-and-
she, and words like "mankind" that stand for all of us.
But, the readers don't have to extend this practice by defining archeologists as "men" who dig. Archeologists are
also women. Why not, simply "people" who dig? A pre-
ponderately female Red Cross Unit is referred to as
"brothers." Why not as "one family?" The built-in sexism
of our common language is loud and clear in a comment
made to the young Oliver Perry on these pages: "You're

already been discussed under "Demeaning the Opposite Sex." That a girl bakes a cake and forgets to serve it can only be funny if you think girls are foolish. The other attempts at humor come through animal escapades, such as a hen who lays square eggs. Again, the females of the species are the silly ones as epitomized by Mrs. Goose who takes a bath without water. Just like a woman!

*The Motivation Gap.* Rarely are we offered an explanation why people behave as they do. Why do boys tease girls? Why are women mean to animals or mothers cross with children? Why are children so unkind and even cruel to newcomers in their midst? People, simply, come in two styles—good and bad. To present the world in this motivationless way implies the even more insidious idea that all these traits and more are inborn, not subject to change. They are presented as *given*, not *created*.

An example of such "motivation explanation" appears in a story about a bully. His abnormal behavior is attributed solely to the fact that his mother works in contrast to the good boy whose mother is home all day. What kind of idea is this, we wonder, to instill in the minds of millions of school children whose mothers work outside the home, and whose families are dependent on that income?

*Physical Appearance.* Boys never seem to care how they look. But, girls have a great need to be beautiful and well groomed. Do the readers attempt to correct this imbalance? On the contrary. Girls are encouraged to dress up and play, to covet clothes and to preen, whereas clothing or physical attractiveness is virtually ignored in relation to boys.

Size is frequently mentioned. Any illustrator of readers knows that girls are invariably smaller than boys. If visitors from Outer Space picked up one of these books, they would have to assume from the illustrations that girls as a species come smaller and younger than boys on planet Earth.

There are many role models for boys to shop among, from which to select a skill, a trade, a profession. Men are shown in almost every conceivable role. For girls, the Reader Seal of Approval is reserved for one form of service or another, with wife or mother the overwhelming

favorite. There are 147 different role possibilities suggested for boys; for girls, a mere 25.

Adult males are job holders and fathers. Adult females
are either job holders or mothers, rarely both. Only direct
necessity drives mother to work, never mere desire or
special skill or burning talent. The entire reader study of
134 books unearths only three working mothers, though
the U.S. Office of Labor statistics tells us that 38 percent
of all working women have children under eighteen.

A young girl is constantly being "sold" on nursing over
doctoring, stenography over business administration,
grade teaching over high-level teaching or school administration, and on motherhood over all alternatives. The
little lamb asks her mother what she can be, and Mother
says: "You can be a sheep. A mother sheep, just like me."
The message is rarely this explicit; it doesn't have to be.

The reader mother is a limited, colorless, mindless creature. She is what we have all been looking for all our lives,
the perfect servant. Not only does she wash, cook, clean,
nurse, and find mittens; these chores constitute her only happiness. In illustration, she frequently appears in the classic
servant's posture, body slightly bent forward, hands clasped,
eyes riveted on the master of the house or the children.

The mother in the readers is more remarkable for
what she doesn't do than for what she does do. She is
never shown making something of her own or working
at some task unconcerned with domestic duty. Children
never hush to allow her to concentrate. They never help
with chores in order for her to have some time of her
own. They never bring her cups of tea while she relaxes
with the papers. They never meet her at the station or the
airport as she returns from some independent expedition. Her unlucky son sits up on a tree for hours waiting
for Father to come home and rescue him with the ladder.
Clearly, one needs masculine resourcefulness to think of
such an ingenious solution.

Father is the "good guy" in the family. He's where the
fun is. He builds things with his children, and takes them
hunting, fishing, and up in planes. He solves the problems.
No wonder he's allowed to rest and relax in his favorite
chair so often. If Mother isn't, it probably doesn't mean
what it seems to mean—that she does no real work. It

must be that her time off comes after the family has gone to bed and before the sun comes up.

Responsibility in the home is rigidly defined. The inside jobs go to Mom, the outside jobs to Pop, along with all the mechanical failures. Father's the fixer, even though Mother actually uses most of the domestic equipment. For Mother to change a tire would be as blasphemous as if Father were to whip up the supper.

Sometimes we wondered during this study why all the marriages shown in the readers are so joyless. There's no closeness between husband and wife—all the interaction is between parent and child. There's virtually no touching between adults. Fathers rarely give wives a hug. Mothers never kiss husband or anybody else. Outside of sad-happy waves from a doorway, and food offering, demonstrations of affection are out-of-bounds.

Single females don't hang around the readers very long. They are in the marketplace, quite frankly, like the girl who attended the king's birthday party because "it might be a good place to catch a husband." One backward nineteen-year-old daughter is prodded by her mother and told she ought to be thinking of getting married. No mother is in a hurry to unload a son, and never are males casting about in search of a wife as their ultimate goal—unless, of course, she has a kingdom attached. If love is woman's *whole* life, it is because her life is, perforce, an incomplete one.

Much of the inspirational material in the readers is found in biographies. They are overwhelmingly male. Governmental leaders as disparate as Alexander the Great, George Washington, and Franklin Delano Roosevelt are portrayed. Yet, women of power such as Cleopatra, Queen Elizabeth I, or Queen Victoria never appear.

To be sure, there is Joan of Arc. There is always Joan of Arc, although one story about her life made a special point of describing how her parents sent her brothers to protect her! Other favorites such as Amelia Earhart, Marian Anderson, Marie Curie, and Helen Keller also bow in at least once.

We're glad to see them and others like them whose lives have shown great personal achievements against great odds. But, we wonder why there is a conspiracy of

silence about women whose lives have had political implications. Where are women like Elizabeth Cady Stanton,
Susan B. Anthony, or Lucy Stone? Or women like
Sojourner Truth, Amelia Bloomer, or Rachel Carson? Or
even favorites like Clara Barton and Florence Nightin-
gale?

The readers give the impression that the only people
who make history are men. Mother, who were those
women walking down Fifth Avenue with placards? Silence. Why were those women chaining themselves to the
White House railings? More silence. One half of the
citizenry of a country founded on freedom win the right
to vote after a long struggle and the whole chapter is
passed over as if history had made a terrible gaffe.

To be sure the readers are not history books and are
under no obligation to show all phases of our national
history. But since they do attempt to provide children
with historical role models, they are obligated to show
women as *people who can change history* and can act in
their own interests. Otherwise we are left with images of
women as spectators and handmaidens of history—Betsy
Ross, for example. We all know what she grew up to be.
A seamstress!

Dr. Edward Hall, in "The Silent Language" finds that
children are indeed assimilating the content and values of
their books as they learn to read, without giving it any
conscious thought. Goodwin Watson and Ruth Hartley
both find that by the age of eight, 99 percent agreement
is found among children of both sexes as to which sex
does which job, what kind of person a girl or boy should
be and what the role limitations and expectations are.

Children are exposed to conventional sex stereotypes
long before they learn to read. Attitudes shown by friends
and family, television and books are among the influences
which have already begun the process of socialization.
School readers have a special place in this process. They
convey official approval. They are presented to children
within a context of authority, in the classroom. Finally,
every child must read them. Through the readers, society
says, "This is what we would like you to be."

This expectation is presented to children at a time when
most of them have not yet attained a critical perspective
on themselves and their backgrounds. The official ver-

sion cannot help but become the norm in childish vision.

The pressure of official expectations has a different impact on those children coming from backgrounds which differ sharply from the "approved." They are left with three choices—condemnation of themselves and their families for being atypical or abnormal, a forced conformity to societal norms, or rejection of a society to which they can never fully belong. For these children and for those who realize that the norms are unrealistic and the ideas harmful, exposure to readers can be an introduction to general disaffection with "official" American culture.

Clearly role models of one kind or another must be used in the process of socialization. For example, Margaret Mead in "Male and Female," and Erik Erikson in "Childhood and Society" have shown clearly that all societies use role models to encourage self-development of their children as individuals and functioning members of the group.

But, when the role models remain static while society changes, they lose their value as educational devices and become instead psychological straightjackets which constrict individual development and preparation for life. When the models deliberately build up the self-images of one group at the expense of another, they become viciously repressive.

In America, such practices are particularly inappropriate to the principles upon which this society supposedly was founded. If socialization has twin goals, to rear fit individuals as well as individuals who fit, the models presented in school readers can be faulted on both counts.

The society into which our children will be expected to fit is very different from that presented by the readers. Dr. Suzanne Keller, professor of sociology at Princeton University, outlines the rapid changes which are reshaping the roles our daughters can expect to fill as adults. Briefly, they can look forward to biological developments which may make family planning safer and more reliable, giving women much greater control over their own lives. They can also expect population pressures to result in small families. According to present trends, children will be born to younger parents, and spaced more closely together, thus giving women several decades of postparenthood freedom in which to follow their own pursuits.

More women will find themselves on their own, either by choice or through divorce or early widowhood. Census figures show a 49 percent increase in single adult households in the last ten years. More than half of these are headed by women. Thus, more women will be driven into the job market by financial or personal needs. Already 48 percent of women between eighteen and sixty-four years of age are working. This percentage increases every year.

The high failure rate of modern marriages, which is now one in four, will probably continue or accelerate and will produce a correspondingly expanded search for alternative living patterns, both within the context of marriage and outside it.

Whether or not we like these trends, we must prepare our daughters and sons to deal with them. We cannot do this by pretending changes are not happening or that they will go away if we adhere to the ideals of some past American Golden Age. That age was never golden, and it certainly cannot be recaptured.

The groundwork for a healthy adjustment to social change has to be laid in childhood. Readers are an important part of this groundwork. Changes in role models and the behavior patterns they depict can have a great impact on the changing images children have of themselves. Few but the strong can function under a constant barrage of self-doubt and social disapproval. If we wish our children to avoid the destructive conflicts in social relationships which can be traced to the effects of sex role conditioning with its dehumanizing consequences for men and women alike, then we must begin now to reform the images with which they will form themselves.

One of the reasons often cited for the overwhelming amount of "boys'" to "girls'" material is boys' lack of reading readiness in the primary grades. Boys, we are told, will only read stories about boys, whereas girls will go along with anything. We seriously question this premise. We are convinced that if girls' stories were not so limp, so limited, so downright silly even, boys would cease to discriminate between boys' and girls' stories. There would only be "good" or "bad" stories. (Harriet the Spy, and Pippi Longstocking have no **trouble mak**ing friends among boys as well as girls.)

Future readers should reflect a sensitivity to the needs and rights of girls and boys without preference or bias. Stories in any given reader should feature girls as well as boys, women as well as men. They should respect the claim of each of us to *all* traits we regard as human, not assign them arbitrarily according to preconceived notions of sex roles. Let the Reader Man and Boy show emotion. Let the Reader Women and Girl demonstrate courage and ambition. Such a reapportionment should not involve any loss of self-regard or blurring of identity for boy readers.

Future readers should not arbitrarily bar women and girls from the rights, privileges, pursuits, and pleasures granted to men and boys, nor deny them abilities and occupations males have dominated until now. Specifically, there should be girls and mothers solving problems unassisted by boys and fathers; girls earning money and getting recognition in the form of rewards and awards; mothers and other women in positions of authority; mothers employed outside the home; independent working women; girls operating machinery and constructing things; girls playing with boys on equal terms; girls in strenuous physical situations; girls travelling; girls depicted as taller, wiser, stronger or older than boys—randomly, as in the actual world. Nobody expects readers to conform to strict statistical probability, but blatant bias must be erased.

In the meantime, teachers can make sure that children using readers are provided with supplementary reading material that will help to counteract the message of the stereotypes. They can guide class discussions upon how the Reader World compares with the real world and an ideal world.

The most effective illustration of the sex-role message can be provided by children themselves in informal discussion. Any doubts about whether a message gets through to them at all will be instantly removed as soon as Johnny talks about his view of Janey, and Janey reveals her career ambitions to Johnny!

# THE SEX PROBLEMS OF SCHOOL MATH BOOKS

*MARSHA FEDERBUSH*

Reading books? Sure, it's easy to see how they can discriminate against girls and women. But math books? Pure, objective, scientific mathematics books couldn't possibly be guilty of sex discrimination. Right?

WRONG!

School-textbook companies are not immune to the survival problems of the more mundane industries. They want their products to sell and to bring in money. To do this, they have to make the pictures, problems, and explanations as appealing as possible so that children will enjoy learning from them. And this is where the trouble begins. For books to be attractive to children, now and then humans or humanoid animals have to appear, and as soon as males and females come into the picture, some artists and writers do not seem to know how to do anything BUT stereotype—sometimes artistically or cutely, but offensively just the same. Because math books are not trying to tell a story or to leave a philosophical message or to dramatize a human experience (although these might be good approaches to teaching math), they are under no compulsion to establish heroines or heroes for young people or to challenge students' highest aspirations (except in math). Instead, they do what comes naturally. They stereotype—according to the artist's most simplistic

*MS. FEDERBUSH organized a task force to combat sexism in the Ann Arbor public schools. She is chief author and distributor of the group's report,* Let Them Aspire.
Copyright © 1974 by Marsha Federbush.

conceptions of what girls do and what boys do, what women do and what men do.

Now, not every page or every book of every series minimizes the abilities and activities of females, but turning that extra page or opening that extra cover will most often produce a striking or a subtle—or a strikingly subtle —example of the devaluation or the neglect of females. Come join us in looking for evidence of math-book sex discrimination in three main categories:

> Stereotyping—standard textbook variety;
> Historic omission; and
> Stereotyping—New Math variety.

Incidentally, sex bias in books is almost certainly committed unintentionally, and without malice (at least, without conscious malice). But because it is frequently so subtle or so ordinary looking, we must continue to make sure that it is exposed and corrected.

When elementary mathematics texts (or spelling, reading, and phonics books, for that matter) indulge in standard textbook stereotyping, they automatically assume that the most obvious and normal activities for girls are cooking, sewing, and watching, and for women, housewifery in all its forms, identified by the presence of an apron plus a mop, an iron, a broom, or an eggbeater. In reality, girls may almost never sit and sew by choice, but that has nothing to do with the artist's impression of "girl." And some of the few career roles, other than elementary teacher, painted for women in standard math books are ones that no girl—well, almost no girl—could possibly hope to achieve, like wicked witch or queen. Mathematics texts have the special requirement of putting people into roles that can be associated with numbers. So the most logical outdoor activity in addition to jumping rope, for math-book book girls is going to the store to buy such and such an amount of material or food to satisfy their cooking and sewing instincts. Men and boys, on the other hand, are stereotyped into constant activity and excellence, somehow associable with numbers. In pictures they do woodwork together (females can work with cloth, males with wood), they sail, they climb mountains, they go to the moon, they plant. They are policemen, they are dancing Indians (also stereotyped), they are circus performers, etcetera, etcetera.

When children of both sexes are pictured together in a classroom, there appears to be general equality—usually until one reads the problems carefully. "Susan could not figure out how to . . ." "Jim showed her how. . . ." The expressions on girls' and women's faces are sometimes the models of bewilderment as they struggle to find a way to put order into a seemingly chaotic or even a simple numerical situation. There are occasional explanations which put it into words quite plainly: "I guess girls are just no good in math," said Joe. One can get the uncomfortable impression that, as with some other areas of school life, such as athletics, maybe some of our math books weren't intended to help girls feel mathematically competent after all.

In the slightly higher and purer mathematics courses, where books no longer have to play games in their pictures and problems to entice students to learn, and when books begin listing some of the leaders in the history of mathematics, it is as though noteworthy females have never existed. Not a word is ever mentioned, for example, about the contributions of the great algebraist, Emmy Noether, to her field. By the time many young women students reach their upper grades, they are already so intimidated by the long-taught notion of female inability in mathematics and science that they desperately need role models of female excellence to convince them that their brains are in first-rate working order.

New, New Math—that's another story. Right?

Wrong again.

New Math has brought with it a lot of new mathematical concepts—and a lot of old social ones.

The important new dimension in elementary New Math is the counting of objects in sets. When artists group triangles, rectangles, circles, and squares, these are fine. It may be boring, but children do learn the names of the geometric figures. When they draw baseball mitts, cats, or sports cars for counting, about the only people they may offend are neglected automobile manufacturers. But as soon as they arrange *people* into sets, they spoil it. They almost invariably limit group membership by sex. And particularly when it comes to placing people in occupational groupings, the traditional sex-role expectations are the rule. "Sets by sex," you might call them. Men may be doctors, firemen, chefs, astronauts, pilots, mailmen, painters, policemen, and you name it. (In some cities, half the bus drivers and mail deliverers are female.) Women may be waitresses (or housemaids, depending upon who is looking at the picture), nurses, stewardesses, and funny-hat-wearers, and not much more. Nowadays the people even come in a number of assorted tints, but they are still fixed into rigid sex roles. From these pictures, children must assume, if they are affected by book pictures at all, that only females may be nurses, only males may be astronauts, and only females may be airplane service personnel. (Remember when men sued the airline companies not long ago to enable them to be stewards as they are in so many other countries?) A mother reports that her first grade daughter said to her, "I can't be a doctor, only a nurse. My book said so," after looking at sets containing large numbers of male doctors and female nurses. If a girl could just for once see a picture of a female astronaut, it might make her say, "Gee, maybe when I grow up, I'll be an astronaut." This way, the idea probably never crosses her mind.

It is not only adults who are stereotyped in these New Math books. Boys run, play ball, and swim. They are ACTIVE! Like some of their real-life college counterparts, all twenty-four instrumentalists in a marching band are boys. Girls jump rope, hold dolls, and hold hands with younger children. When set theory problems become more verbal, youngsters deal with the sets of all boys who play baseball and football, and the sets of all girls with blue eyes and with short hair. Boys are judged by what they do; girls by what they look like.

But all is not hopeless. Textbook companies want business, and they are not eager to be accused of discrimination of any sort—particularly when it is perfectly visible. When told of their book's inadequacies, some indicate with what seems to be remarkable sincerity that they will make the necessary changes in future editions. (It is found to be useless to communicate with the writers after their books are written. "I've never heard anything so ridiculous in all my life," was the comment of one well-known mathematician whose name appears prominently on a popular math-book series, when he was told of some clearcut stereotyping in his texts. Evidently the products of writers' painstaking labors become somewhat sacred to them.)

A few important steps can be taken that should work to produce fairly rapid changes in the future mathematics books available to our children:

(1) Committees should be formed immediately by school systems or by outside (preferably feminist) groups to review the texts and audiovisual materials being used in the school system, for sexual-stereotyping, condescension, humiliation, omission, and so on. These committees should make recommendations to their school systems concerning books found to be least offensive in this regard.

(2) Such a committee, or an individual, should be empowered by the school system to inform book companies that all future books being considered for use will be scrutinized for male and female role portrayal, and those found remiss will not be purchased. Companies should also be told that unless future editions of texts already in use are changed, they will not continue to be bought by the school system. (At least one company has already issued a statement of apology for some sexually offending material in a text and has promised to omit the section in future editions. This action was brought about through the efforts of a feminist group surveying school texts.)

(3) A set of guidelines should be drawn up and presented to companies to use as directives to authors and artists preparing new books. For math texts, this task is less difficult than for reading texts. The main categories would deal with:

> Adult role stereotyping—in occupational and family life;
> Boy-girl activities, values and groupings;
> Problems involving male-female competency in mathematics; and
> Inclusion of female mathematicians.

A good and safe rule of thumb is to divide all roles and activities 50:50 wherever possible. It is certainly more reasonable than the current 100:0 sex-role ratio evident in so many current textbook pictures and descriptions. What is desirable is realism (female taxi drivers) plus a little exaggeration (female astronauts)—and the way life is moving in America, what is extraordinary today may be commonplace tomorrow.

(4) Book-review committees, schools, and private individuals should communicate with publishers concerning each book found faulty with respect to sex discrimination, detailing specifically the page number and the description of each picture, problem, wording, or historical account considered inadequate. It is a good practice for individuals to drop a note to the company each time they come across a page which does females (or males in some cases) a sex-role injustice.

(5) Some state Departments of Education are examining books used by the schools for the adequacy of their racial and multiethnic makeup, for the purpose of offering a list of recommended books to school systems. State superintendents should be pressured hard to include sex-stereotyping in their search. There is reticence among some minority group members to pair the two problems because they tend to feel that their cause will be lost if schools begin to focus on anti-sex-discrimination at the same time they are trying to upgrade programs for minority students. But it seems absurd—and expensive in its duplication of efforts—not to review books for both problems simultaneously. A book that may be excellent in its inclusion of nonstereotyped minority people may be hopelessly sexist. And there is no group more rigidly stereotyped into traditional roles in our textbooks, unfortunately, than minority females of almost any variety namable!

(6) State and local education associations, school systems, and involved citizens should pressure appropriate State legislators and legislative committees to pass a law prohibiting sex discrimination in the schools, included in which should be a provision that all instructional materials used in the state's schools will be free of racial, ethnic, and sexual bias. (The Michigan Education As-

sociation sponsored an "instructional materials" bill of this type, early in 1973.)

Carrying out this sort of program of action will be one more step toward helping our young and our very young women feel like unapologetically capable and aspiring human beings. And where mathematics is concerned, this would be a particularly good aftermath.

# SEX-ROLE PRESSURES AND THE SOCIALIZATION OF THE MALE CHILD[1]

*RUTH E. HARTLEY*

Lawrence K. Frank recently suggested that current changes in women's social roles are likely to lead to feelings of anxiety, inadequacy, and hostility in men because of a lack of synchronization in role-change on their part. Increasingly, others have noted evidence of socialization and adjustmental difficulties stemming from male role demands at the adult and adolescent levels. Differential rates of referral of boys and of girls to child-guidance centers have long pointed to markedly greater incidence of failure in social functioning in boys as compared with girls. Delinquency rates notoriously have favored young males, and recent studies of educational underachievement in the gifted have revealed that underachievement occurs twice as frequently among boys as among girls. Finally, a current study of the development of concepts of women's social roles, originally focused on girls, increasingly has been revealing data pointing to the existence of such exigent stress in the boys' implementation of male roles as to call for serious and systematic examination.

[1] Adapted from a paper presented at the Biennial Conference of the Play Schools Association in October 1958. The investigation referred to here was supported by a research grant, M 959 (C), from the National Institute of Mental Health, Public Health Service. The author wishes to thank Dr. Frank Hardesty for his critical reading of preliminary drafts of this paper and for helpful suggestions during informal discussions.

*RUTH HARTLEY is Professor and Chairwoman of Growth and Development at the University of Wisconsin at Green Bay.*

In this paper we shall attempt a preliminary statement of the problem, based on an integration of theory and research findings in the areas of personality and learning processes, along with illustrative case materials, selected from the protocols of forty-one young male Ss (eight and eleven years old) interviewed in the course of our study.[2]

One definition might be in order at this point. By "social roles" we mean all the personal qualities, behavioral characteristics, interests, attitudes, abilities, and skills which one is expected to have because one occupies a certain status or position; in this case, that of being a male human being. These expectations are usually common to a whole culture and are mediated to the individual child early in life by persons in contact with him—first by his parents and other adults close to him, then by his peers and adults with whom he comes into more casual contact. All sex-connected social roles share in one source of difficulty, that they are defined by forces outside the individual (i.e., the culture into which he is born) without any necessarily appropriate reference to his particular native endowments, presenting a pattern into which he must fit himself. This fact is responsible for discomfort enough; to the male role, however, folk myth and social structure combine to impose additional difficulties.

First of all, demands that boys conform to social notions of what is manly come much earlier and are enforced with much more vigor than similar attitudes with respect to girls. Several research studies, using preschool children as their Ss, indicate that boys are aware of what is expected of them because they are boys and restrict their interests and activities to what is suitably "masculine" in the kindergarten, while girls amble gradually in the direction of "feminine" patterns for five more years. In other

---

[2] Half of the Ss came from professional families and half mainly from the lower-middle and working classes. Ss were interviewed individually by one of seven interviewers, whose minimal education was at the master's level. Ss were asked to respond to a variety of pictorial and verbal techniques, which required from six to ten hours to administer. Responses were story endings to unfinished stories, interpretations of pictured situations, and comments as to "sex-type" on a series of pictures depicting common activities. Ss' teachers were also interviewed.

words, more stringent demands are made on boys than on girls and at an early age, when they are least able to understand either the reasons for or the nature of the demands. Moreover, these demands are frequently enforced harshly, impressing the small boy with the danger of deviating from them, while he does not quite understand what they are. To make matters more difficult, the desired behavior is rarely defined positively as something the child *should* do, but rather, undesirable behavior is indicated negatively as something he should *not* do or be —anything, that is, that the parent or other people regard as "sissy." Thus, very early in life the boy must either stumble on the right path or bear repeated punishment without warning when he accidentally enters into the wrong ones. This situation gives us practically a perfect combination for inducing anxiety—the demand that the child do something which is not clearly defined to him, based on reasons he cannot possibly appreciate, and enforced with threats, punishments, and anger by those who are close to him. Indeed, a great many boys do give evidence of anxiety centered in the whole area of sex-connected role behaviors, an anxiety which frequently expresses itself in overstraining to be masculine, in virtual panic at being caught doing anything traditionally defined as feminine, and in hostility toward anything even hinting at "femininity," including females themselves. This kind of overreaction is reminiscent of the quality of all strong emotion precipitated early in life before judgment and control have had a chance to develop.

This, however, is only one source of difficulty. Another related one comes from the simple fact that fathers are not at home nearly as much as mothers are. This means that the major psychodynamic process by which sex-roles are learned—the process of identification—is available only minimally to boys since their natural identification objects, their fathers, are simply not around much of the time to serve as models. Illustrative of the children's awareness of this state of affairs, many *S*s expressed themselves in the following vein: "My father . . . I don't see him very often." "It's harder to know about boys (than about girls) . . . Father hardly has time to talk to me." "Men are harder to tell about . . . to tell the truth, my father isn't around much."

The absence of fathers means, again, that much of male behavior has to be learned by trial-and-error and indirection. One outcome of this state of affairs is the fact that boys, as a group, tend to resemble their fathers in personality and attitudes much less than girls resemble their mothers. This has been impressively documented by the results of a number of research studies conducted by different workers using different Ss and collecting data by different methods.

In addition to the effect of the relative absence of fathers from boys' experience, we also have evidence that the relations between boys and their fathers tend to be less good than those between girls and their mothers or fathers. Since identification is affected by the quality of relationships existing between the child and the identification model, this diminishes still further the boy's chance to define his sex-roles easily and naturally by using his male parent as a model. Boys having trouble in sex-roles, for example, often report their fathers as the punishing agents, their mothers as protectors. Fathers in general seem to be perceived as punishing or controlling agents.

Where, then, we might ask, *do* boys find meaningful, positive guides for the specifics of their behavior as males? The answer seems to point largely to their peer groups and somewhat older youths. For a boy then,- contact with, and acceptance by, his peers is tremendously important, because he has to look to them to fill in the gaps in his information about his role as a male, and he has to depend on them to give him practice in it. Unfortunately, both the information and the practice he gets are distorted. Since his peers have no better sources of information than he has, all they can do is to pool the impressions and anxieties they derived from their early training. Thus, the picture they draw is at once oversimplified and overemphasized. It is a picture drawn in black and white, with little or no modulation, and it is incomplete, including only a few of the many elements that go to make up the role of the mature male. Thus, we find overemphasis on physical strength and athletic skills, with almost a complete omission of tender feelings or acceptance of responsibility toward those who are weaker. It is, after all, a picture drawn by children and it is not enough. Unfortunately, it is almost all that many boys have to go by, and its power to induce anxiety is amply attested.

And now we come to what is perhaps the source of greatest difficulty for the growing boy—the conflict in role demands that our social structure imposes on him! On the one hand, we have insisted that he eschew all "womanly" things almost from the cradle, and enforced these demands in a way that makes whatever is female a threat to him—for that is what he must not be. Ordinarily, one responds to threat by trying to escape from it or by trying to destroy the threatening object. But this the boy cannot do, for society puts him directly under the jurisdiction of women, without relief, for most of his waking day. On the one hand he is told that he is supposed to be rugged, independent, able to take care of himself, and to disdain "sissies." On the other, he is forced into close contact with the epitome of all sissy-things—women—for most of his day and he is commanded to obey and learn from them. In other words, he is compelled to knuckle under to that which he has been taught to despise. Need we wonder that he tends to rebel at times or has trouble making a smooth adjustment?

Moreover, the demeanor of the women with whom he is forced to associate is often such that the boy feels that women just don't like boys. We found many indications of this belief in our Ss' responses to a hypothetical adoption story that they were asked to complete. Almost invariably mothers were assumed to prefer girls to boys. The reasons given for this were drawn from the boys' own experience with their mothers: "She says boys are rough." "A girl wouldn't be so wild—she would not run so much and play rough . . . a girl is more kind." If a mother is assumed to want a boy, it is for a nefarious purpose, as in the following: "She'd want a boy so she can give him to the Indians . . . girls are always good."

Admittedly, the pressures of male-oriented socialization are not exerted on all equally. Some suffer more than others, notably those with physical endowments or special abilities not congruent with the common cultural definition of the male role, and those who have even poorer opportunities than usual for forming sex-appropriate identifications. Thus, the small boy, the weak boy, the boy whose physical coordination is poor—these are especially penalized.

But the lad with better-than-average endowments also suffers if those endowments happen to be in areas not included in the culture's definition of what is "masculine" —music, for example, or art. It takes an unusually rugged physique to offset the disadvantage of a creative mind.

To illustrate what we mean by the "demands" of the male role, let me quote from the boys themselves. This is what they tell us boys have to know and be able to do— their view of the masculine role at their own age level (eight and eleven years): they have to be able to fight in case a bully comes along; they have to be athletic; they have to be able to run fast; they must be able to play rough games; they need to know how to play many games—curb-ball, baseball, basketball, football; they need to be smart; they need to be able to take care of themselves; they should know what girls don't know—how to climb, how to make a fire, how to carry things; they should have more ability than girls; they need to know how to stay out of trouble; they need to know arithmetic and spelling more than girls do. (The last point is probably the greatest blow of all for an eight-year-old.)

We learn a little more when we ask, "What is expected of boys?" We find that they believe grownups expect them to be noisy; to get dirty; to mess up the house; to be naughty; to be "outside" more than girls are; not to be cry-babies; not to be "softies;" not to be "behind" like girls are; and to get into trouble more than girls do. Moreover, boys are not allowed to do the kind of things that girls usually do, but girls may do the kind of things that boys do.

Going beyond the immediate present, this is what the boy sees as his future, described in terms of the things men need to know and be able to do: they need to be strong; they have to be ready to make decisions; they must be able to protect women and children in emergencies; they have to have more manual strength than women; they should know how to carry heavy things; they are the ones to do the hard labor, the rough work, the dirty work, and the unpleasant work; they must be able to fix things; they must get money to support their families; they need "a good business head." In addition to their being the adventurers and protectors, the burden bearers, and the laborers, they also need to know how to take good care of children, how to get along with their wives and how to teach their children right from wrong.

We are also told that, in contrast to women, men are usually in charge of things; they work very hard and they get tired a lot; they mostly do things for other people; they are supposed to be bolder and more restless, and have more courage than women. Like boys, they, too, mess up the house.

On the positive side, men mostly do what they want to do and are very important. In the family, they are the boss; they have authority in relation to the disposal of monies and they get first choice in the use of the most comfortable chair in the house and the daily paper. They seem to get mad a lot, but are able to make children feel good; they laugh and make jokes more than women do. Compared with mothers, fathers are more fun to be with; they are exciting to have around; they have the best ideas.

One wonders, looking over these items, whether the compensations are enough to balance the weight of the burdens that boys see themselves as assuming in order to fulfill the male role adequately. Looked at from this point of view, the question is not why boys have difficulty with this role, but why they try as hard as they do to fulfill it. Perhaps a glance at the characteristics of the female role from the boys' eye view can give us the answer.

Concerning girls, boys tell us: they have to stay close to the house; they are expected to play quietly and be gentler than boys; they are often afraid; they must not be rough; they have to keep clean; they cry when they are scared or hurt; they are afraid to go to rough places like rooftops and empty lots; their activities consist of "fopperies" like playing with dolls, fussing over babies, and sitting and talking about dresses; they need to know how to cook, sew, and take care of children, but spelling and arithmetic are not as important for them as for boys. Though reeking of limitation and restraint, this picture is not very full. Not until we ask about adult women do we get any sort of depth or reflection of the affective aspects of the female role.

Concerning adult women we are told: they are indecisive; they are afraid of many things; they make a fuss over things; they get tired a lot; they very often need someone to help them; they stay home most of the time; they are not as strong as men; they don't like adventure; they are squeamish about seeing blood; they don't know what to do in an emergency; they cannot do dangerous things; they are more easily damaged than men; and they die more easily than men. Moreover, they are "lofty" about "dirty" jobs; they feel themselves above manual work; they are scared of getting wet or getting an electric shock; they cannot do things men do because they have a way of doing things the wrong way; they are not very intelligent; they can only scream in an emergency where a man would take charge. Women are the ones who have to keep things neat and tidy and clean up household messes; they feel sad more often than men. Although they make children feel good, they also make boys carry heavy loads; haul heavy shopping carts uphill; keep them from going out when they want to go or demand that they stay out when they want to come in. They take the pep out of things and are fussy about children's grades. They very easily become jealous and envy their husbands.

Concerning women's traditional household activities, we get the following reflections: "They are always at those crazy household duties and don't have time for anything else." "Their work is just regular drudging." "Women do things like cooking and washing and sewing because that's all they can do." "If women were to try to do men's jobs the whole thing would fall apart with the women doing it." "Women haven't enough strength in the head or in the body to do most jobs." "In going to adventurous places women are pests—just a lot of bother. They die easily and they are always worried about their petticoats." "I don't know how women would get along without men doing the work." Natural exploiters, women are good people to stay away from because as one boy told us, "If I play with my mother, I'll end up doing the dishes and she'll be playing with my father."

When he sees women as weak, easily damaged, lacking strength in mind and in body, able to perform only the tasks which take the least strength and are of least importance, what boy in his right senses would not give his all to escape this alternative to the male role? For many, unfortunately, the scramble to escape takes on all the aspects of panic, and the outward semblance of nonfemininity is achieved at a tremendous cost of anxiety and self-alienation. From our data we would infer that the degree of anxiety experienced has a direct relationship to the degree of pressure to be "manly" exerted on the boy, the rigidity of the pattern to which he is pressed to conform, the availability of a good model, and the apparent degree of success which his efforts achieve.

Variations in degree of anxiety and in modes of handling it are reflected in the observable range of boys' responses to the socialization pressures put on them. In our sample of Ss, we have identified four major configurations[3] thus far: (a) overstriving, with explicit hostility expressed against the opposite sex and with marked rigidity concerning the differentiation between the role activities assigned to men and those assigned to women; (b) overstriving with less hostility, but with marked rigidity; (c) a tendency to give up the struggle, accompanied by protest against social expectations; and (d) a successful, well-balanced implementation of the role, which is positive in approach, showing clear differentiation between concepts of male and of female roles, but with an understanding of the complementary relationships between the roles, and marked flexibility in relation to the activities assignable to them. The cases below illustrate three of these patterns.

T. D. exemplifies the pattern of hostile overstriving with extreme rigidity of sex-role concepts.

For example, when asked whether women ever do things like fixing electric cords, driving trucks, giving sermons (activities which he reported as assigned to men), he responded, "No, women never do that. I think it isn't right for them to do it. Who asked them to do it? I don't trust women doing anything." When asked what most people thought about women doing "men's jobs," he said, "They're just no good—like women presidents. If we had a woman in Congress and taking over everything, probably the Russians would attack tomorrow if they knew about it—if we had a war, they would tell everybody to put down their

[3] The author identified these configurations by inspection of the protocols and checked her judgment with Dr. Frank Hardesty, who, as Research Associate on the Project, had been intimately involved in planning the collection of data, and who had collected data from at least a third of the Ss.

arms. They'd probably make it life imprisonment for any boy or man who strikes a girl. I wouldn't even trust a woman as a doctor. You never know what they are going to do next."

Concerning girls, T. D. made the following remarks: "They're getting too smart now. Before, only the boys gave wisecracks; now, girls do too. Now, some are too advanced. They use double talk. They talk, well, it's like a college man to a junior high—they make us look like fools in front of everybody."

In a discussion concerning working wives, this boy said: "I don't like women working. They get in the way. I don't care for females. I don't like females. I say that men could live better by themselves." Concerning marriage, T. D. said, "I don't like to. The only way I'll get closest to marriage is being engaged for five years. I don't like the idea."

His ideas concerning activities appropriate for men were just as rigid as his attitude concerning the proper place for women. When asked what he thought about men doing things like cooking, teaching small children, working in a sewing factory [activities he had assigned to women], he said, "It's not right for them [the men] to be at work they are not fitted for . . . just the women think that men should. Most men think they shouldn't do it." Asked if there was anything he thought men should *never* do, he said positively, "Take care of the house."

Concerning mothers working, he was sure they ought not to do it. If his own mother wanted to go to work he would not permit it. Asked to imagine that he might be married in the future, and what he thought he might do around the house, he replied, "Lie around and watch TV, or it's just going to be a losing fight and I'll be washing the floors or shopping. Every boy and man I know hates to go shopping. Men do it but boys put up a fight."

In contrast to T. D. a few brief excerpts from the file of R. J. will serve to clarify what we mean by "rigidity" and "flexibility" in relation to sex-role differentiation. Asked about the appropriateness of women doing the kind of work R. J. had assigned to men, he said, "I think they should know about things like that before they tried it . . . I think it is a good idea that they know, so if they were alone they could do them [meaning traditional "male" home activities like mending electric plugs, etc.] without calling somebody else in." Asked if there were things women should never do, R. J. said, "No, I think it should be fun for women to do things like that, to show other women that women can do hard jobs and take it, too." In response to our question about the appropriateness of men doing "women's work," R. J. replied, "I think a man should do that sometimes and let the wife take a rest [referring to domestic chores]. As for being a secretary and things like that, I think men should, if they know how to do it and like it."

Concerning child care and household activities, R. J. said, "I think they [women] feel responsible for making children happy and helping children to understand. They, well . . . women want to feel that they are needed and someone wants them very much." Concerning domestic routines, he stated, "I don't think they enjoy it but I think they feel they have to make their children happy and to help them along. They do it to help the child grow to be a good mature fellow so that he'll help other people. I don't think most women enjoy working around the house all the time and doing those things, but so someone has to help the family out, and that someone has to take care of the children and things like that, so they'll grow up to be good people."

The tolerance and sensitivity to human values indicated by R. J.'s judgments can be appropriately evaluated in the light of his place among his peers. From his teacher we learn that his self-confidence never seems to falter, he is physically well coordinated, and excels in baseball, basketball, and other sports. On the playground and in the class-room he is the unquestioned leader of his group. Of all our *S*s, this boy seemed to be most at ease and comfortable in all his role activities.

On the other end of the scale from the overstriving lads we find K. M., a boy with transparently damaged self-esteem who, although he clearly perceives the role definitions imposed by society, protests them helplessly.

To begin with, K. M. is certain that grownups prefer girls to boys. He indicates this by telling us, in discussing a story about a hypothetical adoption, that he knows both his mother and his father would prefer a girl to a boy. His mother would want a girl because "she would help around the house . . . a girl is more kind . . . and, well, she knows how wild I am." He thinks his father would prefer a girl because he has a younger sister; his father plays with her more and "is always kissing her." These responses should be evaluated against a background of responses from many other Ss, most of who assume that fathers, at least, prefer boys. K. M. departs from the norm of our sample also by saying that when he marries he would prefer all his children to be girls. This is the reason he gives: "All our neighbors around the block have girls and they are so cute . . . some girls are much smarter than boys . . . Well, in all the grades I had all the girls were smarter than boys . . . just a couple of the boys were smarter."

K. M. indicates an awareness of lack in relation to his own male role by giving himself a mark of eighty in male-role skills and a mark of ninety-five in female-role skills. He explains this discrepancy by saying, "I do know what girls need to know better than what boys need to know. It is harder to know about boys—you get scolded more than girls and the teacher is always yelling at you if you are a boy."

Not only is K. M. aware of his own limitations, but he knows what other people think of them. In discussing the appropriateness of "women's activities" for men he says, "[most people] care, but they don't say anything about it [if a man performs traditional women's activities]. They don't say anything, but they think he is crazy or nuts."

However, K. M. does not think that there are things men should never do—except getting drunk or breaking the law. In contrast to most of his peers, he indicates that he does not think this is the best of all possible worlds. In relation to sex roles, he believes that improvements should be made —with machines, for example. "It makes things easier—if it is a man's job, the women can even do it then." Similarly, although he feels that most vocational activities are satisfactorily apportioned between men and women, he thinks they should do the same things around the home, like washing dishes and taking care of the children.

To a boy in K. M.'s situation, girls who are tomboys present a real threat because they emphasize the boy's own failure. Talking about the "tomgirl" who had been in his class the year before he said, "Everybody was scared of her, even me. She played football and did everything that boys did. She obeyed the stronger boys though . . . One day she gave practically all the boys in class their social-science lessons. I didn't get them, though . . . There is even one in my class this year. There always is. S. E. beats everybody up. Every year there is one in the class." The last statement seems to embody K. M.'s resignation to a permanent secondary place, not only in relation to the other boys, but even in contacts with girlish imitators of boys.

Difficulties with sex roles spill over into the classroom. The teacher of T. D., for example, confesses that she has no idea what he is like. "I have never really been able to reach T . . . I really don't know what he knows, what he does not know, or what he does not care to know. I have not been able to find out too much about him. He is very quiet. He is not really one of the most normal boys in the class and I do not think he associates with most of the boys." Apparently, most of the time T. D. daydreams in class or draws pictures of boats. He evidently has no intention of letting his teacher, who is one of the despised and exploiting females, get close enough to him to sense the quality of his thoughts, nor has he any intention of producing any work for her. He presents a clearcut example of passive resistance. Knowing how hostile he feels about women in general, we are not surprised that he takes refuge behind a blank facade in her presence.

K. M.'s teacher describes him as a "foolish boy who irritates the class through his thoughtless teasing and picking at them." In his bids for attention and acceptance he involves other youngsters in small misdemeanors which bring reprimands from the teacher and result in his rejection by most of his classmates. He tends to shy away from anything that is competitive and challenging and "requires constant prodding in his schoolwork." Poor vision and poor coordination add to his difficulties on the playground and in the classroom. Although he is a gifted musician, this does not seem to help him gain status either with his peers or with his teacher, both of whom seem to regard this as another indication of his lack of manliness.

Although, as we have indicated before, initial difficulties in the male role may be based on constitutional lack and on poor models, the boy's response to his sex-role demands is often complicated by the quality of his intrafamily relationships. T. D.'s younger sister who is receiving more attention than he and his brother may account for some of his hostility, as may his mother's insistence on cooperation in the kinds of things that T. D. thinks a man should never do—cleaning, tidying, and other housework. K. M., on the other hand, feels almost completely bested by the patently stronger appeal of his younger sister, who seems to be preferred by both his father and mother. Added to his lack of physical endowment, this makes a heavy burden—apparently too heavy for him to bear well.

In summary, the implications of the available data are at once encouraging and discouraging. On the positive side we may note the examples of flexible, comfortable, well-balanced implementation of male roles we have found. It is comforting to know that this kind of development is possible even with current socialization techniques. We are also encouraged by the fact that it is apparently feasible to identify some of the child-handling practices that seem to produce unhealthy attitudes in this area. What we can identify, we may be able to change.

On the other hand, the frequency and intensity of cross-sex hostility in our male $Ss$, their manifest anxiety about their adequacy, and the prevalence in them of marked inflexibility, suggest a dismaying prognosis for their future adjustment in a society where feminine roles are changing rapidly. In addition, the widespread prevalence of the socialization practices which seem to be associated with the difficulties we have described, and the intense anxieties shown by adults concerning possible failures in "maleness" by boys, give up little reason to hope that amelioration of those difficulties will be swift or simple.

## Summary

From the interviews of forty-one eight- and eleven-year old males, four adjustment patterns to the male sex role are apparent. Sources of conflict experienced by these young children are lack of adequate models, extensive supervision by women, conflicting nature of multiple role demands, lack of clear, positive definition of the male sex role in socialization practices, and rigidity of role demands.

# SEX-ROLE ATTITUDES
# OF FIFTH-GRADE GIRLS

*GRACE K. BARUCH*

I am presently studying sex-role attitudes of pre- and post-adolescent girls.[1] Findings now available permit some comparisons of fifth and tenth graders with respect to the motive to avoid success, sex-role stereotyping, and career aspirations. Fifth-grade girls were of special interest. Concern about popularity with boys is not yet a major influence upon them, and several mothers of ten-year-old girls warned me that their daughters not only believed that girls could outdo boys in almost every area but also rather enjoyed proving this.

I especially wanted to study the onset and development of the motive to avoid success which Matina Horner[2] has described as an inhibiting fear that success in achievement-related situations will be followed by negative consequences. To avoid using a cue that would merely reflect the

[1] Material reported here is from an ongoing study of sex-role attitudes of approximately fifty fifth-grade girls and fifty tenth-grade girls in relation to their age and to their mothers' sex-role attitudes and child-rearing values. The work is supported by post-doctoral fellowship #5 HD5343501 from the National Institute of Child Health and Human Development. I am grateful for the advice and assistance of Inge K. Broverman, Karen Johnson, and Judy Jordan and for the cooperation of principals, teachers, parents, and children in the schools involved.

[2] See Matina Horner's, "Toward an Understanding of Achievement-Related Conflicts in Women" in Chapter One of this volume.

*GRACE BARUCH is a postdoctoral fellow in psychology at the Worcester Foundation for Experimental Biology.*
Copyright © 1974 by Grace Baruch.

usual superior school performance of girls in all areas, I gave a rather extreme verbal lead sentence. "Anne has won first prize in the science fair for her exhibit on car engines," and asked each student to write a little story about Anne.

To study career aspirations I asked subjects: "What do you think you would like to do when you're an adult; that is, what career do you think you'd like to have?" The third aspect of sex-role attitudes studied was stereotyping, the tendency to polarize males and females in terms of the traits ascribed to each. Using a short version of the Sex-Role Questionnaire developed by Rosenkrantz, Vogel, Bee, Broverman, and Broverman (1968), I asked subjects to rate men, women, and themselves on a series of traits such as independence, ambition, competitiveness, tenderness, and neatness. The traits included on this instrument which have previously been found to be socially valued and associated with males center around competence, independence, and leadership; those socially valued and associated with females center around warmth and nurturance. The questionnaire also indicates how the girl sees herself, as well as men and women, in terms of these qualities.

A warning is necessary before reporting and interpreting the results obtained so far. Most of the fifty-two fifth graders tested were from the middle or upper-middle class. It is true that many professional women would be expected to emerge from among such a group, and therefore their problems and conflicts deserve attention. However, one cannot generalize from these findings about girls in general; differences that are due to social class and/or race are known to be profound.

## Career Aspirations

Of the fifty girls who responded to the question about career goals, about half wanted to be a secretary, nurse, or teacher. Perhaps because of the daily exposure to classroom models, teacher was the most popular choice. Being a stewardess, actress, or singer were also frequently desired. Only twelve girls chose occupations ranking at the top level of the widely used Hollingshead Scale. Of these, four wanted to be veterinarians, three to be physicians, and the others chose scientific specialities like marine biology. No one wanted to be a lawyer, banker, politician, architect, or business manager.

It is unlikely that lack of knowledge about various occupations was a major reason for these results, since tenth-grade girls, who can be assumed to be more familiar with various careers, made almost identical choices. Rosalind Barnett (1973) obtained similar results for girls at all ages between nine and seventeen; boys with similar backgrounds tended to choose much higher ranking occupations. Of course it is possible that, if the study had been done five years ago, many girls might have responded simply, "wife and mother." None did so here.

## Sex-Role Stereotyping and Self-Concept

Previous researchers (Rosenkrantz et al., 1968) have reported a remarkable consensus in perceptions about the differing characteristics of males and females. Despite the fact that traits ascribed to women are consistently seen as less socially desirable, they are nevertheless incorporated into the self-concepts of female subjects. Because a new form of the Sex-Role Questionnaire was used in the present study, exact statistical comparisons with results for other age groups remain to be worked out, but certain gross trends are already apparent. The fifth graders do tend to stereotype men and women along the lines previously indicated. Men are seen as competent, logical, active, but not as gentle, neat, or affectionate, as compared with women. Their perceptions of women are just the reverse. However, the tendency to stereotype is less than that of the tenth graders or of adult subjects. The fifth graders also tend to perceive themselves as lacking the masculine traits, although to a lesser degree than they think adult women do. This tendency too is less pronounced than for older subjects.

In a pilot study of a small number of female college students, David Tresemer and Joseph Pleck found a strong association between sex-role stereotyping and fear of success; preliminary results suggest there will be a similar connection in my sample. It seems reasonable that where great differences between the sexes are perceived, it would be more likely for successful achievement and femininity to seem incompatible.

## The Motive to Avoid Success[3]

Because of the superior school performance and minimal concern for male opinion considered to be characteristic of fifth-grade girls, I did not expect to find evidence of conflicts over success in most stories. Upon first reading them, however, it seemed to me that at least half of the stories did indicate the presence of a motive to avoid success, in terms of the varieties of "serious concern about success" described by Horner (1970). For example:

> All the boys were teasing her for being interested in car engines. I'll show them, she thought. I can make just as good an engine as any boy. And one boy said, I'll bet you can't. So they were going to see. They both brought in their car engines and guess what—Anne won. Now everybody looks at her with new respect.
>
> Everybody thought that Anne would not win because car engines are boys' things but there was not any law about doing it on car engines so she tried her hardest and won.
>
> She is almost crying because she is so happy. The man who was the judge is giving her the reward. Just the day before she was crying because she thought she wouldn't win. Her brother is mad because he didn't win. Her father is one of the happiest people in the world and is going to buy her a present.

I soon realized that, except for the quite realistic acknowledgment of doubts or criticisms about Anne's abilities, these stories contained no suggestion that Anne would be deterred from her goal or become anxious about achieving it. Stories by the fifth graders in which these consequences did occur had a quite different quality:

> She was so happy, her friends were really mad. They also had a good exhibit but Anne won. On the way

3 David Tresemer and Joseph Pleck have pointed out (1972) that, under the present scoring system and in the original Anne cue, anxiety over success in a sex-inappropriate activity is not distinguished from anxiety over achievement in a competitive situation. It should be noted that the cue used in the present study also does not permit a clear distinction of these two sources of anxiety.

home from the Science Fair she was going to walk with someone but she had left so she went to walk with someone else but she ran away. Anne couldn't understand why.

She is a tomboy and she wants to do everything a boy does. Anne lives with five brothers, Micky, Joel, Tom, Art and Keith. Before she was a tomboy she played with Sue Holmes but she moved away. She wants to keep the prize on her dresser. She will get to keep her exhibit in the closet.

Sue and Mary Ellen got very jealous and started being very mean to Anne. They thought they should win because they took the courses for it and Anne didn't. The fair manager called and said that they had made a mistake and Anne won second prize. They made friends again even though Anne was disappointed.

---

### Table 1
## INCIDENCE OF FEAR OF SUCCESS IMAGERY IN FIFTH- AND TENTH-GRADE BOYS AND GIRLS

|  | TYPE OF STORY | | |
| --- | --- | --- | --- |
| NATURE OF THE SAMPLE | *Fear* Present | Coping | *Fear* Absent |
| **FIFTH GRADE** | | | |
| Boys ($n = 40$) | 25% | 0% | 75% |
| Girls ($n = 52$) | 29% | 19% | 52% |
| **TENTH GRADE** | | | |
| Boys ($n = 43$) | 42% | 0% | 75% |
| Girls ($n = 48$) | 33% | 29.5% | 37.5% |

---

Except for the theme of antagonizing a valued male, these latter stories illustrate most of the fear of success categories Horner has described—denial, negative consequences, etc. However, only 29 percent of the subjects wrote such stories, compared with the 47 percent that Horner (1972) reports for seventh graders and the 33 percent I found in my tenth-grade subjects. About 19 percent wrote stories, illustrated in the first group above, that I now have labeled "coping" stories, following Jerome Bruner's distinction between coping and defending. When a problem exists, coping is an adaptive response that requires acknowledging the problem and finding a solution, whereas defending—denying or distorting what is happening—does not permit a solution to be found. The latter group of stories, in which inhibition, denial, and anxiety are described, illustrate a failure to overcome problems.

After making this distinction, I noticed that among the 52 percent of stories that showed neither a fear of success nor an obvious coping theme, there were several stories in which the heroine seems to be *preventing* negative consequences by sharing her success with others, often quite literally:

> Anne: "Oh boy! I know just what I'm going to do with this dollar I won on car engines at the science fair. I'm going to get candy for all the girls." She tells Sally. Sally: "Oh, that's so nice of you, Anne."
>
> Anne is very happy today. It was a cake that she won. The class got to have a piece of cake too. They ate the cake and went back to the classroom.
>
> Anne has been waiting years for this. Her friends Mary Anne and Beth also helped. First they got the car engine from an old car. There was no need for a report. The trio wanted to win first prize but they gave it to Anne because she seemed to do all the work.

It is possible to view this sharing theme in a negative light, perhaps as a sign of anxiety for approval. However, the desire to remain a part of the group after winning is better seen as a valuable, adaptive, and even ancient trait, not so different from the food-sharing behavior which Jane Goodall describes among chimpanzees who have made a kill.

It is interesting that no such theme was found in the stories of the forty fifth-grade boys, to whom I gave a similar sentence cue—with John as the hero—in order to compare responses of boys and girls. About 25 percent of the boys' stories did show a fear of success, a percentage comparable to that of the girls. In the other 75 percent there was no indication of awareness that any problem existed. Since the achievement described was sex-appropriate, those boys not anxious about competition apparently saw no difficulties that required coping. Perhaps girls are more sensitive to and concerned about the feelings of others, for realistically, those confronted with another's success usually do have mixed feelings about it, even (perhaps especially) a friend's success.

Boys' fear of success stories had as the most frequent theme that of revenge from an unsuccessful competitor. For example:

> John brought his exhibit on car engines home and went out to play. One of Tom's friends, Jerry, took it when he wasn't looking.
>
> John won first prize but on the way home he remembered a bully's promise to beat him up and also wreck his model-car engine if he won first prize. So the bully came up. He said, "This engine is real and if you try to hurt me I'll throw it at you and it will explode." The bully really believed him.

However, stories in which the motive to avoid success was absent did not differ much for boys and girls; themes usually concerned the winner's happiness or future achievements.

A typical boy's story in which the motive was absent was:

> He was so happy he could cry. As he saw the blue ribbon coming toward him, how glad he was he worked real hard. And here comes his reward.

A typical girl's story was:

> She is so glad she won because she had no first prizes before. When she gets older she is going back to the science fair for she is going into the 7th grade and the teacher would like her to come back again to show the people the engine. The people were thinking that she would become a car fixer when she grows up.

For purposes of comparison, it is helpful to look at responses of tenth-grade subjects. Although this study is not longitudinal and we can expect the rapid change in attitudes in this area to continue, differences between the two age groups are still of interest and suggest that, with the onset of adolescence and interest in boys, there is increased concern that achievement and femininity can be incompatible. Only 33 percent of the stories clearly indicated a motive to avoid success, but this is an increase over the 29 percent in the fifth grade. There was also an increase in coping type of story, from 19 percent to 29.5 percent. In only 37.5 percent of the stories, as opposed to 52 in the younger group, was there no evidence of either fear of success or problems to be coped with.

An example of a story in which the heroine is defeated by the consequences that follow her success is:

> She is standing in front of her exhibit, smiling and feeling proud, yet she also feels sort of funny because she is a girl, and girls don't usually think about car engines. Her girlfriends all look at her because they think she is weird and all the boys are laughing at her because they don't think she's feminine. Now she feels hurt and alone and wishes she had gotten the prize for almost anything else. She even feels that she doesn't even want the prize now at all.

While some coping stories are similar to the 5th graders, others suggest that the problems, usually concerning boys' reactions, are becoming harder to overcome or ignore:

> Anne made a bet with Paul she would be able to win first prize at the science fair for her exhibit on car engines. Anne put a lot of time and thought into it. Paul didn't think she could do it. But Anne did a good job on it and was very thrilled just in thinking how easy it really was to win, after she had finally started it. Paul is a poor loser and said he will never sit with Anne again, because she is too smart for him.

Horner has pointed out the powerful influence of the significant male; this is surely one reason that fear of success increases with age. Thelma Alper has reported a story, told to a picture cue of two women scientists at work in a laboratory, in which the women are described as winning the Nobel Prize and using the money to go on a cruise to meet men.

As is indicated in the table, tenth-grade boys wrote a

*higher* percentage of stories showing fear of success (42 percent). Conflicts over success are a frequent problem for males as well as females. However, the nature of the conflict seems qualitatively different; the usual theme in the boys' stories was that John had cheated:

> He has worked hard on this engine to win, setting it up perfect, but his friends helped him out with his writing and others helped him with the engines. The judges found this out and took the prize away. John didn't like it. So he killed all the judges. John is now in the state pen serving a life sentence.
>
> John has just brought a converted aircraft turbine to the fair. John has just received the engine from his father at Rolls Royce. The judges do not think that any boy there would cheat so they think that John is a genius and give him first prize. John will show the prize to his father and say that he won it fairly.

This theme may indicate jealousy of John, perhaps out of inability to identify with him because of feelings of incompetence. Unfortunately no data on ability was available for the male subjects, so I cannot test this hypothesis. (Although recent studies have indicated an increasingly negative attitude toward success among males, the studies have used the medical school cue and have elicited a quite different type of criticism of John—that he is greedy, insensitive, etc., apparently because of his association with the medical profession.)

After this account of the pervasiveness of the motive to avoid success, it is important to resist a tendency to "blame the victim." The focus on women's inner psychological conflicts over success, Clara Mayo has pointed out, must not allow us to forget that this anxiety about the consequences of success and the portrayal of barriers to its enjoyment reflect the true situation facing women. We must avoid locating the problem as solely in the victim's head, for to do so is to conclude, at least implicitly, that the remedy is also there rather than in social change.

A second danger is the tendency I have noticed to view concern about the opinions of others as a (mainly feminine) flaw or weakness. The human condition involves long years of dependency on others and a perhaps biologically supported need to be accepted. These insure that the attitudes of significant other people will have a profound effect upon the individual, and the mitigation of this effect requires more than preaching the virtues of ignoring what others think. When parents as well as males do not support a girl's ambitions, she requires assistance in maintaining them rather than criticism for her lack of independent thinking.

## Implications

In offering any interpretations of or remedies for the findings presented so far, concerning children's views of sex roles, certain points should be kept in mind. First, although the sexist content of such influences on the elementary-school child as books, television, and school policies is well documented in this volume and elsewhere, it is important to note that these are a reflection of social realities rather than a plot, conscious or unconscious, by the people responsible. In real life, men do tend to go out to work and to have adventures while their wives do housework. Even more relevant is the structure of many elementary schools, in which all-female teaching staffs are supervised by a male principal. In asking school personnel to fight against sexism, we are asking them to improve upon real life, to initiate social change.

Second, while it is widely acknowledged that influences other than the school and the mass media affect children —for example, whether the mother works or the father is deeply involved in child care—it is less widely recognized that the child, as Piaget has shown, is actively engaged in *constructing* reality, in seeking out rules, overgeneralizing them at first, and clinging to them rigidly. Walter Emmerich has suggested a parallel between sex-role learning and language acquisition. The preschool child produces such sentences as "I goed out," or "I maked a cake," yet the child has never heard such forms; they result from overgeneralization of the most common form of the past tense. Analogous examples with respect to sex-role attitudes are numerous. In one elementary school I worked in, the only male teacher is constantly called "Mrs." instead of "Mr." by the younger children. Many professional mothers are horrified by their young children's insistence that girls can't be doctors, boys can't be nurses, and so on. When the determined mother takes the child to a woman doctor, the child then insists that the doctor cannot be a Mommy. Alleen Nilsen (1971) reports that her sister's six-year-old son and five-year-old daughter cried when their mother was accepted to medical school. To be a doctor, they said, she would have to turn into a man, and then they wouldn't have a mother any more. A general tendency for doctors to be men and teachers to be women has become an absolute when filtered through the child's mind.

To make this point is certainly not to defend the status quo. In fact, the urgency for more than token changes in the social structure becomes more apparent; token changes are simply not noticed by children.

I have assumed a connection between various sources of sexist input affecting children and the problems and conflicts adult women have in achievement-related areas. While the evidence still remains circumstantial (or correlational), since we have not examined the connection directly in this study, the traditional content of sex-role attitudes in the fifth graders supports our belief that they are profoundly affected by the input. However, it is also apparent that there are major individual differences in girls' sex-role attitudes, and my study is now proceeding in analyzing influences on these, especially the role of the mother.

My research confirms the need for social changes that have been urged by others. Furthermore, this study makes it clear that a major source of individual strength in the face of sex-role problems and other important human concerns is the ability to cope with one's need to win approval, to be like others, and to avoid criticism. This ability guards against the tendency to incorporate and adopt social attitudes that are harmful to the self, a tendency which, as I have already indicated, should not be seen as shameful. It should be possible to make even young children aware of this tendency to conform, of its negative as well as positive side, and of ways to reduce and deal with such conflicts between the self and society. These conflicts occur in many areas. An example is Huck Finn's fear that he is wicked because he does not carry out or fully share his society's laws and views on slavery, which conflict with his tie to Jim. One reason that the price of dissent and of breaking out of old patterns has always been high is that individuals themselves tend to add to the penalties society exacts.

## REFERENCES

BARNETT, R., "Vicissitudes of Occupational Preferences and Aversion Among Boys and Girls Ages 9 to 17." Paper presented at meeting of the American Psychological Association, Montreal, Canada, August 1973.

HORNER, M., "Femininity and Successful Achievement: A Basic Inconsistency." In J. Bardwick, E. M. Douvan, M. S. Horner, and D. Gutmann (eds.), *Feminine Personality and Conflict*. Belmont, California: Brooks-Cole, 1970.

HORNER, M., "Toward an Understanding of Achievement-Related Conflicts in Women." *Journal of Social Issues*, 1972, *28*, 157–175.

NILSEN, A. P., "Women in Children's Literature." *College English*, 1971, *32*, 908–921.

ROSENKRANTZ, P., S. VOGEL, H. BEE, I. BROVERMAN, and D. BROVERMAN, "Sex-Role Stereotypes and Self-Concepts in College Students." *Journal of Consulting and Clinical Psychology*, 1968, *32*, 287–295.

TRESEMER, D., and J. PLECK, "Maintaining and Changing Sex-Role Boundaries in Men and Women." Paper presented at Radcliffe Institute Conference, *Women: Resource for a Changing World*, Cambridge, Massachusetts, April 1972.

# IV.
# Sexism in
# High School

# HIGH-SCHOOL WOMEN:
# OPPRESSION AND LIBERATION

*JENNY BULL*

More and more in the Movement, people are seeing the way capitalism and this society not only create oppressive institutions but also warp each of us. I think the Women's Liberation movement fully understands how institutions warp individuals, and thus has a clear sight of the way women must work to be equal and human with each other and with men on the personal level, as well as working together on the political level to change the institutions in this society that create that oppression. What I want to talk about in this article are the more specific ways high-school women are oppressed in this society—[by the schools, by their families, and by the social scene.] I also want to talk about liberation—liberation as the personal strength to control one's own life, resist social pressures, and work together politically to change those pressures. I want to talk specifically about how this can be done in high schools.

First to start with the schools. Compulsory attendance means that students are subjected to the system's way of training people in capitalism—a system based on competition, status consciousness, conformity, and unquestioning obedience to authority. For women students, there is added oppression—not only are they unequal because they are students, but they soon learn to know their unequal place as women, both academically and socially.

Schools train people to fit into this society as it exists—therefore courses of study in school reflect the traditional subservient roles women are expected to play. For exam-

ple, I took a year of required home economics (cooking
and sewing) in high school, and many schools still either
require or strongly urge home economics for women.
Rarely are men allowed to take these courses, and few
want to. In other words, schools basically see women as
future homemakers—"If you're going to get stuck with
the shit work, might as well be trained to accept it." Besides homemaking, the other use women serve is that of
servant to men in business—as secretary or clerk. Therefore, you will find a large majority of women in business
typing and shorthand classes. The school is in effect saying
to women students, "Your claim to business competence
is that you are Mr. So-and-so's servant." On the other
hand, there are various skills which men learn, such as
woodworking and other shop courses, which women cannot take—again, this is not their role in society; they don't
have the choice. In the academic areas men are encouraged to take more intellectual subjects, especially math
and science. It's OK if a woman does poorly in these subjects; she is not expected to be as competent. On a more
general level, guidance counselors often limit women's
academic aspirations, recommending less ambitious
courses or colleges. So, men are generally prepared for
leadership, authority roles and women trained to be their
assistants in preparation for a male-dominated country
and economy.

In general, what I am saying is that schools view wom-
en's education as training for subservience rather than as
equipping her to choose her own potential by exploring a
wide range of possibilities. One of the purposes of this
subservient training is that if women get jobs it keeps
them from questioning their traditional roles. The secretary is trained in school to be a slave, to know she must
obey the boss' orders, not to be independent, and to expect
low wages. By teaching these attitudes, women are not a
threat to the job hierarchy and can be easily exploited.

The other part of the way schools oppress women students is more personal; it has to do with the attitudes
women have toward their intelligence and academics.
The first and most important thing to say is that women
have just as much intelligence as men, although few men
or women act as if they believe it. This is one reason why
women have just as good grades, if not better, than men

in high school. However, being a "good student" in high school has little to do with intellectual ability and creative use of the mind. The good student in school is passive, does it the "right" way, is neat, follows directions, says what the teacher wants to hear—and all of these are attitudes women know well because they are expected to act this way all of the time. The obedient woman and the obedient student are both "good" in society's and the school's terms—and both lack creativity and independent thinking.

Women in high school often react to these oppressive attitudes in school in basically two ways: they either stay "feminine" or they try to become men intellectually. Neither is open or fully human. The "feminine" student never acts too smart, and especially never shows it if she knows more than a male student. This game has a lot to do with the male ego. Men don't like to admit that a woman is smarter than they are, and so any woman who wants to be popular knows how to be tactful and at least let the guy *think* he thought of it first. Not only are such games dishonest, manipulative, and inhibiting, but they eventually persuade the woman she *isn't* as smart. Basically, social acceptance for the woman means accepting intellectual inferiority in school.

The other reaction to intellectual oppression is for the woman to think of herself as a man, rejecting popularity as a woman for acceptance in male terms. She rejects one false definition of herself only to take on another. I was like this in high school—since I wasn't popular socially I decided to get even by competing intellectually with men, by showing them how smart I was. Not only was this compensating for my failure as a woman in society's terms, but it was defining intellectual success by male standards, not by my own. In competing intellectually with men I was letting them set the standard for me to reach. As a result, I disliked other women, thought they were stupid, and got great joy out of showing how smart I was. I was sort of like a middle-class black—rejecting my origins, putting on all the outer signs, but at the same time still seen as inferior—trying to make it in someone else's scene. One of the most important things I have learned since I have been involved with Women's Liberation is that the liberated woman is *not* a man! The aggressiveness and competitiveness with which men relate to each other and to intellectual things is a long way from the human ideal of respect for people, as equals. Men too often use their intelligence to prove superiority and to play the game of "oneupsmanship"—and women who try to play the same game only succeed in becoming more warped by capitalism's view of people as superior or inferior—never equal. This competition at the root of capitalism is obvious in school where competition for grades, social status, IQ scores, college entrance, sports, all stress being better or worse than someone else.

All this is to say that the male roles in this society are often negative ones that do not treat people as equals. The woman who does not accept the inferiority assigned to her must also reject the competitive male role and learn how to relate to her mind in a *human* way, allowing her to share ideas with people, rather than using her mind as a weapon or status symbol.

All of the various kinds of oppression I have been talking about deal with school—however there are at least two other institutions in which high-school women are equally oppressed: the dating game and the family.

First I want to talk about the social attitudes women and men have held traditionally. Just the slang tells the story. Women try to "catch" guys, "seduce" them, "lead them on." While men "make it with a chick," or "get a lay." Such terms show how our personal relationships are based on competitiveness, manipulation, and ownership just as much as our intellectual relationships. We see other people as property, "my broad," or status, "she dates a good-looker." These attitudes mess up both men and women. In addition, the women must be passive and the man aggressive. Women have to play the whole game of "let *him* take the initiative." Both sexually and socially the man must at least look as if he has made the first move—either in asking for a date or in making out. This game means that neither men nor women can be open about their feelings toward each other and their roles work against genuine humanness of personal relations. In addition, the whole dating game breeds a lot of jealousy among women. If a woman's status is defined in terms of her popularity with men, then all other women are seen as competition for male attention. Such a scene not only separates women from each other, but it undermines the self-confidence of women—if they can't win at the dating game they are of less worth as a person according to society's standards.

All of this is fairly traditional, and I realize that some very good changes are happening socially today. Dating is more casual, roles less rigid—but I want to emphasize that I feel most of the stuff I was just talking about is still very much present, just a little more subtle. Men and women dressing more alike and having the same length hair still doesn't change the basic pattern of female passivity and men viewing women as possessions.

Another change for the better is the greater sexual freedom, honesty, and openness today. It is a step forward when people learn how to touch without playing a game, when people learn how to love without feeling guilt. However, men still use women to prove their virility. Manliness which depends on the submission of another person is oppressive and lacks humanness. All of this goes to say that women must learn how to "play the game" if they hope to be "accepted."

Now about the family. Women who are still living at home face a double problem. They are young and therefore considered unequal, and they are women and thus expected to be more passive than their brothers. When a high-school woman moves toward greater freedom, responsibility, and self-determination, this is often very threatening for her parents, who see themselves as authorities and superiors. Her parents, especially her mother, whose relationship with their daughter is not built on mutual love and respect, feel a neurotic need for dependency from her. They feel threatened when she lives by values different from their own, often because they are unsure enough about their own values and worth. When she rejects status and material possessions as goals in life, this questions one of the basic reasons for living of many parents.

A mother in this society often lives *through* her husband and children—she has no life of her own. Because her children are her only emotional outlet a mother sees in her daughter the hope of what she cannot be. In so doing she *uses* her, instead of respecting her for what she is. A mother lacks respect for herself, and judges her worth in terms of her children, so she feels a failure if they don't come out "right."

In many ways the parent/child relationship belongs in the whole list of unequal relationships that this society creates: man/woman, white/black, teacher/student, etc. In fact, just as with the schools, it's easy to view the family as a training institution for fitting into society. Since most parents don't accept or respect the different values of their children, they use their energies in training the children in traditional roles. The girls learn manners, how to cook and sew, learn career expectations, how to dress "attractively," etc. In fact, in all instances I am familiar with, the family is working against the goals of women's liberation—often because it is so threatening to the parents' relationship.

So high-school women are oppressed in a variety of ways. I have linked that oppression basically to our capitalist system, which sees people in terms of status, possessiveness, competition, and inequality. I have talked about how these values are taught in schools, by the family, and in the social dating scene. These institutions train women to fit into society as it exists, not respecting them as equals who should be liberated to live as they wish and relate as human beings. What I'd like to do now is go on to the second half of this article—how that liberation can be achieved for high-school women.

First of all, let me say that I see Women's Liberation as understanding the deep and essential connection between true personal liberation and true political liberation. This society warps each of us, so each of us must work to change our own lives as well as resisting and working politically to remove the causes of that oppression. In other words, institutions shape people, and thus must be resisted on the personal and institutional level. I'd like to compare this concept of liberation with the Resistance. Five years ago Resistance meant "resist the draft," and was narrowly limited to saying "no" to an oppressive institution. But people have found it takes courage, individual strength, and commitment to say "no." Often resisters have formed or joined communities for strength and support. People have found that in not letting a social institution run their lives, in placing their actions where their convictions were, they had a positive, creative personal freedom, even if they ended up having to spend time in jail.

I see Resistance as an approach by which many different people can unite as they come to understand that their individual hangups are caused by the institutions which oppress them, by the total system under which they live. A draft resister, a black, a woman, and a high-school student are all struggling against an oppressive society. More important, these people can talk on a personal level about their individual struggles to free themselves from the patterns in which they have been trained to think. Resistance need not be defined in a narrow political and negative sense, but should be broadened to include all those people in this society who are struggling for self-definition and personal freedom and control over their own lives in this society.

What does Resistance mean for women in high school? In school, it implies the personal decision to define education in one's own terms, based on personal needs, and disregarding competitive, social, and vocational pressures to comply with the status quo. In the family, Resistance means standing up for yourself as an equal human being, making up your own mind, and trying to communicate at this level with your parents, especially your mother, about her role. In social relationships Resistance means being honest with men, not compromising your integrity, avoiding competition for men, jealousy among other women— valuing yourself *not* in terms of "seductiveness" or "popularity with men," but your own ability to love, and give, and think. In all of these things Resistance means you have to take the consequences: bad family squabbles, unpopularity with men, wrath of the school administration, "F's," and all the other various pressures people and institutions can bring to bear on people who dare to resist. The amount of force in the arsenal for oppressing high-school women is vast indeed. Taking the initiative in resistance is difficult and requires a lot of strength and group support. In fact, people usually come to resist in gradual steps. The more a woman student deviates from the accepted role, the more she becomes aware of the oppressive nature of our society, and the harsher is the oppression. One special problem for high-school women is the tendency to say, "I'll wait it out, one or two more

years and I'll be free—away from home, in college, etc."
First, such an idea is illusory, in that women are always
treated unequally, and often those college years just put
off marriage and the conventional housewife role for four
more years. The more basic point though is a woman's
response to her immediate oppression in high school.
Waiting it out does not build the strength to resist later,
and that strength is especially important during a period
when social, vocational, and intellectual roles are being
learned.

How can women find the strength to resist? My basic
conviction is that women can find strength in community.
We have all been so messed up by schools, family, and
society that it is foolish to believe that we can straighten
ourselves out and become conscious of our problems
without the help of others, much less begin to change
institutions. The whole women's liberation movement is
based on small discussion groups or cadres, through which
women come to recognize and deal with their common
oppression as well as to act on it politically. The Vietnamese use this same cadre structure as they fight together for freedom. They realize that the community,
group strength, and support provided by a close-knit
group of people who trust each other, see each other as
equals in the struggle, and share a common goal, is essential to the revolution. The Vietnamese have gone a long
way toward liberation for women. Women are an integral
part of the NLF forces and form their own resistance
cadres. Mutual trust, support, respect, and comradeship
are essential for a new *human*, socialist society in which
all are equal.

Many young people today find a real need for community—communal living for high-school people is growing more and more frequent as people find family
oppression unbearable. More and more people are dropping out of school, or seeking a real community for
learning outside of school. This community, because it is
an attempt to live with equality and mutual respect and
sharing, can be a situation in which women can come to
deal with their oppression and learn new, liberated ways
of relating. I am part of the Learning Action Center, a
community in Baltimore that is trying to relate to each
other as equals, to work together to find direction in our

learning and relate it personally to our lives, and to use that community as a base for various political activities and involvements. This is just one of several "free schools" here on the East Coast that find their basis in community and various kinds of resistance. One of the things I find most exciting about the Learning Action Center is the way it is helping men and women to change the social roles they have been taught, and to learn more honest, open, and equal ways of relating to each other. Not only are there no "teachers" at the center, but men and women share equal responsibilities in the groups—in fact the thing is based on a shared responsibility for making it work. The Center also provides a base where people in high school can have political meetings, as well as some time away from school, family, and the usual social scene. This center not only gives people strength to resist in school, but it helps people find a vision of a better way, a hope for *now* which gives strength in the struggle for the future. The Learning Action Center is not a women's liberation group but it does draw people together for strength in various resistance struggles.

I feel that especially for high school women a women's group could help focus a specific kind of resistance. Let me describe my ideas on how such a group could operate. First of all, it would meet somewhere away from school and family—somewhere women can relax and gain some perspective on themselves and these institutions. If the group felt strong enough it could meet with an older woman active in women's liberation or a radical woman teacher. However, in doing this it is important to work on the old/young, teacher/student gap, and be sure enough of yourselves that you won't let an older person or teacher dominate or "run" the group. But if the group comes together *as women*, their other roles in society should not get in the way of relating as women to common problems. I feel that the group should stay small—no more than ten or so, starting another cadre if more women want to join, but maintaining close contact for political actions.

There are all sorts of things such a group can explore —they can really study the whole fashion, glamour racket, "What does *Seventeen* offer and why?", and try to explain this to others. They can read teenage romance stories as examples of the way society views sex and love, and again point out the falsities of this literature to others, the same time increasing their own understanding of how we are trained to think and act. The whole school social calendar of proms, homecoming queens, club "sweethearts" and the like can be publicly opposed. Beautiful and effective guerrilla theater or demonstrations can be held around such public "popularity" events that view women as ornaments and sex objects, not as people. Women can make a thorough study and critique of the curriculum and guidance facilities at their school, bring these inequities to the school's attention, and *fight it!* They could publicly challenge teachers who degrade women, even asking that a teacher be fired on the basis of male chauvinism (just as teachers have been fired for blatant racism!). Women can start their own women's history course, and demand credit for it. As much as possible, these activities should start as self-educating, freeing, *human* things.

When acting politically in schools, I don't necessarily see confrontation as the first step, but rather *acting* in the midst of the system in ways that help strengthen understanding, humanize relationships, and point out the inhumanity of that system. If women can find the strength to direct their own education, social life, and family life they will gain support from other students and draw other people into a greater awareness of their unfreedom and give them strength to join with them. Of course, from such actions oppression and confrontation will follow, but that confrontation will be as a result of a creative, freeing action, one which helps people gain understanding and strength.

In addition to these political and institutional activities, the women's groups could support each other in their personal efforts to relate honestly and equally with men, and in efforts to be treated as an equal in their families. Often the group is a place where women can share their frustrations as they struggle in these personal areas. In overcoming the traditional jealousy and competitiveness among women, women can realize that even if their parents don't respect them, and men reject them, here is a group that will accept them as an equal and with respect.

Let me say again that I see this group as functioning

both politically and personally. If it is only personal it will turn into another gossip club, not relating to the institutions that cause these problems. If it is only political it will suffer from the same hangups of jealousy and competition and lack of community that other political groups do. The women's movement is talking about a whole redefinition of roles in this society—destroying the hierarchical patterns in which this society places people. When we talk about changing institutions we are also talking about redefining the whole way we relate to each other as human beings—as man to woman, as teacher to student, as parent to child. The women's movement emphasizes sharing, equality of leadership and responsibility, the ability to *listen* to one another, to see beyond intellectual analysis to common problems. In struggle against oppression we can often become very rigid and defensive about our actions. We need to accept the fact that people in the movement can struggle in different ways and that doesn't need to threaten us. We need to work together from different fronts as we deal with our own problems and come to understand the ways this country messes us all up. And as we come together in small groups we can hope, from the positive things we discover, to find strength to know the way for the future, a future of liberation for women, a future of liberation for people!

# DOWN THE UP STAIRCASE

*RICHARD ROTHSTEIN*

*Education is commonly viewed as the key to upward mo-
bility in America. High schools channel students into
appropriate occupations, ostensibly according to their interests and aptitudes. In reality, one of the best predictors
of curriculum choice is sex, not ability; girls go into home
economics and commercial tracks, boys into agriculture
and industrial arts. This text demystifies the high-school
tracking system, distinguishing its rhetoric from its actual
social function of maintaining society's rigid class, race,
and sex divisions.*

From the Post Office rack, you can get this glossy pamphlet:

## WOULDN'T IT BE THE SMART THING FOR *YOU* TO STAY IN SCHOOL?

It's a great, big world out there.

And there's a place in it for you.

Trouble is, a lot of other guys will be out scratching for the same spot.

It's sort of like a basketball, football, or baseball game.

You've got to have the moves to beat out those other guys.

To get out into the open and score. Or make the double-play or hit it up the alley.

And you know what that takes.

Training. A stick-to-it attitude. An education. The kind you're getting right now by staying in school.

SAY YOU DROPPED OUT OF SCHOOL TO LOOK FOR A JOB?

You ought to be able to get a job of some kind.

Whether it's what you want, or would like to keep, is another question.

As a high school dropout, you'll have three general types of jobs open to you. Farm jobs. Unskilled labor. Service jobs.

Openings in these jobs seem to increase slightly year after year. But then, so do the number of people looking for them. So even here, you'll have to beat out the next guy.

*(Prepared and distributed in the public interest by the United States Army)*

Most Americans accept the assumption of the Army pamphlet: that people can rise in life by getting an education; that to get a better job, stay in school. This belief in upward mobility through education is widely accepted not just for individuals but for groups as well. In the late 1960s liberal Americans held that black ghetto poverty resulted from the failure of blacks to obtain a good education which would prepare them for well paying jobs. As the Kerner Commission said, "the schools have failed to provide the educational experience which could overcome the effects of discrimination and deprivation."

Upward Mobility is Limited—Everyone Can't Get Ahead of Everyone Else. However, widespread mobility through education is mythical. And like many social myths, this myth retains its strength not by its sophistication but by our failure to question an obvious contradiction. The emperor has no clothes. In any "basketball, football, or baseball game" there are as many losers as winners. When you make the double play, two other guys are out. And while a pep talk can sometimes determine which side wins and which side loses, it can never make a winner out of everyone. If the same pep talk is given to everyone, it probably won't even affect who wins.

Think about the Army pamphlet for a minute. What if every kid followed its advice and stayed in school? Would the number of farm jobs, unskilled jobs, and service jobs decrease? Ultimately, the pamphlet's myth of upward mobility implies that these jobs will disappear if everyone graduated from high school. If they all went on to college, we would have a society where everyone was a doc-

tor, lawyer, teacher, or business executive. Nobody would
have to car-hop, run a punch press, or harvest lettuce.
Absurd.

*Tracking* is the "American or indirect" way of assign-
ing occupational roles through manipulation of the school
systems of the country. This paper is about how tracking
works.

If everyone stayed in school, what mechanism would
neatly choose those most qualified for the better jobs?
Everyone can't stay in school if the system is to function.
The effect of the Army pamphlet depends on the refusal
of large numbers of young men and women to heed its
advice; moreover, they must know that they refused to
heed it. For an essential ingredient of this nation's man-
and woman-power channeling system is the belief by
those stuck with lousy jobs that it's their own fault—I
can't do better than a farm, unskilled, or service job because I was too dumb to stay in school. If only I'd listened to that pamphlet . . .

If the poor believe that their poverty and alienation is
the result of their own stupidity, their own failure to
achieve, and their own unwillingness to stick it out in
school, they will be less likely to squawk about their
condition and less likely to question the occupational
structure which assigns poverty and alienation to those
who do the majority of the country's necessary work.
And if those who are secure financially believe their success is the result of hard work rather than a favorably
stacked deck, they are likely to be more self-righteous and
rigid in defending the status quo.

The economic structure of our society requires a system of vastly differentiated educational opportunities for
those destined for different jobs; combined with the myth
that the top educational opportunities are open to all who
try to make it. In the elementary and high schools of the
nation, *tracking* is the mechanism which fills this function.
Students are assigned to tracks; the track sizes are pro-
portional to the job openings in the occupations to which
those tracks lead. We will show in this paper that students are effectively assigned to reading groups, special

classes, and special schools on the basis of income, race, and sex. Yet there is a complex mechanism which persuades those involved (teachers as well as students and parents) that the assignments are made on the basis of "ability."

Tracking is not unique. It is similar to other systems whose purpose is to manipulate people to adjust to national economic policies. In 1965, the Selective Service System issued a memorandum to local draft boards justifying the use of draft deferments to pressure men into civilian occupations which were short of voluntary manpower:

> From the individual's viewpoint, he is standing in a room which has been made uncomfortably warm. Several doors are open, but they all lead to various forms of recognized, patriotic service to the nation. Some accept the alternatives gladly—some with reluctance. The consequence is approximately the same . . .
>
> The psychology of granting wide choice under pressure to take action is the American or indirect way of achieving what is done by direction in foreign countries where choice is not permitted. Here, choice is limited but not denied, and it is fundamental that an individual generally applies himself better to something he has decided to do rather than something he has been told to do.

* * *

The tracking system in American elementary and secondary education is not meritocratic. In addition to the rational occupational channeling functions of a meritocratic system, American educational tracking also serves a second function; the maintenance of rigidities in the social class, race, and sex-role divisions of American society. It is an essential purpose of the tracking system to prevent significant mobility between rich and poor, white and black, male and female. Tracks do insure that schools certify students for occupational openings in the required proportions, but they do this by insuring that the "upper" tracks leading to more prestigious occupations have proportionally more whites, men, and rich students;

and that the "lower" tracks leading to blue-collar (and now to technical, service, sales, and clerical) jobs include proportionally more blacks, women, and poor or working class students.

Sometimes this tracking to inhibit mobility is explicit. Most high schools assign classes in home economics and typing to girls and classes in "shop" to boys. Most large cities have special high schools for girls and boys, in which specialized male technical or female secretarial skills are taught. However, most tracking is more subtle. Because girls are socialized (in school and out) to defer to male intelligence and leadership, they not only learn how to act dumb but become dumb. Girls who are "underachievers" in high school usually begin to be so at the onset of puberty—when social pressures to defer to boys also begins. Boys score about sixty points higher than girls on College Board math-aptitude tests. But girls improve their math scores if the same math problems are reworded to deal with cooking and gardening.

Neighborhood schools are tracks which in themselves inhibit mobility. An academic high-school diploma from a black-ghetto high school has a very different value as a ticket to college from a middle-class school diploma in the same city. The ghetto diploma, even with high grades, is relatively worthless in the eyes of college admissions officers, when compared with the same grades on a transcript from a "good" white school. Indeed, the correct perception of this situation by large numbers of white middle-class parents has been a chief cause of population movements in the last two decades. The massive shift of white families from cities to the suburbs is in large part due to the conscious attempt by these families to nullify the results of increasing "equal educational opportunity." By moving to a suburb with a "good" (i.e., prestigious) school system, families can protect for their children privileges (like admission to prestigious colleges) which would be denied if they only earned an honors urban diploma.

Sometimes this tracking to inhibit mobility is suspiciously coincidental. For example, we noted that tracking rigidity within schools was increased rapidly after 1958. Throughout the country, high schools were divided into advanced placement, honors, academic, vocational, general, and essential tracks. School systems received extra government and foundation grants if they would set up special programs for the "gifted child." We suggested earlier that this was inspired by the military decision to invest rapidly in space technology and the need for increased numbers of engineers and scientists to make American rocket capacity competitive with Russia's. But the late 1950s was also a period when racial integration was becoming significant in large urban areas. Migration of blacks from the south to northern cities had reached a level where the participation of black children in many formerly white urban schools was no longer "token." The beginning implementation of the 1954 Supreme Court desegregation decision seemed, to many whites, to "threaten" even more widespread school integration. In the face of these racial trends, the increased emphasis on "ability" tracks within schools had the effect of nullifying racial integration. Segregation was transformed from an interschool phenomenon to an intraschool one. "Honors" and "general" tracks served to provide a convenient mechanism for separating white from black students within a school, while at the same time providing a seemingly objective ability test which monopolized college and career privileges for the white students in the honors tracks.

Men and women were also segregated by this tracking. As "advanced placement" and "gifted children" tracks were established in high schools, A.P. science and math classes were overwhelmingly populated by boys, while girls filled the new high-school poetry or comparative-literature classes. (There was some mixture in what were usually called "problems of democracy" or "contemporary civilization" advanced placement social studies classes.) Today, the male products of 1960 advanced placement tracks are engineers, while the female graduates are most often highly literate secretaries or housewives.

Explicit, near-explicit and "coincidental," the results are clear:

### Table 1
## PER CENT OF HIGH-SCHOOL GRADUATES GOING TO COLLEGE THE FOLLOWING YEAR, BY ACADEMIC APTITUDE, SOCIOECONOMIC BACKGROUND, AND SEX, 1960

| ACADEMIC APTITUDE | *Socioeconomic status* | | | | | |
| | LOW | LOW-MID | MID | UP-MID | HIGH | ALL |
|---|---|---|---|---|---|---|
| **MALES:** | | | | | | |
| Low | 10 | 13 | 15 | 25 | 40 | 14 |
| L-Mid | 14 | 23 | 30 | 35 | 57 | 27 |
| Mid | 30 | 35 | 46 | 54 | 67 | 46 |
| U-Mid | 44 | 51 | 59 | 69 | 83 | 63 |
| Upper | 69 | 73 | 81 | 86 | 91 | 85 |
| ALL | 24 | 40 | 53 | 65 | 81 | 49 |
| **FEMALES:** | | | | | | |
| Low | 9 | 9 | 10 | 16 | 41 | 11 |
| L-Mid | 9 | 10 | 16 | 24 | 54 | 18 |
| Mid | 12 | 18 | 25 | 40 | 63 | 30 |
| U-Mid | 24 | 35 | 41 | 58 | 78 | 49 |
| Upper | 52 | 61 | 66 | 80 | 90 | 76 |
| ALL | 15 | 24 | 32 | 51 | 75 | 35 |

SOURCE: Christopher Jencks and David Riesman, *The Academic Revolution*, New York, Doubleday, 1968, p. 103.

If meritocratic reforms were politically possible their chief effect would be to increase access of black students to the privileges of an obsolete system. Since we are likely to be stuck with this system for some time, this increased access is an essential element of justice for which all should fight. But, for the purposes of building a long-range movement, teachers should also be aware of how faulty even a "fair" tracking system would be.

Even a "fair" tracking system would rest on dubious assumptions; e.g., that "objective" ability testing is possible in this society. We are not prepared to say that this assumption is false, but only that it is impossible to justify its truth. Objectivity in ability testing has never been achieved—all our supposed tests of "ability" are in fact tests of different socialization, class, race, and sex.

Even if we developed a relatively objective ability test for a meritocratic tracking system, at what age are children to be put in tracks? Since there is no way of measuring ability except by measuring achievement under some attempt at standard conditions, the liberals hope to create as uniform as possible an environment for all children so that competition for the top tracks will be based on genuinely "equal" opportunity. But unless this track placement is done at a very late age in a child's life, many kids will be cut off from opportunities because of their own rate of development. Even among children of relatively equal background and environment, teachers often spot "late bloomers"—kids who, for one nonstandardizable reason or another, become highly motivated relatively late in their school careers. Even if race and class could be eliminated as the determining factors in track placement, this problem alone would prevent any truly objective system of early childhood ability testing. Even for a single individual with a relatively constant environment, I.Q. scores can vary throughout life.

Even more important is the fact that we have no way of defining ability for American children. Every test we have—I.Q. scores, reading tests, etc.—are in fact so infected with cultural assumptions that we are not testing ability but race, class, and sex. Liberals assume that this problem will be eliminated if early childhood socialization can be standardized. But how much standardization of socialization (and by whom?) is required to justify the tracking system?

This question may seem panicky. But there is in fact talk among the nation's educational planners of attempting to fully standardize child-rearing practices for the entire population. This form of totalitarianism is closely related to the "cultural deprivation" theories we described earlier. If one believes (as does the Coleman Report, the Moynihan Report, and the Ford Foundation) that poor urban education stems primarily from "defects in the learner," there is no limit to how early the meritocratic state should intervene in the homes of racial minorities.

Thus, in April 1970, President Nixon sent to the Department of H.E.W. a recommendation of his personal physician that all children be tested at age six to identify criminal potential; and that the potential criminals be "treated" by being placed in state-run camps. And in the same month, the Commissioner of Education, Dr. James Allen, proposed that all American children should be "diagnosed" at age two and a half for "home and family background, cultural and language deficiencies, health and nutrition needs, and general potential as an individual." This information would then be computerized and sent to a "team of trained professionals whose job it would be to write a detailed prescription for the child and, if necessary, for his home and family as well."

Within our current political structure, this kind of emphasis on improving "ability" testing is more likely to lead to cultural annihilation than to equal opportunity. The second assumption of meritocratic tracking—that different occupational categories require different levels of educational attainment—is so deeply rooted in modern American ideology that many will find it strange even to question. But the assumption is false.

At a commonsense level, many of us teachers realize that little in our formal school training was relevant to our teaching roles. Life experience—in the world of work —rather than college or education school would have been better preparation for teaching. We know that many competent teachers with real skills to teach are kept out of the schools because they don't have the formal education credentials; while many incompetent teachers fill the schools simply because they have persevered to get a B.A. and a dozen education credits.

Sixteen years of formal education is not the best qualification for a good teacher. It should not be surprising, therefore, that in other occupations as well, formal schooling has little relevance to the real requirements of the job. A recent statistical study has shown that workers with more schooling do not do better jobs than workers with less. For textile workers, utility installers, auto workers, paper technicians, secretaries, insurance agents, bank tellers, electrical engineers and scientists, higher educational levels did not improve job performance.

Air-traffic personnel working for the Federal Aviation Agency [need] the characteristics that technical college training might be expected to develop. . . . Yet half of the 507 air controllers who had attained government rating 14 or above had no formal schooling beyond high school.

Further, there was no pattern /of differences in job grades among men with different school records. . . . Non-college graduates *without* managerial training earned the most awards. Nevertheless, FAA officials expect to raise the schooling requirements for new employees in the future. . . .

That formal schooling has little relationship to job performance does not mean that a high degree of skill is not required for many jobs. Teaching requires skill, but most of us feel that we gained our most important teaching skills on the job—not in education classes. Apprenticeship under the careful eye of a respected master is a much more effective way of gaining skills—be they teaching or air traffic skills, surgery or auto mechanics.

If formal schooling does not qualify occupational skill, why is school tracking used to select out different categories of workers, and why are educational requirements for most jobs increasing? Simply because school attendance is more a means of restricting access to good jobs than a means of qualifying people to do jobs well. The nation's first high schools, established in Massachusetts in the 1840s, were set up in order to keep Irish immigrants out of competition for expanding managerial opportunities in the industrial revolution—not because a high-school education was necessary for job success. In 1910, "only a little better than an eighth of all adults had twelve or more years of schooling, yet a third of the labor force was employed in white-collar occupations (which now require at least a high-school diploma), while many others were employed in demanding, skilled, technical jobs." As competition for good jobs increased, so did educational requirements.

Compulsory education laws were passed and increased over the last 150 years, not primarily because school was good, but because child labor was bad. Compulsory school laws were the reverse side of the coin of child-labor prohibitions—with work forbidden, school was needed to keep kids out of trouble. Today, there is talk of raising the compulsory attendance age to eighteen—not because of increased educational levels required in the economy, but because youths who can be kept in school cannot swell the unemployment or delinquency lists.

Again, we can use our own experience to guide us. School teaching is not becoming more complicated, not requiring increased education. But master's degrees are more and more helpful in getting teaching jobs because there is a surplus labor pool in the teaching field.

So the assumption that better jobs require more (or "better") school education is false. Even a tracking system which created "fair" competition for school honors would be irrational in its own terms—it would have little to do with qualifying graduates for job performance.

. . .

Schools could meet their social responsibilities by helping to train students of all ages to do work which served the needs of all the people. If all workers were entitled to an adequate and decent standard of living the rational channeling tasks which would still be performed would have none of the competitive or punitive characteristics of tracks today.

Schools could help people find purpose in life which was not defined by the need to earn a living. Not only is this task of equal relevance to all students, regardless of race, class, and sex, but it is hardly separable from the living of life itself. The present tracking system could disappear and schools cease to be isolated institutions whose inmates were defined as children not yet prepared to live. At what age(s), if any, citizens should get formal, school-like training would be an open question. Society would be "deschooled."

There is no short-run reform program which can eliminate the tracking system with its breeding of competitiveness, false hopes for upward mobility, antisocial feelings of superiority and inferiority. So long as schooling is a scarce material reward which serves as a ticket to other, more important scarce material rewards, the tracking system in some form or other will separate those rewarded in school from those not. The frustrations of tracked schools are a reflection of the class structure of a capitalist society. So long as we have doctors earning $30,000 a year alongside dishwashers earning $3,000, we will have a school system which separates the dishwasher from the doctor at an early age. And so long as we have a political system which is dominated by corporate interests, the schools will also serve to insure that the sons of doctors have a better crack at privileges than do the sons of dishwashers.

Teachers upset about the tracking system and their role in it ultimately must look to the broader structure of society for the cause of their frustrations. A school-reform movement which does not also become an economic-structure-reform movement is bound for defeat, caught up in its own contradictions.

• • •

# REALISTIC COUNSELING
# FOR HIGH-SCHOOL GIRLS

*IRIS M. TIEDT*

Data distributed by the U.S. Department of Labor indicate that over half of today's high-school girls will work full time for up to thirty years, and 90 percent of these girls will be employed for other significant periods of time. At present women comprise 40 percent of the workforce in this country; 10 percent of the families in the U.S. are headed by women.

Women are, however, concentrated in jobs that pay poorly. According to census statistics in 1969, the median salary for women was $4,977 compared to $8,227 for men. Further, the unemployment rate for women is much higher than that for men. Forty percent or 1.8 million of the families with incomes below the poverty level were headed by women in 1970 (U.S. Department of Labor, 1970).

Few high-school girls seem to be aware of these facts. They are not, therefore, preparing seriously for positions that will enable them to earn a living and, in many cases, to support a family. Here is a problem with which the counselor and teacher need to be concerned as they work with high-school girls during the years when important decisions are being made.

Studies find that high-school girls consistently have low aspiration levels compared to boys at this level. They are not motivated to achieve largely because of their poor self-concepts. A statewide survey of California teenagers in

*IRIS M. TIEDT is Director of Teacher Education, University of Santa Clara, Santa Clara, California.*

1968 found that in general girls had a negative self-image. Forty-two percent of the girls doubted that they could be successful. They saw marriage as having priority over a career and usually did not consider the possibility of both marriage and a career. Only one-third planned to continue any kind of college course-work. The researchers concluded (Morgan, 1970):

> The teenage survey revealed that today's girls are unaware that, married or not, most of them will be employed for many years, that many will never marry, that many will be widowed for many years, that probably three in ten will be divorced, that more than one in ten will be heads of families, that adequate and reliable child care at modest cost is in very short supply, and that if current childbearing trends continue, forty potentially productive years of life will lie ahead after their youngest child is in school [p. 5].

Girls from low socioeconomic backgrounds, furthermore, were even less certain about their potentials. Forty percent of the sample were unsure that they would complete high school. All of them planned, however, "to get married" after graduation, and none of them planned to continue their education after high school. Even more pessimistic is their expectation that they would be on welfare if something happened to their husbands (Advisory Commission, 1971).

Through the socialization process the child learns from birth to differentiate behaviors appropriate to the sex roles. From early childhood little Jimmy knows that he will be an active member of the labor force of our country. When asked what he will be, he answers, "a pilot, a policeman, a farmer . . ." He does not answer, "a daddy." By contrast, a small girl, playing with her dolls, almost surely will reply, "a mommy" (Boocock, 1971).

Ginzberg and others (1966) substantiates this attitude toward a career in his study of mature educated women:

> One of the striking differences that we found between our parallel investigations of the career development of men and women was that men followed a relatively simple and straightforward pattern compared with the

much more complex career and life patterns characteristic of the majority of our women [pp. 4-5].

Cultural expectations tell a girl in many ways that she should marry and have a family. She is taught to be feminine—which is usually interpreted to mean passive, submissive, dependent, docile, and narcissistic (Boocock, 1971). She is conditioned not to be assertive and competitive and to consider herself intellectually inferior to men. To defy these expectations obviously requires an especially strong personality.

Few girls, furthermore, see models of women who are intelligent, attractive, and respected in their careers. Instead they observe well-dressed men in positions of responsibility as they make decisions and assume leadership roles. They see women more typically as housewives dependent on a husband's money and position. They come in contact with women teachers and librarians who have been frequently caricatured. They know secretaries, beauticians, clerks, waitresses, and household workers who hold the lower-paid jobs in society that require minimal training.

Our aim must be to improve the self-concept of girls as early as possible. In order to be effective, the counselor's efforts should not be passive, but active; in other words, the counselor should not wait for girls to ask for help. They do not know that they need it. As we have pointed out, they are largely unaware of the problems that are involved.

The counselor needs first of all to be informed about the problems of young women, as well as about the problems of the mature woman that the girl will become. To operate best, furthermore, he must be she, for studies show that male counselors tend to provide male-oriented counseling that is not in the best interests of women (Chesler, 1971).

Counseling in this case will involve much more than the one-to-one consultation. The counselor should experiment with varied approaches such as:

1. Developing a file of inexpensive materials for the counseling center or the school library, including items such as (a) *Mademoiselle's* college and career articles; (b) information about the National Organization for women (NOW); and (c) careers in the Armed Services.

2. Helping girls form discussion groups about mutual problems, alternative futures, etc.

3. Speaking to classes of mixed sexes about the problems of women in our society, encouraging questions and discussion.

4. Inviting speakers to come to school to address large or small groups; for instance, a woman lawyer to provide a career model for girls, a member of NOW to discuss the work of this organization, a panel of women to discuss today's woman.

5. Brainstorming with teachers to discover ways of helping girls through daily contacts, books studied in the curriculum, classes offered, and so on, including the selection of texts that present real women, not stereotypes.

6. Publicizing opportunities available to girls—materials in the library, interesting kinds of jobs, group meetings, speakers.

7. Recommending books for purchase by the library, including books about the feminist movement and equality for women such as *Born Female* by Caroline Bird, and good biographies such as *Eleanor and Franklin* by Joseph Lash.

8. Instigating curricular changes that permit girls to enroll in any vocational courses available in school; avoiding segregation by sexes as much as possible, considering, for example, how many courses in physical education can be coeducational.

9. Designing courses specifically to aid girls, particularly those in lower socioeconomic families; designing instruction to provide information that will help girls plan for a career, that will help motivate them to achieve and to consider themselves as individuals of considerable worth.

10. Subscribing to some of the newer publications for women; for example, *The Spokeswoman*—an independent monthly newsletter of women's news—and *NOW Acts*—a monthly publication that covers issues and actions related to the equality movement.

Counselors should also encourage girls themselves to work with any of the activities described. They will learn much and gain confidence as they develop a bibliography of books about women or make contacts by phone or letter to invite a speaker to come to the school. They will also have ideas about how the counselor can best help high-school girls.

## REFERENCES

Advisory Commission on the Status of Women. *California Women*. Sacramento: Author, Documents Section, 1971.

BOOCOCK, s. s., "A Funny Thing Happened on the Way to Maturity." *Association of American University Women Journal*. November 1971.

CHESLER, P., "Men Drive Women Crazy." *Psychology Today*. July 1971.

GINZBERG, E., et al. *Life Styles of Educated Women*. New York: Columbia University, 1966.

"High school women: Three views." In Robin Morgan (ed.), *Sisterhood is Powerful*. New York: Random House, 1970.

TIEDT, I. M., "Improving Self-Concepts of Young Women Through English Instruction." Paper presented at California Association of Teachers of English Convention, San Francisco, February 1972.

U.S. Department of Labor. *Bureau of Labor Statistics*. Washington, D.C.: U.S. Government Printing Office, December 1970.

# THE USE AND ABUSE
# OF VOCATIONAL TESTS

*CAROL TITTLE*

The Women's Movement has alerted us to the ways in which girls are socialized for traditional female roles, both in the family and at school. But vocational counselors and educational psychologists also contribute to the socialization process. Recent research suggests that the manner in which psychological measures in the vocational/occupational area are presented and interpreted for women closes options to women and reinforces sex-role stereotypes.

Those who are concerned with eliminating these stereotypes need to reexamine the methods and conceptual framework of psychological measurement.

Studies in educational and psychological measurement are particularly vulnerable to the problem of values and misinterpretation since most of these studies are descriptive: the results are a function of, or are embedded in, the society in which they are obtained. The methodology is largely correlational in nature, and hence subject to all the limitations this method has in inferring causality, and when used for prediction, in the assumptions of an underlying system which is stable or static. The terminology in measurement, "norms," "stable," "adjustment," are value-laden words, derived typically from descriptive data of *what is*, which often becomes prescriptive of *what should be*.

To understand how vocational inventories limit women's

*CAROL TITTLE is Project Director at the Office of Teacher Education, City University of New York.*
Copyright © 1974 by Carol Kehr Tittle.

choices it is instructive to examine in some detail the interpretive material and the scales which are provided on an interest measure such as the *Kuder*. The *Kuder DD, Occupational Interest Survey* (1966, 1970) is used here only for illustrative purposes. Other interest inventories have been criticized for similar faults.[1]

Starting from the woman's viewpoint, the interpretive leaflet tells her: "Your interest pattern should be one of the major considerations in making important education and vocational decisions. . . ." The next paragraph makes the distinction that there are OCCUPATIONAL SCALES, WOMEN; COLLEGE MAJOR SCALES, WOMEN; OCCUPATIONAL SCALES, MEN; COLLEGE MAJOR SCALES, MEN. The clear and ever present distinction for women is reinforced: "In addition to scores under the headings marked WOMEN, women will have scores under the headings marked MEN in selected occupations and college majors where men predominate but opportunities for women are increasing." (Kuder, 1970, p. 1).

An examination of the Occupational Scales shows that there are seventy-seven for men, and a total of fifty-seven for women (including twenty on the men's scales). However, close inspection shows that only sixteen scales overlap (i.e., only sixteen categories are identically stated occupations on both men's and women's scales).

The example given in the interpretive leaflet for "Maxine Faulkner" shows another way of closing possibilities for women. Looking at the scales on which she is highest on the men's occupational scales would indicate

---

[1] N. K. Schlossberg and J. Goodman, "Resolution to the American Personnel and Guidance Association: Revision of the *Strong Vocational Interest Blanks*." Presented to the American Personnel and Guidance Association, Chicago, March 1972.

This resolution asked the APGA to request revision of the *Strong* to eliminate discrimination and that counselors be instructed to refuse to administer the *SVIB* until it was determined that sex discrimination is eliminated. The resolution was referred to the Association on Measurement and Evaluation in Guidance for recommendations. An attachment details the following criticism of the *SVIB*: the men's and women's lists of occupations differ substantially, and discrimination appeared to enter; in addition, women's occupations are, on the whole, of lower status or salary. It was noted that census data seem to indicate that in many instances, adequate samples of women would be available to provide data on the opposite sex in an occupation reserved for one sex on the Strong.

interests in the occupations of optometrist, pediatrician, physician, psychiatrist, dentist, and pharmacist. However, on the college major scales for men, Maxine could *not* show an interest in the major of premed, pharmacy, or dentistry, since scores for women are not reported for that major. On the women's occupational scales, she is presented a spectrum of occupations typically suggested to women: dietitian, nurse, dental assistant, physical therapist, etc. We don't know Maxine, her abilities and skills, but we do know that this inventory is reinforcing the status quo in society for her. And we do know that the major professions with power and prestige in our society have been omitted for her in the college major scales: law, business management, marketing, finance, government, and premed, dentistry, and pharmacy.

While there is no direct evidence, in the sense of longitudinal data on defined samples, of the effect of using vocational/occupational interest inventories with women, some indirect evidence may be available in the statistics provided by the Bureau of Labor. The statistics for women in professions is available for comparison purposes. These data show proportionally fewer women in the professional and technical occupations in 1968 than in 1940. This is the only major occupation group in which women's representation was less in 1968 than in 1940 (Handbook of Women Workers, 1969). It is not unreasonable to suggest that the interest inventories initially developed in the 1930s have gone along with the rest of the trends in American society to limit the career possibilities considered by women. These measures now lag behind the general trend to end discrimination and stereotyped, biased views of various groups in American society.

The argument against the interest inventories includes limitations in technical development, in interpretive and normative data, and in the image of woman that is presented to the girl making occupational choices. Several types of studies are relevant to the argument that these inventories need to be changed: studies which examine the structure of interests for men and women; studies which have examined the relationship between occupational level and masculine and feminine interests; studies which have given modified instructions to women—that is, the possible influence of context or set on the interests expressed by women; and studies which have examined counselor behavior with women.

Cole (1972) has conducted a series of studies that examine the similarity between the patterns and interrelationships of women's interests as compared to those found for men. The purpose in these studies was to see whether it was possible to make inferences from data for women to the entire range of men's occupations, and thus eliminate the limiting effect of using only the traditional women's vocations. The work summarized in this 1972 report indicates that a common structure of women's interests is found which parallels that for men. Cole suggests that this information should be used to give women information about how their interests relate to the full spectrum of occupations.

Studies by Diamond (1971, 1972) have examined the area of the relationship between occupational level (high-low) and masculine and feminine interests, using the *Kuder*. In general, sex differences in interests are minimized at the high end of the occupational continuum and differentiated at the low end. This meant that persons with scores high in the occupational hierarchy (i.e., physicians, lawyers, etc.) were more frequently classified correctly on the basis of scores on a high occupational level scale than on the basis of sex. This was not true for persons with scores low in the occupational hierarchy (mechanics, secretaries, etc.). Diamond attributes this to the fact that the occupational structure is far more sharply dichotomized on the basis of sex at the low end of the structure (Diamond, 1972.)

A study by Farmer and Bohn (1970) examined the influence of instructions to reduce home-career conflict for women. Using the *Strong* (*SVIB-W*), scores of career scales increased after the experimental instructions. The experimental instructions gave these role-playing suggestions: (a) pretend men like intelligent women, and (b) pretend a woman can combine a demanding career with raising a family and perform both well. These instructions raised the measured career interest of women in six occupations—author, artist, psychologist, lawyer, physician, and life-insurance saleswoman. Career interests were lowered in eight occupations—buyer, business-education teacher, steno-secretary, office worker, elementary-school teacher, housewife, home-economics teacher, and dietitian.

In a somewhat related study, Stanfiel (1970) administered the *SVIB* men's form to women. Although the number of subjects was small, the results showed that the men's blank yielded more high-interest ratings than the women's blank, and would, therefore, have suggested a greater range of vocational prospects for the woman.

Two studies provide some evidence that counselors may work with women with "atypical" career goals differently than women with more traditional goals. Thomas and Stewart (1971) used secondary-school counselors who were presented with taped interviews of female clients with traditionally feminine (home economics—conforming) and traditionally masculine (engineer—deviate) goals. Counselors (male and female) rated conforming goals as more appropriate than deviate and rated girls with deviate goals as more in need of counseling. Pietrofesa and Schlossberg (1970) describe a study where counselor trainees interviewed a (coached) college girl having difficulty deciding between teaching and engineering. Taped interviews were rated by three persons (two males, one female). Results indicated that there was counselor bias against women entering a "masculine" occupation. Female counselor trainees displayed as much bias as males.

These studies of what may be termed "counselor bias" suggest an important area for study. The interpretive materials presented to the girl or woman and the counselor's views should be as much subject to study as the theoretical and technical issues in career interest measurement. Studies in counseling should also examine the reduction of conflict for women to enable realistic planning and decision making. Studies of the attitudes of men and women (see Kaley, 1971) toward working women should further the understanding for both sexes of the changing role of women (and men).

In conclusion, it is incumbent upon psychologists working in the field of education and psychological measurement to respond to the needs of women. In interpretation and presentation of studies, less emphasis should be placed on the implicit prescription of what is, and there should be examination of values to bring them in alignment with "higher valuations"—equality of opportunity and rights. This would be encouraged by focusing on individual development, rather than on group differences, and by emphasizing the cultural context in which psychological measurements are embedded. The emphasis on the status quo should be tempered by values oriented toward what ought to be in the "good" society.

In the area of occupational/vocational counseling, the interpretive materials presented to students need to be examined for stereotypic statements and examples. If publishers and counselors cannot adapt current psychological measurements in this area so that they present the full occupational spectrum to women, then the materials should be withdrawn or labeled, "Caution, this instrument may limit your choices!"

## REFERENCES

AIKEN, L. R., JR., "Attitudes Toward Mathematics." *Review of Educational Research*, 1970, *40*, 551–596.

ANASTASI, A. and J. P. FOLEY, JR., *Differential Psychology*. New York: Macmillan, 1949.

CAREY, G. L., "Reduction of Sex Differences in Problem-Solving by Improvement of Attitude Through Group Discussion." Ph.D. dissertation. Stanford University, 1955.

CLIFFORD, M. M., and W. R. LOOFT, "Academic Employment Interviews: Effect of Sex and Race 1." *Educational Researcher*, 1971, *12*, 6–8.

COLE, N. S., *On Measuring the Vocational Interests of Women. ACT Research Report No. 49.* Iowa City, Iowa: American College Testing Program, 1972.

COLE, M., and J. S. BRUNER, "Cultural Differences and Inferences About Psychological Processes." *American Psychologist*, 1971, *26*, 867–876.

DIAMOND, E. E., "Occupational Interests: Male-Female or High Level–Low Level Dichotomy?" *Journal of Vocational Behavior*, 1971, *1*, 305–315.

DIAMOND, E. E., "The Masculinity-Femininity Scale in Interest Measurement: An Idea Whose Time Has Passed." Paper presented at the meeting of the American Psychological Association, Honolulu, September 1972.

DONLON, T. F., "Content Factors in Sex Differences on Test Questions." Paper presented at the meeting of the New England Educational Research Organization, Boston, June 1971.

FARMER, H. S. and M. J. BOHN, JR., "Home-Career Conflict Reduction and the Level of Career Interest in Women." *Journal of Counseling Psychology*, 1970, *17*, 228–232.

FIDELL, L. S., "Empirical Verification of Sex Discrimination in Hiring Practices in Psychology." *American Psychologist*, 1970, *25*, 1094–1098.

*Handbook on Women Workers 1969*, Women's Bureau Bulletin 294. Washington, D.C.: U.S. Government Printing Office, 1969.

HOLTER, H., *Sex Roles and Social Structure*. Oslo, Norway: Universtist-forlaget, 1970. (U.S. Distribution: Box 142, Boston, Massachusetts 02113.)

KALEY, M. M., "Attitudes toward the Dual Role of the Married Professional Woman." *American Psychologist*, 1971, *26*, 301–306.

KELMAN, S., "Sweden's Liberated Men and Women, a Nonchalant Revolution." *New Republic*, March 13, 1971, 21–23.

*Kuder DD Occupational Interest Survey Interpretive Leaflet*. Chicago: Science Research Associates, Rev. ed. 1970.

KUDER, G. F., *General Manual, Kuder DD Occupational Interest Survey*. Chicago: Science Research Associates, Rev. ed. 1970.

MACCOBY, E. E., (ed.) *The Development of Sex Differences*. Stanford: Stanford University Press, 1966.

MACCOBY, E. E., and C. M. JACKLIN, "Sex Differences in Intellectual Functioning." Paper presented at the ETS Invitational Conference in Testing Problems, New York, October 1972.

MILL, J. S., *The Subjection of Women*. Cambridge: M.I.T. Press, 1970 (Orig. ed., London, 1869).

MYRDAL, G., *Objectivity in Social Research*. New York: Pantheon, 1969.

NAGEL, E., "The Value-Oriented Bias of Social Inquiry." In M. Brodbeck (ed.), *Readings in the Philosophy of the Social Sciences*. New York: Macmillan, 1968.

PETERSON, E., "Working Women." In R. J. Lifton (ed.),

*The Woman in America*. Boston: Houghton Mifflin, 1965, 144–172.

PIETROFESA, J. J., and N. K. SCHLOSSBERG, "Counselor Bias and the Female Occupational Role." Detroit: College of Education, Wayne State University, 1970. (ERIC CG 006 056)

ROSSI, A. S., "Equality Between the Sexes: An Immodest Proposal." In R. J. Lifton (ed.) *The Woman in America*. Boston: Houghton Mifflin, 1965, 98–143.

SCRIVEN, M., "Values of the Academy: Moral Issues for American Education and Educational Research Arising from the Jensen Case." *Review of Educational Research*, 1970, *40*, 541–549.

STAFFORD, R. E., "Hereditary and Environmental Components of Quantitative Reasoning." *Review of Educational Research*, 1972, *42*, 183–201.

STANFIEL, J. D., "Administration of the SVIB Men's Form to Women Counselees." *Vocational Guidance Quarterly*, 1970, *19*, 22–27.

THOMAS, A. H., and N. R. STEWART. "Counselor Response to Female Clients with Deviate and Conforming Career Goals." *Journal of Counseling Psychology*, 1971, *18*, 352–357.

WALSTER, E., T. A. CLEARY and M. M. CLIFFORD, "The Effect of Race and Sex on College Admission." Paper presented at the 78th annual meeting of the American Psychological Association, Miami, September 1970.

ZWERDLING, D., "The Womanpower Problem." *New Republic*, March 20, 1971, 11–13.

# WOMEN IN U.S. HISTORY HIGH-SCHOOL TEXTBOOKS

*JANICE LAW TRECKER*

Early in our history, enterprising groups of English gentlemen attempted to found all-male colonies. The attempts were failures, but the idea of a society without women appears to have held extraordinary appeal for the descendants of those early colonists. Throughout our history, groups of intrepid males have struck off into the wilderness to live in bachelor colonies free from civilization and domesticity.

The closing of the frontier and the presence, even from the earliest days, of equally intrepid females ended these dreams of masculine tranquility. Yet, the hopeful colonists may have had their revenge. If women have had their share in every stage of our history, exactly what they did and who they were remains obscure. Ask most high-school students who Jane Addams, Ida Tarbell, or Susan B. Anthony were, and you may get an answer. Ask about Margaret Sanger, Abigail Duniway, or Margaret Brent, and you will probably get puzzled looks. Sojourner Truth, Frances Wright, Anna Howard Shaw, Emma Willard, Mary Bickerdyke, Maria Mitchell, Prudence Crandall, and scores of others sound like answers from some historian's version of Trivia.

Interest in the fate of obscure Americans may seem an esoteric pursuit, but this is not the case. History, despite its enviable reputation for presenting the important facts about our past, is influenced by considerations other than

*MS. TRECKER is a freelance writer who writes and speaks often about the role of women in American history.*

the simple love of truth. It is an instrument of the greatest social utility, and the story of our past is a potent means of transmitting cultural images and stereotypes. One can scarcely doubt the impact of history upon the young in the face of recent minority groups' agitation for more of "their history."

A reasonable place to start, considering the admitted obscurity of most women in American history, is the United States history text. Are the stereotypes which limit girls' aspirations present in high-school history texts?

The answer is *yes*. Despite some promising attempts to supplement the scant amount of information devoted to women in American history texts, most works are marred by sins of omission and commission. Texts omit many women of importance, while simultaneously minimizing the legal, social, and cultural disabilities which they faced. The authors tend to depict women in a passive role and to stress that their lives are determined by economic and political trends. Women are rarely shown fighting for anything; their rights have been "given" to them.

Women are omitted both from topics discussed and by the topics chosen for discussion. For example, while only a few women could possibly be included in discussions of diplomacy or military tactics, the omission of dance, film, and theater in discussions of intellectual and cultural life assures the omission of many of America's most creative individuals.

Women's true position in society is shown in more subtle ways as well. While every text examined included some mention of the "high position" enjoyed by American women, this is little more than a disclaimer. Wherever possible, authors select male leaders, and quote from male spokesmen. Even in discussions of reform movements, abolition, labor—areas in which there were articulate and able women leaders—only men are ever quoted. Even such topics as the life of frontier women is told through the reminiscences of men. When they are included, profiles and capsule biographies of women are often introduced in separate sections, apart from the body of the text. While this may simply be a consequence of attempts to update the text without resetting the book, it tends to reinforce the idea that women of note are, after all, optional and supplementary. Interestingly enough, the increase in the amount of space devoted to Black history has not made room for the black woman. In these texts Black history follows the white pattern, and minimizes or omits the achievements of the black woman. Like the white woman, she is either omitted outright, or is minimized by the topics selected.

These assertions are based upon the examination of over a dozen of the most popular United States history textbooks. Most were first copyrighted in the sixties, although several hold copyrights as far back as the early fifties, and one text is copyrighted back to 1937. Included are the following:

BALDWIN, LELAND D., and MARY WARRING. *History of Our Republic*. Princeton, New Jersey: Van Nostrand, 1965.

BRAGDON, HENRY W., and SAMUEL P. MCCUTCHEN. *History of a Free People*. New York: Macmillan, 1965.

BROWN, RICHARD C., WILLIAM C. LANG and MARY A. WHEELER. *The American Achievement*. New Jersey: Silver Burdett, 1966.

CANFIELD, LEON H., and HOWARD B. WILDER. *The Making of Modern America*. Boston: Houghton Mifflin, 1964.

FROST, JAMES A., RALPH ADAMS BROWN, DAVID M. ELLIS, and WILLIAM B. FINK. *A History of the United States*. Chicago: Follett Educational Corporation, 1968.

GRAFF, HENRY E. and JOHN A. KROUT. *The Adventure of the American People*. Chicago: Rand McNally, 1959.

HOFSTADTER, RICHARD, WILLIAM MILLER, and DANIEL AARON. *The United States—The History of a Republic*. Englewood Cliffs, New Jersey: Prentice-Hall, 1957.

KOWNSLAR, ALLAN O., and DONALD B. FRIZZLE. *Discovering American History*. 2 Vols., New York: Holt, Rinehart & Winston, 1964.

NOYES, H. M., and RALPH VOLNEY HARLOW. *Story of America*. New York: Holt, Rinehart & Winston, 1964.

TODD, LEWIS PAUL, and MERLE CURTI. *Rise of the*

*American Nation.* (1 Vol. & 2 Vol. editions) New York: Harcourt, Brace & World, 1966. 2 Vol. edition includes selected readings.

WILLIAMS, T. HARRY, and HAZEL C. WOLF. *Our American Nation.* Ohio: Charles E. Merrill Books, Inc., 1966.

### COLLECTIONS OF DOCUMENTS

HOFSTADTER, RICHARD. *Great Issues in American History.* 2 Vols., New York: Vintage, 1958.

MEYERS, MARVIN, ALEXANDER KERN, and JOHN G. CARVELTI. *Sources of the American Republic.* 2 Vols. Chicago: Scott, Foresman & Company, 1961.

All entries indexed under "Women" were examined and various other sections and topics where information about women might reasonably be expected were examined. Particular attention was paid to women in colonial and revolutionary times, education, the women's rights movement and suffrage, reform movements, abolition, the Civil War, labor, frontier life, the World Wars, family patterns, the present position of women, and all sections on intellectual and cultural trends. The resulting picture is a depressing one.

Based on the information in these commonly used high-school texts, one might summarize the history and contributions of the American woman as follows: Women arrived in 1619 (a curious choice if meant to be their first acquaintance with the new world). They held the Seneca Falls Convention on Women's Rights in 1848. During the rest of the nineteenth century, they participated in reform movements, chiefly temperance, and were exploited in factories. In 1923 they were given the vote. They joined the armed forces for the first time during the second World War and thereafter have enjoyed the good life in America. Add the names of the women who are invariably mentioned: Harriet Beecher Stowe, Jane Addams, Dorothea Dix, and Frances Perkins, with perhaps Susan B. Anthony, Elizabeth Cady Stanton, and, almost as frequently, Carry Nation, and you have the basic "text." There are variations, of course, and most texts have adequate sections of information on one topic, perhaps two, but close examination of the information presented reveals a curious pattern of inclusions and neglects, a pattern which presents the stereotyped picture of the American woman—passive, incapable of sustained organization or work, satisfied with her role in society, and well supplied with material blessings.

## Revolutionary and Early Federal Periods

There is little information available in most texts concerning the colonial woman, or on her daughters and granddaughters in the revolutionary and early federal periods. The amount of information ranges from one textbook's two paragraphs on women's legal and social position to another textbook's total absence of anything even remotely pertaining to women during the early years of American history. Most texts fall in between. Some attention is commonly paid to the legal disabilities inherited from English law, although one textbook limits itself to "tobacco brides" and a note about William Penn's wife. Usually, little is said about the consequences of the social, political, and legal disabilities of the colonial woman, although the sharp limitations of the nineteenth century and the exploitation of the working-class women in the early industrial age were a direct result of woman's lack of political influence and her gradual exclusion from "professional" and skilled jobs. The texts are especially sensitive to the problem of religious and clerical prejudices against women. The long opposition of most American religious groups to women's rights is almost never suggested.

The perfunctory notice taken of women's education in the early period is discussed below. It should be noted, however, that few texts take any note of sectional differences in women's education or in other aspects of the position of women.

Although a number of texts mention the high regard in which the colonial woman was held, few are named and only one gives much information about the amount of work done outside the home by colonial women. Women mentioned are Pocahontas and Anne Hutchinson. Sections on Pocahontas tend to favor discussion of such questions as "Did Pocahontas really save John Smith?", rather than on any information about her life or the lives of other Indian women. Anne Hutchinson is almost always subordinated to Roger Williams. In one book, for example, she is described as another exile from Massachusetts. In more generous texts, she may receive as much as a short paragraph.

In general, the treatment of the early periods of American history stresses the fact that the America of the colonies, and early republic, was a "man's world." The authors wax eloquent over the "new breed of men." Any doubt that this might be merely linguistic convention is soon removed. The colonial farmer is credited with producing his own food, flax, and wool, in addition to preparing lumber for his buildings and leather goods for himself and his family. What the colonial farmer's wife (or the female colonial farmer) was doing all this time is not revealed, although plenty of information exists. Such passages also convey the unmistakable impression that all the early planters, farmers, and proprietors were male.

Education is important in consideration of the position of women because, as Julia Cherry Spruill points out in *Women's Life and Work in the Southern Colonies*, lack of opportunities for education finally ended women's employment in a variety of areas as technology and science made true "professions" of such occupations as medicine. In the early days, women, despite stringent legal restrictions, participated in almost all activities save government, the ministry of most religions, and law (although the number who sued and brought court cases is notable).

Usually, if any notice at all is taken of the education of girls and women, it is limited to a bland note that ". . . girls were not admitted to college" or "Most Americans thought it unnecessary or even dangerous to educate women." These statements are presented without explanation. A mention of the existence of the dame schools completes the information on women and education.

After the colonial-revolutionary period, it is rare for more than one paragraph to be devoted to the entire development of education for women. Often, none of the early educators is mentioned by name. The facts that women literally fought their way into colleges and universities, and their admission followed agitation by determined would-be students, and that they were treated as subservient to male students even at such pioneering institutions as Oberlin, are always absent. The simple statement that they were admitted suffices.

## Sections on Rights and Reforms

The most information about women appears in two sections, those on women's rights and suffrage and general sections on reform. Yet a full page on suffrage and women's rights is a rarity and most texts give the whole movement approximately three paragraphs. The better texts include something on the legal disabilities which persisted into the nineteenth century. These sections are sometimes good, but always brief. Most of them end their consideration of the legal position of women with the granting of suffrage, and there is no discussion of the implications of the recent Civil Rights legislation which removed some of the inequities in employment, nor is there more than a hint that inequities remained even after the nineteenth amendment was passed.

Leaders most commonly noted are Susan B. Anthony, Elizabeth Cady Stanton, and Lucretia Mott. Aside from passage of the nineteenth amendment, the only event noted is the Seneca Falls Convention of 1848. Even less space is devoted to the later suffrage movement. Anna Howard Shaw is seldom mentioned and even Carrie Chapman Catt is not assured of a place. The western leaders like Abigail Duniway are usually absent as are the more radical and militant suffragettes, the members of the Woman's Party. Alice Paul, leader of the militants, is apparently anathema.

This is perhaps not too surprising, as the tendency in most texts is to concentrate on the handicaps women faced and to minimize their efforts in their own behalf. One textbook, which dutifully lists Seneca Falls, Stanton, Mott, Wright, Anthony, Stone, and Bloomer, tells very little about what they did, noting "the demand for the right to vote made little headway, but the states gradually began to grant them more legal rights. The text mentions that by 1900 most discriminatory legislation was off the books and describes the post-Civil War work of the movement in these terms: "the women's rights movement continued under the leadership of the same group as before the war and met with considerable success." Later two lines on suffrage and a picture of a group of suffragettes complete the story. Lest this be considered the most glaring example of neglect, another textbook devotes two lines, one in each volume, to suffrage, mentioning in volume one that women were denied the right to vote and returning to the topic in volume two with one line on the nineteenth amendment in the middle of a synopsis of the twenties. This book actually includes more information on the lengths of women's skirts than on all the agitation for civil and political rights for women.

Other texts show a similar lack of enthusiasm for the hundred years of work that went into the nineteenth amendment. One places woman suffrage fifth in a section on the effects of the progressive movement. Catt, Anthony, and Stanton are mentioned in a line or two, while whole columns of text are devoted to Henry Demarest Lloyd and Henry George.

> At times there appears to be a very curious sense of priorities at work even in textbooks which give commendable amounts of information. One book uses up a whole column on the Gibson Girl, describing her as:
> . . . completely feminine, and it was clear that she could not, or would not, defeat her male companion at golf or tennis. In the event of a motoring emergency, she would quickly call upon his superior knowledge . . .

The passage goes on to point out that this "transitional figure" was politically uninformed and devoted to her traditional role. One would almost prefer to learn a little more about the lives of those other "transitional figures," the feminists, yet there is almost no mention of their lives, their work, or their writings.

Only one text quotes any of the women's rights workers. It includes a short paragraph from the declaration of the Seneca Falls Convention. The absence in other texts of quotes and of documentary material is all the more striking, since a number of the leaders were known as fine orators and propagandists. Books of source materials, and inquiry method texts, are no exception; none of those examined considers woman suffrage worthy of a single document. One book is exceptional in including one selection, by Margaret Fuller, on the topic of women's rights.

The reformers and abolitionists are slightly more fortunate than the feminists. Three women are almost certain of appearing in history texts, Harriet Beecher Stowe, Jane Addams, and Dorothea Dix. Addams and Stowe are among the few women quoted in either source books or regular texts and, along with the muckraking journalist Ida Tarbell, they are the only women whose writings are regularly excerpted. Addams and Dix are usually given at least one complete paragraph, perhaps more. These are sometimes admirably informative as in certain sections on Dix. Other reformers, including the women abolitionists, both white and black, are less fortunate. The pioneering Grimké sisters may rate a line or two, but just as often their only recognition comes because Angelina eventually became Mrs. Theodore Weld. None of the female abolitionists, despite their contemporary reputations as speakers, is ever quoted. Interest in Black history has not made room for more than the briefest mention of Harriet Tubman, whose Civil War services are deleted. Sojourner Truth and the other black lecturers, educators, and abolitionists are completely absent. The texts make little comment about the nineteenth century's intense disapproval of women who spoke in public, or of the churches' opposition (excepting always the Quakers, from whose faith many of the early abolitionists came).

Women journalists are given even less notice than the early lecturers. The women who ran or contributed to newspapers, periodicals, or specialized journals and papers for abolition, women's rights, or general reform are rarely included.

The reform sections of these high-school texts frequently show the same kind of capriciousness that in sections on the twenties assigns more space to the flapper than to the suffragette. In discussions on reform movements, they give more prominence to Carry Nation than to other more serious, not to say more stable, reformers. The treatment of temperance is further marred by a failure to put women's espousal of temperance in perspective. Little stress is placed on the consequences for the family of an alcoholic in the days when divorce was rare, when custody of children went to their father, and when working women were despised. Nor is there much mention of the seriousness of the problem of alcoholism, particularly in the post-Civil war period.

## Neglected Areas

The most glaring omission, considering its impact on women and on society, is the absence of a single word on the development of birth control and the story of the fight for its acceptance by Margaret Sanger and a group of courageous physicians. The authors' almost Victorian delicacy in the face of the matter probably stems from the fact that birth control is still controversial. Yet fear of controversy does not seem a satisfactory excuse. The population explosion, poverty, illegitimacy—all are major problems today. Birth control is inextricably tied up with them as well as with disease, abortion, child abuse, and family problems of every kind. Considering the revolution in the lives of women which safe methods of contraception have caused, and the social, cultural, and political implications of that revolution, it appears that one important fact of the reform movement is being neglected.

A second, largely neglected area is the whole question of woman's work and her part in the early labor movement. Although the American woman and her children were the mainstays of many of the early industries, for a variety of social and political reasons she received low wages and status and was virtually cut off from any hopes of advancement. The educational limitations that gradually forced her out of a number of occupations which she had held in preindustrial days combined with prejudice to keep her in the lowest paid work. Whether single, married, or widowed, whether she worked for "pin money" or to support six children, she received about half as much as a man doing the same or comparable work.

Obviously under these conditions, women had exceptional difficulties in organizing. Among them were the dual burden of household responsibilities and work, their lack of funds, and in some cases their lack of control over their own earnings, and the opposition of male workers and of most of the unions.

Despite these special circumstances, very little attention is paid to the plight of the woman worker or of her admittedly unstable labor organizations. Information on the early labor leaders is especially scanty; one textbook is unique with its biographical information on Rose Schneiderman. On the whole, the labor story is limited to the introduction of women workers into the textile mills in the 1840s. As a caption in one book so concisely puts it, "Women and children, more manageable, replaced men at the machines." Others note the extremely low pay of women and children, one text calling women "among the most exploited workers in America." Anything like a complete discussion of the factors which led to these conditions, or even a clear picture of what it meant to be "among the most exploited," is not found in the texts.

Several things about women and labor are included. Lowell mills receive a short, usually complimentary, description. The fact that the Knights of Labor admitted women is presented. There then follows a hiatus until minimum wage and maximum-hour standards for women workers are discussed. The modern implications of this "protective legislation" is an area seldom explored.

Despite the fact that abundant source material exists, the sections on labor follow the familiar pattern: little space is devoted to women workers, few women are mentioned by name, and fewer still are quoted. Most texts content themselves with no more than three entries of a few lines each.

The absence of information on the lives of women on the frontier farms and settlements is less surprising. In the treatments of pioneer settlements from the colonial era on, most texts declare the frontier "a man's world." This is emphasized by the importance the authors place on descriptions and histories of such masculine tools as the Pennsylvania rifle and the ax, the six-shooter, and the prairie-breaker plow. One textbook is perhaps the most enthralled with these instruments, devoting five pages to the story of the six-shooter. Scarcely five lines is spent on the life of the frontier woman in this text, and most other works are also reticent about the pioneer woman.

Only "man's work" on the frontier is really considered worthy of description. This is particularly puzzling, since there was little distinction in employment, and marriage was a partnership with lots of hard work done by each of the partners. On pioneer farms, typical "woman's work" included, in addition to all the housework, the care of poultry; the dairy—including milking, feeding, tending to the cows, and making butter and cheese; the care of any other barnyard animals; the "kitchen" or vegetable garden, and such chores as sewing, mending, making candles and soap, feeding the hired hands, and working in the fields if necessary.

Considering these chores, it is hard to see why discussions of pioneer farming content themselves with descriptions of the farmer's struggles to plow, plant, and harvest. The treatments of the frontier period also omit mention of the women who homesteaded and claimed property without the help of a male partner. According to Robert W. Smuts in *Women and Work in America,* there were thousands of such women. Information about the women on the frontier tends either to short descriptions of the miseries of life on the great plains frequently quoted from Hamlin Garland or to unspecific encomiums on the virtues of the pioneer woman. One text states:

> . . . [the women] turned the wilderness into homesteads, planted flowers, and put curtains in the windows. It was usually the mothers and school teachers who transmitted to the next generation the heritage of the past.

The relationship between women's exertions on the frontier and their enlarged civil and political liberties in the Western states and territories is often noticed. Their agitation for these increased privileges is generally unmentioned.

With little said about women's life in general, it is not surprising that few are mentioned by name. Sacajawea, the Indian guide and interpreter of the Lewis and Clark expedition, shares with Dix, Stowe, and Addams, one of the few solid positions in United States history texts. Occasionally the early missionaries to Oregon territory, like Nerissa Whitman and Eliza Spaulding, are included, and one book even adds a "profile" of Nerissa Whitman. Most, however, only mention the male missionaries, or include the fact that they arrived with their wives.

*Civil War Period*

Like the frontier experience, the Civil War forced women from all social strata into new tasks and occupations. In *Bonnet Brigades*, a volume in the *Impact of the Civil War Series*, Mary Elizabeth Massey quotes Clara Barton's remark that the war advanced the position of women by some fifty years. Great numbers of women dislocated by the war were forced into paid employment. The war saw the entry of women into government service, into nursing, and into the multitude of organizations designed to raise money and supplies for the armies, to make clothing, blankets, and bandages. The result of this activity was not only to force individual women outside of their accustomed roles, but to provide the experience in organization which was to prove valuable for later suffrage and reform movements. The war helped a number of women escape from the ideas of gentility which were robbing women in the East of much of their traditional social freedom, and brought women of all classes into the "man's world." In addition to the few women who served as soldiers, women appeared in the camps as nurses, cooks, laundresses, adventurers; they served in the field as spies, scouts, saboteurs, and guides; they worked in the capitals as the "government girls"—the first female clerks, bookkeepers, and secretaries. Women opened hospitals, set up canteens, and developed the first primitive forms of what we know as USO clubs and services. After the war, they served as pension claims agents, worked to rehabilitate soldiers, taught in the freedman's schools, entered refugee work, or tried to find missing soldiers and soldiers' graves.

Of all these activities, women's entry into nursing is the only one regularly noticed in the texts. The impact of the war upon women, and upon the family structure, is barely mentioned, although a few texts include a paragraph or two on the hardships which women faced during the conflict. The only women mentioned by name are Clara Barton and Dorothea Dix, who held the position of superintendent of women nurses. Other women, like Mary Bickerdyke, who was known both for her efforts during the war and for her work for needy veterans afterwards, are omitted. No other women, black or white, are named, nor is there any information on the variety of jobs they held. The special problems of black women in the post-war period rarely get more than a line, and the efforts by black women to set up schools and self-help agencies are omitted.

## The Two World Wars

While women in the Civil War era receive little attention, even less is given to them during the two World Wars. In both cases, their wartime service is glowingly praised, but few details are presented. At least half of the texts examined make no note at all of women's wartime activities during the first World War; in a number of others, the story of women's entry into what were formerly labeled "men's jobs" is dealt with in a captioned picture.

As far as social changes between the wars, a number of texts devote several paragraphs to the "liberation of women" and to their changing status. In one textbook there are four paragraphs devoted to these liberated ladies—the only two mentioned being Irene Castle and Alice Roosevelt. Like other texts, this one devotes a considerable amount of space to fashions and flappers and to the social alarm which they occasioned.

There is little about the later stages of the rights' movement, although two textbooks note the relationship between women's wartime service and the increasing willingness of the nation to grant rights and privileges to women. One limits itself to three sentences, noting women's work "in factories and fields" and their efforts behind the lines overseas. "Women's reward for war service was the Nineteenth Amendment which granted them the franchise on the eve of the 1920 election." Readers might wish for greater elaboration.

The period from the depression to the present day receives the same laconic treatment in the texts. The one woman sure of notice in this period is Frances Perkins, Roosevelt's Secretary of Labor. She receives at least a line in most texts and some devote special sections to her. Frances Perkins appears to be the "showcase" woman, for no other American woman is regularly mentioned—this includes Eleanor Roosevelt, who is omitted from a surprising number of texts and who is mentioned only as Roosevelt's wife in quite a few more.

The World War II era marked the beginning of the Women's Military Corps. This fact is invariably mentioned, usually with a captioned picture as an accompaniment. As in World War I, women entered factories, munitions plants, and "men's jobs" in great numbers. This development rarely gets more than a paragraph and the differences between the experience in World War I and the longer exposure to new jobs in World War II are seldom elucidated. The impact of the war on women and specific information about the variety of jobs they held is sketchy or nonexistent.

Information on women in the post-war era and in the present day is hardly more abundant. The history texts definitely give the impression that the passage of the nineteenth amendment solved all the problems created by the traditional social, legal, and political position of women. Contemporary information on discrimination is conspicuously absent. The texts are silent on current legal challenges to such practices as discriminatory hiring and promotion and companies' failures to comply with equal-pay legislation. They do not take account of agitation to change laws and customs which weigh more heavily on women than on men. There is nothing about recent changes in jury selection, hitherto biased against women jurors, or reform of discriminatory practices in criminal sentences; there is no information on the complex problems of equitable divorce and guardianship, nor on the tangled problem of separate domicile for married women.

A number of texts do, however, provide good information on changes in the structure of the family, or provide helpful information on general social and political changes. The impression, insofar as these sections deal directly with American women, is a rosy picture of the affluence and opportunities enjoyed by women. Many books note the increasing numbers of women employed in the learned professions, but never the percentage decline in their numbers. While women undoubtedly enjoy more rights, opportunities, and freedoms than in many previous eras, the texts give an excessively complacent picture of a complex and rapidly changing set of social conditions.

*Intellectual and Cultural Achievements*

A final glimpse of the position of the American woman may be gained from sections dealing with intellectual and cultural trends and achievements. Since most texts extol the role of women in preserving culture and in supporting the arts, one might expect women to be well represented in discussions of the arts in America. A number of factors, however, operate against the inclusion of creative women. The first, and one which deprives many creative men of notice as well, is the extreme superficiality of most of these discussions. Intellectual and cultural life in America is limited to the mention of a few novelists and poets, with an occasional musician or playwright. Only a few individuals in each category are ever mentioned, and the preference for male examples and spokesmen, noticeable in all other topics, is evident here as well. In individual texts, this leads to such glaring omissions as Emily Dickinson and Margaret Fuller. To be fair, the text guilty of ignoring Miss Dickinson appears to feel that John Greenleaf Whittier was one of our greatest poets, yet ignorance of American poetry is hardly an acceptable excuse.

Dickinson and Fuller, however, are among the small, fortunate circle including Harriet Beecher Stowe, Willa Cather, and Margaret Mitchell who are usually named. The principles governing their selection and decreeing the omission of other writers like Edith Wharton, Ellen Glasgow, Eudora Welty, and Pearl Buck are never explained. Apparently their presence or absence is determined by the same caprice which decrees Edna St. Vincent Millay the only modern female poet.

Only a handful of texts discuss painters and sculptors, but of those that do make some effort to include the visual arts, only one reproduces a painting by Mary Cassatt. Georgia O'Keeffe is also represented in this text. Other texts, even when including Cassatt's fellow expatriates, Sargent and Whistler, omit her—an exclusion inexplicable on grounds of quality, popularity, or representation in American collections. Contemporary art is totally ignored and everything after the Ashcan School is left in limbo. This omits many painters of quality and influence, including the many women who have entered the arts in the twentieth century.

More serious than the sketchy treatment given to the arts covered by the texts is the omission of arts in which women were dominant or in which they played a major part. Dance is never given as much as a line. This leaves out the American ballerinas, and, even more important, it neglects the development of modern dance—a development due to the talents of a handful of American women like Isadora Duncan, Martha Graham, and Ruth St. Denis.

There is a similar neglect of both stage and screen acting. If film or drama are to be mentioned at all, directors and writers will be noted. It hardly seems necessary to point out that acting is an area in which women have excelled.

Music sees a similar division with similar results. Composers and instrumentalists, chiefly men, are mentioned. Singers, men and women, are omitted. This particularly affects black women. Only one textbook mentions Marian Anderson and Leontyne Price. White classical singers are ignored as are the black women jazz singers.

If intellectual and cultural developments are limited to areas in which men were the dominant creative figures, it is obvious that American women will not receive credit for their contributions. It also seems clear that such superficial accounts of the arts are of questionable value.

## Summing Up

Although it is tempting to imagine some historical autocrat sternly decreeing who's in and who's out—giving space to Harriet Beecher Stowe but not to Marianne Moore; to Dorothea Dix but not Mary Bickerdyke; to Pocahontas but not Margaret Brent; to Susan B. Anthony but not Abigail Duniway—the omission of many significant women is probably not a sign of intentional bias. The treatment of women simply reflects the attitudes and prejudices of society. Male activities in our society are considered the more important; therefore male activities are given primacy in the texts. There is a definite image of women in our society, and women in history who conform to this image are more apt to be included. History reflects societal attitudes in all topics, hence the omission of potentially controversial persons like Margaret Sanger or that militant pioneer in civil disobedience, Alice Paul. Sensitivity to social pressure probably accounts for the very gentle notes about religious disapproval of women's full participation in community life and for omission of contemporary controversies, especially on sexual matters, which would offend religious sensibilities.

Another factor which affects the picture of women presented in these texts is the linguistic habit of using the male pronouns to refer both to men and to men and women. While this may seem a trivial matter it frequently leads to misunderstanding. Discussing the early colonists, for example, solely in terms of "he" and "his" leads to the implication that all early proprietors, settlers, planters, and farmers were men. Given the cultural orientation of our society, students will assume activities were only carried on by men unless there is specific mention of women.

To these observations, authors of high-school texts might reasonably respond that their space is limited, that they seek out only the most significant material and the most influential events and individuals; that if dance is omitted, it is because more people read novels, and if such topics as the role of female missionaries or colonial politicians are neglected, it is for lack of space. One is less inclined to accept this view when one notices some of the odd things which authors do manage to include. One feels like asking, "How important was Shays's Rebellion?" Should the Ku Klux Klan receive reams of documentary material and woman suffrage none? Do we want to read five pages on the six-shooter? Is two columns too much to give to Empress Carlotta of Mexico, who lived most of her life in insanity and obscurity? Is the aerialist who walked a tightrope across Niagara Falls a figure of even minor importance in American History? Is Henry Demarest Lloyd more important than Carrie Chapman Catt? Are the lengths of skirts significant enough to dwarf other information about women?

There are other questions as well: How accurate is the history text's view of women and what images of women does it present? The texts examined do very little more than reinforce the familiar stereotypes.

It should be clear, however, that changes in the construction of high-school-level history texts must go beyond the insertion of the names of prominent women and even beyond the "profiles" and "special sections" employed by the more liberal texts. Commendable and informative as these may be, they are only the beginning. Real change in the way history is presented will only come after those responsible for writing it, and for interpreting the finished product to students, develop an awareness of the bias against women in our culture, a bias so smooth, seamless, and pervasive, that it is hard to even begin to take hold of it and bring it into clear view. Until this awareness is developed, until the unquestioned dominance of male activities and the importance of male spokesmen and examples is realized, texts will continue to treat men's activities and goals as history, women's as "supplementary material."

One sees this quite clearly in the existence of sections dealing with women's rights, women's problems, and women's position, as if women's rights, problems, and position were not simply one half of the rights, problems, and position of humanity as a whole, and as if changes in women's position and work and attitudes were not complemented by changes in the position, work, and attitudes of men. A sense of the way the lives and duties and achievements of people of both sexes is intermeshed is needed in expositions of life in all periods of American history.

To do this it is clear that material hitherto omitted or minimized must be given more consideration. For example, information about mortality rates, family size, and economic conditions must be included, along with more information on the impact of technological change, on the mass media, and on moral and religious ideas. More information about how ordinary people lived and what they actually did must be included as well as information drawn from the ideas and theories of the educated classes.

This is not to deny that certain developments have had far more effect on women than on men, or that women's experience might be different from men's: for example, the early struggles to form unions. Nor is it to deny that more information on women leaders is needed and more space for their particular problems and achievements. More information on all aspects of women's life, work, and position—legal, social, religious, and political—is needed, but more information alone, no matter how necessary, will not really change histories. What is needed, besides more information, is a new attitude: one which breaks away from the bias of traditional views of women and their "place" and attempts to treat both women and men as partners in their society; one which does not automatically value activities by the sex performing them; and one which does not relate history from the viewpoint of only half of the human family.

# HIGH-SCHOOL SEX(IST) EDUCATION

*JANICE ALBERT*

I used to think one of the most wonderful things about the New York Public School System was that it dealt with sex education. I remember my counselor telling my mother and me that this was a progressive school and they felt there were certain things every teenager should know. I looked forward to taking hygiene. I was sure it would be everyone's favorite class. I thought I'd be able to ask questions and discuss attitudes with the other kids in my class. I wondered why the kids who were taking the course didn't seem to talk about it much.

I know now that the only progressive thing about high-school sex-education classes is that they exist. The classes are not coed. I was first put in a boys' class by mistake and very much regretted having to leave because they were having such a good time. When I finally registered in the girls' class I found that there were forty girls seated so that we couldn't see each other (the boys' class had about ten students seated in a comfy semicircle). Our teacher was not trained in the subject and had read only our text. No one took the class seriously though it is required for graduation and sex is certainly among the most important topics teenagers need to discuss.

We spent the first few weeks on "meal planning" and "family living." I wondered what that had to do with sex until I realized it was a class in sex roles, not sex itself. We saw films and read about the great joy of cooking hearty meals for one's children and husband. Our book,

*Modern Sex Education*, emphasized the role of women as mothers and wives:

> In our society the father assumes the major financial and legal responsibility for the family, while the mother concerns herself with physical and emotional comforts of her husband and children. But these roles are often easily shared by both parents. However, even when a boy or girl doesn't grow up in this "ideal family setting" [quotation marks are mine], it is possible to understand the roles played by both sexes. A boy who can say to himself, "I'm glad to be a man" and who can anticipate experiences of manhood will be a better man. A girl who understands all that it means to be a woman, and who has learned about the tender and helpful role that a happy mother plays in the family will be a happier person.

Why is the subject of womanhood restricted to the subject of motherhood?

Later we read that although the "normal" woman stays home, it is still possible to be happy if you "must" work. I was amazed to hear this very middle-class attitude taught in a class of very poor black and Puerto Rican girls. The experience of daddy bringing home the bread is so farfetched it has become a common joke.

We never actually discussed sexual intercourse, orgasm, or masturbation, though our book did mention masturbation: "It is possible to avoid or control this practice by directing one's thoughts to more constructive activities." (I didn't know *anyone* still believed that!) Surprisingly my 17- and 18-year-old classmates knew very little about sex or their bodies and even believed the ancient myths about menstruation. This class never taught them anything to dispel those stories. The little anatomy that we were taught dealt only with pregnancy. Although we discussed the development of a fetus, we never discussed the development of our own sexuality. For the purposes of this class, the uterus was the only part of our bodies related to sex.

Our class was fortunate enough to be given some information about birth control. (I have heard of only one other class where this was even mentioned.) Of course, we weren't told where or how to get birth-control devices. Abortion was an even more taboo topic, because, we were told, "It's illegal."

Venereal disease was one of the few topics thoroughly covered and it was taught in such a way as to scare us about sex and to perpetuate the "double standard." We were shown a film comic strip about a boy who caught syphilis from a girl he "picked up" one night. The moral of the story was that it is evil to sleep with a "tramp." Premarital sex, we were told, also causes unwanted pregnancy, social ostracism, promiscuity, and worst of all, disrespect from boys. We were advised not to have sex before marriage, but to understand and forgive our boy-friends if they had their fling with the "bad girls" and came back to us, the "good girls," for clean, healthy fun.

During the last week of my class we were finally allowed to ask questions. I tried to ask about things pertaining to sexual intercourse, but our discussion was directed into the safe subject of how to feed a baby. We spent an hour discussing the merits of allowing the baby to hold the spoon. If some parents are worried about their children learning too much in sex-education classes, they needn't be. The class couldn't be better at not fulfilling a teenager's needs.

You might say that the sex-hygiene classes bring into the open many of the stereotyping attitudes toward women implicit in the rest of the school curriculum. It is the high school's last chance to indoctrinate girls and put us in our place. It is probably fortunate that the last word is so dull and empty.

# V.
# Are Colleges
# Fit for Women?

# PRESENT TENDENCIES IN WOMEN'S COLLEGE AND UNIVERSITY EDUCATION

*M. CAREY THOMAS*

*Nineteenth-century pioneers in women's higher education had to combat deep-rooted popular prejudices. M. Carey Thomas, President of Bryn Mawr College from 1894 to 1922, devoted her life to proving that women were both physically and intellectually fit for college. She subjected Bryn Mawr students to the same academic rigors as their Harvard or Yale counterparts and was thrilled by their achievements. Addressing the Association of Collegiate Alumnae in 1907, Thomas rejoiced over women's victory in the battle for higher education. This excerpt from her speech contrasts sharply with the next essay in which Liz Schneider indicts Bryn Mawr for betraying its feminist commitment in the '60s.*

. . . I doubt if the most imaginative and sympathetic younger women in this audience can form any conception of what it means to women of the old advance guard, among whom you will perhaps allow me to include myself, to be able to say to each other without fear of contradiction that in the twenty-five years covered by the work of the Association of Collegiate Alumnae the battle

*M. CAREY THOMAS (1857–1935), a Baltimore-born Quaker, was a Phi Beta Kappa graduate of Cornell, class of 1877. She received her Ph.D., summa cum laude, at Zurich, 1882, and returned to become Dean and Professor of English literature at Bryn Mawr College, where she served as President from 1894 to 1922.*

for the higher education of women has been gloriously, and forever, won.

The passionate desire of the women of my generation for higher education was accompanied throughout its course by the awful doubt, felt by women themselves as well as by men, as to whether women as a sex were physically and mentally fit for it. I think I can best make this clear to you if I refer briefly to my own experience. I cannot remember the time when I was not sure that studying and going to college were the things above all others which I wished to do. I was always wondering whether it could be really true, as everyone thought, that boys were cleverer than girls. Indeed, I cared so much that I never dared to ask any grownup person the direct question, not even my father or mother, because I feared to hear the reply. I remember often praying about it, and begging God that if it were true that because I was a girl I could not successfully master Greek and go to college and understand things to kill me at once, as I could not bear to live in such an unjust world. When I was a little older I read the Bible entirely through with passionate eagerness, because I had heard it said that it proved that women were inferior to men. Those were not the days of the higher criticism. I can remember weeping over the account of Adam and Eve because it seemed to me that the curse pronounced on Eve might imperil girls' going to college; and to this day I can never read many parts of the Pauline epistles without feeling again the sinking of the heart with which I used to hurry over the verses referring to women's keeping silence in the churches and asking their husbands at home. I searched not only the Bible, but all other books I could get for light on the woman question. I read Milton with rage and indignation. Even as a child I knew him for the woman hater he was. The splendor of Shakespeare was obscured to me then by the lack of intellectual power in his greatest woman characters. Even now it seems to me that only Isabella in *Measure for Measure* thinks greatly, and weighs her actions greatly, like a Hamlet or a Brutus.

I can well remember one endless scorching summer's day when, sitting in a hammock under the trees with a French dictionary, blinded by tears more burning than the July sun, I translated the most indecent book I have ever read, Michelet's famous—were it not now forgotten, I should be able to say infamous—book on woman, *La Femme*. I was beside myself with terror lest it might prove true that I myself was so vile and pathological a thing. Between that summer's day in 1874, and a certain day in the autumn of 1904, thirty years had elapsed. Although during these thirty years I had read in every language every book on women that I could obtain, I had never chanced again upon a book that seemed to me so to degrade me in my wonanhood as the seventh and seventeenth chapters on women and women's education of President Stanley Hall's *Adolescence*. Michelet's sickening sentimentality and horrible over-sexuality seemed to me to breathe again from every pseudo-scientific page.

But how vast the difference between then and now in my feelings, and in the feelings of every woman who has had to do with the education of girls! Then I was terror-struck lest I, and every other woman with me, were doomed to live as pathological invalids in a universe merciless to woman as a sex. Now we know that it is not we, but the man who believes such things about us, who is himself pathological, blinded by neurotic mists of sex, unable to see that women form one-half of the kindly race of normal, healthy human creatures in the world; that women, like men, are quickened and inspired by the same great traditions of their race, by the same love of learning, the same love of science, the same love of abstract truth; that women, like men, are immeasurably benefited, physically, mentally, and morally, and are made vastly better mothers, as men are made vastly better fathers, by subordinating the distracting instincts of sex to the simple human fellowship of similar education, and similar intellectual and social ideals.

It was not to be wondered at that we were uncertain in those old days as to the ultimate result of women's education. Before I myself went to college I had seen only one college woman. I had heard that such a woman was staying at the house of an acquaintance. I went to see her with fear. Even if she had appeared in hoofs and horns I was determined to go to college all the same. But it was a relief to find this Vassar graduate tall and handsome and dressed like other women. When, five years later, I went to Leipzig to study after I had been graduated from Cornell, my mother used to write me that my name was never mentioned to her by the women of her acquaintance. I was thought by them to be as much of a disgrace to my family as if I had eloped with the coach-man. Now, women who have been to college are as plentiful as blackberries on summer hedges. Even my native city of Baltimore is full of them, and women who have in addition studied in Germany are regarded with becoming deference by the very Baltimore women who disapproved of me.

During the quarter of the century of the existence of the Association of Collegiate Alumnae two generations of college women have reached mature life, and the older generation is now just passing off the stage. We are, therefore, better prepared than ever before to give an account of what has been definitely accomplished, and to predict what will be the tendencies of women's college and university education in the future.

# OUR FAILURES ONLY MARRY: BRYN MAWR AND THE FAILURE OF FEMINISM

*LIZ SCHNEIDER*

> By upholding a standard of scholarship and culture that is difficult and not easy to attain, she will inevitably lose many students, but she will not regret the loss. Bryn Mawr has faith to believe that as long as her grey towers stand there will never be wanting youthful enthusiasm and youthful love of learning to inhabit them. Future generations will turn to her for inspiration. Be it her part never to betray her trust.—Alumnae Magazine, 1908.

Here are the voices of the women who followed, responding to the promise of meaningful education implicit in the feminist founding of Bryn Mawr:

> I think that men's institutions are different from women's in that men's are constantly trying to build up their students; at Bryn Mawr I feel as though I'm being beaten down all the time. My mind is viewed as some kind of input-output mechanism; as though I'm being trained to perform well and be a good scholar so that I can come back and teach here. Bryn Mawr capitalizes on women's oppression by trying to give women the Truth.—Student, Class of 1970

*LIZ SCHNEIDER is a law student at New York University and a planner of the Vera Institute of Justice Project on Women in the Criminal Justice System. She is active in the women's rights and legal-education movements in New York City.*

The only thing that has made my last year at Bryn Mawr bearable has been women's liberation. Now I feel like I have something in common with other girls here, and that we have something that we are fighting for together. We are a community and I feel like I have real friends; I know that my problems are not only mine, and I want to work with other women, instead of competing against them, to solve those problems. Until women's lib, I thought of Bryn Mawr as a cloistered retreat from anything real.— Student, Class of 1972

The most outstanding part of my "Bryn Mawr experience" was Haverford—to get a Haverford boyfriend whom I could be an extension of and whose achievements and respect and friends I could acquire by association, and to be "known" at Haverford. My reputation at Haverford was of primary importance and fundamentally shaped my self-image.—Class of 1968

Who were our models? Professors. The successful and popular and well-liked and intellectually respected professors. And except for a few token women (mostly eccentrics from another age) these professors were *men*. There were a few wonderful women, but most were faculty emeriti (over sixty) or low-level instructors (like in Baby Languages) but the really inspiring professors were known to be men, or at Haverford.—Class of 1965

I feel insecure about myself here and I have for four years. I don't understand why Bryn Mawr has been so bad for me; it was supposed to be what I was working for for twelve years in school. I feel like the administration and faculty think that being a woman is something you are supposed to overcome. The expectations that they've placed on me are totally unrealistic. . . . They've told me that the world is my oyster and yet I feel unhappy being in the dorm and not being with a man. The conversations at dinner are so deadening and stupid, my classes are so boring. They tell me I'm supposed to go on to graduate school, but I feel like I'm being prepared to be a good conversationalist or make some man a good wife. The only good thing about

Bryn Mawr is Haverford. In my Haverford classes professors keep on asking questions and I feel like some intellectual responsibility is being demanded of me.—Class of 1966

The alienation that we felt from each other was inextricably bound with the alienation we felt from our education. We had heavy academic loads; four courses, all with long papers and exams. We sat in lecture classes, taking notes on the professors' wisdom. Rarely did we venture a differing opinion, fearing to be found wrong. We only felt confident in our ability to read extensively, digest the various facts and ideas, and organize them into lengthy, well-documented essays. The outstanding memory that remains from my philosophy course, an introductory survey required of everyone, is not any set of ideas, nor even a concept of what philosophy as a discipline is, but rather of the girl in front of me drawing an elaborate T.G.I.F. during every Friday lecture. We all commented on the recklessness of Haverford students who boldly challenged their professors whenever they disagreed or didn't understand. They seemed to feel that they had every right to an opinion and some even felt that they had to have an opinion to satisfy their egos. We accepted the authority of professors and books much too easily, but we didn't have the confidence to trust ourselves. We continued to be passive recipients just as we had been raised to be.—Class of 1963

The official rhetoric of Bryn Mawr College, an elite Seven Sisters school, reflects a firm commitment of feminism. Yet Bryn Mawr women, like their sisters in other female institutions, are discovering more and more that this rhetoric lacks substance, and they feel betrayed. The discrepancy between the official intellectual credo and the neurotic, hypersensitive, self-absorbed seriousness that pervades the college's atmosphere poses a problem. Its elitist rhetoric pretends that Bryn Mawr women are special, that their intellectual and class privilege and mobility transcend the political reality of their situation as women. Its emphasis on individual status and achievement denies that there is any collective problem for women in this society. Bryn Mawr women's supposed intellectual superiority places them above ordinary women. Its academic emphasis is accompanied by an intellectual rejection of all that is traditionally feminine—displays of emotion, signs of insecurity or fear, concern with practical good works or human suffering—and a snobbish attitude toward traditionally feminine professions such as teaching or social work, despite the existence of the Bryn Mawr School of Social Work. These attitudes are rarely made explicit but they are subtle and pervasive, and women at Bryn Mawr, if they do not already share them, soon internalize them in much the same way that women with working-class or regional accents learn to speak in a mellow, sophisticated style and voice.

Byrn Mawr's excellent academic reputation, which its founders fought so hard to establish in order to prove that women could take on the same intellectual work as men, now makes for an atmosphere of what is essentially pseudointellectualism, one in which scholarship is parroted, rather than realized. For the Bryn Mawr student finds herself primarily a study in twentieth-century female problems, and Bryn Mawr, founded as a feminist institution, does not permit feminism to exist as an issue. Bryn Mawr's nineteenth-century illusions of uniqueness and intellectual superiority make it unable to see the peculiar turn that its "special" situation as a woman's college has taken. In selecting a woman's college, students at Bryn Mawr may have been asking the school to relate to their needs and problems as women. However, trapped in the circularity of the "let's not admit that we're special, because then we'll be seen as inferior" problem that pervaded the black movement for so long, Bryn Mawr, in its cultural myopia, has become, if anything, antifeminist.

The reasons are complex and make Bryn Mawr an instructive microcosm of the plight of educated women in sexist society. Obviously, the college itself cannot appreciably change the society for which it is educating its women. The education of women—no matter how rigorous or inspiring—cannot overcome the wholesale prejudice of a society entrenched in its belief that women are inferior and properly excluded from the positions a first-class education might prepare them for. Once it is made clear—and it is eminently clear in present-day America—that women will not be accorded positions of responsibility, their education begins to develop all the attributes of irrelevance: it becomes sterile, unspontaneous, academic, and ornamental rather than useful. The students themselves are acutely aware that their expensive educations will be of marginal use to society, and their already considerable feelings of uselessness (coexisting with traditional feminine desires for self-validation through altruism) are compounded by this apparent squandering of resources in pursuit of egotistical self-improvement. These feelings of guilt lead to further self-denigration and self-abnegation and produce strong conflicts with the competitiveness required for academic success. Thus, while creative and imaginative work is not unusual at Bryn Mawr and academic achievement quite common, the fact is that the Bryn Mawr woman who genuinely feels that her intellectual work is meaningful, or ultimately important, is rare.

In reality, a great deal of the Bryn Mawr woman's actual attention is focused on her emotional life, as well as on men and the need to find a husband. The atmosphere is charged with "sensitivity" and emotionalism. And yet the women learn to hate this—their emotions, their insecurities, their fears, their helpless concentration on all of it—because the college perpetuates the very functional myth that emotionalism is a sign of individual weakness. Thus, the Bryn Mawr woman finds herself in the classic female bind. Intellectualism is a constant—and unreached—goal, and therefore a cause for self-hatred. It functions to advance the pretense that "achievement means equality" (the line that the administration supports), while at the same time it deepens self-doubt and anxiety since intellectual pursuits never seem as satisfying as they should. The statement "Our failures only marry" (once made by M. Carey Thomas, the first president of the college) has long been distorted to "Only our failures marry"; this distortion reflects the real pressure the college exerts to deny such solely marital desires as do in fact exist. Most Bryn Mawr women are trapped in a fundamental ambivalence: do they want to be the doctor or the doctor's wife? In this confusion they are not different from most American women. But Bryn Mawr has only deepened the contradictions and failed to provide an environment in which these questions can be openly asked (or one in which it can be admitted that the question is even there).

Now, for the first time, Bryn Mawr has chosen a man

as president, claiming that no "qualified" woman was able to free herself from her family commitments to take the job. Alumnae wrote in opposition, angry that the college had admitted failure on its own terms since it had not produced one woman graduate capable of serving as its president. Similarly, three women "who have lived with famous husbands" addressed the class of 1970 on Class Day. Thus, it is clear that the true condition of American women is now at Bryn Mawr's doorstep; the college's failure is only a grotesque expression of its time.

Bryn Mawr's early feminism has failed, but the real question is why? Bryn Mawr was founded to provide equal education for women; its first president was actively involved in the woman's suffrage movement and was known as the leading feminist educator of her time. The failure of feminism at Bryn Mawr is an illustration of the natural degeneration of nineteenth-century feminism; the history of Bryn Mawr's feminism provides a clear example of the class-bound contradictions and limited perspectives that resulted in the demise of nineteenth-century feminism. The inability to come to grips with the fundamental economic and social issues of marriage and the family and woman's position in those institutions, to analyze the institutional and psychological oppression of women, and to construct radical alternatives for socialized life—these were the vital failures, and they arose from the fundamental limitations of Bryn Mawr's early feminism.

Bryn Mawr's failure to maintain its position as a feminist institution is deeply connected to the failure of the larger feminist movement to transcend the suffrage issue with a more radical analysis of the structural causes of women's oppression. More basic, however, to the school's feminist confusions is the elite role which the founders of the college saw for it. The fundamental motivation for Bryn Mawr's founding was the demand for education made by wealthy, leisured women who felt that their lack of a higher education was the barrier to the realization of their human potential. The men who first organized the college acted out of the Quaker belief that "women must be sensible and able; they should be equal to taking part in the thought and discussion of the vital things with which

Friends were constantly occupied." Bryn Mawr was to be "a truly great experiment in American education, the proving of how far women's minds could go, once the limits of opportunity were removed," but it was, nonetheless, "a college for the advanced education and care of young women and girls of the higher and more refined classes of society."

M. Carey Thomas, the person most involved in the direction of Bryn Mawr College, was remarkable for the power of her vision and the strength of her commitment to the "advancement of women." Even as a child, she was enraged by the inferior position in which women were placed. "I can remember weeping over the account of Adam and Eve because it seemed to me that the curse pronounced on Eve might imperil girls' going to college. . . . I read Milton with rage and indignation; even as a child I knew him for the woman-hater he was." If she wrote "boys and girls" in her diary, she quickly crossed it out and substituted "girls and boys." Her anger reached a fevered pitch when a friend of her father walked home with her from a meeting talking about "the sacred shrine of womanhood."

> He said that "no matter what splendid talents a woman might have she couldn't use them better than by being a wife and mother" and then went off in some high-faluting stuff about the strength of women's devotion, completely forgetting that all women ain't wives and mothers, and they, I suppose, are told to fold their hands and be idle waiting for an eligible offer. Stuff! Nonsense!

Carey Thomas' commitment and single-minded devotion to building Bryn Mawr resulted from her own struggle to get an education. Her adolescent obsession with going to college was undoubtedly heightened by her fear that there might be some truth to the prevailing belief that women were made to be wives and mothers.

At twenty-seven she was determined to become president of Bryn Mawr. Her father and uncle were on the college's Board of Trustees; the three of them convinced the board to appoint her professor of English and dean, with the understanding that she would eventually become president. Her motive in applying for the presidency, in fact her whole purpose in life, is summed up by an entry in her diary when she was ill as a child:

> If I ever live and grow up my one aim and concentrated purpose shall be and is to show that women can learn, can reason, can compete with men in the grand fields of literature and science and conjecture; that a woman can be a woman and a true one without having all her time engrossed by dress and society.

Bryn Mawr became Carey Thomas' vehicle for realizing her aim. She was determined to make its curriculum "just as stiff as Harvard's," "to show that women could compete with Harvard men." Her requirement that all faculty have Ph.D.'s (except Woodrow Wilson) was mocked by Harvard's president, who claimed that "there was an intuitive something in ladies of birth and position which enabled them to do without college training, and make on the whole better professors for women college students than if they themselves had been to college." She even devised an entrance exam every bit as rigorous as Harvard's, much to the horror of other women's colleges.

Carey Thomas' view of feminism was complicated. Her concern for the situation of women, regardless of class, was real, but her understanding of the political responsibility of a college like Bryn Mawr, had been founded on principles of feminism, and was, like the understanding of most nineteenth-century feminists, confused. She did not understand the basis of woman's degradation in her position in the family and underestimated the strength of sexual conservatism in action throughout the society. This limited her perspective on the college's function with regard to its students. She could not see that Bryn Mawr existed in a vacuum, that the deeper truths of woman's condition in society remained untouched, unaddressed, unchanged. Her basic drive was to prove that women are intellectually equal to men; Bryn Mawr was the vehicle she used to prove it. Her belief in the intellectual capacities of women was radical at the time the college was founded, and she was instrumental in changing the then widely held position that women were biologically and naturally unsuited to a life of the intellect. She was an unusual woman, for she let no one stand in the way of her goals. In order to get women admitted to Johns Hopkins Medical School, she raised $500,000 and contributed it to the school when they promised to take women students.

She did not, however, have a radical view of education. Bryn Mawr was designed to reinforce the symbols of education, the "good student" syndrome—"diligence, obedience, and complete faith in the school and its teachings." Scholasticism was the rule at Bryn Mawr, but then again it may be true that "pedantry is not to be despised in an oppressed class as it indicates the first struggle of intellect with its restraints and is therefore a hopeful symptom." Carey Thomas "never understood that she and her sister educators, at the same time that they made it possible for women to secure a first-class education, had helped establish a ceiling above which few women could rise. Carey Thomas' own accomplishments were born of rebellion; at Bryn Mawr there was no room for rebels." It was exactly that "quality" education for which Miss Thomas had striven so hard that kept women down.

Bryn Mawr was an important institution during the years of the suffrage movement; Carey Thomas saw the school as an integral part of the women's struggle. She assumed, however, that both suffrage and the advent of educational opportunities for women would herald the coming of full freedom for women; in this respect she was representative of the larger feminist movement. She was not concerned with analyzing or changing the structural bases of women's oppression, and it was this failure that fostered the growth of an institution whose vestigial feminism had as its aim the development of a class of privileged women who would find a place in a male-dominated world. Miss Thomas' overinvolvement in academic achievement, her blindness to the political realities of sexism (which would prevent even women with "quality" educations from being equal to men), and her basic commitment to elite education obscured her vision.

Carey Thomas' feminism was unquestionably elitist. For the last forty years Bryn Mawr has maintained her elitism without her feminism. It is true that the women's rights movement was not sustained during these years, and that Bryn Mawr only succumbed to the general cultural atmosphere. Those members of the administration and faculty who retain feminist ideals have received little support or reinforcement from the society at large. Social history since World War II seemed to prove beyond contradiction that American women want nothing more out of life than a cloistered home, motherhood, and the role of loyal supporter of children, husband, and community. And certainly husbands, psychologists, sociologists, and pundits require nothing more for them. The students themselves have strongly internalized the social ideal of woman as supportive, altruistic, and self-sacrificing and thus have tended to view "old-fashioned" feminists as strident and selfish. Nevertheless Bryn Mawr had a distinctly feminist tradition and responsibility which it has subsequently failed to uphold.

Marion Park, Carey Thomas' successor as president of Bryn Mawr, never showed any significant feminist concern; on the contrary, her feminist confusion was painful to behold, a perfect example of the degeneracy of the college's original ideas. She praised Virginia Woolf's *A Room of One's Own* as a book in which "a woman writes as a woman and presents her sex not in relation to men but in relation to all the other interests in the world, just as men are presented." At the end of this speech, Miss Park urged the students "to give this book to your woman friends and read it yourself. I only advise you not to give it to men because it is very much the sort of book that you can use and fit in delightfully in dinner conversations." A 1941 speech on the special problems of women's colleges further reveals her extraordinary ambivalence and its limitations with regard to feminism. Miss Park praised the anthropological discovery that the mental capacities of men and women are not fundamentally different and concluded that colleges should not act as though there were two homogeneous groups to be trained. She conceded that the problems of men and women are different; that professional women faced a more difficult time in their careers than men, and that "a woman who marries needs to be prepared to encounter interferences with her unified individual life and must be given intellectual techniques which will allow her to acquire interests readily after she has solved the immediate problems of bringing up a family." This fully stated recognition that Bryn Mawr's function is to train women to use their leisure time constructively while they assume full and primary responsibility for raising a family implicitly admitted the degeneracy of Bryn Mawr's feminism.

Two articles written by the students over the last fifteen years reflect the same degeneracy, and reveal the extent of the student body's acceptance of this position. Describing a conference in 1951 on "Women in the Defense Decade," a student writes that "the conference did not mention women's rights (thank god) but only women's responsibilities. It is time for women to stop complaining about lack of opportunity!" Most Bryn Mawr women probably feel this way during college, for they are told that they are "special," and they believe that their privilege makes feminism irrelevant to them. Another student, writing on "The New Feminism" in a 1963 issue of the Alumnae Magazine, describes her experience at Harvard Medical School:

> The young men worried about us, rushed to protect us. . . . They were young men who believed women should be educated and should take up careers or jobs susceptible of easy termination upon marriage or childbearing, and perhaps easy renewal at age 45 or so. They did not envisage a man's world wanting to make a place for us on feminine terms and so they feared the sacrifice of our femininity to our careers in a man's world.
>
> We were then what I like to call the New Feminists, no longer militant but engaged in a sort of passive resistance movement in a man's world, our personal difficulties compounded by demands not only for professional acceptance . . . at least by one man per woman.
>
> Bryn Mawr is . . . an ivory tower, an artificial temporary community in which feminine capabilities can be expressed fully without social pressure (and which) allows one to go on even in the face of ordinary pressures and develop into a feminine and attractive

person. . . . Because it was taken for granted that I
was a person of serious purpose and great ability, I
acquired an enriched self-image.

At Bryn Mawr, no one, in class or out of class, ever
discusses what femininity means, what are the sources of the
problems faced by women, and what would be needed to
change the situation. Characteristically, the author does not
deal with any of those problems. She internalizes the male
image of her role, yet rebels against it. Passive resistance
would appear to mean a compromise for acceptance, based
on the assumption that men could be cajoled or seduced
into accepting women as equals. Bryn Mawr was an ivory
tower that fooled her (and many other women) into believing that such a situation is possible and workable. As
a product of an elite school, the author was able to secure
one of the few places offered to women at Harvard Medical
School. What relevance does passive resistance have for a
secretary? For that matter, what relevance does passive
resistance have for the average Bryn Mawr graduate?

Bryn Mawr's implied philosophy is that it is sufficient
for a woman's college to provide a haven for women so
that they can develop enough confidence to tackle the
obstacles facing them in a man's world. If Bryn Mawr were
providing that confidence-building haven to its students it
would qualify as an important first-rank feminist institution. But, in fact, Bryn Mawr has capitulated utterly to
society's regressive view of women and is actually producing intellectual decorations, women of "sensitivity," who are
rising to the challenge of "managing career and family"
and developing into feminine and attractive people. Bryn
Mawr as it is today is a metaphor for the discrepancy
between women's apparent freedom and their actual social
and psychological entrapments.

A woman's college that does not relate to the needs of
its students and pretends that its education will solve the
"inequalities" of women within the society is *dishonest*.
Most prestige colleges train wives for the ruling and professional classes. If Bryn Mawr claims to do more, to train
women to take a place alongside men in the present social
structure, it is deluding its own students by not openly
admitting and exposing the problems that women have
faced and will continue to face until there is real liber-

ation. Were the college to deal actively with sexism, the ramifications of their problems would begin to be apparent. Few women students would gear their struggle to their own self-interest so narrowly defined. Prestige education does offer the pretense of freedom and equality to many women; more important, however, is the distance that it creates between the "ordinary" woman and the Bryn Mawr woman. As long as the pretense of individual achievement (tokenism) is maintained, as long as the rhetoric of "uniqueness" is not exposed for the lie that it is, collective action will be made impossible by this very elitism.

Many of us as students believed that all of Bryn Mawr's problems could be solved by adding men, and the pressure for coeducation is still strong. Many women still feel that women (like blacks in the early stages of the civil rights movement) must integrate with men in order to prove that they are equal. How Bryn Mawr will deal with this pressure from many of its students and weigh it against its responsibilities as a woman's institution is unclear. What *is* clear, however, is that if Bryn Mawr chooses to remain an all-woman's college, it must radically redefine its responsibilities and choose to deal actively with the political and psychic oppression of its women students as a group.

Minimal steps toward becoming a feminist institution must be taken. The college must critically examine itself in order to deal honestly with sexism in its course and goal orientation, as well as in its own attitudes toward its students. It should devote resources toward developing a broad-based women's movement, whether through research, publication, or activism, and should establish a Women's Studies department which would include courses in history, sociology, psychology, and literature. The courses should be oriented toward developing ideas on structural change necessary for the liberation of women as a group, regardless of class.

At present, the reasons for remaining a woman's college are never discussed; they are justified purely by snobbery and tradition. The decline in the number of applications and the increase in the number of women who drop out or seek psychiatric help reflect the individualism that is a major stumbling block to Bryn Mawr's feminism. A woman's college, no matter how excellent it pretends to be, cannot evade its fundamental feminist responsibilities without doing serious damage to its students. Today, such a school can only genuinely reactivate its feminism by declaring active commitment to the struggle of all women for their liberation. Only by repudiating parochial interests can the school become a place where women can learn together, deal with their problems together, and act collectively in their struggle to assume their rightful positions as functioning adults in the world.

# THE SECOND SEX
# IN ACADEME

*ANN SUTHERLAND HARRIS*

I am only one of thousands of women who believe that Congress will be increasingly occupied in the 1970s with the legislation necessary to insure that women have equal rights and equal opportunities in the United States. Women are organizing now as they have not since their battle for the right to vote fifty years ago, more and more women having realized that they are treated as second-class citizens. The word "sex" was added to Section 702 of Title VII of the Civil Rights Act as a joke, but equality for women is not a joke. It is a serious issue, although many otherwise fair-minded individuals still refuse to believe that discrimination against women is a serious problem or is a problem that should be taken seriously.

That the overall distribution of women in institutions of higher education is highly suggestive of discriminatory attitudes and practices no one can deny, but research into the problem of discrimination against women in higher education is handicapped at present by the scarcity of studies of individual colleges and universities. This study concentrates therefore on those institutions for which it has been possible to obtain up-to-date statistics. Some of these have just been prepared by senate committees; others have been collected by women's groups in the institutions concerned. There is an urgent need for more statistical data

*ANN SUTHERLAND HARRIS is Assistant Professor of Art History in the Graduate Faculties at Columbia University and is active in the National Organization for Women, Women's Equity Action League, and Columbia Women's Liberation.*

of this kind, especially for such information which extends
beyond the areas of faculty distribution, student admissions,
and fellowships to those of staff and administrative employment, salaries, relative rates of promotion, and distribution
by individual subject.[1]

Several remarks by men famous in the academic world
reveal all too clearly how women are regarded in academe.
When President Nathan Pusey of Harvard realized that the
draft was going to reduce the number of men applying to
Harvard's graduate school, his reaction was, "We shall be
left with the blind, the lame, and the women." Harvard has
no tenured women professors, and its excuse for limiting
its female undergraduate enrollment to 25 percent of the
total is that there is insufficient accommodation for more
women. What this really means is that the institution is
reluctant to give a man's place to a woman. At Yale,
when the new women undergraduates recently protested
the quota on female undergraduates and made the modest
demand for an additional fifty women at an alumni dinner,
one of the male alumni was cheered when he said, "We
are all for women, but Yale must produce a thousand male
leaders every year." Those men alumni did not think that
women have similar leadership potential, or, as Kingman
Brewster put it, "Much of the quality that exists at Yale
depends on the support of people who don't believe strongly
in coeducation." But Yale is slowly learning that women are
fed up with only vicarious participation in aspects of human
activity outside the home.[2] Charles de Carlo recently succeeded Esther Rauschenbusch as President of Sarah
Lawrence, in one of many recent instances in which women
presidents have been succeeded by male presidents. He
said, shortly after his appointment, that "feminine instincts
are characterized by caring qualities, concern for beauty
and form, reverence for life, empathy in human relations,
and a demand that men be better than they are." President
de Carlo apparently thinks that women are myths—muses,

---

[1] Berkeley's recent study is an admirable model. The Higgins Committee report on salaries at Kansas State Teachers College is the
only detailed study of this aspect of discrimination against women
that I have come across so far.

[2] See the articles by students and faculty in the April, 1970, *Yale
Alumni Bulletin.*

madonnas—but not people with the potential and full range of characteristics ascribed to men.

Sometimes there appears in serious publications what may to the uninitiated seem to be a perfectly reasonable objection to giving women the same opportunities as men. For example:

> Too many young women are casually enrolling in graduate schools across the country without having seriously considered the obligation which they are assuming by requesting that such expenditures be made for them. And they are not alone to blame. Equally at fault are two groups of faculty—undergraduate instructors who encourage their women students to apply to graduate school without also helping them consider the commitment that such an act implies, and graduate admissions counsellors who blithely admit girls with impressive academic records without looking for other evidence that the applicant has made a sincere commitment to graduate study.[3]

That women who go to graduate school do make a serious commitment is proved by studies that have taken into account the degree of education of working women. Such studies show that the amount of education a woman has received is a more important factor with respect to her decision to work than either marriage or children. The higher her level of education, the more likely she is to be working full time. Helen Astin found that of the almost 2000 women doctorates she surveyed ten years after they completed their Ph.D.'s, 91 percent were working, 81 percent of them full time. The percentage of men who work full time is not, incidentally, 100 percent, as most of us think, but was, in 1968, 69.4 percent of all men of working age.

The attitudes of mind reflected in the foregoing quotations are not uncommon. Responses to a questionnaire published by the AAUW (American Association of University Women) in its January *Journal* showed that the

[3] Edwin C. Lewis, assistant to the vice-president for academic affairs and a professor of psychology at Iowa State University, quoted in *The Chronicle of Higher Education*, February 9, 1970.

majority of the over 3000 men who replied believed "that woman's first responsibility is to be the feminine companion of men and a mother, but women have less need to achieve in the working world, that they have adequate opportunity to develop their potential, that the job turnover rate and sick-leave rate of women is higher than that of men, [and] that women have difficulty dealing with males in subordinate positions" (McCune). The majority of the women did not agree with those statements, however, and they were right not to. With women now comprising over a third of the work force, more women of working age are working than are staying at home. It is working women, and not the suburban housewives, who comprise the silent majority. For some time, women have voted with their feet to get out of the home, even though the jobs that they are offered are for the most part menial and poorly paid. Those women, however, who wish to become professors, lawyers, and doctors can hardly have less need to achieve in the working world than men, for they will need far more determination than men need to reach the same status and enjoy the same opportunities and compensations. The sick-leave rate and turnover rates for women are in fact, according to the latest figures from the Women's Bureau of the Department of Labor, slightly lower than those of men, when those rates are standardized, as they must be, for occupation and income. Shirley McCune remarks, "If males bring this mind-set to employment situations, it undoubtedly affects their behavior towards females." That is an understatement. That men's notions of women's "place" and women's "roles" do affect the way men treat women in employment situations in academe is made abundantly clear by the statistics showing the distribution of women in the academic world, as it has been also by Lawrence Simpson's recent study (discussed later).

The rule is a simple one: the higher, the fewer. Although more women than men finish high school (and this has been true since 1920), fewer women than men go on to college, partly because it is harder for a woman to gain entrance to college with the necessary financial support.[4] Fewer women than men go on to get higher

---

[4] In 1967, 71 percent of male high school graduates went on to college but only 54 percent of women high school graduates did.

degrees, again largely because graduate departments discriminate against women in admissions policies and in the distribution of fellowships. Once they qualify, the higher-the-fewer rule continues to apply: the higher in terms of rank, salary, prestige, or responsibility, the fewer the number of women to be found. Moreover, their numbers have been declining since 1946, despite the increase in the numbers of M.A.'s and Ph.D.'s going to women in the 1960s. Only 1 percent of presidents of colleges and universities are lay women and their proportions are declining still.[5]

## Students

My discussion of discrimination against women students at undergraduate and graduate levels will treat both covert and overt discrimination. I shall begin with a collection of quotations garnered from various institutions this year:

> I know you're competent and your thesis advisor knows you're competent. The question in our minds is are you *really serious* about what you're doing.
>
> The admissions committee didn't do their job. There is not one good-looking girl in the entering class.
>
> Have you ever thought about journalism? [to a student planning to get a Ph.D. in political science]. I know a lot of women journalists who do very well.
>
> No pretty girls ever come to talk to me.
>
> A pretty girl like you will certainly get married; why don't you stop with an M.A.?
>
> You're so cute. I can't see you as a professor of anything.
>
> The girls at [X university] get good grades because they study hard, but they don't have any originality.
>
> [Professor to student looking for a job] You've no business looking for work with a child that age.

[5] According to a list published by the National Beta Club, which does not attempt to list only accredited institutions of higher edu-

We expect women who come here to be competent, good students, but we don't expect them to be brilliant or original.

Women are intrinsically inferior.

Any women who has got this far has got to be a kook. There are already too many women in this Department.

How old are you anyway? Do you think that a girl like you could handle a job like this? You don't look like the academic type.

Why don't you find a rich husband and give all this up?

Our general admissions policy has been, if the body is warm and male, take it; if it's female, make sure it's an A— from Bryn Mawr.

[To a young widow who had a five-year-old child and who needed a fellowship to continue at graduate school] You're very attractive. You'll get married again. We have to give fellowships to people who really need them.

Somehow I can never take women in this field seriously.[6]

Women graduate students at the University of Chicago were so angered by these and similar statements that they collected a page of them and appended to it a page addressed to their professors explaining why such comments are offensive and harmful. I quote part of their excellent analysis:

Comments such as these can hardly be taken as encouragement for women students to develop an image of themselves as scholars. They indicate that some of our professors have different expectations about our performance than about the performance of male graduate students—expectations based not on our ability as individuals but on the fact that we are women. Comments like these indicate that we are expected to be decorative objects in the classroom

6 Seve
the U

that we're not likely to finish a Ph.D. and if we do, there must be something "wrong" with us. Single women will get married and drop out. Married women will have children and drop out. And a woman with children ought to stay at home and take care of them rather than study and teach.

Expectations have a great effect on performance. Rosenthal and Jacobson (1968) have shown that when teachers expected randomly selected students to "bloom" during the year, those students' IQ's increased significantly above those of a control group. Rosenthal and Jacobson (1966) had already shown that experimenter expectation made significant differences in the performance of the subjects—even when verbally identical instructions were read to the groups of subjects. The teachers and the experimenters stated that they had treated all subjects or students exactly alike. They were, however, giving both verbal and nonverbal cues about what was to be the appropriate behavior (R. Rosenthal and L. Jacobson, *Pygmalion in the Classroom: Teacher Expectation and Pupil's Intellectual Development*, New York, Holt, Rinehart and Winston, 1968). It would be surprising to find that graduate schools are immune to this phenomenon. When professors expect less of certain students, those students are likely to respond by producing less.

Rosenthal and Jacobson also found that experimenters who were told that one group of white rats was more intelligent than another identical group of white rats discovered in the tests they ran that the supposedly brighter rats did in fact perform better than the supposedly dumb rats. If male scholars believe that women are intellectually inferior to men—less likely to have original contributions to make, less likely to be logical, and so on—will they not also find the evidence to support their beliefs in the work of the women students in their classes, evidence of a far more sophisticated nature than the speed at which one rat finds its way through a maze? Their motives will be subconscious. Indeed, they will firmly believe that their judgment is rational and objective.

One remark above all is repeatedly made to women

students. Although one professor noted that he found it difficult to take women in his field "seriously," women students are asked again and again, "Are you really serious?" Since the vast majority of women students are as serious as the men students, the women start questioning themselves. Are they supposed to be more serious than men are? Are male students more serious than women students? How serious do you have to be? It is even asked of women who have completed Ph.D.'s at great personal and financial cost when they apply for their first jobs, which in my field were being advertised at last year's convention with the label "man preferred." (And the women investigating jobs not so labelled in interviews learned that men were generally preferred when the employer could afford to discriminate against women.) The study just completed by the Women's Committee at the University of Chicago confirmed what most of us have known from personal experience for a long time, namely, that women receive significantly less perceived support for career plans than men do, and that a large number of women in various institutions have met or have heard of discriminatory experiences.

Accurate statistics documenting the attrition rates of either male or female students are difficult to come by. The statistics that I have seen suggest that the overall attrition rates of men and women during a course of study are not very different, the majority of women dropping out not *during* a course of study but after completing one stage —after finishing high school, after finishing college, or after completing an M.A. program.[7] Studies also indicate that the attrition rate for both sexes is higher in the humanities and social sciences than in the physical sciences and professional schools. Since women are more often found in the former two fields, their overall attrition rate is higher than that of men, but when the figures are com-

[7] A higher proportion of undergraduate women than of men completed four years at the University of Michigan (Shortridge). In the class of 1965, 60.8 percent of the men graduated, compared with 76.5 percent of the women, but women undergraduates at cation, there are 2847 colleges a
One hundred and ninety-eight
twenty-three are lay women. I w
dent of Alverno College in Mi
these figures for me.

pared by field, the differences are small.[8] The Chicago study provides the first published breakdown that I have seen of the dropout rates of students in selected departments. A cohort analysis for students in various fields who entered in 1962, 1963, and 1964 showed the following:

## ATTRITION RATES OF GRADUATE STUDENTS
### (University of Chicago)

| FIELD | *Percentage* MEN | WOMEN |
|---|---|---|
| Biological Sciences | 26% | 33% |
| Physical Sciences | 16 | 20 |
| Social Sciences | 40 | 51 |
| Humanities | 24 | 19 |

The overall difference in attrition rates of men and women graduate students was in fact rather minimal, with women actually having a lower attrition rate than men in the humanities. The College of Physicians and Surgeons at Columbia provided Columbia Women's Liberation with the information that the attrition rate of men students was equal to or higher than that of the women students. The proper study of attrition rates is, however, in its infancy. Other factors, such as the greater availability of fellowship support in the physical and biological sciences than in the social sciences and humanities, almost certainly contribute to the lower attrition rates in the two former fields. Women are more likely to be studying in fields where there are fewer fellowships available. This should make it more difficult for them to complete their graduate studies. However, conversations between women faculty members and administrators at some institutions have revealed that women have a higher completion rate without fellowship support than men do, a discovery that I fear can be used to justify

[8] This was one of the results reported by Rudd and Hatch in their analysis of men and women in Great Britain who received their B.A.'s in 1957 (E. Rudd and S. Hatch, *Graduate Study and After*, London, 1968).

further discrimination against women when awarding fellowships. I regard it as additional evidence that women who go to graduate school are likely to be more highly motivated than men who do.

One institution had statistics on the numbers of men and women applying to graduate school for admission and for financial aid, on the numbers of each sex awarded places and fellowships, and on their relative attrition rates, but it refused to release them to the appropriate local faculty committee because the figures would be "misinterpreted." I think, however, that if the picture were rosy for women, the opportunity would be taken to prove that women are not discriminated against. It might be pointed out in such a case that women were probably discriminated against when fellowships were handed out, and, moreover, that such discrimination was fair because women were less likely to finish than men were. One might respond in turn that denying women fellowship support will almost certainly increase their attrition rate, thus making the prophecy self-fulfilling.

In my opinion, and in the opinion of others who have thought about this problem, the slightly higher attrition rates of women graduate students are largely explained by the lack of encouragement and by the actual discouragement experienced by women graduate students for their career plans. They are continually told that they will not finish, that women's minds are not as good as men's minds, that the "difficulties of combining the career [*sic*] of marriage and motherhood with a career as a scholar and teacher" will be beyond the physical and mental energies of all but the "exceptional woman" (but never, of course, of men, who are presumed to spend no time at all being husbands and fathers). Women are told that they are welcome first and foremost as decoration for the male academic turf. Even in academe, women are sex objects. Repeatedly accused of being intellectual delinquents, overtly and covertly, women are consequently more anxious than are men students about their work and futures, and this anxiety helps to stifle a great deal of the pleasure many of those women felt for the subjects that they had chosen to pursue. It is not surprising that some women decide that they are not cut out to be scholars and teachers. Rather, it is surprising that the dropout rates of women are not far higher than they are. That they are not, I take to be evidence of women graduate students' higher degree of commitment, which arises in part from a natural defense mechanism in response to the sexual discrimination that they meet in their daily lives.

It is generally assumed that it is more difficult for a woman than for a man to get into college, let alone into graduate school.[9] My first acquaintance with the problem of discrimination against women in academe came in conversations with older faculty women who were complaining about the fact that their women undergraduates needed A or A— records to gain admission while their men undergraduates could obtain places with B averages. Evidence that this was indeed the case came from one institution at which the students in a department drafted a bill of rights for students and included the word "sex" in the discrimination clause. The senior faculty were puzzled because that department had more women than men graduate students and awarded more than 50 percent of its Ph.D.'s to women. A senior faculty member told the following story to try to allay the students' fears. He said that faculty dealing with graduate admissions in the department had noticed that the worst women applicants were considerably better than the worst men applicants. All the women applicants were, in fact, highly qualified. Suspecting that the administration, which does a preliminary sifting of all graduate admissions applications, was holding back the folders of qualified women in order to keep up the numbers of men in a subject that attracts a majority of women students, the faculty called for all the folders in

[9] Caroline Bird's statement, "A girl needs higher marks to enter college than a boy" (*Born Female: The High Cost of Keeping Women Down*, New York: Pocket Books, 1969) is substantiated by statistics such as those for the University of Michigan (Shortridge, *passim*), by those for state institutions in Virginia provided in the 1964 report of the Commission for the Study of Educational Facilities in the State of Virginia, and by statements such as the following from a publication issued by the Office of Undergraduate Admissions at the University of North Carolina: "Admission of women at the freshman level will be restricted to those who are especially well qualified." According to testimony given by Dr. Bernice Sandler before the House Special Subcommittee on Education on June 19, there were 1893 men but only 426 women in the freshman class of the General College of the University of North Carolina in 1969–1970.

order to do the preliminary sifting themselves. As a result, a number of women were admitted who might not otherwise have been offered places. The moral of the story was, "We don't discriminate against women but the administration does." Nor should it be assumed that the administrations of universities are worse than faculty with regard to sexual discrimination. Lawrence Simpson in his study of employment practices found that there was no difference between the attitudes of administrators and faculty.

The Chicago report contains evidence (p. 93) that it is easier for a man than for a woman to get into graduate school. The most conclusive evidence is the grade average of the women, which is significantly higher than that of the men.

### GRADE AVERAGES OF STUDENTS ENTERING GRADUATE SCHOOL
#### (University of Chicago)

|       | A     | A—    | B+    | B or lower |
|-------|-------|-------|-------|------------|
| Men   | 6.8%  | 20.1% | 31.6% | 41%        |
| Women | 9.1   | 24.9  | 32.2  | 30         |

My own experience and that of colleagues suggest that such results are to be expected, for women students who request letters of recommendation for graduate school have, on the average, much better records than do the men students. And they all know that they will need better grade averages to get in; in fact, they expect to be discriminated against.

Analysis of published admissions figures provides additional evidence in support of the widely held assumption that on balance you have to be better to get a place in graduate school if you are a woman than if you are a man. Before examining the statistics, it is worth remembering that women candidates for graduate school are the survivors of a long sifting process. Although more women than men finish high school, women's socially approved lower self-aspirations insure that fewer women than men will even think of going on to college. Those women who do must leap another hurdle of double standards, and even then they are either denied places or are allowed only a small number of places at America's most prestigious undergraduate colleges: Harvard, Yale, Princeton, Columbia, Notre Dame, and Dartmouth. Moreover, the range of subjects offered, the facilities (libraries, laboratories), the endowments, and the faculties of the supposedly equivalent women's colleges do not measure up to those of their male counterparts. About 43 percent of the B.A.'s awarded in the United States now go to women. Again, the lack of social approval for women's careers will insure that many able and capable women will stop their professional training with a B.A., which will, as is well known, entitle them to become the secretary of the male college graduate who has just collected his B.A. Women who have definite career plans and consequently choose to go on to graduate school are, therefore, a very special group of women. With all this, it is not surprising that Jessie Bernard commented that "only the very best of the good women students" go to graduate school. Out of these, only the hardiest survive.

## Faculty

There is considerable evidence, in many reports by women's groups at particular institutions, in support of the contention that women faculty are systematically discriminated against with regard to hiring practices, promotion, and salaries, and such reports seem to be further supported by previous scholarly research on the question of the status of faculty women. Dissertations by Lawrence A. Simpson and Helen Berwald came to the conclusion that, in seeking employment as faculty, women are discriminated against by all kinds of institutions of higher education. Dr. Simpson summarized Berwald's research as follows: "When all variables were equal except sex, the male candidate was typically chosen for employment." And to quote Simpson's summary of his own more recent study:

Prospective academic women must recognize that they should, in effect, be more highly qualified than their male competitors for higher education positions. Additionally, women should be aware of the attitudes that may be expected from employing agents in the academic fields which typically employ few females. Perhaps the most important application of the study is that employing agents in higher education must seriously re-examine their own attitudes regarding academic women and be keenly aware of any prejudices or rationalizations which cause academic women to be treated in any other way than as productive human beings. In a period when higher education faces a shortage of qualified teachers, the denial of a teaching position to a qualified female applicant, based solely on the negative attitudes toward women of an employing agent, is open to serious question.

Women earned about 13 percent of all the Ph.D.'s awarded in the 1960s (and now earn just under 40 percent of the M.A.'s) and comprised about 22 percent of the faculty in all institutions of higher education. In all kinds of institutions, however, women are distributed unevenly, clustered in the lower ranks, in part-time positions, and in institutions or programs considered by some to be low-prestige. This uneven distribution was discussed in testimony presented to the House Committee by Dr. Bernice Sandler (footnote 10). I will concentrate on the "elite" schools, from which women are most systematically excluded, and on the "elite" of the women's schools, where we would at least expect to find women in the majority of the controlling positions.

Columbia awards more doctorates to women than any other American university. In 1956–1957, when the national percentage of Ph.D.'s going to women was 11 percent, Columbia awarded only 4.6 percent of its Ph.D.'s to women. In the last two years, almost 25 percent of its Ph.D.'s have been awarded to women, a figure considerably above the national average of 14 percent (in 1968). There has been, however, no comparable change in the number of women employed by Columbia. The percentage of women with tenure in the graduate faculties has remained steady at just over 2 percent. And although in theory Columbia could draw its faculty from all the graduate schools in the country and does in the case of male faculty, it is also significant that the small number of women with tenure are almost all Columbia products.

Men may be and are encouraged to teach at women's schools. It is rare indeed to find women in full-time teaching positions in men's undergraduate colleges. Of the Seven Sisters colleges, in fact, only Wellesley has more female than male faculty in tenured ranks and in chairmanships. In the other colleges, male faculty dominate the upper levels and in some cases the lower levels as well. At Vassar the percentage of women dropped from 55.6 percent of the faculty in 1958–1959 to 40.5 percent in 1969–1970. The number of women with full professorships dropped during the same period from thirty-five to sixteen. At Vassar it was thought that a coeducational faculty provided a healthier atmosphere for women students. The reverse does not apparently apply to Harvard, Princeton, Yale, or Brown. Barnard has two more female than male full-time faculty, but the men hold 78 percent of the full professorships and chairmanships. To quote the Columbia Faculty Report, "even the . . . educational institutions founded to give women access to professional careers do not, after more than fifty years of activity, serve as models demonstrating to the community the ability of women to manage demanding careers." The consistent exclusion of women from positions on the faculties of the Seven Brothers schools is probably the most obvious example of employment imbalance to be found in academe. Women learn to confine their job applications to coeducational institutions and to women's schools. Men may work anywhere, on the other hand, and can even expect to receive preferential treatment at some of the best women's colleges.

When John Parrish reported in 1962 on the 1960 distribution of women faculty at ten high-endowment (Chicago, Columbia, Cornell, Harvard, Johns Hopkins, M.I.T., Northwestern, Princeton, Stanford, and Yale) and ten high-enrollment (Berkeley, C.C.N.Y., Indiana, Illinois, Michigan, Michigan State, Minnesota, N.Y.U., Ohio, and Pennsylvania State) institutions of higher education in 1960, he gave the following statistics. At the eight reporting high-endowment institutions, 2.6 percent of the full professors were women, 7.5 percent of the associate professors, 8.5 percent of the assistant professors, and 9.8 percent of the instructors. At the ten high-enrollment institutions, women constituted 4.3 percent of all full professors, 10.1 percent of all associate professors, 12.7 percent of all assistant professors, and 20.4 percent of all instructors. I have not seen the same statistics computed for 1970, but the statistics that I have seen from individual institutions in those two groups indicate that the overall percentages of women have remained constant or have declined.

Most students of this problem are reluctant to compute relative rates of promotion for women and men faculty. At Columbia, we tried the crude but we think useful procedure of simply counting the numbers of men and women on the faculty in full-time positions who received their Ph.D.'s in the 1960s and then studying their distribution by rank:

|                      | MALE        | FEMALE     |
|----------------------|-------------|------------|
| Assistant Professor  | 91 (47%)    | 24 (96%)   |
| Associate Professor  | 74 (38%)    | 1 (4%)     |
| Professor            | 30 (15%)    | 0 (0%)     |
|                      | 195 (100%)  | 25 (100%)  |

Well over 50 percent of the men who earned their Ph.D.'s in 1963 and 1964 have been given tenure. None of the women in that group has been promoted to the rank of associate professor with tenure, although one woman is an assistant professor with tenure.

The lower median salaries of women in academe (the gap between sexes is widening, not decreasing, are partly explained by the exclusion of women from the better-paying jobs and higher ranks, but even with such factors standardized, women in academe still earn less than men with comparable qualifications.[10] When the faster promotion rates of male faculty are also taken into account, then the differences are even greater. The idea that

[10] At Kansas State Teachers College (Higgins), women had longer average periods of service at all ranks except that of professor: professor—men, 19.37 years, women, 15.25 years; associate professor—men, 10.70 years, women, 14.26 years; assistant professor—men, 4.51 years, women, 7.22 years; instructor—men, 2.54 years, women, 3.72 years.

women, married or single, don't really need jobs or don't need them as much as men do is a hard one to kill. A friend of mine who happens to be an assistant professor married to an assistant professor has a daughter. When she and her husband have paid for child care five days a week and for housecleaning help, and by the time they have paid the higher taxes to which their double income entitles them, she has $1,000 left of her $11,000 salary with which to pay for books, fees for professional periodicals and for memberships in professional associations, taxis, clothes, and all the other overheads of a career. Wives are worth a good deal of untaxed income, but the male professors who distribute departmental budgets generally think that double-income couples are rich. They forget that working couples have to buy on the open market the services many wives perform in return for their keep. If, as happens frequently, the wife is denied full-time employment on account of *de facto* or *de jure* nepotism rules, it will actually cost that couple money for her to work, for the money she brings into the home will not cover the cost of her replacements. Considering the tax deductions which are permitted to businessmen, working couples are unfairly penalized at present, and these unfair tax laws undoubtedly prevent some highly trained women from working, simply because they know that it would not pay their family for them to do so. Other women work for small financial rewards simply because their work is a pleasure for them. Single academic women are penalized financially but for different reasons. It is always assumed that they are only supporting themselves, although the same financial penalties do not apply to the same extent to bachelors. The idea that money should be distributed equitably is nearly always raised when women's salaries are discussed. A man may earn as much as he likes. Here, as in so many areas affecting men and women, double standards apply.

One area of academic employment where the percentage of women employed often tops the 19 percent average of women now employed at all levels is part-time teaching and/or research. Positions in this area do not have the status or fringe benefits of full-time positions and are thus comparatively poorly paid. They also are rarely tenured. When men hold such positions, it is nearly always because they have another full-time job. Such arrangements permit the university to invite men who may have unusual expertise in some relevant area to teach one or two courses a year in that specialty. Women in part-time positions, however, often do not have other full-time jobs, although some have other part-time jobs. In my experience, women with part-time positions carry heavier work loads than men do. Some teach as many as, or more hours than full-time faculty.[11] The administrations and faculties of universities know, in fact, that academic men often marry academic women, and that faculty wives provide a good captive labor market, seldom in a position to demand the full-time position that they deserve because they cannot threaten to leave and go elsewhere. In New York City, there is a sufficient number of institutions of higher education for most couples to find two full-time jobs, but few cities in the United States offer such a range of choices within a small geographical area. Apart from women working in the administration, part-time women faculty are, I believe, the most financially exploited group of women in academe. The women at the University of Pittsburgh discovered that by working for lower salaries than those men with their qualifications would receive, they were saving the University $2,500,000 a year. It is not difficult to see how they could have arrived at such a figure.

A regular complaint of women in academe concerns the punitive effects of nepotism rules, for these almost always mean that the wife, not the husband, is denied employment. The advisability of hiring husband and wife in one small department may be debated. All other forms of nepotism rules (husband and wife may not both have tenure; may not both have full-time jobs; may not both work at the same institution, period) should be declared null and void by Section 805 when it is applied, for nepotism rules constitute *de facto*, if not *de jure,* discrimination against women. (Harvard, incidentally, will employ and has employed father and son but not husband and wife in

---

[11] This may be particularly true in language departments where it seems to be common practice to hire women on a part-time basis to take care of most of the elementary language instruction.

full-time tenured posts.) Nepotism rules often lead to farcical situations. The most famous case is that of Dr. Maria Goeppert Mayer, the first woman to win the Nobel Prize for physics since Marie Curie. Her husband is also a physicist. Department after department hired him, while graciously allowing her to use the laboratory facilities free.[12] Nor have things improved, to judge by the experience of a young female theoretical physicist known to me, also married to a scientist, who, despite a doctorate and several publications, has been unemployed all year while watching men with fewer qualifications than her own being given the research posts for which she applied in her husband's institution. An unwritten nepotism rule is much harder to fight than a written one.

I was told last month about a psychology department in Pennsylvania which is using a college junior to teach freshmen and sophomores rather than employing a faculty wife who has an M.A. Another recent case known to me illustrates both sexual discrimination and covert nepotism rules (many institutions claim not to have them and do not print them in official literature). A brilliant European couple were invited to teach in one department, for they specialize in different areas. He did not have a Ph.D.; she did. He had not published a book; she had. He was hired as a visiting Associate Professor; she, after considerable hassle, as a visiting Assistant Professor. Throughout the negotiations, they were told that the nepotism rule would prevent the institution's offering her a full-time position in the same department as her husband, although, in reply to a questionnaire circulated by the AAUW a few years ago, the institution declared that it did not have any nepotism rules. The couple concerned has since returned to Europe where she has just been given a distinguished appointment to a rank above that of her husband, an appointment to which her academic achievements clearly entitle her. She has remarked that she does not think a married academic woman will receive such fair treatment in America for many years.

12 Bird, *op. cit.*, p. 58.

## Coeducation

The passing of Section 805 will call into question the existence of any institution that limits its enrollment to members of one sex, whether male or female, as well as those institutions now "going co-ed" on a quota system. At present 92 percent of all women attend coeducational institutions of higher education. The majority of sex-segregated schools are run by religious foundations, however, which explains why only 28 percent of Roman Catholic women attend coeducational institutions.[13] Thus it will be seen that we are dealing with a minority group of institutions, albeit a highly visible one, the Seven Sisters and their Ivy League brothers being among the most famous educational institutions in the world. The admission of a limited number of students of the opposite sex to men's and women's schools will not, in theory, permit those institutions to make that change a gradual one, aiming at, say, 33 percent female and 67 percent male enrollment. They will be required to select applicants on the basis of demonstrated ability and potential and will have to accept whatever the resulting sexual proportions are. I predict a greater reluctance on the part of male than of female institutions to do this, with the result that there will be fewer places available overall for women until the situation is adjusted. Both men and women's schools will plead lack of dormitory space and will conceive of coeducation as an extension and expansion of their facilities rather than a sharing of existing facilities. Lack of accommodation must be recognized, however, as a false defense against true coeducation.

One painful point must be made. Sex-segregated education does not benefit women. The Gourman Institute ratings for all women's schools are at least two hundred points (on an 800 scale, 400 being accreditation level) below those of their supposedly equivalent men's schools, with the Catholic schools collecting the lowest ratings of all. The kinds of courses offered and the philosophies behind the majority of these schools are effectively dissected in Kate Millett's essay, *Token Learning*. Especially revealing is a comparison of the introductory blurbs in

[13] C. Westoff and R. Potvin, *College Women and Fertility Values*, Princeton, New Jersey: 1967, ch. I.

the catalogues of twin institutions. Women undergraduates are also "protected" by a myriad of rules that do not exist for male undergraduates. Even at the best-known women's schools, the smaller endowment, more limited facilities, and smaller range of courses, especially in male-dominated fields, affect all women students. Our society does not yet value the education of women as highly as it values that of men, and consequently we do not invest as much in female as we do in male education. As with racially segregated education, sex-segregated education works to the disadvantage of the group which is discriminated against. I am certain therefore that it will benefit women if all educational institutions are opened to them.

Lifting the barriers will not, as some may fear, empty the Seven Sisters or fill them with the also-rans of the race to get into the Seven Brothers. As now, all educational institutions will have and preserve their own particular character and identity, to which size, location, faculty interests, and available facilities will contribute. The feminist heritage of the women's schools should provide an excellent foundation for genuine coeducation, although the alumnae of these schools (and some faculty) will resist the idea strongly to start with. The main argument for retaining the women's schools is that they provide women with a supportive atmosphere as long as our society is male-dominated and male-oriented. However, few of the women's colleges now take such responsibilities very seriously, and most are male-dominated, if not male-oriented, as we have seen. I am not sure why the women's colleges abandoned active support of the feminist cause, although Betty Friedan has suggested some reasons in her chapter, "The Sex-Directed Educators," in *The Feminine Mystique*. Faculties and administrations now prefer a neutral stance, and as a result provide their women students with little or no preparation for the discriminatory world of employment outside.

## De Facto and De Jure Sexual Discrimination

If the government is willing to take steps to enforce this new legislation, the law will no doubt be regarded as primarily applicable to the kinds of problems outlined above.[14] To show which way the feminist wind is blowing these days and to show how difficult it often is to define sexual discrimination, I should like to summarize briefly some other areas where women's groups believe that discrimination exists.

Some women are arguing, and I am among them, that the almost complete lack of serious study of women by academics constitutes *de facto* sexual discrimination. Women are seen as part of the social background against which the main events of (women would say "masculine") history are played out. Women are seen from a male perspective (Freud's distortions are among the most obvious examples) and their roles are misunderstood or undervalued. Philosophy, religion, psychology, biology, history, literary criticism, sociology, anthropology, and art history are all disciplines that could contribute a great deal more than they have in the past to our understanding of women. The faculty and administration of many schools may regard "women's studies"—like black studies at their inception—as a pseudointellectual fad at first, but I think they will change their minds. Cornell ran a full and varied program this year using visiting experts from a wide variety of fields, and the resulting course was enormously popular with undergraduates of both sexes.

Women both inside and outside academe have to cope with discriminatory health services, lack of paid maternity leave, and lack of child-care facilities. The first of these items may surprise readers, but it is a fact that the male body is regarded as the norm, and women students and faculty as a rule pay extra for gynecological services, while men are treated for genito-urinary tract health problems as a matter of course. Women students are now demanding that their health fees cover the services of a gynecologist. The idea of paid maternity leave will be

[14] So far the government has shown extreme reluctance to enforce existing legislation with regard to discrimination against women. National Organization for Women has filed 1200 compliance suits against federal contractors under Executive Order 11246, amended by 11375, but none has been investigated so far. Similarly Women's Equity Action League has filed over 100 compliance suits under the same executive orders against colleges and universities. Only one case has so far been investigated.

resisted at first (it is almost nonexistent in the United States, after all), but considering the various ways in which institutions of higher education try to accommodate and help other disadvantaged groups, it seems reasonable to expect them, as well as other employers of women, to compensate women for their distinctive biological function. Academic women find, as do other highly trained women who stop work in order to have children, that they must drop out of ladder positions to which they may never be able to return. One minor but helpful concession has recently been made by Princeton, where nontenured women faculty may, at *their* option, delay their tenure decision if they find that family responsibilities make it difficult for them to complete the necessary publications within the normal seven-year limit. Some men might appreciate similar concessions, but I think the ready availability of high-quality child care facilities on the Swedish model would be a better solution for all academic parents. Colleges and universities, unlike big business firms, will find the financial burden of providing such facilities difficult to bear. I predict federal and state funds for such facilities eventually, for most people concerned with such programs think it is ideal for the facilities to be near the parents' place of work so that parents can spend time with their small children during the day.

Jo Freeman's trenchant dissenting comments at the end of the Chicago report summarizes *de facto* discrimination as follows:

> As long as the University does not concern itself with the variety of life styles prevalent among academic women and the many needs they have that differ from those of men, it will inevitably discriminate against otherwise qualified women. The life styles of the population of intelligent highly educated women is much more heterogeneous than those of intelligent, highly educated men. The University is geared to serve the needs of the latter and those of the former group who most closely resemble these men or who can organize their lives, however uncomfortably, into the environment created for intelligent, highly educated men. Failure to realize that women as a

group have a wider diversity of life styles than men
as a group will result in an exclusion of those women
whose life styles least resemble those of men.

I have discussed in some detail here the widespread
discrimination against women in all strata of higher education.[15] As students, as faculty and staff, and as concerned women, we have a keen interest in changing
institutional values and policies. Higher education as a
whole will benefit if we succeed.

[15] Those on campus responsible for investigating charges of sexual
discrimination should also check the representation of women in
the following areas: faculty honors and awards; commencement
speakers and recipients of honorary degrees; bylaws of alumni associations (the Graduate Alumni Association of Columbia has many
women members but women may not hold office in that organization); the composition of the Pulitzer Prize Committee, administered
by Columbia University trustees, etc. The Chicago report (p. 63ff.)
has an interesting appendix with data of this kind. As is to be
anticipated, there are few women represented in any of these
categories.

# WOMEN AND THE LITERARY CURRICULUM

*ELAINE SHOWALTER*

President Pusey of Harvard once remarked that the draft for Vietnam might take so many young men that the graduate schools would be left with the blind, the lame, and the women. Whether the blind and the lame have indeed moved in, I do not know; but the women we have always with us. In the graduate schools they are in fact a majority. As for undergraduate schools, the trend toward coeducation makes it likely that we will all be teaching women before long, if we are not doing so already. Therefore I would like to look at the literary curriculum today, not from the viewpoint of the administrator or the professor, but from the viewpoint of the woman student, who is its prime consumer.

Let us imagine a woman student entering college to major in English literature. In her freshman year she would probably study literature and composition, and the texts in her course would be selected for their timeliness, or their relevance, or their power to involve the reader, rather than for their absolute standing in the literary canon. Thus she might be assigned any one of the texts which have recently been advertised for Freshman English: an anthology of essays, perhaps such as *The Responsible Man*, "for the student who wants literature relevant to the world in which he lives," or *Conditions of Men*, or

*ELAINE SHOWALTER is an Assistant Professor of English at Douglass College of Rutgers University. She read this paper at the MLA Forum on the Status of Women in the Profession, Dec. 27, 1970.*

*Man in Crisis: Perspectives on the Individual and His World*, or again, *Representative Men: Cult Heroes of Our Time*, in which the thirty-three men represent such categories of heroism as the writer, the poet, the dramatist, the artist, and the guru, and the only two women included are the Actress Elizabeth Taylor, and The Existential Heroine Jacqueline Onassis.

Perhaps the student would read a collection of stories like *The Young Man in American Literature: The Initiation Theme*, or sociological literature like *The Black Man and the Promise of America*. In a more orthodox literary program, she might study the eternally relevant classics, such as *Oedipus*; as a professor remarked in a recent issue of *College English*, all of us want to kill our fathers and marry our mothers. And whatever else she might read, she would inevitably arrive at the favorite book of all Freshmen English courses, the classic of adolescent rebellion, *Portrait of the Artist as a Young Man*.

By the end of her freshman year, a woman student would have learned something about intellectual neutrality; she would be learning, in fact, how to think like a man. And so she would go on, increasingly with male professors to guide her. What would she encounter for the next three years? I looked at the syllabi for all the courses offered in the English Department of the women's college I attended as an undergraduate. In the twenty-one courses beyond the freshman level offered by the department, there were listed 313-male writers, including such luminaries as William Shenstone, James Barrie and Dion Boucicault; and seventeen women writers: Lady Mary Wortley Montagu, Anne Bradstreet, Mrs. Centlivre, Fanny Burney, Jane Austen, Charlotte and Emily Brontë, George Eliot, Margaret Fuller, Emily Dickinson, Sarah Orne Jewett, Lady Gregory, Virginia Woolf, Dorothy Richardson, Marianne Moore, Gertrude Stein, and Djuna Barnes. This list is in some respects eccentric, I assume; Mrs. Centlivre and Lady Gregory may not be universally popular, and surely there are departments somewhere teaching Christina Rossetti, Edith Wharton, and Ellen Glasgow, to name a few surprising omissions. But I think we can all recognize the truth of the relative proportions of men to women on the reading lists. A quick check of some standard two-volume anthologies reveals a similar imbalance; the *Norton Anthology*, for example, includes 169 men and six women: *American Poetry and Prose* lists eighty-six men and ten women.

In the gallery of the literary curriculum, there will thus be very few portraits of the artist as a young woman. Women will figure much more prominently in literary history in their relation to male artists, as martyred mothers, pathetic sisters, and difficult wives: Frances Trollope, Dorothy Wordsworth, Alice James, Zelda Fitzgerald, Caitlin Thomas. And they will be still more conspicuous as subjects of the male intellect and imagination. Students will surely encounter the myths of female sexuality as seen by Hardy and Lawrence, and the wonders of childbirth as seen by Sterne and Hemingway. As they study the long and honorable tradition of literary misogyny, women students will learn to suppress their partisan fury towards Milton and Swift. Feminism as a political philosophy will be mentioned apologetically, if at all, with regard to Mary Wollstonecraft or Virginia Woolf, and passed over entirely with regard to John Stuart Mill or Shaw.

Women students will therefore perceive that literature, as it is selected to be taught, confirms what everything else in the society tells them: that the masculine viewpoint is considered normative, and the feminine viewpoint divergent. In the literary curriculum the woman writer is by definition "minor," recommended perhaps, but not required; likely to be a recluse, childless, or even mad, and yet lacking the phosphorescent glamor of the doomed male artist. In short, a woman studying English literature is also studying a different culture to which she must bring the adaptability of the anthropologist.

What are the effects of this long apprenticeship in negative capability on the self-image and the self-confidence of women students? The masculine culture, reinforced by the presence of a male author and, usually, a male professor, is so all-encompassing that few women students can sustain the sense of a positive feminine identity in the face of it. Women are estranged from their own experience and unable to perceive its shape and authenticity, in part because they do not see it mirrored and given resonance by literature. Instead they are expected to identify as readers with a masculine experience and perspective, which is presented as the human one. As critics, too, they are required to maintain this identification.

Since they have no faith in the validity of their own perceptions and experiences, rarely seeing them confirmed in literature, or accepted in criticism, can we wonder that women students are so often timid, cautious, and insecure when we exhort them to "think for themselves"? Women notoriously lack the happy confidence, the exuberant sense of the value of their individual observations as a check upon the abstractions in the classroom, which enables men to risk making fools of themselves for the sake of an idea. Indeed, women are all too frequently passive and dependent in class, not only with hostile male professors, but also with indulgent ones; not only with embittered female professors, but also with encouraging ones.

We have customarily dealt with these problems, with the reverent hush of the women students, with their reluctance to clash with each other or with their professors, by sympathetic attention to individuals, or by coercion, or by emphasizing, à la Huxley, the need for some dependable academic Betas. One professor was recently quoted, for example, as saying that his women graduate students were dull, of course, but "more patient and systematic than men," and likely to do very well with bibliographic problems. The ideal for education has been to treat all students alike, to teach the same curriculum in the same way to everybody, with the pretense that this guarantees each student equal opportunity. But women do not have equal opportunity either in the society or in the classroom, where they learn that with a handful of exceptions, writers of their own sex are ignored, ridiculed, or scorned. Preferable to the myth of equal opportunity is a curriculum which recognizes differences and attempts to compensate for a socially limiting self-image at the same time that it teaches an important and neglected area of culture.

The concept of Women's Studies has already had considerable impact in other disciplines. Over 100 courses dealing with women have been introduced at the college level; more than a quarter of these are in the field of literature. My own experience has been with a variety of courses in English literature concentrating on feminine identity and achievement.

To freshman women I have taught three versions of a course called "The Educated Woman in Literature." Its purpose is three-fold: first, to study the image of the educated woman in twentieth-century literature; second, to consider the relationship between social and political change and literary stereotypes; and third, to enable women students to confront in their own lives the effects of sex-role conditioning on the educational process. In general, I have tried to structure the class to allow students the maximum degree of self-determination, because it seems to me essential that they overthrow their inertia and learn how to direct their own education, that they gain some experience in decision-making; that they learn how to discuss and debate ideas forcefully, and that they write with strength, confidence, and commitment. In short, the reading about educated women is related to the students' own development, and both the reading and the structure of the class are designed to help students overcome their feelings of inadequacy and passivity, and to begin to take themselves seriously as competent and articulate individuals.

We begin by extensive reading and discussion of non-fiction about contemporary feminism, ranging from texts as familiar as *The Feminine Mystique* to the more recent, specialized, and controversial publications of the Women's Liberation Movement. This introductory reading is essential, because it raises the students' consciousness of their feminine identity, and awakens them to awareness of their own experience. Catholic girls, for example, begin to see a distinctive, potentially literary shape to their lives, which they can then recognize as expressed by Mary McCarthy or Bernadette Devlin. Most of the semester is devoted to reading fiction and poetry concerned with the education and the vocation of women; merely discovering that such literature exists can encourage students who have grown accustomed to the fictional female stereotypes of the beautiful and the damned.

Two of the three required papers demand analysis of feminine themes in modern literature. For the third paper, I try to experiment more with the possibilities inherent in the title of the course, "The Educated Woman." The students decide together what they will write for this paper, individually or as a group, about their own education. This past semester they decided to write a history of their shared experience in the course—their evolving consciousness of a feminine perspective as well as their responses to the reading and discussion—and have it reproduced for distribution to the next class in the spring.

My students have been enthusiastic and highly motivated, in part because they have the opportunity to participate in a pioneering field; good papers not only circulate in the classroom, but many hold interest for the college community, and occasionally, for the press. One result of their involvement is that the students' critical ability and particularly their writing has improved significantly during the semesters of this course. My primary concern is to foster such improvement. I do not, however, recommend that freshmen courses on women be established merely for the sake of better writing. Women are not just another special-interest group among students who can be lured into identification with their reading, and thereby motivated to produce better criticism. Ideally, introductory courses focusing on women could serve as the academic equivalent of decontamination chambers, helping freshmen women unlearn some of the damaging patterns of behavior to which they have been conditioned, and preparing them to make the fullest use of their education and their lives.

Entirely different emphases, however, prevail in upper-level courses, in which the essential questions relate to achievement, rather than identity. This spring, for example, I am teaching a lecture course on the woman writer in the twentieth century, in which we are discussing thirty-five American and English authors from Kate Chopin to Susan Sontag. Such segregation may be offensive to traditionalists, who feel that Kate Chopin should fight for her place against Stephen Crane on an open market; or to some feminists who resent any implication that the woman writer is a different species than her male counterpart. Yet there are practical and intellectual reasons for establishing some separate courses dealing with women writers, who represent, after all, the second oldest female profession.

To the feminists, first, I would say that we cannot

change literary history or reinterpret a tradition overnight. We cannot create women writers where they do not exist, and we must recognize that in English literature few exist before the nineteenth century. Women writers should not be studied as a distinct group on the assumption that they write alike, or even display stylistic resemblances distinctively feminine. But women do have a special literary history susceptible to analysis, which includes such complex considerations as the economics of their relation to the literary marketplace; the effects of social and political changes in women's status upon individuals, and the implications of stereotypes of the woman writer and restrictions of her artistic autonomy.

To the traditionalists I would say that the contribution of women writers has been ignored too long. Although I would like to see more women on the reading lists, I would not anticipate more from that sort of reform at present than appeasement or tokenism, the addition of Aphra Behn or Elizabeth Barrett Browning. An entire course makes more sense, because when women are studied as a group, their history and experience reveal patterns which are almost impossible to perceive if they are studied only in their relation to male writers. In the modern languages, where 55 percent of the graduate students are women, it seems important to recognize that this experience and this tradition exist; to acknowledge that women have created literature and are not merely handmaidens to it.

Finally, there are vast curricular possibilities for thematic courses or seminars dealing with sexual identity and literature. My husband and I taught a seminar together on "Sexual Themes in American Novels of the 1960s," in which we considered sexual stereotypes, literary treatment of the erotic, obscenity and pornography in contemporary fiction, contrasting uses of sexual themes by male and female authors. Reading included *Couples, The Group, The American Dream*, and *Portnoy's Complaint*, as well as a wide selection of underground and popular fiction, most of it chosen by students; and background material in psychology, sociology, and law. We discovered several consistent and irreconcilable differences of critical interpretation which depended on the sex of the reader. Men, for example, liked the lyrical rhapsodies on erotic themes in *Couples*, while women found them slightly absurd; on the other hand, men found the sexual descriptions in *The Group* deliberately mocking and sardonic, while women insisted that they were merely realistic.

Topics for such seminars, many of which would offer excellent opportunities for team teaching, are numerous. The MLA membership has in fact voted in favor of the resolution for new courses in the humanities, as described by Lillian Robinson in the *Newsletter* last March, courses investigating "stereotypes of sexual attributes; social influence of literary fantasy; gender as a factor in critical point of view; the female body as symbol; literary investigations of female psychology; literature intended for the female audience; and literary relations between sex and style."

Therefore, for those who cannot wholeheartedly adopt my approach to teaching, an admittedly radical one which concerns itself with the effects of education on the students' lives, as well as on their minds, there are yet many possibilities in courses for women and about them. Even a conservative literary curriculum should include consideration of the woman writer, the image of women in literature, and the literary treatment of feminism. We can at least rid our disciplines, and ourselves, of antifeminine bias. The very term "feminine," applied to literature, has been a pejorative. It is simply not true, as a colleague once told me, that women have written no autobiographies worth teaching, or, as Norman Mailer claims, that all lady writers are quaintsy, dikey, or bitchy.

Further, we can all develop sensitivity to the masculine tone of much of our literature and criticism. Anaesthetized to a masculine terminology, we often overlook its implications. In Wordsworth's dictum that "the poet is a man speaking to men," for example, the poet is male and the audience is mixed, since Wordsworth invariably used the term "poetess" for a woman, and since women of his day figured significantly as an audience for poetry, but not in its composition. Such a distinction becomes meaningful when Wordsworth's statement is quoted in criticism of Anne Sexton, as in a recent issue of the *Partisan Review*.[1] Literary history affords us infinite contrasts of masculine

---

[1] G. S. Fraser, "Public Voices," *Partisan Review*, no. 2, 1970, p. 300.

and feminine experience, from the broadest considerations of the themes of courtly love, romantic love, and seduction, to biographic contrasts between individual writers.

Having their experience dignified by inclusion in the literary curriculum would not work miracles for women students, but it would be an important recognition of the value of the feminine perspective. For the more radical teacher, male or female, teaching women could be the new frontier of education. The willingness of women teachers to make relevant aspects of their personal lives accessible to their students, the willingness of men teachers to forego the privileges of male authority, could have enormous influences on the ways women students visualize themselves and their future roles. Through the discovery of women's history and achievements, they might develop a new faith in the validity of their own thoughts and feelings. At the least, we might anticipate such attention to produce livelier classes, serious and committed writing, and a higher level of ambition in women students. But I think it would also carry over to other areas of the students' lives, and that a generation of confident women students might produce a new and exciting feminist criticism, and perhaps even a new literature.

# SEXISM IN HISTORY

*RUTH ROSEN*

For centuries, historians have paid homage to the female muse Clio as their source of genius. This Goddess of History, however, has shared the fate of most women; she has quietly served and inspired while her own history has remained unwritten.

Today, the role of woman as muse is growing increasingly unacceptable. Rather than inspiring historians, women are now reshaping history itself. Stimulated by their rising social and political consciousness, women are beginning to rethink and rewrite their past from a feminist perspective. Clio is finally being liberated.

Despite the spiraling interest in Women's History, however, many attitudes which inform the writing of history have remained unquestioned and, even worse, undiscussed. How, for example, do we begin to recreate the past? Which sources do we explore? Which movements and which women do we emphasize? What are the personal and political implications of such study? Unless we seriously consider the attitudes, methods and content that will create Women's History, we may end up perpetuating the very sexist attitudes we would ideally destroy.

To begin with, let's consider the nature of sexism. It is a word that has been overused and underdefined. Sexism, like racism, is an ideology of oppression. Sexism includes

*RUTH ROSEN is a doctoral candidate in history at the University of California, Berkeley, where she teaches a course on Women in American history.*

all ideas and attitudes which are based on the fundamental belief in the natural inferiority of women.

The sexism in historical writing is not much different from the sexism that one encounters in daily situations. When women appear at all in history texts, they are usually regarded as the domestic scenery behind the real actors and real action of national life. This should hardly be surprising. History, after all, is usually written by professional historians whose ideas and values reflect the attitudes of our dominant white male culture. It is they who have defined both the "nature" of history *and* the "nature" of woman.

What is the "nature" of history? Traditional history has been most concerned with the recreation of the elite intellectual, military, economic, and political powers who controlled other people's lives. The "history" books which proudly line our library shelves mostly described diplomatic decisions, military maneuvers, and economic exchanges.

Recent social pressure by minority groups, however, has created a new awareness of cultural voids in historical writing. New interest in working class culture, black, and Chicano studies, and yes, even Women's History, has led historians to question the nature of this traditional concept of history. Resurrecting the history of the oppressed, recreating the voice of the inarticulate, and giving life to the muted discontent of the enslaved have more and more become the subject of socially dedicated history.

Though the nature of history has been challenged, the "nature" of woman has not. The American woman still sees herself defined primarily as a female who happens to be a human being, while men are viewed as human beings who happen to be male.[1] Women's biological function of childbearing still justifies their meager participation in society, while men's ability to father children is only of incidental relevance to their social and economic status. Most forms of written and visual media still portray the American woman as the happy recipient of a biologically determined destiny. In short, American men and women continue to be

[1] Aileen Kraditor, *Up from the Pedestal*, Chicago: Quadrangle, 1968, p. 24. This is another way of stating what Aileen Kraditor describes as an old myth: "that men are male *humans* whereas women are human *females.*"

educated, conditioned, and bombarded with images of woman's natural inferiority.

Consequently, there is a serious problem in the writing of Women's History. While historians are beginning to resurrect women's past, they are burdened with their stereotypes and prejudices of the present. Unless historians' own experiences challenge their conditioned responses concerning the proper role of women in society, they have little but their prejudices with which to guide them into the unfamiliar world of female feelings, motivations and ideas.

It is no wonder, then, that Women's History has been the Waterloo for many a competent and sincere historian. Recreating the past has never been an easy task. Recreating women's past is an especially formidable job. It is no accident that women (as well as blacks, Chinese, immigrant groups) have been characterized as mysterious, deceitful, or childlike and capricious. Those without any real power must resort to all indirect means of survival. Women's past, like their present, is filled with the unfamiliar language of the oppressed.

Coy behavior, for example, can be interpreted as an example of woman's generally sweet nature, or it can be seen as a skill developed for manipulating men's power. In a society where women obtain no real social or economic power of their own, such manipulation is every woman's means for survival. As another example, a woman's written desire to be a man can be viewed as evidence of her lack of womanly fulfillment or as her expressed desire for the social, economic, and political privileges of a male-supremacist society.

The language with which women have expressed their feelings, then, has often been deliberately developed to avoid male comprehension. Writers of Black History soon learned that the external obediency of the lackey often concealed the inner rage of the slave. Writers of Women's History will also have to learn to decipher the language and actions of women in the past.

When scanning general historical texts, I am no longer shocked to find women characterized as docile, passive, fragile, inane creatures. I am no longer surprised to find an author dismissing a woman with the easy familiarity of a superior or discussing a woman's appearance instead of her achievements. In serious monographic studies on women in history, however, I expect more serious consideration of women and their past. Unfortunately, my expectations have remained unfulfilled.

Too often historians write about women without the slightest sympathy for or understanding of their subject, which is, after all, women. Their forewords and prefaces —of which I·am an addicted reader—often reveal their most basic attitudes about women. Such biases indicate a lack of the sympathy and understanding necessary for an adequate and competent treatment of women in history. William O'Neill, for example, wrote the following passage in the preface to his *Everyone Was Brave: The Rise and Fall of Feminism in America* (1969):

> This book, then, is first of all an inquiry into the failure of feminism. . . . To begin with, I have avoided the question of whether or not women ought to have full parity with men. Such·a state of affairs obtains nowhere in the modern world and so, since we cannot know what genuine equality would mean in practice, its desirability cannot fairly be assessed.[2]

We need only substitute the word black for women, and white for men, to see the level of sympathy he reveals:

> This book, then, is first of all an inquiry into the failure of the *Black Movement*. . . . To begin with, I have avoided the question of whether or not *blacks* ought to have full parity with *whites*. Such a state of affairs obtains nowhere in the modern world and so, since we cannot know what genuine equality would mean in practice, its desirability cannot be fairly assessed.

I begin to wonder whether this would still be considered serious history or simply racist propaganda.

Page Smith, in his introduction to *Daughters of the Promised Land* (1970), not only revealed his private opinion of

2 William O'Neill, *Everyone Was Brave: The Rise and Fall of Feminism in America*. Chicago: 1969, p. viii.

his wife, but also the smugness of his attitude toward women's past:

> The writing of this book owes nothing to my wife. She viewed the whole enterprise with undisguised skepticism, interrupted me frequently to ask if the Joneses would make good dinner partners with the Browns, or whether the Thompsons will go with the Johnsons, seduced me from my labors with delicious meals (so that my girth grew with my book) and, most unnerving of all, said periodically, "How you could pretend to know anything about women . . ." Which of course I don't.[3]

Professor Page then goes on to prove this ignorance in the following three hundred and ninety-two pages of his eight dollar and ninety-five cent book.

The problem is that most historians begin their journey into women's past with a sexist definition of women's nature. In his chapter on "The Nature of Women," for example, Page Smith announces that "Anyone who writes about women has to confront, sooner or later, the question of the nature of woman."[4] The assumption that women, or any other social group, have an "identifiable nature" is a crude form of pseudo-biological determinism. Such assumptions are always at the root of racist and sexist thought.

Smith's definition of woman's nature leads him to make conclusions that will surely return to haunt his reputation as an historian. Consider, for example, the following declarations on woman's nature:

> A woman "is"; a man is always in the process of becoming.

and

> A man wishes for an audience of millions; a woman will create for one man she loves.[5]

---

[3] Page Smith, *Daughters of the Promised Land.* Boston: Little, Brown. 1970, p. v.

[4] *Ibid.,* p. 307.

[5] *Ibid.,* p. 318.

Such conclusions are not analyzed as the socially conditioned responses of an underprivileged and oppressed social group; they are stated as the eternally true, biologically determined facts of the female condition. Historical writing about women should instead determine what forces and attitudes in the socialization of women in American society create such female behavior.

Most of Smith's conclusions are simply outrageous because he accepts woman's socially conditioned role and behavior as her real and inherent "nature." Women, he decides, are not as sexually motivated as men, because they do not respond to traditional pornography. It never occurs to him that women may be less stimulated by such performances because females are usually depicted as the victims and slaves of sexual abuse, rather than as equal participants in sexual pleasure. In yet another historical gem, Smith states that women rarely make great chefs. "A woman's cooking is personal," he declares, "she cooks for those she loves and wishes to nurture; thus her cooking is sacramental."[6]

This is the same kind of historical analysis that not so long ago concluded the black slaves were the happy, contented, mindless servants of their beneficent masters. Women, in Smith's view, love their "natural" position as domestics. The fact that women are socialized from infancy to accept cooking and cleaning as acts of personal devotion is never mentioned. The fact that women are systematically discouraged from receiving professional and economic status for their labors as cooks, janitors, teachers in the home, etc., is ignored.

In one final admonition, Smith authoritatively defines the natural boundaries of the female role. "Unless women respect this order," he warns, "childhood, girlhood, motherhood, and grandmotherhood, they will end up frustrated and unhappy wayfarers in the valley of the dolls."[7] Their biological "nature" as mothers determines their social position. Women are not "meant" to be lawyers, historians, or chefs.

Such nonsense is by no means a rarity in historical writing. William O'Neill, for example, repeatedly used the

[6] *Ibid.,* p. 313.

[7] *Ibid.,* p. 315.

term "spouse surrogate" to define the intense relationships that suffragists had with one another and with the movement in general. He could not view women outside of their relationship to and need for a "spouse." If women are viewed only as mothers, wives, daughters, and sisters, then historical writing must result in flagrant distortions of their past.

Women's Histories are filled with such false assumptions about woman's nature. And these attitudes are not always held by male historians. Mary Massey (*Bonnet Brigades*), for example, in her study of women during the civil war, asserted that it is "woman's nature to prefer working with a group."[8] Mildred Adams (*The Right to Be People*) wrote how Mrs. Catt's organizing efforts were impeded by "the innate frivolity of feminine minds."[9] The examples are numerous; the conclusions disappointing.

Writing and thinking about Women's History, however, is not an impossible task. It does require serious consideration of the subject . . . women. Eleanor Flexnor, in her narrative of the women's suffrage movement, *Century of Struggle* (1959), treats women's intellectual activities, economic position, and educational needs as serious historical problems. Though a fairly dry narrative, her book is noticeably free from assumptions about women's nature and mocking condescension. Interested in women's activities and ideas, Flexnor does not dwell on women's marital status, sex life, or children unless such information has direct historical relevance. Unlike William O'Neill, who emphasized every woman's social and sexual relationships to men, Flexnor treats intellectual and activist women as she would have treated their male counterparts, that is, seriously.

In the *Emancipation of the American Woman*, Andrew Sinclair explores more topical problems in Women's History, such as the "Lady" in American culture and the effects of religion on women's lives. This serious investigation into women's social history successfully integrates women into the broader context of American social movements.

A final example is Aileen Kraditor's work in both *Up from the Pedestal* (1969) and *Ideas of the Women's Suf-*

---

[8] Mary Massey, *Bonnet Brigades*. New York: Knopf, 1967. p. 33.

[9] Mildred Adams, *The Right to Be People*. Philadelphia: Lippincott, 1966, p. 96.

*frage Movement* (1965). Both books are fine intellectual and social histories which analyze the racism and xenophobia of feminist Progressive ideas, and the social and economic origins of their thought.

These works are only a few examples of what can be done in the writing of Women's History. To approach women's past, we must recognize two things; first, the objective facts of women's oppression according to their age, race, and class position, and secondly, that while women may tend to exhibit certain well conditioned behavior patterns, this far from constitutes a readily indentifiable nature.

Furthermore, the history of women must not focus solely on men's images of women, as in Kate Millet's literary history, *Sexual Politics*. Studying society's general mythology and folklore about women is only one side of women's past. Women's History is also the resurrection of women's *own* past thoughts and actions.

There has also been a tendency to study only one group of women in history. We should not, for example, focus our study solely on the exciting but limited ideas and actions of the women's rights movement of the nineteenth century. Women's past is also the history of the silent and inarticulate; your grandmother and mine, garment workers and housewives, seamstresses and saloon keepers. To resurrect these forgotten voices, we must be creative with our sources; humor, folk-music, magazines, letters, and diaries should be explored.

In seeking the history of lost women in the past, however, we should not ignore those more privileged women who articulated what many women could not and dared not say. Women's History is also the history of these capable voices from the past. Women of all classes offer insights into the kinds of oppression and humiliation that women have experienced, as well as into the system which perpetuates such brutality.

Finally, we must be alert to the dangers of whitewashing women's past. The history of the women's movement in the United States, for example, is shamefully filled with racist argument for suffrage. That is, many white women argued that women should be allowed to vote in order to outvote blacks in the South and immigrants in the North. Such a plea for liberation based on the continued exploitation of others must be exposed and examined for its important implications for the women's movement today. We should not shy away from such ugliness in women's past. Not every woman is a sister. Not every woman is a saint. Every woman is simply human.

One cannot assume that every woman was either a docile servant or a rebellious feminist. Obviously, some women could and did accept the limitations of their narrowly defined social role. Other women boldly risked ridicule and condemnation in their serious efforts to broaden the boundaries of those female roles. Most women, however—terrified of losing men's physical and economic protection—concealed their rage in ways that have yet to be identified.

Women's History is the record of all these responses to the female's role in society. Sometimes it is the story of untold tragedy; the history of wasted lives. Other times it is the story of untold greatness; the history of hidden genius and actions. One thing is certain; if one is serious about women, then serious history will be written.

# VI.
# View from
# the Desk

# TEACHING IS A GOOD PROFESSION ... FOR A WOMAN

*ADRIA REICH*

You're a young teacher, and you're in the middle of the first semester, explaining to your tenth-grade history class how the U.S. began bombing North Vietnam; you've been describing the government's duplicity with passion, using the Pentagon Papers to support your point; you pause for a moment, reflecting, and someone in front of you observes calmly, "You've got a run in your stocking, Mrs. Marks." You flush, say thanks, and finish up on American foreign policy in 1964, deflated.

"I always thought I would be a teacher. At least as far back as sixth grade, when I had my first male teacher and had a mad crush on him. But, by the time I got out of high school, I had given up on the idea of being a teacher, because teachers were so straight and oppressive. I hated women teachers especially. They were always so tense and nervous. Then I got out of college, and what else could I do? Working in an office would drive me even nuttier than teaching does. I could not type twenty-two words a minute. I was overqualified for stuff like factory work or nontyping clerical work. It wasn't so much that I wanted to be a teacher, but I couldn't imagine being anything else."

*"My family was lower class. My brother and I and the kids from one other family on the block were the only ones to go to college from our neighborhood. I was programmed*

*ADRIA REICH is an editor of* The Red Pencil, *a Boston-area radical teachers' journal.*

*to either nursing or teaching. These seemed like good things—they would provide security in case I had to support a family. Since I didn't like blood, teaching was the best option. It was one step beyond civil-service jobs."*

"My mother was always telling me: 'Teaching is a good profession for a woman' or 'Teachers have such good hours' or 'It's a career you can always go back to.' And I knew what she meant by that. She wanted me to get married, and she thought teaching would combine well with marriage— you get home early enough to cook a good dinner for your husband; you can take five or ten years off to raise your kids, and then when they are ready for school, you too can go back to school, and be home in time to take care of them. It never sounded like such a great deal to me. I thought there had to be more to life than spending it in school. But I never did find any other decent options. The hardest part was doing what my mother wanted me to do."

*"I felt somehow that teaching would be less compromising than a lot of other things; that working with kids would mean something. It had social value. But there were a lot of feelings, when I dropped out of graduate school to become a teacher, that I was inadequate, that deciding to be a schoolteacher was a failure in some way. I remember that my boyfriend at that time said that he felt he had to keep telling people I had dropped out of school. That there was something that really upset him about my becoming a teacher."*

Why do women become teachers? Channeling from Mother, guidance counselors, teachers; a lack of other options; social concern, a desire to work with people; feelings of academic inadequacy; a B.A. and no typing skills. Emerging from this mixture of positive, but mostly negative reasons comes the decision to be a teacher. Given the options, it's a choice that makes sense.

Teaching is one of the only jobs available to women with a "mere" B.A. that does not put us directly at the service of a man. It is one of the only jobs in which women are more than adornment. Responding to impersonal bells all day may be horrible, but bells are clearly preferable to a boss telling you to hurry up with his coffee. Teaching from a prescribed curriculum guide may be constraining, but it is certainly preferable to typing words you had no part in writing. And once a teacher is in the classroom, behind a closed door, she does have some discretion over what goes on.

In other words, teaching, because it is a profession (albeit low status) does offer some job control, some prestige; and, the teaching profession, because it is predominately women, avoids some of the blatant sexism common to other jobs.

> *It is true that sentimental reasons are often given for the almost exclusive employment of women in the common schools; but the effective reason is economy . . . If women had not been cheaper than men they would not have replaced 9/10 of the men in American public schools."*
>
> CHARLES ELIOT
> *President of Harvard*

The process which eventually led to women standing in front of a classroom began over a century ago in America. Between 1840 and 1860, the percentage of men teaching school in Massachusetts went from 60 percent to 14 percent. Although crude, Eliot's statement that this was an economy measure seems essentially correct. The feminization of the teaching profession coincided with several important changes in the economic and social character of America.

Growth of American business and industrialization was creating new job opportunities for men; the increase in the number of immigrants expanded the population that primary schools had to serve, without expanding the tax base. Obviously something had to be done to expand the number of teachers without increasing the funds available to the schools. The school boards saw the solution in (1) feminizing and expanding the primary-school teaching force; and (2) decreasing the number of masters (always men) needed for those well-to-do students pursuing further education, by creating centralized high schools.

In other words, women were hired because it seemed natural for them to work with little children and because they would be cheap . . . not because those doing the hiring believed that women were capable of doing important work, making important decisions. Hence, there have always been more women in the primary schools than in the secondary schools, and there have always been very few women in administrative positions.

The current statistics are reflective of these trends. In 1967, 85 percent of primary school teachers were women, 68 percent of the profession as a whole. In secondary schools, men held a bare majority. Women are 25 percent of elementary, 4 percent of junior high, and 10 percent of senior-high principals. In both elementary and secondary schools, the percentage has declined since 1950. According to the NEA, there are at most a handful of women superintendents in the country. Furthermore, women in 1960 constituted only 10 percent of school board members. More than half of all school boards have no women members.

This is more than interesting background; these statistics have very real consequences for women teaching in the public schools. They indicate that while women are in the majority in most schools, we don't have the power that derives from numbers, because we are underrepresented in the decision-making positions. Ironically, the imbalance between women and men teachers is used to justify the opposite imbalance (more men than women) in the authority positions. The logic goes something like this: we need more men in the schools. In order to bring in and retain men, they have to be given some incentive. Men have families to support; men have to be able to move up, both in salary and prestige.

All of us have heard this argument. It might be used as an explanation of why a woman did not get to be class adviser (which may carry with it several hundred dollars) or why a woman was not chosen to be part of a curriculum workshop (which often means release time and extra pay). Or we might simply have overheard such conversations in teachers' rooms. It is hard for a woman to respond in that situation—hard to sort out our own interests and anger, our view of what the best learning situation would be for the kids, and the interests of the administration in proposing the change in ratios.

On a certain level it does seem important to have integrated teaching staffs (especially in the elementary schools where imbalance is greatest). If any type of sex equality is to be achieved in America, people have to see that working with children is not simply women's work. And children should see that men as well as women can be responsive, sympathetic, capable of tenderness; that these are human qualities, not just male or female qualities.

These, however, are not usually the reasons the educational authorities and administrators favor male advancements. They tend to take basic sex roles in society as given and desirable. Men are (and should be) aggressive, bold, inventive, energetic, strong. Women are (and should be) passive, shy, gentle, sweet, and kind. By this logic, if boys are to grow into healthy adult men, they need "real men" around them, providing a model for them. And, conversely, it is harmful for boys to attend school in a predominately feminine environment where they will be weakened, made effete.

If women teachers create such a narrow, "prissy" environment, why aren't the administrators similarly concerned about what will become of the girl students? Why is there no worry about how girls will relate to all these "masculine" new teachers? The assumption underlying all of this seems to be that it's the boy students who count. They will be the future leaders, the men who will build our tomorrow, while the primary function for girls will be as wives and mothers.

In reality, of course, as any of us who have worked in sex-integrated faculties can attest, there are both male and female teachers who limit the interest, potential creativity and strengths of both boys and girls by stressing obedience to all the minute regulations of the school, neatness, and punctuality. And there are both male and female teachers who react against those standards and try to help their students question and analyze. If the first type of teacher predominates over the second, we need to look beyond sex-imbalance or feminization for an explanation.

Those fearing the "feminization" of boys in school are forgetting the important point that schools educate both girls and boys for social roles and for jobs in the labor force. All children are being channeled into a bureaucratic and corporate America. Workers are expected to perform narrow, impersonal tasks, to meet regulations someone else fixes. The behaviors and values traditionally associated with "real men" may have no place in this society. When you look for basic causes for the problems of schools, you have to look at the demands of the society, not at particular sex ratios.

Certainly, increasing the number of male teachers will not change these realities. In fact, if the only way to bring more men into the schools is to create more hierarchies and hence more chances for promotion, (both the state Department of Education and the Massachusetts Teachers Association have made proposals calling for team leaders, master teachers, etc.) the schools will become an even more efficient training ground for the corporate bureaucracy than they are now. Students will see their teachers jockeying for position, competing for advancement.

Women teachers can't afford to ignore these proposals, or the assumptions and fears that underlie them. As the unemployment rate (especially among college graduates) grows, so does the "teacher surplus." Women are no longer facing just the question of promotions, but rather of who gets hired, retained, and finally given tenure. It seems almost the reverse of the situation in the 1840s and '50s, when the expanding industrial and commercial opportunities lured men away from teaching. As men find their way back into the schools, where does that leave us?

Everywhere we go to apply for teaching positions we are made to feel guilty that there are so many of us—young women teachers, with lots of ideas, and often with little or no experience. Sometimes they are even honest with us; they tell us that if a man comes along with the same qualifications, he'll almost certainly get the job. After all, these are "tough kids," or it's a "tough school," or the kids could use a man to relate to. If we're married they seem suspicious we might have a baby; if we are single, they wonder when we'll get married and quit.

And even if we get a job, it is harder for us to hold on to it. In trying to integrate into the life of the school, women face built-in (structural) difficulties. Because the teachers' rooms are usually sex-segregated, and often the tables in the lunchroom are, we don't get to have a smoke with or joke with the "people who count"—the coaches, the Union representatives, the Department Chairmen. We can never be "one of the guys."

Furthermore, for the most part, the "guys" don't feel comfortable around us. They don't know what to make of a young, intelligent, aggressive woman (which is what you have to be to get the job in the first place!) Sometimes we can overcome this discomfort, by getting to know the few women they do accept, by working for the Union and having beers before Union meetings, by smiling sweetly at the right times. But it's hard—much harder than for a new male teacher. And, of course, hanging over us always, is the threat that they will have no trouble replacing us with someone who does fit in better.

There have been attempts by women in the school systems in this area to do something about this situation. In cases where there is clear discrimination, women are trying legal actions. Most school systems have laws requiring a woman to stop teaching by her fifth or sixth month of pregnancy and forbidding her to return to her position until a year from the first September after the baby is born. (All without any compensation, of course.) In Newton, a case has been filed by a woman who gave birth in August, and a male teacher at the same school, whose wife gave birth the same month. As a man, he, of course, faces no restrictions on his return to work.

Women in several liberal high schools (Lincoln–Sudbury, Newton South) have succeeded in getting the schools to set up nursery programs, to which they can bring their children. By approaching a school system in pairs, some women have managed to convince administrators to hire two part-time people for one job. In several suburban systems (Weston, Brookline, Newton) women teachers have begun to find new ways to talk to each other and female students by offering women's courses, mini-courses or discussion groups.

But for most women teachers, for whom none of these special actions are possible or appropriate, the best immediate step is to get together with other teachers facing a similar situation. Several groups of women teachers who met at a workshop at the Teacher Center (a drop-in storefront for teachers) have begun meeting regularly to support each other, to talk about teaching, and particularly the problems of being a woman teacher. In the short run, such discussions make it easier to survive in the schools; in the long run they may lead to some programs for action.

# THE HARVARD ED SCHOOL

*BETSEY USEEM*

By comparison with other graduate schools at Harvard, the Education School seems a haven for women in a male dominated university. There are more women enrolled there—46 percent—than in any of the other professional schools or in the Graduate School of Arts and Sciences. And in fact, women at the Ed School don't experience some of the more blatant aspects of male chauvinism that plague other graduate women at Harvard.

But on closer inspection, it is obvious that men dominate the school's administration. Too, male faculty and students receive preferential treatment in hiring and admissions. It should be clear first of all that women are welcome at the Ed School not because of any commitment on its part to train large numbers of female "educational leaders" but simply because so few qualified men (until very recently) have been attracted to careers in education. For decades public-school teaching has been considered a "woman's field" and the low pay and prestige associated with it has kept men out of that occupation. Second, within the Ed School it is obvious that women are predominantly enrolled in programs that won't train them for positions of "leadership" in education. For example, while women comprise 63 percent of the students in the Master of Arts in Teaching program, they constitute only 31 percent of the doctoral candidates.

Furthermore, in certain doctoral programs, women are shockingly underrepresented, particularly in the Administrative Career Program which "prepares candidates primarily for positions of major administrative responsibility in American education . . ." (HGSE Catalogue, 1969–1970). Only 6 percent of the students in that training program are women. A survey of the alumni of the Ed School carried out in 1964 indicates that this merely continues a traditional pattern—the percentage of women graduates who become administrators has always been very low. Of those alumni who are still in education, 36 percent of the males are administrators; only 9 percent of the women are.

According to knowledgeable sources in the Ed School, the problem isn't just that few women apply to the administrative training program—they have been systematically discouraged all along the line from doing so; it is also that the competent women who *do* apply are often discriminated against on the basis of sex. Male faculty members in Administration have a sexist notion of the ideal school administrator and this attitude provides a convenient rationalization for maintaining a male-dominated department and profession. There seems to be a curious double standard at work in the matter of whether or not to recruit men or women to certain programs of study. Men are encouraged to apply to the teacher-training programs because Ed School officials believe it's important to have adult male role models for young male students in public-school classrooms. On the other hand, despite the fact that women are as underrepresented in administrative roles as men are in teaching roles, there seems to be no attempt to recruit women to become educational administrators so that they can serve as models for girls to emulate.

Faculty members admit that doctoral programs that have traditionally had high percentages of female students—e.g., Human Development, with 73 percent female enrollment this year—seek out male candidates, and are likely to accept a less qualified male applicant over a female one.

Those women who are in the Ed School's teacher-training program are rarely exposed to a classroom discussion of the problems that will confront them as women in the teaching profession. For example, women are usually forced to leave their teaching jobs regardless of their own wishes soon after they become pregnant. Moreover, women who want to continue teaching on a part-time basis after they have children find it extremely difficult to locate half-time teaching positions. And even if they find such a job, they cannot find inexpensive day care centers for their children. These reforms will never be gained unless women teachers collectively put pressure on school and community officials. But the need for this kind of pressure is seldom discussed in teacher-training courses.

One reason issues relevant to women are so infrequently dealt with by the faculty is that almost all of the faculty members are men. There is only one female full professor—and only one female associate professor. Twenty-one percent of the assistant professors and 19 percent of the lecturers are women. Altogether, in a school where almost a third of the doctoral students are women, only 15 percent of the faculty members are female.

There are other more subtle ways in which women who are students at the Ed School are treated by males as something less than equals. Many male professors appear to be as interested in a student's physical attractiveness as in her intellectual capabilities. It is reported that in one "shop," expressions of male-chauvinist attitudes reach an annual high when faculty members are choosing their advisees—comments like "I'll take her; she's good looking," are not uncommon. And male faculty often crack "clever" jokes about the academic prowess or "inherent" personality characteristics of women. For example, one professor opened his class with the following joke—"A professor can always distinguish his male from his female students . . . when he says 'good morning' to a class, the men reply 'good morning,' and the women just write it down."

There are clear signs that in at least one respect the position of women at the Ed School will get worse before it gets better. Because of a budget crisis, the Ed School is going through a period of rather drastic retrenchment. It is expected that a substantial percentage of the faculty will not be rehired in the next few years—perhaps as many as one third of the faculty members will be forced to leave and no replacements will be hired. This cutback will primarily affect junior faculty—and since all but two of the women who are currently teaching are either lecturers or assistant professors, this means that they will be among those not rehired. Hence the percentage of women on the faculty, already ridiculously low, will most likely be reduced even further. And that curtailment will merely serve to reinforce the atmosphere and the channeling notions that prevail at all levels of the school.

# WOMEN AND THE PDKs

*JOHN ASKINS*

> *Phi Delta Kappa's light preserve,*
> *Where men the sons of men do serve.*
> *Loyal hearts have lit the flame*
> *Where shines the beacon of her name . . .*
> — *"Phi Delta Kappa's Light"*

Yet another front: A small, drab office in the University of Michigan's School of Education building containing Eric Warden and his indignation over the reluctance of Phi Delta Kappa to admit women members.

Phi Delta Kappa is an honorary fraternity for male educators only. It used to be for WHITE male educators only, but that was changed in the 1940s. Now a growing but still minor number of its members want to eliminate the last restriction.

PDK is supposed to be a professional fraternity, they argue, and women comprise 70 percent of the teaching profession. But so far the 85,000-member international organization has not exactly embraced the idea of sexual integration.

When the UM chapter sent in an initiation list with the names of two women on it a couple of years ago, the list was sent right back for correction.

After a good deal of discussion the local chapter sent back a revised list sans women that was accepted.

*JOHN ASKINS is a staff writer for the Detroit Free Press.*

The two women were initiated locally, however, and more have been added since then.

There are organizations like Phi Delta Kappa for women but they don't have as much clout professionally. Most high-level educational administrators are men and PDK provides contacts the others can't. A New York woman has filed suit in federal court against the international, claiming her career had been damaged by her inability to become a member.

Men who wanted women in PDK made their first run at the international in 1969, at the 32nd Biennial Council in San Diego, where out of several hundred votes they managed to muster twenty-two. At the 33rd biennial last December the vote was 321–394.

That council also voted to suspend chapters that insist on sending initiation lists with women on them. The Cornell University chapter did that and was suspended.

It sounded as though the nation's male educators did not like women. One recalcitrant Kappan is reported to have said that allowing women would be like "letting in black widow spiders."

"You get all kinds of silly rationalization," Warden says, "Like one person said, 'If you let women in this organization, do you really think your wife is going to let you come to these conventions?' "

Still, he thinks the delegates to the biennial councils are not representative Kappans. The dice were loaded against women, he says. "The Biennials have always been held immediately after Christmas. The kind of guy who would leave his family on December 26 or even the night of the 25th so he can go to a fraternity meeting is not the kind of guy you want voting on the admission of women to Phi Delta Kappa."

A survey of PDK members nationally showed that nearly 40 percent favor the admission of women, so Warden may be correct. But 40 percent is still not all that overwhelming. One wonders what the other 60 percent is teaching students about women.

The main opposition to opening membership to women comes from PDK field chapters, Warden says—small-town units of as few as twenty members, whose meetings he characterizes as more social than professional.

They just hate to give up the "night out with the boys," he thinks.

Other big campus chapters around the country, however, have been initiating women locally and pressing the international to change its stance, including Harvard, Stanford and Columbia. The future of Phi Delta Kappa may be at stake.

An editorial in the fraternity's respected magazine, "The Kappan," this past February urged dissidents to stay in PDK and work for change instead of leaving. "Note that the favorable vote two years ago was just twenty-two," it said. "The ninety-five votes for admission of women registered by delegates at the Urbana council represents a growth of 332 percent in just two years.

"If that change rate were to be maintained—and it is not impossible in this volatile period—then approval at the 34th council in 1973 would be inevitable."

Warden says: "I think if that doesn't happen, they're going to lose some of the most important chapters they have, including us.

"When you come right down to it, the organization just isn't that important. If it can't get in step with admitting women, it ought to just fold up and wither away."

# PARA-PROFESSIONAL

*CLEO SILVERS*

When I worked as an Educational Assistant at Public School 51 in the Bronx a few years ago, my salary was $50.00 a week. This is still the salary of the majority of Educational Assistants working in New York City schools. When I worked as a Community Mental Health worker at Lincoln Hospital, my salary was $6,000 and the psychiatrists' salaries were from $13,500 to $15,000, a sizable difference.

Along with these poor salaries we para-professionals do not even receive any degree of respect for our work inside these agencies. In PS 51, my first para-professional job, I was expected to assist the teacher inside the classroom, take attendance, make pretty bulletin boards, act as policewoman in the hall, control the children, and go into the homes of problem children to speak to their parents. Often I had to calm down parents who had come to school to protest over a teacher's violation of their child's rights or about a cultural insult his child had received in the classroom. I was also expected to represent the school in the community meetings, telling the community people all of the good things about the school. As a community person I went from classroom to hall, expected to administer corporal punishment to loud and overanxious children, since there are laws prohibiting the teachers from doing this.

Even with all of these teacher-related things, I was refused a key to the teachers' restroom. I was told by most teachers on staff that para-professionals really should not share the teachers' lounge for eating lunch as there really wasn't much for us to do or talk about in there. All of the para-professionals in that school went to the children's bathroom (unless a teacher occasionally agreed to lend us her key). I ate lunch with the children, which was much more to my interest, but I always thought the rule was unfair.

At this point another important factor should be brought into the over-all picture. Most para-professionals are women. We make up close to 90 percent of all non-professionals employed in the so-called Human Service fields: hospitals, schools, welfare centers, community agencies, legal service centers, etc. The reason has to do with the nature of the black and Puerto Rican communities and their relationship with the professionals who come into them. Our men are not hired because the administration and its representatives fear their response to this kind of treatment. It would be extremely difficult to continually dehumanize our men without an eventual response. Furthermore, with such inadequate salaries a man could not possibly support a family (although many female para-professionals are the sole support of their families!) We women fall victim to being used to oppress our people since we are seen to be more suitable in this regard than men.

It must be pointed out here that my experience as an Educational Assistant was not unique. The degrading incident I described before is not an isolated experience, as some might want to claim or believe. This kind of thing, small but telling, is experienced every day whether in the schools, hospitals, Welfare Department, or any other Human Service agency. Its occurrence should not be surprising, because the para-professionals exist precisely to solidify the position of the professionals and their agencies.

# PORTRAIT OF A TEACHER
from *Good Morning, Miss Dove*

*FRANCES GRAY PATTEN*

*American novelists have typically caricatured female teachers in one of two opposite ways, as the pretty young thing or the dried-up old spinster. In reality, these caricatures portray the same woman at different stages in her life. They hark back to a not-so-distant past when, for a woman, marriage and teaching were deemed incompatible. (See the teacher's contract, quoted by Waller, in the Introduction.) Miss Dove is one of the kinder portraits of an aging school marm. Even so, she illustrates the cultural stereotype: to succeed as a teacher, one must fail as a woman.*

At eight-twenty, Miss Dove crossed to the corner of Maple and Grant, where Cedar Grove School sat—redbrick, stolid, with only one cedar left to soften its ugliness, for its grove had been chopped down long before in the interests of level playgrounds. Bill Holloway, the traffic cop on duty, saw her. "She looked as natural as nature," he reported later in a tone of wonder. "I tipped my cap and said: 'Good morning, Miss Dove' and she says, genteel like always, 'Good morning, William.' "

By eight-thirty, some two hundred and fifty children, ranging in age from six to twelve, were safely inside the school building. In various homerooms they gauged, with the uncanny shrewdness of innocence, the various moods of various teachers. How far dared they go today?

But as the morning progressed and the classes went, in turn, to spend forty-five minutes in the geography room with Miss Dove, they dropped their restless speculation.

For Miss Dove had no moods. Miss Dove was a certainty. She would be today what she had been yesterday and would be tomorrow. And so, within limits, would they. Single file they would enter her room. Each child would pause on the threshold as its mother and father had paused, more than likely, and would say—just as the policeman had said—in distinct, formal accents: "Good morning, Miss Dove." And Miss Dove would look directly at each of them, fixing her eyes directly upon theirs, and reply: "Good morning, Jessamine," or "Margaret," or "Samuel." (Never "Sam," never "Peggy," never "Jess." She eschewed familiarity as she wished others to eschew it.) They would go to their appointed desks. Miss Dove would ascend to hers. The lesson would begin.

There was no need to waste time in preliminary admonitions. Miss Dove's rules were as fixed as the signs of the zodiac. And they were known. Miss Dove rehearsed them at the beginning of each school year, stating them as calmly and dispassionately as if she were describing the atmospheric effects of the Gulf Stream. The penalties for infractions of the rules were also known. If a child introduced a foreign object—a pencil, let us say, or a wad of paper, or a lock of hair—into his mouth, he was required to wash out his mouth with the yellow laundry soap that lay on the drainboard of the sink in the corner by the sand table. If his posture was incorrect he had to go and sit for a while upon a stool without a back-rest. If a page in his notebook was untidy, he had to copy it over. If he emitted an uncovered cough, he was expected to rise immediately and fling open a window, no matter how cold the weather, so that a blast of fresh air could protect his fellows from the contamination of his germs. And if he felt obliged to disturb the class routine by leaving the room for a drink of water (Miss Dove loftily ignored any other necessity) he did so to an accompaniment of dead silence. Miss Dove would look at him—that was all—following his departure and greeting his return with her perfectly expressionless gaze and the whole class would sit idle and motionless, until he was back in the fold again. It was easier—even if one had eaten salt fish for breakfast—to remain and suffer.

Of course, there were flagrant offenses that were dealt with in private. Sometimes profanity sullied the air of the geography room. Sometimes, though rarely, open rebellion was displayed. In those instances, the delinquent was detained, minus the comfort of his comrades, in awful seclusion with Miss Dove. What happened between them was never fully known. (Did she threaten him with legal prosecution? Did she beat him with her long mappointer?) The culprit, himself, was unlikely to be communicative on the subject or, if he were, to overdo the business with a tale that revolved to an incredible degree around his own heroism. Afterward, as was duly noted, his classroom attitude was subdued and chastened.

Miss Dove had no rule relating to prevarication. A child's word was taken at face value. If it happened to be false—well, that was the child's problem. A lie, unattacked and undistorted by defense, remained a lie and was apt to be recognized as such by its author.

Occasionally a group of progressive mothers would contemplate organized revolt. "She's been teaching too long," they would cry. "Her pedagogy hasn't changed since we were in Cedar Grove. She rules the children through fear!" They would turn to the boldest one among themselves. "*You* go," they would say. "You go talk to her!"

The bold one would go, but somehow she never did much talking. For there in the geography room, she would begin to feel—though she wore her handsomest tweeds and perhaps a gardenia for courage—that she was about ten years old and her petticoat was showing. Her throat would tickle. She would wonder desperately if she had a clean handkerchief in her bag. She would also feel thirsty. Without firing a shot in the cause of freedom she would retreat ingloriously from the field of battle.

And on that unassaulted field—in that room where no leeway was given to the personality, where a thing was black or white, right or wrong, polite or rude, simply because Miss Dove said it was, there was a curiously soothing quality. The children left it refreshed and restored, ready for fray or frolic. For within its walls they enjoyed what was allowed them nowhere else—a complete suspension of will.

And what did David see as he looked at Miss Dove? How did any of Miss Dove's pupils, past or present, see her? Off hand, that would seem an easy question. There was nothing elusive about Miss Dove's appearance and it had, moreover, remained much the same for more than thirty-five years. When she had begun to teach geography her figure had been spare and angular and it was still so. Her hair was more shadowy than it had once been but, twisted into a meagre little old-maid's-knot, it had never had a chance to show much color. Her thin, unpainted mouth bore no sign of those universal emotions—humor, for instance, and love, and uncertainty—that mark most mouths in the course of time. Her pale, bleached-out complexion never flushed with emotion—a slight pink-ness at the tip of her pointed nose was the only visible indication that ordinary human blood ran through her veins. She wore round-toed black shoes with low, rubber-tapped heels that did not clatter when she walked. Her dress, of some dull-surfaced dark material, was close cousin to the one in which she had made her pedagogical debut: It had the same long sleeves, the same high neck, and the same white linen handkerchief (or one very like) fluted into a fan and pinned to its left bosom. (The hand-kerchief was not for use—Miss Dove did not cough or sneeze in public—, nor was it for ornament. It was a caution to its owner's pupils that it behooved each of them to possess a clean handkerchief, too.) All in all, in bearing and clothing and bony structure, Miss Dove suggested that classic portrait of the eternal teacher that small fry, generation after generation, draw upon fences and side-walks with nubbins of purloined chalk; a grown-up stranger catching his first glimpse of her, might be in-clined to laugh with a kind of relief, as if he'd seen some old, haunting ogress of his childhood turned into a harm-less joke. And then Miss Dove would look at him and all the comedy would ebb from his mind. Her large eyes were quite naked (for she had retained perfect vision) and gray like a flat, calm sea on a cloudy day. They were shrewd and unillusioned; and when one stood exposed to their scrutiny feeling uncomfortably that they penetrated veil upon veil of one's private life and perceived, without astonishment, many hidden—and often unlovely—truths in the deep recesses of one's nature, it was impossible to see anything about Miss Dove as ridiculous. Even the elevated position of her desk—a position deplored by modern educators who seek to introduce equality into the teacher-student relation—was right and proper. The dais of aloof authority suited her as a little hill near Ratisbonne suited Napoleon Bonaparte.

But there was more to Miss Dove. There was something that defies analysis. She had an extra quality as compelling as personal charm (which she did *not* have and would have scorned to cultivate) that captured the imagination. She gave off a sort of effulgence of awe and terror. But the terror did not paralyze. It was terror that caused children to flex their moral muscles and to dream of enduring, without a whimper, prolonged ordeals of privation and fatigue. Sometimes, if their ideal of courage was high, it caused them even to dare Miss Dove's disapproval.

The little ones, the six-year olds, whose geographical primer was entitled "At Home with Birds and Beasts," often pictured Miss Dove in the guise of some magnificent creature, furred or feathered. She was a huge black grizzly reared on its hind legs to block a mountain pass; she was a camel—bigger than other camels—leading a caravan across the desert; she was a Golden Eagle on a crag in Scotland. Later, when they had progressed to the intellectual sophistication of the fourth, the fifth, or the sixth and final grade of Cedar Grove School they were likely to cast her in the image of symbol. (One fanciful child had likened her to the Pharos watching little skiffs in the harbor of Alexandria.) But David Burnham was not fanciful; he was scared. Had he been pressed, at the moment, to describe Miss Dove, he would have said: "She looks like a teacher."

Miss Dove would have been gratified. A teacher was what she was and what she wished to be.

# ACADEMIC WOMEN
*MARY ELLMANN*

Since their political equality was secured by the suffragettes, American women have toyed with the idea, the
possibility in nature, of entering college teaching, and all
other fields of educated work formerly reserved for men.
But as Mrs. Jessie Bernard points out in her recently published *Academic Women*,[1] their first happy flush of pro-
fessionalism in the 20s dwindled in the 30s, and almost
disappeared in the 40s in what might have been regarded
as a new vagary, a revived enthusiasm for femininity and
its most convincing proof, the bearing of many children.
But now, presumably, college women have grown calm
about parturition too, settling down to a much less feverish purpose, really to emulate men at last in being both
sexual and highly educated. This new endeavor, though it
suggests a perfect union of opposites, may be more attain-
able in college teaching than it appears at first. Of this
fresh group of women the honorary president might well
be Mary McCarthy—always beautiful (and her profile is
strong), always married, and always making the most
industrious use of a quick, informed intelligence.

But then she teaches only sporadically, and her con-
nections are closer with art than with pedagogy. The
troubles of academic women arise from their formal
training and their formal use of training as teachers.
There the difference, or the problem, lies. Other activities

[1] University Park: Pennsylvania State University Press, 1964.

*MARY ELLMANN has taught English at Wellesley College and
Roosevelt University. She is the author of* Thinking About Women.

of body and mind have been allowed to women in the past. Their rightful share of gross physical exertion has always been inalienable. An absolute equality here, in fact, has been obscured only by the one condition, that they should not be seen enjoying it. Most heavy *outdoor* work in the city has always been confined, therefore, to men. And for at least two centuries Western women have been free to think—as long as, again, they carried on the activity in discreet privacy. They became novelists because novels could be written in sitting rooms and because until the nineteenth-century, novels, written or read, were something male relatives indulged as a female pastime. Women wrote letters and lyrical poems. "How do I love thee? Let me count the ways," asserts a small arithmetical skill as well. And women's minds became pleasantly associated, of course, with a superior intuitive power, a befitting faculty since it was untrained, instinctive, mysterious. In the past a man might be guided by this quality in a wife as warriors before him were advised by a sheep's entrails.

But in their invasion of academic education in the twentieth century, women have relinquished the intuitive faculty, so effortlessly come by ("slattern thought," Adrienne Rich calls it), to train themselves consciously and methodically as logicians and anatomists. The sexual and social effects of their new preference have been felt gradually, but now the initial response, uncertain and curious, would seem to have coalesced for some in an intense dislike. Dislike, at any rate, is the judgment, not of Mrs. Bernard's study, but of our novels of the 60s, which find it repulsive that women should bare their minds in public. This reaction is, of course, not wholly modern: the hint of rationality in the female has frequently been found distasteful in the past (see Chaucer's Pertelote). And yet there seems to be no recalling the old peaceful allotment of faculties between the sexes. To suggest, like a character in Wallace Markfield's *To an Early Grave* ("You couldn't think up his stories and he couldn't make your coffee"), that each sex can be happy in its own forte, has come to sound fatuous. Formal training has destroyed that old clarity of separate aims and separate gratifications.

But the loss, as it seems to some, is repeatedly lamented. Just when women have reached a fairly stable position in the universities (holding to at least a steady 10 percent of the Ph.D.'s each year), one becomes aware of a tremulous, and yet concerted, outcry in fiction for the old duality of learned man and lovely woman. And this new turbulence of dislike for formally educated women is still to some extent based on the old assumption that study desiccates women, renders them ugly, bespectacled, angular. So, in *A Severed Head*, Iris Murdoch has Martin Lynch-Gibbon refer to Honor Klein, the Female Don, as "looking like a haystack," and one of the first isolated details about her is "a stout crepe-soled shoe." (Not that Honor hasn't still some avant-garde surprises up her rough tweed sleeve.) And Quentin, in Arthur Miller's *After the Fall*, subscribes to a degree of this old assumption in deploring the fact that Louise, the bacteriologist, holds an ugly, angular conviction that to be a "separate person" is "maturity." Between her microscope and her analyst, she has lost all her husband's warm, mystical sense of human complicity.

As learning used to be thought spiky, ignorance was charming, and Quentin echoes this early association as well in his bathetic utterance to Maggie: "Honey, you know how to see it all with your own eyes; that's more important than all the books." But both teams of ideas began to break up in the late nineteenth century and are really only souvenirs now. George Eliot was learned and ugly (so far, so good) but she managed to bowl over one of the first of the conservative American writers, Hawthorne, by her sexual shenanigans. She set a pattern, evidently, in the minds of several novelists to follow her, since the new assumption is that learning turns a woman, not angular, but dissolute. If Bellow's Madeleine reads Soloviëv instead of folding her husband Herzog's undershirts, it follows that she will betray him with Valentine Gersbach. The classics scholar, Dorothy Murchison, in John Aldridge's *The Party at Cranston*, is "the author of three definitive works on the literary culture of Greece and Rome," and "her qualifications for bed were no less impressive." Her union with Waithe, the wraithlike narrator, happened to be "consummated to the accompaniment of the shelling of Cherbourg—an activity which she had likened, between moans, to the siege of Troy."

The effects of study upon the body itself, apart from its diversions, have also been freshly interpreted. The academic torso grows now more grotesque than pallid. Herzog can tell when Madeleine is excited by ideas because then her voice sounds "positively like a clarinet." And when she reads her Russian encyclopedia, her nose twitches. What she says to Shapiro in the garden is apparently invalidated by Herzog's noticing that Shapiro notices her behind. And Shapiro, who offends by answering her is punished by the same argument *ad corpus*: whatever *he* says seems invalidated by his having an ulcer. Breasts, above all, are considered to be at odds with the pursuit of knowledge. Delivering a formal lecture, Dorothy Murchison wore "a black and very low-cut evening gown beneath which she obviously had nothing on whatever" and "her large breasts bulged threateningly out upon the desk at which she sat." Profanation of a desk. And Bernard Malamud, in his somber way, carries this point on to pathology. Pauline Gilley, heroine of Malamud's *A New Life,* is given to simple, untutored profundities: "I married a man with no seeds at all." In her final, pregnant happiness with the seedy Levin, she is developing new breasts and she smells like "fresh-baked bread." But Levin's colleague, the instructor Avis Fliss, smells of orange blossom perfume and tobacco; and her life, dedicated to remedial grammar, will never be new. Her breasts are extraordinarily depressing, even among academic women characters: hanging "like water-filled balloons," scarred by one bout of surgery and due for another. Levin is obliged to examine a second "benign fibroma."

Sorely afflicted with all these physical distortions, educated women are found to be generally malformed in character as well. They are bad-tempered; they fume and rage and tear sheets. Avis Fliss is a snoop. Madeleine Herzog is a bad housekeeper—she leaves veal bones under the sofa. But her successor in Herzog's affections, Ramona (perhaps because she never did finish that M.A. in art history), remains sweetly, very simply sexy, and a great little cook to boot. And Madeleine is a fraud: what she really likes to read, Herzog confides, is murder mysteries. (But she has at least *that* in common with Sartre.) Louise, the first lady in Miller's *After the Fall*, is a fraud too: it was Quentin, of course, who got her an *A* by writing her paper on Roosevelt. Both women are jealous of their husbands' talents and try to steal attention away from them. Quentin, with saintly restraint, tells Louise:

> I wasn't *angry*; I simply felt that every time I began to talk you cut in to explain what I was about to say.

Herzog is frankly annoyed:

> Madeleine, by the way, lured me out of the learned world, got in herself, slammed the door, and is still in there, gossiping about me.

Holga, the third lady in *After the Fall*, is educated too (Quentin can tell when she is upset because then she talks "desperately" about architecture), and the thorough approval accorded her is therefore puzzling at first. But the play furnishes reasons why she is right in being educated while Louise is wrong. (1) Holga is an archaeologist, not a bacteriologist (Louise has said, "Quentin, I saw you getting angry when I was talking about that new antivirus vaccine.") (2) Between Louise and Holga comes Maggie, a massive dose of knownothing even for a man with a taste for it. (3) Finally, Holga, like Quentin, can survive higher education because she, like Quentin, is loaded with emotional insight: "I think one must finally take one's life in one's arms, Quentin."

If the less joyful ladies of these tales are not capable of this solipsistic embrace, it is perhaps because they are already encumbered with the lives of others, or with the hatred of themselves emanating from those other lives. Herzog achieves the most eloquent venom. Arthur Miller is reduced once again to the predictable; at the end of an argument with Louise, Quentin thunders, "Bitch!" The reader is guiltily relieved (because the scene is unmistakably perorative in tone) when Dorothy Murchison gets her come-uppance, her bruised breast (one of those which threatened the lecture audience) and her bloody nose.

Young women scholars, quailing before this modern fiction, might well retreat into Jane Austen's propriety of "acomplishments accustomary to the sex." But fortunately ambition in women as in men is often ruthless, and often indifferent to literary judgments. Moreover, with excellent timing, Mrs. Bernard appears now on the book scene, to reassure and encourage. Reading her cheerless but dispassionate statistics, the thesis of the current novel (that intellectual women are bound to be hateful) begins to seem a temporary and eccentric inflammation of male self-pity in fiction, rather than an index of general feeling in the actual society. The truth of the matter must be, as always, less histrionic. What interests Mrs. Bernard is not so much the disturbance caused to lovers and husbands by women's education, as the disturbance caused to the women themselves. Their real problem in teaching is not that they cease to be women, but that they *cannot* cease to be women. The academic woman, as she enters her profession, is visualized by sociologists as wheeling before her, in a mental grocery cart, all the stock impedimenta, the staples, of her feminine role. Far from losing them, she cannot get rid of her passivity, her diffidence, her compliance, her leniency, her "conserving, stabilizing, appeasing" nature.

If she speaks as inoffensively seldom as possible, her colleagues find her "withdrawn." If she teaches part-time in order to tend husband and children as well, her colleagues feel she is not seriously "involved" in the profession. If she teaches full-time and devotes herself to the nurture of students, she reveals a new shortcoming: a tendency toward "momism" in what the academic men believe should be as stark and rigid a training as that of the Coldstream Guards. If she consults members of her "field" freely, they assume that she is making advances. If she keeps a decorous distance, they consider her outside the real pulsing life of the subject. Even if she speaks eloquently, she finds it difficult to hold undivided attention. A man teacher reports to Mrs. Bernard:

> There she [his colleague] stands. A beautiful woman. Above her neck she is talking about the most abstruse subject. From the neck down her body is saying something altogether different.

And undeniably, even if she dresses in a spacesuit, the academic woman is always at some physical disadvantage. It is not, of course, as great as some men imagine it to be. Another male witness, confined to a sanatorium, his life evidently an intravenous illusion, announces in Mrs. Bernard's report that he now understands what it is like to be a woman. But all well women must demur: being female is not quite or not always a postoperative sensation. Moreover, the profession has never been noted in either sex for its great strength. But still, these women are aware of minor physical deterrents. Menstrual schedules do not yield priority to class schedules. The nine months of pregnancy are, as likely as not, the nine months of the school year. In fact, the problems which women create by attempting to lead both sexual and intellectual lives, attract so much sociological concern that one is left with an impression of willful self-divisiveness in contrast with the disciplined wholeness and continuity of male careers. The coincidence that men too are repeatedly diverted from study by the marital act is obscured by the women's monopoly of child care. Most academic husbands, with the exception of Herzog, are therefore ready to report they are glad to be married; quite a few academic wives record less contentment.

Their physical difference causes the familiar difference between the careers of academic husbands and wives. College teaching careers depend more than others upon regularity. The academic law is that the first seven steady years of famine guarantee thirty-three more of tenure. The instructor who meets every class, corrects most of the papers, publishes an article a year in the trade journal, and escapes being seduced by a student, cannot fail. At worst, he will transfer at a higher rank to a lower institution.

But women do fail, because their careers are notorious for interruption. The irregular history of most rouses suspicion of all from the start. Even as young, unmarried, and gifted applicants, women look treacherous to a fellowship committee. The male body holds no academic swindles in store. Its square bulk in the chair immediately suggests to the committee the uneventful filling of some job somewhere for the next half century. Unless the women applicants promise celibacy (a pious solution offered by David Riesman in his introduction to Mrs. Bernard's book—offered, at least, as an alternative to marrying "dreadfully inadequate men") or, married, promise to be barren, there is always that risk of their quitting before the fellowships have, in a way, been paid back. And if they *are* hired as instructors, women are capable of madcap romances—with other members of the faculty or, worse, with members of the faculty in their own departments. In the event of so thoughtless a marriage within the profession, the wife, in the past, invariably resigned. Now nicety yields gradually to necessity, to the shortage of teachers, and some of these brides are allowed to stay on. But still, married women teachers are prone to resigning. They reproduce and resign, they make beds and resign, they trail along after their husbands wherever their husbands' jobs erupt on the globe, and resign again.

The hapless women whom Mrs. Bernard describes make clear, nevertheless, that the profession is not quite forgotten, that it nags and pulls at them, and that—totally dismissed from the minds of their old colleagues—they reappear one day to sign a new (and, of course, punitively meager) contract. By having to leave their work so often, these women become distinct, too, in their compulsion to resume it. In four, ten, sixteen years the trauma of marriage is healed. And like Jane Eyre, that most academic heroine of all, the wives are no sooner nursed back to sensibility than they open their mouths and teach again. College deans have no way of guessing this lurking, dormant intention. Lovers and husbands confuse it with sexual invitation or sexual rebuff—a regrettable, though rather touching, single-mindedness. The personal accounts of the dilemma furnished to Mrs. Bernard are dreary, repetitive, threnodic for many paragraphs, but they all conclude with the decision to study and teach again. Once put to graduate school, women evidently harbor thereafter, until death do part, an implacable instrumentality of mind.

# DISCRIMINATION AND DEMOGRAPHY RESTRICT OPPORTUNITIES FOR ACADEMIC WOMEN

*ALICE ROSSI*

Women faculty members have always posed some perplexing questions for the administrators of colleges and universities. In this study on assessing the female contribution to higher education, I will review the status of women in our institutions during the past three decades, placing particular emphasis on the future trends as I see them, and, on the basis of my research with 15,000 women college graduates, evaluate how the twin factors of motivation and discrimination bear upon the role of women in both higher education and the job world.

The greatest change since the turn of the century has been the narrowing of the gap between the sexes in obtaining the first degree: Women obtained only 19 percent of the bachelor's degrees at the turn of the century, 40 percent by the early 1960s, and about 43 percent during the last five years. At the master's level, the increase has been from 19 percent at the turn of the century, to a high of 38 percent in 1940, then down to 32 percent by the early 1960s. At the doctorate level, the number of women graduates increased from 6 percent at the turn of the century to peak at 16 percent in the early 1930s, then slip to 13 percent in 1940, then down to a low of 11 percent in the early 1960s, where it has remained.

Women faculty members must be recruited from

*ALICE ROSSI is a professor of sociology at Goucher College, Baltimore, Maryland. Her article is adapted from a paper presented to the 37th conference of the Academic Deans of the Southern States; her research was supported by the National Institute of Mental Health.*

bachelor's and higher degree holders. What is interesting to note is that at the turn of the century, when women made up only 19 percent of the bachelor's degree holders, they represented 20 percent of the teachers at the college and university level. This suggests that a much larger proportion of women college students had college teaching as a career goal than is true in our own era. By the early 1960s, women represented 22 percent of these teaching faculties, down slightly from a peak of 28 percent in 1940. While the national figures are higher than those from the very large and most prestigious universities, it is clear that teaching at the college level has not kept pace with the increasing rate of college attendance and graduation of American women.

There has been a noticeable expansion of part-time faculty over the last 25 years, as colleges and universities responded to the growing demand for their services. Early in the 1960s, of all the teaching and professional personnel in institutions of higher education, 44 percent were full-time faculty, but a hefty 37 percent were part-time faculty. It is among the part-time faculty that women are heavily represented, and this is clearly an insecure hold on positions in higher education—an expendable labor supply for colleges and universities to add or drop from their staffs in response to variations in the size of the student body and budgetary appropriations.

Many women in the 1960s owe even their small and insecure foothold in academia to the fact that Ph.D.s have enjoyed a long period of a sellers' market. For twenty-five years, the institutional need and desire for Ph.D.-holding faculty has been in excess of the number available, hence there was need for non-Ph.D. women teachers to fill out the faculty staff. But this situation is expected to undergo rapid change in the 1970s; after 1970, there will be a buyers' market in which the number of academic teaching posts to be filled will be lower than the number of Ph.D.s available. This does not mean Ph.D.s will go unemployed, since there are many spheres away from the college and university where their skills are badly needed. From this perspective, the future looks dim indeed for academic women since academic employers will have an ample market of male Ph.D.s to fill new positions. Unless a woman has a Ph.D., and perhaps even then, she may find an even more competitive situation facing her in academia in the next decade than she has had during the last few decades of great expansion in institutions of higher education.

Taking all teachers—elementary, secondary, and college—as the educational pool, statistics show there has been an increase in their number between 1930 and 1960 of some 87 percent. But, between the respective educational levels, much variation is apparent. There has only been a 36 percent increase in the number of elementary-school teachers, while the number of secondary-school teachers has grown 146 percent, and the number at the college and university level has increased 360 percent. Furthermore, sex differences appear at each educational level: Women high-school teachers increased only 83 percent during the 30 year period, but men high-school teachers increased by 260 percent, shifting the field from predominantly female to one in which men are now a slight majority. At the college level, the two percentages are a 265 percent increase for women, but a 395 percent increase for men.

Any rapidly expanding occupation must draw from those in the labor force with the necessary educational qualifications. This is typically white males, and it is this tendency that leads to the decline of the representation of women at the secondary and college level of teaching. Education below the college level is exerting increased pressure for higher levels of knowledge and skill: Many high-school biology teachers today are equivalent in knowledge and skill to college science teachers in the past. Any field which undergoes such knowledge expansion is most likely to draw more heavily from men than from women as long as women aim their aspirations for schooling and working at a lower level than men do. The crisis that may lie ahead for women aspiring to college teaching in the 1970s is not peculiar to this segment of the female labor force. Much of the great increase in the numbers of older married women in the labor force over the last 20 years is rooted in the peculiarities of the demographic structure of the American population during these particular years. Up to 1940, the traditional source of the female labor force had been young unmarried women. During the 1950s and early 1960s, a pattern of earlier marriages developed and schooling was extended, thus shrinking the size of the available labor pool of unmarried women. Even more important, the young women of the 1950s were born in the 1930s, when the birth rate was very low, while at the same time there was a vast increase in the numbers of young children being born during the baby boom of those post war years. As a result, the traditional pool of female labor shrunk during those twenty years from six million to three million while every other age category was increasing in size.

It would be comforting to believe that the shift in women's employment over the past twenty-five years, with an increasingly large proportion of married older women in the work force, was essentially due to changes on the supply side of the economic equation, with women pressing for entry and seeking wider horizons than those provided by the home and family. In an economy as hard-nosed as ours, this is a highly unrealistic economic assumption. The shift had as much if not more to do with employer demand as with women assertively seeking jobs. Employers flung doors open, beckoning women in.

Looking ahead to the 1970s, there will be a reverse in this demographic pattern: The birth rate is now on the decline, age at marriage is creeping upward, and the time interval between marriage and childbearing is widening. In the 1970s there will be more young unmarried women or childless married women seeking jobs; at the same time middle-aged married women will also be very numerous, for the baby-boom females will have grown to maturity. Some expanding service occupations may well be able to absorb large numbers of both categories of women, but it is less clear what the situation will be in academic circles.

Ambitious women who aspire to careers on what has been masculine turf must have thick skins and the utmost inner security to withstand what they so often experience, subtle and overt forms of punishment rather than encouragement and support. Yet highly committed career women are in even greater need than men of such support and encouragement during the early years of their careers. My analysis of the background of the highly committed career graduate women shows them to differ from women who enter traditional feminine fields in ways that depress their confidence in themselves in early adulthood. Indeed, my major hypothesis was that deviant choices in adult roles are rooted in other kinds of deviance earlier in the life line. (By deviance I mean merely departure from a cultural expectation of appropriateness for one's sex, age, class and so forth.) The message derived from my study seems to be that young American women with serious professional goals have a special need to obtain compensatory rewards through adult socialization that can build up their confidence and stoke their motivation to reach the goals they set for themselves. Yet the qualitative quotes are full of ego-depressing rather than ego-building experiences. It is little wonder that so many women learn to hide their ambition, to redirect their energies into non-occupational activities or lower their sights and try patiently to accept positions below their ability. In the words of one such woman:

"We take jobs far below the salary and title we deserve, just to get a foot in the door. All too often, that's all we get in—a foot."

Looking at this situation from the point of view of the employer, what are the factors involved that make so many men prejudiced against ambitious professional women or simply insensitive to the fact that they are discriminatory toward women? A major figure in this situation in academia is the department chairman, and a perspective on his attitudes toward women colleagues can be gleaned from a review of what it has taken him to reach the position he now enjoys. Typically, his success comes after long years of hard work: struggling to finish a degree; getting a promising teaching post, and writing and publishing while his wife carried most of the responsibilities for home management and child rearing.

As an academic researcher myself, and also as the wife of a department chairman, I have been in a position to observe some of the more subtle processes that cause such men to look unfavorably and with erroneous assumptions on young aspiring women in academia. For example, a mutual friend had recently been made chairman of his department at a Midwestern university, some seven years after he first entered that department. This is the complaint he brought out in the course of a conversation:

"I have worked damned hard for seven years to become a tenured professor at this place and chairman of the department. Now I earn $20,000 and along comes a fresh new Ph.D. with a brand new appointment in the department as an assistant professor at $12,000. But his wife has the same appointment at another college nearby. Why between them they now earn $4,000 more than I do after seven years of hard work!"

When pressed to explain what bothered him about this, he explained:

"They are now building a better house than I'll ever be able to afford. They serve vintage wines, take off for ski trips week-ends while we are at home with the kids. . . . I don't think he'll amount to much though. It's not good to start off so well. He'll drift I'm sure, postpone writing, because there's no pressure on him to publish in order to live well or better."

Sensing a tortured rationalization, my husband laughed, and the man finally blurted out: "Well, it's just not fair!" Underneath his protestations about his young colleague's probable low productivity was merely a peevish personal gripe. It is much the same pattern that often lies behind the refusal to increase the salary of an academic woman. Since most academic women, if married, have husbands in academic or professional fields with more than adequate incomes of their own, department chairmen are sometimes motivated not by a woman's performance on the job, but personal resentment of the higher style of life a joint household of career people can enjoy.

There is also another element in employers' handling of professional women on their staffs: their inability to distinguish between these women and their own homemaker wives. They overlook the fact that these professional women have no psychic need to make a fuss about their home duties as their own wives do in order to match the busyness of their ambitious husbands, and they overlook the fact that the professional women's husbands are often ideologically committed to helping in home maintenance and child care.

One more example will serve to underscore the special situation of the young academic woman. This case comes not from my research files, but from personal correspondence with a friend and former research assistant of mine, who is now a young faculty member at a California university. This woman worked for me for two years while she had one small child and through her second pregnancy. She did all her graduate work in record time while her two children were preschoolers. During the spring and summer prior to her move to California, she completed all the analysis of data for her dissertation, which she planned to write the next summer. When she arrived in California, she was able to set up a household, settle her two children in school, arrange household help, and prepare her lectures during a few weeks before the beginning of the fall term. She has been teaching full time and loving it. Yet, she has been told by her department chairman that she is not being kept on next year because he doubts that her dissertation will really be completed.

This young woman has several young male colleagues who will be kept on, even though their dissertations are still far from complete. Had her chairman taken the trouble to review her pattern over the last five years—her ability to hold down a full-time job through a pregnancy, to move from a job to graduate training and maintain a normal pace along with family responsibilities—he might have realized that she was the one young faculty person who was *most* rather than *least* apt to complete her dissertation and receive the doctorate during that year.

This also illustrates one way in which college administrators can help their women faculty: by getting to know each new woman who joins their faculty, keeping well enough informed of her progress to raise hard direct questions if she is not retained or promoted by her department.

The question of academic productivity is often raised when women faculty members are discussed: How adequate are our criteria of productivity in comparing men with women, and what is it in men's productivity that we want more women to emulate?

Academic productivity has been traditionally measured by the number of published articles and books completed by the academic man or woman. But, if there is any institution in modern society that should place quality above quantity, it should be the university. Many of us share Jacques Barzun's charge that what we have been witnessing in recent years is not so much a knowledge explosion as a publication explosion. I suggest the university should push and push hard to assess quality, not merely quantity. One fine article can often equal a dozen mediocre ones, or one book surpass three. Married academic women may indeed write and publish less often than their male colleagues. Since many women are supplementary rather than exclusive breadwinners, they have had the luxury of avoiding the trap of publish-or-perish thinking. Before we push women into such a competitive race, we should be sure it is a race either sex should be in.

Universities should depart from a narrow time perspective in judging faculty productivity. The contemporary college is no longer a local, parochial, social community turned in upon itself, but a cosmopolitan national community of talented professionals. In making this transition from a local to a cosmopolitan institution, we should not lose sight of the teaching goal of the enterprise by merely valuing teaching equally with research. We should show a willingness to value the delayed impact on the younger generation of women students that may flow from having young married women on the teaching staff. For college students to have such a woman as a teacher and model may influence them to persist in their own professional careers rather than withdraw from them, and raise their goals to more demanding positions than they have considered for themselves. To truly value this mission and the potential influence of women faculty upon women students, a university must depart from the parochial concern for immediate status pay-off in the form of current faculty productivity by sharing a societywide goal of encouraging greater social contributions from young women a generation hence.

In brief, concern for productivity must make room for the role of the teacher as model to the young, for charisma and style of teaching, for the quality and not merely the quantity of research and scholarship produced by faculty members. Until these factors are taken into account, it is too early to judge women faculty as less productive than men.

What of the price paid for high productivity among faculty members following the conventional focus on publications, honorary awards, national commission participation, and all the other high-prestige activities our jet age professors engage in outside the office and classroom? To be productive in this modern sense exacts a great price: a lopsided life of almost all work, little play, and little family or community life.

The important point is this: Many women do not want such a life, and the woman student watching her professor juggle frequent flying trips with class and research schedules may conclude that college teaching is not for her. More than men, women may seek a better-rounded life style that permits significant but not excessive commitment to work, with time and energy for the pleasures of sociability with friends and their own children, time and energy for cultivating a garden, walking or swimming, and doing what they can in political and community affairs.

The men and women who manage our academic institutions should answer this question: Isn't it time the university, as the most far-seeing of our social institutions, prepared itself for life in the postindustrial world? I hope that world is not merely "post" something, but "for" something—a compassionate world with the time, room and flexibility to create a style of living that permits both men and women to live deeply and meaningfully at play and at home, as well as at work.

# VII.
# The Feminist Response

# FEMINIST EXPERIMENT IN EDUCATION

*BARBARA HARRISON*

Several years ago, when my children—now seven and eight—were small, I shopped around for an alternative to the public schools. Remembering my own joyless elementary-school days I went in search of someplace where teachers actually liked kids, where my children's uniqueness would be respected.

I ended up sending my son and a daughter to a school in which their needs would be understood. But who, in our sexist society which defines social role according to gender—has determined what my daughter's needs are? Attitudes about a female's "nature" are culturally influenced and determined—by men. Most education *authorities* are men (just as most of the elementary-school *teachers* who sit at their feet are women). Few, up to now, have troubled to observe the facts of early childhood education from a feminist point of view, to explore what "education for the entire *man*" does for the girl-to-be-a-woman, to question the validity of a curriculum that integrates all learning into a "study of *man's* development."

At the beginning of the 1970–1971 school year, feminists at the Woodward School in Brooklyn, the parent-teacher cooperative in which my children are enrolled, formed a "sex-roles" committee to explore ways in which Woodward might be perpetuating stereotypical sex roles, reflecting the culture of a society in which women are

*BARBARA HARRISON, a freelance writer, is the author of* Unlearning the Lie.

molded to be passive, decorative, supportive, and, ultimately, powerless in a male-dominated world. Woodward feminists want—and are beginning to get—a "free school," one that will free their daughters (and therefore their sons) from the mind- and spirit-debilitating vise of sexist education. But first a word about the setting in which this revolution grew.

Visitors to Woodward, warmed by its open, expansive disposition, tend to sum up the school's ambience in a word: happy. The 200 children are housed in a Civil War mansion, a brightly decorated limestone building full of odd turns and corners and whimsical flights of stairs that terminate in unexpected rooms. It is a sunny, nook-and-cranny, window-seat place. Interracial (40 percent of its students are black) and nonsectarian, Woodward attracts children from the upper-middle-class homes of Brooklyn Heights as well as from the inner city (tuition grants keep it from being a preserve of the liberal well-to-do). Both counterculture young parents and more staid middle-class types are comfortable within a framework of an innovative educational philosophy that refuses to acknowledge a dichotomy between playing and learning, one that is in fact noncompetitive and noncoercive.

Knowledge is not regarded at Woodward as a consumer commodity, bought by discipline and drills. "Learning" is not something a child is "taught." Not much is laid on the kids; they are participants in a process in which a teacher is less an instructor than a catalyst for the development of the children's potential. The school, which pioneered in interaging, does not grade pupils or issue report cards, and *homework*, for most Woodward children, is an exotic activity engaged in by their public-school friends; the pleasures and ardors of *research*, however, are familiar.

Woodward offers a wide range of options—"choosing" is a school pastime; whether to grant the freedom not to choose at all is usually determined by the individual teacher. Ms. Goldstein, Woodward's director, calls this "freedom with limits." In one sixth grade class I visited last year, each kid had chosen an individual social-studies project: women's fashions, Eskimos, drugs, primitive tribes, Declaration of Independence, crime, prehistoric man, citizenship, Africa, the Panthers, pollution, Women's Lib.

What parents have loved about Woodward is that their children love it. So, what, according to feminists, is wrong?

When the founding members of the sex-roles committee first announced meetings and encouraged attendance, the response was largely aggrieved bewilderment. It had never occurred to most women to question whether their daughters might be victims of subtle discrimination. Feminists were suspected of inventing issues to provide outlets for their new-found militancy, or, at the very least, of being overzealous. Woodward's parent body is energetic; many women were deeply committed to the Black Parents' committee, a militant group that was engaged in sensitizing the staff to the needs of black children. The demands of black parents for a curriculum that was relevant to their children were seen as far more pressing than complaints of irate feminists.

But once the feminists suggested that there was reason for concern, it was not easy to ignore them. They confined their approach, initially, to other women, honoring the revolutionary precept that one addresses oneself to one's own oppression. When you think about it, of course, it is only mothers one is likely to see at school: mothers deliver the kids, mothers pick the kids up. The PTA is for all practical purposes an organization of mothers. When kids of two working parents are sick, it's mother who stays home. When there is a problem with a child, the director calls in the child's mother. Ms. Goldstein admits that it had been her inclination, when a father came to see her about a child, to assume that "there was something wrong at home." Since mothers spend a great part of their lives talking to other mothers, when the sex-roles committee was formed it was as natural as it was practical for it to become a topic of conversation with mothers one met or spoke casually with every day. The telephone grapevine and an informal network of school-based relationships became vehicles for agenda-less "consciousness-raising" among all mothers. As Woodward women began to share experiences, it became more and more apparent that there were grounds for exploration, if not for complaint.

By the time of our first (leaderless) sex-roles committee meeting, at which about thirty women joined the founding core of six, we were all eager to discuss the implications of our observations. At the first meeting, these are the things we talked about:

*Teachers' expectations of girls are different from their expectations of boys.* A number of kindergarten children are working at a carpentry bench. A girl shows her teacher (male) her handiwork. "These nails aren't hammered in far enough," he says; "I'll do it for you." A boy shows the teacher his handiwork. "These nails aren't hammered in far enough," the teacher says; "Take the hammer and pound them in all the way."

*Boys are expected to be physically aggressive:* A sixth-grade class trip to an ice-skating rink; a boy pushes and shoves a girl, who, falling, retaliates by calling him a four-letter word. A concessionaire who has witnessed the incident later refuses to serve the girl, because "ladies don't talk like that." The girl, irate, complains to the school's director; the director, sympathetic to the girl's feeling of having been messed over, nevertheless counsels her to have a "decent respect for the opinions of others," and suggests that the sensibilities of a hot-dog vendor who is appalled by a girl's using street language have got to be taken into consideration. . . . Somehow, the initial provocation—the boy's physical aggression—is overlooked in the discussion of the girl's verbal response.

*Styles differ according to sex:* Boys erect massive block structures; girls tend to build nesty, small-scale constructions. . . . A nursery-school teacher takes a radio apart. The boys rush over, clamoring to see how it works. The girls, happily festooning one another with the laces and cast-off jewelry of the costume box, stay put. Boys are mobilized by the opportunity to see how things function: girls seem content to engage in passive, ornamental activities.

*Girls relate to esthetics; boys relate to scientific principles:* A group of first- and second-grade children is in the playground, observing clouds. The boys discuss the movement of the clouds, the wind, the power that pushes them across the sky. The girls say, "Oooh, aren't they pretty?"

*Sex-role stereotyping is unquestioned:* Eighth-graders discuss *The Grapes of Wrath.* A young girl, asked to define the qualities of Steinbeck's characters, says, "Rose of Sharon is completely obsessed with her pregnancy. That's what she's about." "Ma," says a boy, "gets it all together. The family couldn't make it without her." "Apple-pie mother," interjects another boy, with a laugh that is rather sly. "No, not really," corrects the teacher (a man); "Steinbeck sees woman as earthmother, as a pillar of strength, nurturing, supportive. . . ." "Right! Apple-pie mother," says one of the girls.

*When boys violate girls' physical integrity the girls are held equally to blame:* Embarrassed third-grade girls complain of boys' "pinching their bottoms" and of boys' peering over lavatory walls to "spy on them." The teacher (female) suggests to the girls that they were "teasing" the boys, and to the parents that the girls were being "provocative." A parent questions her girl: "Mommy, I was teasing. I guess. But I don't know what I *did*. I don't know *how* I teased. I never touched *them*." *When girls are assaulted, they feel guilty.*

Were these isolated incidents? Did they reflect no more than individual teachers' styles? It would be anathema, of course, to suggest to a feminist that boys are innately assertive, intellectually curious, achievement-oriented leaders, and that girls are natural followers. If gender does not account for behavior patterns, how, in a free school, do we account for them? How do we change the patterns?

After the initial session, the sex-roles committee aggressively solicited the attendance of fathers and of teachers. Together, as an ad hoc committee of the PTA, we returned again and again to the original observations that had led to the formation of the group, to what we perceived to be differences between boys and girls, and to a consideration of the ways in which parents and teachers alike had helped to foster differences, which were then accepted as innate.

For many weeks we centered our semimonthly discussions on aggression and intellectuality. An example: By the time boys reach third grade, they are demonstrably more exuberant and physically aggressive than girls. In organized wrestling—a teacher-directed activity—boys play to win; girls are concerned about alienating their friends. When a girl becomes identified as a "tomboy" and shares in boys' activities, she is highly respected, both by

boys and by girls. But physical girls are socially acceptable only if they lose a fight with a boy. "Don't hit her,
she's a girl." Boys learn to despise girls for their weakness
and to require weakness of them. Is the cliquishness of
girls, their concern for popularity, the importance they
attach to alliances, another form of aggression, a manipulative and punitive technique? By requiring that our girls
become physically assertive, are we sanctioning the kind
of violence we castigate in adult male society? Do we
equate sensitivity with softness and lack of assertiveness?
Are we sufficiently concerned with the suffering of a boy
who is not physically aggressive, who cannot live up to the
Superman image? When we comment on a girl's pretty
dress, pretty hair-style, are we, by rewarding her, forcing
her to "think pretty," to draw her satisfactions from esthetics rather than from dominance over her world? Do we
reward girls for strength and mastery? Observations seem
to confirm the results of psychological tests. Girls are
early achievers, only to fall behind boys in academic skills
during puberty. Why is this so?

After several months, core members of the committee
started providing resource materials for the staff, with a
view to putting women, their role in history and in society
into Woodward's curriculum. Sex-roles committee meetings continued to be a forum for consciousness-raising.
Simultaneously, just as women's liberation groups as they
refine a feminist analysis engage in political activity,
Woodward feminists saw areas in which direct, immediate
action was called for.

*Books.* Woodward's library reflected the overwhelming
"maleness" of children's books. Boys celebrate life by living
it fully and reaching out to the world; girls reach out to
boys. Early-childhood readers celebrate stereotypical
nuclear-family roles. Mothers and girls stay home and
clean, fathers go off to work, and boys have adventures.
Not only is this demeaning, it does not even accurately
reflect a child's objective reality. Many Woodward mothers
work and many are professionals. One of the few textbooks
(a first-grade reader) that showed a woman working
placed her in her daughter's school cafeteria—cooking.

The sex-roles committee invited the Feminist Collective
on Children's Media (a group of young women in publishing) to present a slide-and-talk program at a general meet-

ing of the PTA. Hundreds of illustrations from children's books were projected, in all of which girls were depicted as dependent, passive, beribboned, ruffled, playing "little-mother" housekeeping roles, playing wide-eyed little sister to boys who were physical, dominant, intellectually aggressive, courageously in control of their world. The evidence was massive and incontrovertible: a girl's world is narrow; she must take delight in small, homely pleasures. A boy glories in pushing against constrictions, leaping over boundaries, thrusting himself against his ever-widening world. Bibliographies of nonsexist children's books had been compiled and were distributed. Books carefully selected both for their story appeal and for the unstereotypical way in which they delineated girls and women were displayed. The school committed itself to reevaluating its library and its readers and to ordering nonsexist books.

*Physical setup of nursery/kindergarten classrooms.* Heavy blocks, trucks, and carpentry equipment were in one well-defined section; "dress-up," dolls, and homemaking equipment in another. The boys obviously considered the heavy "doing" stuff their turf; when a girl wandered over to the carpentry table she was easily intimidated and likely to be shut out. For many children, crossing the invisible boundary line between "boys' things" and "girls' things" was an emotional impossibility.

Feminists protested a physical setup that encouraged grouping according to sex. As a result, classrooms were rearranged to facilitate the movement of children without regard to boy/girl definitions.

*Parent-staff relationships.* The humdrum but necessary mechanics of keeping a school functioning had always fallen to women, designated at Woodward as "class mothers" who didn't even have names. On grade lists, parents were identified thus: Mr. and Mrs. John Smith. Feminists urged the director to encourage fathers to perform some of the exacting and time-consuming tasks that had previously been entirely the province of women. Accordingly, "class mothers" are now "grade parents," five out of seventeen of whom are men. Class lists now include the names of both parents (Joan and John Smith).

Several fathers found themselves momentarily at a loss for words when their grade chairperson telephoned to ask if they would contribute a casserole to the school bazaar. We weren't inundated with manmade casseroles, but we had, we felt, by not allowing men to assume that this was their wives' job, raised their consciousness. Just as we stepped out of our male-defined roles by suggesting, at a PTA meeting, that the lone man present (the treasurer) be the one to take notes.

These were token victories. Feminists were concerned about a climate. We sought to create an alternative to sexist education in the context of which teachers' expectations of girls are different from their expectations of boys. Hopefully, we thought our year-end presentation to staff would engender such a climate, by heightening the awareness of the staff and by providing work tools and resources for a nonsexist curriculum. But resistance had, not surprisingly, been building all along.

Parents—male parents in particular—began to insist upon the libertarian nature of the school as an argument against feminist change: "I agree with you about a lot of things, but I don't think you should force your values on the kids. Any conscious imposition of feminist values impinges on kids' freedom. Woodward's a free school, isn't it? Leave them alone. Why do we have to make value judgments for them?" "If you encourage girls to do traditional 'boy' things, you run the risk of squashing the child's essence."

Feminists countered his argument, which they considered disingenuous by contending that Woodward, while free, was not a moral vacuum. War toys, for example, are not allowed at Woodward because adults have made a value judgment that war is bad. If an adult makes the judgment that sexism is bad, then that is the adult's reality; is it really possible, or desirable, to educate or to socialize children without making them aware of their parents' or their teachers' reality? To speak of allowing children freedom of choice when options have not been made available to them is to miss the point entirely. At the age of eight or nine, children have already gotten the message that only certain choices are available, and that these choices are based on sex. Our concern was, if anything, to "squeeze back in," rather than to "squash out."

Feminists also had to contend with the charge that

they were overrating intellectuality. We were warned (often, ironically enough, by men with Ph.D.s) against falling into the trap of intellectual elitism: "The screwdriver," we heard, "is just as important as the pen . . . the frying pan is just as important as the screwdriver." Why was it so difficult to convince men that what we were saying was that the freedom to choose freely among the screwdriver, the pen, and the frying pan was the most important thing of all?

In matters directly pertaining to curriculum, it was suggested to feminists that Woodward's nonsexist orientation could be deduced from the fact that boys (studying Northwestern Indians) were as happy to work at bead looms as were girls, and that boys (studying pioneer times) baked bread and made patchwork quilts and dipped candles.

Feminists responded that, while a coeducational arts and crafts program was delightful, we wanted more. We wanted our children to have a sense of the "dailiness" of women's‘ lives in the past, which was notably missing, not just from Woodward's curriculum but from history textbooks as well. We wanted an awareness of women to permeate every subject under discussion. If eighth-graders were studying constitutional law, we wanted the teacher to be able to illuminate women's place under law. We wanted seventh-graders studying black history to be made aware of women's place in that history—the organic relationship between the abolition movement and the suffrage movement, for example. When third- and fourth-graders discussed American Indians, we wanted the oppression of female Indians to be made clear—even at the expense of demythicizing Indian braves.

Feminists deplored the absence of women from history books. We were asked (again by men) why it was necessary to have heroines. Wasn't it possible to teach history as a process rather than as a succession of great men (or great women).

Feminists, angered, responded that it was all very well for men to talk—after all, they *had* their heroes; we couldn't allow our heroines to be taken away from us before we even had them. (Do our daughters know who the Grimke sisters were? Do they read the poetry of Anne Bradstreet? Is Sojourner Truth's name a household word?) We suggested that we wanted to provide our daughters not with heroines, but with models. And teaching history as a process was fine—provided that it was acknowledged that women, as a class, had a place in that process. As it was, we were stuck with a male version of history that made it appear as if women arrived on these shores; they got the vote; a few deranged women agitated for suffrage and for prohibition; and women worked in defense plants during World War II. That version of history would not do.

One of the happier results of resistance to our giving a place to women in the curriculum was that it served to diminish the resistance of black women at Woodward to what many had previously regarded as an essentially frivolous white middle-class preoccupation. The more we discussed women's absence in the male version of history, the more clearly black women saw that the fight was theirs too. The participation of black mothers at working sessions, our striving for a mutual understanding of the dynamics of oppression, our increasing openness with one another, was one of the more gratifying aspects of the struggle for female liberation at Woodward. We often reflected on the words of Sojourner Truth: "If colored men get their rights, and not colored women theirs, you see the colored men will be masters over the women, and it will be just as bad as it was before. . . . Consider on that, chil'n."

As the end of the school year drew near and the time for the sex-roles committee's formal presentation to staff approached, we had a final ideological battle. Some fathers took the familiar we-are-all-victims-this-is-a-human-problem line, to argue that they should help determine the program and make the presentation to staff. The men-and-women-are-equally-victimized argument went hand in hand with the "practicality" argument: "As long as it's still a man's world, your approach to the staff will have more weight if men share the platform."

It did not seem to feminists that men could logically argue, on the one hand, that they were equally victimized, and, on the other, that they had more "weight"—or more power—than did women. If they were willing to surrender their power, the first step would be for them to acknowledge that women would have to speak for themselves. After all, it was women, not men, who had questioned the status quo in the first place; women, and their daughters, who had the most to gain or to lose. Feminists, adamant that the oppressors could not speak on behalf of the oppressed, were accused of being more concerned with themselves than with the welfare of their kids. But their point of view prevailed, and those who thought passion had triumphed over reason were in the minority.

June, 1971. Feminists came to Woodward to present the results of their labors, the evidence of the overwhelmingly anti-female bias of media influences to which our daughters are subjected every day of their lives, a rigorous analysis of sexist education, and tools for radical change in our daughters' education.

Working with edited video tape, a media group showed a seemingly endless number of commercials directed at girls and women, a mind-numbing barrage of trivia; the relief that was expressed when boy-oriented commercials were shown said a great deal about the claustrophobic world girls live in (the message: boys—the world is yours; girls—the womb and the kitchen and the toilet bowl are yours).

Feminists urged the staff to cooperate with them to bring into the school more visiting outside resource people whose presence would counteract gender type-casting— male nurses and dancers, for example, and female scientists.

As part of a discussion of women in history, one feminist read affectingly from the poignant diary of her great-grandmother, who had left a Philadelphia townhouse and a promising musical career to pioneer in the western plains with her husband. It gave a sense of the dailiness of her life, childbirth, the death of her ambitions, her accomplishments, her pain; one saw in it the face that a strong, sturdy, uncomplaining wilderness-defeating pioneer woman never allowed the world to see.

Because woman's history is to be found, not in history books, but in their journals and diaries, the feminists were prepared for a field-work project. They proposed to tape-record the experiences of older women—immigrants, for example, children of pioneers, and black women who had come to the urban North from the rural South, some of whom are the daughters of slaves—the tapes to be given to the school to be used as living texts, to supplement whatever written journals and diaries we are able to find. This is our heritage, and it is dying; we should no longer countenance alienation from our past.

A woman presented an overview of the image of women in literature, ranging from the fairy tales of Hans Christian Andersen (how many wicked step*fathers* do their kids in? how many *male* witches dangle curses over cradles?) to the literature of the Victorians (which abounds in sprightly, bright, independent heroines who long to offer up their independence to a man—because they know the world will break them if they do not), to contemporary best-sellers (what was *Mrs.* Portnoy's complaint?). Feminists agreed to make themselves available to participate in upper-grade literature discussions if a teacher so desired.

A psychologist took the assembly through the labyrinths of psychological testing, and particularly those tests that indicate gender-based differences in modes of perception and cognition. Her presentation made painfully explicit the terrible double bind women find themselves in. A girl is afraid of failure, she is equally afraid of success —because success implies incorporating qualities she has come to think of as "masculine," thus subjecting her femininity to doubt. To redeem our female children from the pain and bewilderment of this double bind must be the goal of parents and educators.

In the discussion that followed the feminist presentation, a teacher protested that before the school committed itself to a liberationist point of view, "we should get the agreement of all the parents." A black woman responded, "We didn't wait till we got the agreement of every parent for a black-studies program and we're not going to wait for this." Ms. Goldstein said, "We were integrated before other schools were, and we didn't ask the parents' permission to integrate. Some parents still complain because we don't push their first-graders to read and write. Some of our parents don't like interaging. We act on the best evidence available and we are committed to what we think is right for our children, and we hope we can carry the minority of protesting parents along when they see the results."

Feminists took that for a commitment.

At this writing a beginning has been made toward honoring that commitment. No longer is the legitimacy of feminist concerns questioned. At a meeting this month a feminist lawyer will accompany Woodward feminists to discuss women and the law; teachers will then be able to incorporate the information into a curriculum which already reflects the results of a year of consciousness-raising. Such meetings with staff will be held regularly; their content will vary, but their purpose—the liberation of our daughters—will remain the same. When feminists, early this year, delivered to a general meeting of the PTA —the whole school body—the presentation they made to the staff last June, they did so not as a "special interest group" but as partners in the education of their children.

At the beginning of the 1971–1972 school year, parents received from Ms. Goldstein this letter:

"In the study of man's development at all levels we plan to be increasingly aware of the contributions of groups long overlooked. This includes the vast contributions to the entire non-Western, nonwhite, and non-Christian world.

"Attention also needs to be focused on the changing roles of women and men and the part that women have played in building our civilization."

If Woodward feminists have anything to say about it, our liberated children will speak of the study of *human* development, and our daughters will speak with pride of women.

# TWELVE AND TURNED-ON

*SHARON WOLFSON*

I have been teaching a once-a-week elective course on "The Role of Women in Society" to seventh- and eighth-grade girls at a Quaker school in Washington, D.C., and I find twelve-year-olds among the most turned-on, thoughtful, stimulating young women I know. The course is divided in four sections: the socialization of women, the family in other cultures, women's history, and "Women, technology, and ecology." I started with no background in sociology, anthropology, or women's history (despite a B.A. in history) and have made up materials and revised the course outline from week to week.

How do you learn to be a girl? This first assignment read: "Find a game, toy, book, or advertisement that you think teaches children or teenagers what they should be, or how they should act, specifically as a girl or boy." It was so easy, examples so blatant. A Golden Book called "Little Mommy": a coloring-book-manual on how-to-buy-the-perfect-wedding called "Pretty Bride": a careers game for girls offering ballerina, stewardess, and nurse as models: a novel called *Fifteen*, which begins, "Today I will meet a boy," and ends, "She was Stan's girl. That was all that mattered." A question and answer exchange in *Seventeen* (September, 1969) which encourages girls to compete with each other:

> Beware that when girls reach the dating stage, the most devoted friendships may be strained, sometimes

to dissolution, by the tension and competitiveness growing out of new social challenges.

In a study of advertising we discussed two questions: What different emotions do advertisers play on to get us to buy their products, and how do advertisers both *use* and appeal to women in particular? The students were eager and well prepared to respond from their own TV-saturated experience. They surprised and encouraged me by being so aware of the manipulated persuasion of advertisements.

We discussed economic reasons for keeping women out of the wage labor economy under the existing system, and Erich Fromm's analysis of the impact of a market economy on human life:

> In a culture in which the marketing orientation prevails, and in which material success is the outstanding value, there is little reason to be surprised that human love relations follow the same pattern of exchange which governs the commodity and labor market.

I taught one class on psychology—Freud's theory of penis envy, and the recent experiments indicating that all behavior is socially conditioned, which Naomi Weisstein describes in her paper *Kinde, Kuche, Kirche*.

At the end of the section on socialization, after a discussion of *The Feminine Mystique* and the job situation, I asked the students, "Who does the housework and child care in your family? What will you do similarly or differently in your own life?" Their answers forced me to think about who they are and where they're really at.

"Well, I have a full-time maid," said one girl . . . and another said, "An *au pair* girl from Sweden lives with us." The discussion proceeded as I sat silently stunned. Young turned-on girls, but I had forgotten, daughters of the upper middle class, with professional fathers *and* mothers. They argued with each other: "We need a maid. Both my parents work." "We don't have a maid, and both my parents work too. My sisters and I help do the work."

"I don't think having a maid is wrong. After all, she needs the money."

Sheltered from hunger and poverty, they knew nothing of power, and why they were rich instead of poor in a class society. I wondered, are they really the rebellious young women of their generation's revolution? Or are they "upper middle class," sharing their parents' stake in preserving the existing system?

I told them that my experience was different, that I was honestly shocked that so many of them had maids. "*I* don't have one!" "What do you mean, shocked?" Both girls spoke at once, and I saw two dangers. I could make each of them feel personally guilty for their parents' decision, which they cannot change. Or I would unintentionally invite them to repeat a radical rhetoric or put each other down. Kids learn teacher-pleasing in order to survive in school, and they would do it to me if they felt pressure. I wanted *not* to manipulate feelings or force them to parrot back conclusions they had not really reached, but rather to present them with alternatives for their own lives.

I asked the girls to describe an ideal society for taking care of housework and children, using any kind of machine, any definition of family, and any source of money they could imagine.

One general theme emerged from their answers the following week: "In my ideal society, kids will get treated better." One girl mentioned population control, and another the end of wars, but they were exceptions. Parents respecting kids, an end to restrictions on movies, and being allowed to be friends with people of any age were priorities in their ideal societies.

Where were the Engelian, Kibbutzian, ideal, future-age societies I had hoped they would imagine? Humbled, I realized two things. First, their own immediate oppression as women is real, happening to them every day—and they are eager to think about their role and liberation as women. But mostly they *feel* the helplessness of their role as children in an adult world. Second, I as a young girl had never been able to imagine a different society. I have included *Coming of Age in Samoa* precisely because of its impact on me, in college—the emotional, intellectual shock of realizing that we all could have grown up differently. I have learned as a young radical to think in terms of change and alternatives. I had almost forgotten that kids are taught that life is as it is, and always will be, and that their limited years have shown them little different.

So at present we are studying the family in other cultures. I am teaching Engel's *Origin of the Family, Property, and the State* as a theory, a way of thinking about the development of the nuclear family. Samoa, the kibbutz, and Sweden are primitive and modern examples of alternatives. We will also study urban and rural communes in the U.S.

I am in the midst of preparing material for the last two sections. The history section will include an introduction to the suffrage movement, using *Women on the March,* and inviting a local elderly suffragist to speak. I hope to teach some of the songs of women in the labor movement, like "Bread and Roses" and "The Death of Mother Jones." In this section we will also discuss Virginia Woolf and Isadora Duncan as examples of women in the arts.

The last section, "Women, technology, and ecology," has been added since the beginning of the course, and comes out of the thinking and learning of the health and ecology work groups of Women's Liberation in Washington. I hope to introduce questions of health, abortion, birth and population control, and the politics and priorities of environmental management.

Miracles—or major revolutions—don't happen within the conforming walls of a junior high. Cliques, competition for grades and boys, middle-class-private-school isolation, and personal growing pains are reality for these twelve-year-old girls. But they are questioning, thinking —gaining the strength to be different, the confidence that there *are* alternatives—and they may yet join our struggle for political, economic, and human revolution.

# JUMPING THE TRACK
## ALICE LELAND DI RIVERA

Before I went to John Jay High School I hadn't realized how bad the conditions were for students. One of the things that changed my outlook was being involved with the hostilities of the New York City teacher strikes in the fall of 1968. Students were trying to open the school and the teachers were preventing them. I was disillusioned by the low-quality, high-pay teaching we received afterwards, and soon became involved with expressing my discontent.

It was then I found that students had no rights. We had no freedom of the press: many controversial articles were removed from the newspapers by the teacher-editors. We were not allowed to distribute leaflets or newspapers inside our school building, so that press communication was taken away from us. We also had no freedom of speech. Many teachers would put us down in class for our political ideas and then would not let us answer their charges. If we tried to talk with other students during a free period about political issues, we were told to stop. The school was a prison—we were required by state law to be there, but when we were there we had no rights. We had to carry ID cards and passes. We could be suspended; we were considered guilty before proven innocent.

It was this treatment which made me as a student want to change the schools. When I talked to students from

*ALICE LELAND DI RIVERA was fourteen when she wrote this article. She is now a biology major at a Massachusetts college and will be a doctor.*

other public high schools in the city, I found they had been oppressed within the schools in much the same way.

I have been writing about the student's plight in general because it was my first encounter with oppression. It is such a familiar experience to me now, that I think I can try to define it. Oppression, to me, is when people are not allowed to be themselves. I encountered this condition a second time when I realized *woman's* plight in the high schools. And for the second time I tried to help change the schools so that I and other girls would not be hurt.

The first time it really occurred to me that I was oppressed as a woman was when I began to think of what I was going to be when I was older. I realized I had no real plans for the future—college, maybe, and after that was a dark space in my mind. In talking and listening to other girls, I found that they had either the same blank spot in their minds or were planning on marriage. If not that, they figured on taking a job of some sort *until* they got married.

The boys that I knew all had at least some slight idea in their minds of what career or job they were preparing for. Some prepared for careers in science and math by going to a specialized school. Others prepared for their later jobs as mechanics, electricians, and other tradesmen in vocational schools. Some just did their thing in a regular, zoned high school. It seemed to me that I should fill the blank spot in my mind as the boys were able to do, and I decided to study science (biology, in particular) much more intensively. It was then that I encountered one of the many blocks which stand in the woman student's way: discrimination against women in the specialized science and math high schools in the city.

Many years before women in New York State had won their right to vote (1917), a school was established for those high-school students who wish to specialize in science and math. Naturally it was not co-ed, for women were not regarded legally or psychologically as people. This school, Stuyvesant High School, was erected in 1903. In 1956, thirty-nine years after New York women earned the right to vote, the school was renovated; yet no provision was made for girls to enter.

There are only two other high schools in New York which specialize in science and math: Brooklyn Technical, a school geared towards engineering, and Bronx High School of Science. Brooklyn Tech moved from the warehouse, where its male-only classes were started, into a modern building in 1933. It was renovated in 1960, yet still no provision was made for girls.

This left only Bronx Science. Bronx High School of Science is the only school where girls can study science and math intensively—it is co-ed. It became so in 1946, the year it moved into a new building. However, although it admits girls, it still discriminates against them; it admits only one girl to every two boys.

Out of these three schools I could try out for only one. This one, Bronx Science, is one and one-half hours travel time from my home. It presents very stiff competition because of the discriminatory policy* which allows only a certain number of girls to enter, and also because all the girls who would otherwise be trying out for Stuyvesant or Brooklyn Tech have Bronx Science as their only alternative. I became disgusted with this, not only for my sake, but for all the girls who hadn't become scientists or engineers because they were a little less than brilliant or had been put down by nobody having challenged those little blank spots in their minds. After talking about it with my parents and friends, I decided to open up Stuyvesant and challenge the Board of Education's traditional policy.

I took my idea to Ramona Ripston, co-director of the National Emergency Civil Liberties Committee, and she accepted it warmly. Pretty soon I became involved in trying to get an application for the entrance exam to Stuyvesant filled out and sent. It was turned down and we—NECLC, my parents, and I—went to court against the principal of Stuyvesant and the Board of Ed.

The day on which we went to court was the day before the entrance exam was scheduled to be given. The Board of Ed granted me the privilege of taking the test for Bronx Science (which is the same as the one given for Stuyvesant), and the judge recognized that the results of this test would be used in another court hearing to resolve whether or not I would be admitted. Five days after the other students had received their results, we found out that I had passed for entrance into both Stuyvesant and Bronx Science.

We went to court again a couple of months later, in

April. Our judge, Jawn A. Sandafer, seemed receptive to our case, but he reserved his decision. Later we were told that he wished an open hearing for May 13. This was a great break for us because if what the judge needed was public support, we had many important people who were willing to argue in my favor. However, on April 30 the New York City Board of Education voted to admit me to Stuyvesant High School in the Fall. The superintendent had wanted to continue the court fight.

This seemed a victory to us at first, but in actuality it would have been better if we could have continued the case and received a court order. We hoped to establish that public funds could not be used to support institutions of learning which discriminate against women. Such a ruling would have been the key to opening up the other sexually segregated high schools in New York City.

There are a great many battles yet to be fought. Aside from being discouraged to study for a career, women are discouraged from preparing for jobs involving anything *but* secretarial work, beauty care, nursing, cooking, and the fashion industry. During my fight over Stuyvesant, I investigated the whole high-school scene, and found that out of the twenty-seven vocational high schools in the city, only *seven* are co-ed. The boys' vocational schools teach trades in electronics, plumbing, carpentry, foods, printing (another example of Board of Ed traditional policy—there is hardly any work for a hand-typesetter today), etc. The girls are taught to be beauticians, secretaries, or health aides. This means that if a girl is seeking entrance to a vocational school, she is pressured to feel that certain jobs are masculine and others feminine. She is forced to conform to the Board of Education's image of her sex. At the seven co-ed vocational schools, boys can learn clerical work, food preparation, and beauty care along with the girls. But the courses that would normally be found in a boys' school are not open to girls. There are only two schools where a girl can prepare for a "masculine" job. Charles Evans Hughes High School in Manhattan is co-ed for teaching technical electronics. Newtown High School offers an academic pre-engineering course of study for boys and girls. However, this school is zoned for the Borough of Queens only.

In conclusion, there are three types of schools, twenty-nine in number that the Board of Ed has copped out on. These schools are composed of the specialized science and math school Brooklyn Tech, twenty vocational schools which teach students their trade according to what sex they are, and the eight traditionally non-co-ed academic schools.

These eight academic schools are zoned schools which admit only boys or only girls. The argument against these schools is that "separate but equal" is not equal (as established with regard to race in the Brown Decision). The psychological result of the school which is segregated by sex—only because of tradition—is to impress upon girls that they are only "flighty females" who would bother the boys' study habits (as a consequence of girls not being interested in anything but the male sex). This insinuates immaturity on the part of girls—and certainly produces it in both sexes. A boy who has never worked with a girl in the classroom is bound to think of her as his intellectual inferior, and will not treat her as if she had any capacity for understanding things other than child care and homemaking. Both sexes learn to deal with each other as nonpeople. It really messes up the growth of a person's mind.

Out of the sixty-two high schools in New York City, twenty-nine are now sexually segregated. I believe that it is up to the girls to put pressure on the Board of Education to change this situation. I myself cannot live with oppression.

All girls have been brought up by this society never being able to be themselves—the school system has reinforced this. My desire at this time is to change the educational situation to benefit *all* the students. But I'm afraid changes *could* be made that benefited male students, leaving the status of females pretty much as it is. Female students share the general oppressive conditions forced upon everyone by the System's schools, plus a special psychological discrimination shown to women by the schools, the teachers, *and* their fellow students. So, since I don't want *my* issues to get swallowed up in the supposed "larger" issues, I'm going to make women's liberation the center of my fight.

# IT'S TIME FOR EQUAL EDUCATION

*ANN SCOTT*

This year the face of American education will be irrevocably changed. For the first time in American history, it is possible that women will be guaranteed equal *educational* opportunity.

Two pieces of legislation passed by Congress are responsible for this new outlook: The Equal Rights Amendment and the Higher Education Act of 1972.

The requirements of both are going to have to be spelled out so that both university administration and students see what they have to do to ensure that the new right to equal educational opportunity for women becomes a reality. While a great deal of work has been focused on remedying illegal employment inequities among women in universities, to my knowledge, no plans have been proposed to remedy discrimination in *education*. The affirmative action plan we propose here could do just that.

Educational discrimination against women by universities and colleges has been so pervasive and damaging that the costs to women in stunted aspirations and depressed self-esteem, and the loss to the nation in terms of skilled womanpower, can never be fully tallied. According to the Ford Foundation's *Report on Higher Education*, discrimination against women is manifest in three ways: *First, overt discrimination by faculties, deans, and others acting in official capacities; second, practical institutional*

*ANN SCOTT is legislative vice-president for NOW.*

*barriers, such as rigid admissions and residence require-*
*ments, and a lack of campus facilities and services . . .;*
*and third, the ingrained assumptions and inhibitions on*
*the part of both men and women* [reinforced by curriculum and counseling] *which deny the talents and aspira-*
*tions of* [women].

Actual examples of what the *Report* is talking about
are everyday occurrences. Look at admissions practices.
A general admissions policy is to gerrymander the numbers of entering students by sex to keep a 50-50 balance.
In this common but little-known method, the university
takes the entrance examinations, divides them by sex, and
admits equal numbers of top-scoring men and women.
This is disadvantageous to women, as they generally
score higher than men.

Discrimination in admissions policies also results from
the setting of quotas in programs and departments—only
10 percent of the students entering a law school, for example, can be women. Indeed, many professional schools
exclude women altogether. One veterinary college professor defended a policy not to admit women by saying,
"After all, they can't handle animals such as an elephant
in heat." I'm still wondering who can.

Still another inequity is to admit women based on how
much—or how little—housing there is. State residence
requirements are also used against women. In Pennsylvania, for example, a lifelong resident is suing the state
university because she lost her residency status upon
marrying a man from Ohio and was charged the higher
out-of-state tuition.

Women are shortchanged on financial aid, too. Educational Testing Service discovered that grants to women
average $518; those to men $769. Married women are
often denied grants and scholarships on the assumption
that their husbands will provide for them; married men
are frequently given priority on the premise that they have
families to support.

When it comes to health, the reality is much the same.
At most universities a woman's sex-related health needs
are not considered valid medical problems, and therefore are not included in the university's health services
(53 percent of colleges do not provide gynecological serv-

ices and 72 percent do not prescribe birth control for women).

But the new legislation that women worked so hard for can rectify such discriminatory practices; it sets the legal framework for change.

The Equal Rights Amendment, now well on its way to ratification (20 states down, 18 to go), will ensure that "equality of rights under the law shall not be denied or abridged . . . on account of sex" by any governmental action—state or federal. Since states have jurisdiction over school systems, and since both states and the federal government largely finance state universities and colleges, the ERA will prevent all tax-supported schools from favoring students of either sex in virtually all the services they provide. The Equal Rights Amendment is, however, a broad statement of a general principle of equality, and does not spell out how this equality under the law is to be achieved. Explicits must wait for "implementing legislation."

The Higher Education Act of 1972, signed into law June 23, provides in its Title IX for sex equality both in employment in educational institutions and in education itself. We are concerned here only with those sections which cover education (as distinct from employment)—the rights of women as consumers in the educational marketplace that they themselves support with their tax dollars. While it has no direct relationship to the ERA, The Higher Education Act may be looked at as an anticipatory implementing law which describes specific kinds of discrimination and what can be done about them.

The Higher Education Act states that: *No person in the United States shall, on the basis of sex, be excluded from participation in, be denied the benefits of, or be subjected to discrimination under any education program or activity receiving federal financial assistance. . . .*

Digging through the 150 pages of the Act's legal language, we find that it applies to almost all schools receiving federal grants and loans—preschools, elementary or secondary schools, vocational or professional schools, and both public and private undergraduate and graduate institutions. It prohibits discrimination in admissions, financial assistance, use of facilities and other areas. The only exception is that private undergraduate and single-sex public institutions are exempted from the admissions requirements of that Act, though they are subject to all its other antidiscrimination provisions. The federal government is empowered to withhold funds from any university found guilty of violating any of the above provisions of the Higher Education Act.

Clearly problems will arise in defining gray areas such as whether the existing practices of a university do, in fact, violate the Act and what measures must be taken to correct violations. Whether the specific problems are confronted and or dealt with depends upon how the Higher Education Act is enforced. Now that the Act is passed, the next step is for those federal agencies giving grants to issue "implementing rules and regulations" delineating how they intend to enforce the Act. Since the Department of Health, Education and Welfare is the primary source of university grants, it will take the lead in enforcing the Act; other agencies will undoubtedly model their rules on HEW's. Since legislation lives or dies by how it is enforced, it is incumbent on women to make sure that the Act is implemented by rules and regulations which will ensure real change in educational opportunity.

In this article, therefore, we are proposing what we think would be the most effective plan for implementing the Higher Education Act. We believe that HEW should require universities to develop an affirmative action plan —heretofore applied only to employment practices—to realize educational opportunity. To arrive at an affirmative action plan, a university

(1) analyzes its services and student profile to see where women are underrepresented;

(2) sets reasonable goals and timetables for correcting underrepresentation;

(3) makes up a program of specific measures and techniques through which it will achieve these goals. Because an affirmative action plan means little unless something is done to change attitudes, a plan should contain measures (such as women's studies courses and faculty-student groups to raise consciousness) for educating administrators and ourselves out of those ingrained and less obvious assumptions about women.

A model affirmative action plan follows. It is important

to note that this kind of plan can be adapted to cover all minorities.

*An Affirmative Action Plan For Equal Educational Opportunity For Women*

I. RESPONSIBILITIES OF UNIVERSITY ADMINISTRATION

 A. *Statement of policy of nondiscrimination*

 The president of the university shall develop a statement of policy of nondiscrimination containing at least the following elements:

 1. a guarantee of equal educational opportunity regardless of sex, age, marital or parental status, pregnancy or possible pregnancy, and

 2. a commitment to remedy the present effects of past discrimination against women students through a vigorously pursued program of affirmative action.

 B. *Dissemination of policy:*

 The statement of policy shall be signed by the president, deans, and department chairpersons and published in the student handbook, given out to all applicants and incoming students, and posted in each academic department, countersigned by the department chairperson.

 C. *Development of an Affirmative Action Plan:*

 In order to carry out these commitments, the university shall develop a program of affirmative action for women designed to correct all practices which discriminate against women students in recruitment and admissions, curriculum, extracurricular activities, and supportive services. The "AAP" shall include goals and timetables whenever it is shown that women are underrepresented among the students.

 It shall assign specific responsibility for implementation to the heads of each organizational unit within the university (i.e., provosts, deans, department chairpersons).

II. MEANS OF ACCOUNTABILITY: RECORDS AND REPORTS

 A. *Recordkeeping:*

 The president shall require each academic and administrative department (1) to maintain records by sex on applications and admissions, financial aid, scholarships, fellowships, and graduate assistantships applied for and granted, and (2) to identify areas where women are underrepresented.

B. *Affirmative action report:*

Each department shall be required to submit at the end of each school year an affirmative action report describing its record in achieving equal educational opportunities for women students.

## III. MEANS OF ENFORCEMENT: SANCTIONS

A. *Grievance procedure:*

The university shall establish a grievance procedure by which students who feel they have been denied equal educational opportunity on the basis of their sex can appeal. The grievance procedure should follow established rules of due process; one procedure, not several; and should allow the aggrieved party to file grievance with the unit who made the decision under review. If grievance cannot be resolved at this level, the formal procedure—after hearing, right of confrontation, cross-examination, and knowledge of the evidence being used—follows. Failing this, the procedure shall lead to outside binding arbitration, either through the courts or through federal administrative remedy, the costs of which shall be borne by the university.

B. *Faculty and administration:*

For all those assigned responsibility for carrying out the program, affirmative action achievement or failure shall be considered a major criterion in granting or withholding promotion or merit raises. Failure to fulfill specific affirmative action requirements that are delegated shall be considered a failure to do one's job, and therefore shall be grounds for dismissal.

C. *Budget:*

The university shall hold in reserve a part of the operational budget (i.e., for supplies, travel expenses, speakers' fees, etc.) and shall grant these moneys to departments which show genuine progress in carrying out the purposes of the affirmative action plan.

**IV. OFFICE ON THE STATUS OF WOMEN**

In order to carry out its affirmative action plan, the university shall establish an adequately funded and staffed women's advocacy office which shall be administered by a vice-president and shall report directly to the president. Its responsibilities will be:

1. to develop and oversee the affirmative action plan with the aid of an advisory council composed of women faculty and students;

2. to assist students in developing intradepartmental sensitivity seminars to enable students and faculty to discuss and identify sexist content and attitudes in courses, particularly in the social sciences, arts and letters, and medicine;

3. to investigate complaints and initiate reviews of departments;

4. to advise women students;

5. to represent students in educational grievances;

6. to investigate and coordinate women's studies.

**V. EDUCATIONAL ACTIVITIES**

*A. Review of admissions and enrollment:*

1. Analysis of admissions policy:

The university shall make public its admissions policy, including a complete description of all criteria and selection processes at all levels of the university, and shall ensure that none of these are discriminatory on the basis of sex, age, or marital status. (*N.B. Domicile.* No resident of the state, on marrying a resident of another state, shall lose her residency status or be required to pay nonresident tuition or fees.)

A review of admissions shall appear in the annual report of the Office on the Status of Women.

2. Analysis of student profile:

The university shall conduct, department by department, an annual analysis of its student profile to determine where women are underrepresented.

3. Factors determining underrepresentation:

Underrepresentation of women can be defined and reasonable goals arrived at by considering the following factors:

a. percentage of acceptable women applicants to both the department and university;

b. percentage of women students in the university;

c. representation of women in the professions taught by the departments.

B. *Action-oriented measures to eliminate discrimination:*

1. Upon completion of analysis of student profile, the university shall establish reasonable goals and timetables to increase representation of women.

2. Where women are underrepresented in a profession (for example, engineering), the department should make an active effort to recruit more women to that profession. At least one senior member of the faculty shall be assigned overall responsibility for developing the recruitment program and specific techniques for bringing women students into its program, such as making presentations in high schools or among undergraduates; and conducting counseling sessions for women students on opportunities for them in that particular field.

3. Programs shall be designed to recruit and counsel older women wishing to return to school on a full or part-time basis. The university shall establish criteria whereby it shall evaluate the application process and recognize for academic credit the services of women in volunteer work and community service.

C. *Curriculum:*

1. Women's studies:

The university shall encourage departments to establish programs of courses and research into the status and socialization of women, and/or to establish a separate degree-granting department of women's studies. Under the women's advocacy office, the university shall establish an adequately funded center to act as a clearinghouse for information on curriculum development, resources, funding, and research into all questions—social, economic, political, psychological, educational, literary, historical, medical—having to do with women's role in society. This research center shall be available to all students on campus wishing to use it in conjunction with course work in any department or program, and to any students who wish to undertake independent research projects for credit under the women's studies program.

2. Athletics programs

a. The university shall examine the policies of its Department of Physical Education to determine if and where women are being denied the opportunity to participate in existing programs. Recommendations shall be submitted for new programs to be designed for the benefit of women (i.e., self-defense).

b. The athletics budget shall be examined to see what its per capita dollar expenditure is by sex. Where gross inequity exists, the university shall reallocate moneys to fund more, or larger, programs for women, or coeducational programs designed for teamwork and cooperation rather than competition (i.e., jogging, volleyball).

c. Athletics scholarships shall be reapportioned to provide, where indicated, more opportunities and professional training for women (i.e., in tennis and swimming).

3. R.O.T.C.:

The university shall not permit the Department of Defense to carry on any R.O.T.C. program which does not allow women to be enrolled on an equal basis with men.

D. *Extracurricular activities:*

Women shall not be denied participation in any regular programs of extracurricular activities, such as playing in the band, joining honorary societies, managing athletic teams, working on student publications in any capacity.

E. *Support services:*

The university shall review all criteria for making support services available to all students on an equal basis, and eliminate those which discriminate on the basis of sex, marital or parental status, pregnancy or possible pregnancy. It shall publish and make available to all students the criteria and procedures for applying for and receiving such services, and shall maintain full records by sex.

1. Financial aid:

All grants, loans, scholarships, and fellowships shall be publicly posted, and shall be awarded according to clearly established and published criteria. Sex shall not be a criterion for the awarding of financial aid.

2. Counseling:

The Office on the Status of Women shall evaluate all existent counseling services for women, and make recommendations for their improvement. In conjunction with university departments, it shall offer counseling in high schools and elementary schools as well as college—with a view toward encouraging women to enter traditionally male professional fields, and discouraging them from entering fields with a surfeit of trained professionals. In cooperation with local industry and government, it shall undertake a coordinated program of vocational counseling and job development in entirely new employment fields for women. It shall offer counseling to the older woman, and provide nonsexist counseling to all students.

3. Medical services:

Population control center: the university shall offer medical services to women which shall include gynecological examination, complete birth-control counseling and prescriptions, and, with the repeal of abortion laws in the various states, shall prepare for realistic unwanted pregnancy counseling and all related medical care allowed within the law. University health-insurance policies should include maternity benefits regardless of marital status.

4. Child care:

The university shall establish a child-care facility free to the children of all faculty, staff, and students. It shall be open to children from birth to twelve years and shall provide educational programs for the children. It shall remain in operation at those times when libraries are open, classes are in session, or women are working at the university.

5. Housing:

Housing shall be available to men and women on an equal basis. Rules of behavior, and curfew shall apply equally. Availability of housing for women shall not be a criterion for controlling admissions.

6. Placement and employment:

The placement office shall not maintain separate job listings for men and women, but shall make known all jobs to both sexes. The university shall not accept any listings from employers who state preference for applicants of one sex. The university shall not allow any company to interview on campus which does not agree to see all students, regardless of sex.

## What You Can Do:

1. Write or visit the Secretary of Health, Education and Welfare, urging him to implement the Higher Education Act by requiring universities receiving federal assistance to submit Affirmative Action Plans guaranteeing equal educational opportunity to women, and including goals and timetables.

Send him this plan as a possible model. His address is:

Secretary, Department of HEW

Washington, D.C. 20201

Lobby your Congressperson and Senators through personal and group visits; letters; and telegrams to support Affirmative Action Plan implementation.

2. Work with other women to push your university to put into practice its commitment to equal rights for women by *voluntarily* developing such a plan, which will bring it into compliance with the Higher Education Act. Analyze your university for instances of discrimination against women—document your case, and demand that the administration come up with an Affirmative Action Plan which will correct its practices. Make sure that women students are included at all stages of the process.

# FEMINIST STUDIES: FRILL OR NECESSITY?

*MARILYN WEBB*

## Why Feminist Studies Anyway?

When I think about Feminist Studies, I think more about "Feminist" than I do about "studies." Although this may be a false way of saying it, I think Feminist Studies Programs should be more closely tuned to an on-going feminist movement than to the university proper. What has come to be considered the operating assumptions of American universities seems greatly divergent from the aims of a feminist movement, although this means more of a necessity for consciousness of our own situation than for splitting with established universities right now.

Each of us has her own theory of what feminism is, but somehow we hope they all can mesh. In mine I assume that the prime goal of a feminist revolution is the elimination of patriarchal rule. Although other sisters have already written books on the subject, I consider patriarchy the first class division between people, giving one group, by birthright, the authority to rule over another. Historically, once this authority was acknowledged, the groundwork was laid for groups to split into further refined rulers and ruled. So we saw the development of a slave class, then serfs, then an industrial working class, and more currently, colonized nations. We have alternately called this same power dynamic racism, sexism, and im-

*MARILYN WEBB teaches English in the Feminist Studies program at Goddard College, Vermont.*
Copyright © 1974 by Marilyn Webb.

perialism, but what is basic to all is the right of hierarchal rule. This is the basic challenge of a feminist movement.

In formulating this challenge we need to do two things: (1) learn about our condition and recapture an identity out of our colonized state, and (2) avoid hierarchal distinctions between us as an example of a new society we plan to create. Some call this last part the development of female collectivity. I would agree, but stress that implicit in collective action is the development of each individual's strengths and potential, and this is where Feminist Studies fits in.

As part of a feminist movement, the goals of a Feminist Studies program should be for each woman to learn as deeply and as broadly as possible the historical, literary, biological, and psychological roots of our collective colonization and to formulate theoretical perspectives of what female nature is and could be. Implicit in intellectual learning should be the development of a process of collective thought, study and action: form and content. One of these goals is no more important than the other.

Now this is precisely the antithesis of what universities are all about. Rather than building collectivity, they divide by competitiveness and grade hierarchies. Rather than creating group solidarity, they create an intellectual elite whose social status, but not real power, is meant to be above those who have never received a higher education. This is not done by accident or through faulty educational theory, but to serve a society that demands a highly technical yet compliant working class.

If we are not careful, rather than making any dent in a partriarchal class system, we will instead create careers in academic studies on women and have no relationship with the great majority of women to whom we will become like overseers. So divided, we will all fail to change so pervasive a power dynamic.

So we need to clarify two things: What is it we teach and how. I think the two are not separate. What I hope to "teach" my students is that they can develop a solid core of themselves, they can learn their past history in connection with women of all times, and that they can learn better together than they can apart.

But I have reached the end of my thought process too quickly. Let me go back. I was trained at a very scholarly

institution. When we learned history, we learned only
from authorities who had done the finest research and
who lectured on their findings. Their stories were always
those of the most powerful in a society; the rationalizations the powerful used to stay in power, or when the
hands of power changes (say from land rich to merchant
wealth), the reasons for the decline of one class and the
rise of another. Their stories left huge gaps. Why was it
that there were classes anyway? What were those not in
the ruling classes doing? If there were struggles what were
they about?

Since women have never been in power, of course it is
never the history of women we learn. We rarely know
how a woman's day was spent in 1600. We have little idea
how industrialism profoundly changed her relationship
with the world or with her husband and kids. We don't
know how her life changed at the movement of industry
away from her home. We have no histories of the development of the "modern" nuclear family through the eyes
of women who lived through these changes. And thus we
have no view of how those not in the ruling classes—the
common people—saw their own struggles for survival.

Furthermore, the way whatever information we were
given was presented (i.e., lectures by only the most
knowledgeable experts), reinforced in form what was
being taught in content. We learned that there has always
been a system of authority in the world, and that those at
the top must remain unchallenged, while those at the
bottom must consider themselves insignificant at the feet
of those enlightened few.

When we teach about sexual politics, it's a class hierarchy we are attacking. If we recreate this class division
within our teaching, our analysis is devoid of form. That's
why as feminist teachers, it's just as important for us to
look at how we teach as to look at what we teach.


*Feminism as a Philosophy of Knowledge*

We come from a different place than most "departments"
or "Programs" within universities. We have an analysis
and a direction in which we feel change should occur. By
university definitions, we are hardly "Objective" (read:

willing to take *what is* as immutable). But we shouldn't crumble before this charge, because we are doing profound and scholarly thinking in areas never touched by most university scholars, only we have a context in which to fit our research. It is the fact of having this context that makes what we are doing so vital.

Feminism is a philosophy of knowledge. It is the intellectual understanding of the historical struggle between domination and submission; between what Kate Millet calls that group of people born to rule and that born to be ruled. Questions such as: "What is the psychological dynamic that accepts submission?" "What are the forms of passive and active resistance used to combat a colonized state?" "What are the basic units of social organization that develop systems of authoritarianism?", are as current today as they were in prehistory.

As a philosophy of knowledge, feminism is concerned with the forms and functions of power and how it has been wielded. Such a philosophy cuts across so-called "disciplines" to include psychology (both of the individual and in groups; the colonizer and the colonized); sociology (social forms of power and class development); economics (uses of power with varied economic bases in history); biology (is there such a thing as biological inferiority?); and of course the study of history, literature and the arts. But this study is from a wholly different context: it is the history of what was created both by the dominated and the dominator to sustain or struggle against that domination.

Feminism is also a dialectical understanding, in the Marxist sense of dialectic. Among any colonized group a dynamic develops between those aspects of their situation produced by the colonized state and those aspects inherent in their collective identity, and produced out of struggle against colonization.

We have no sense yet what part of feminist cultural identity is created by captivity, and what part is indeed created out of some notion of female principle strengthened by collective resistance. (Empathy, for example, as a female trait.) We really don't know what the true nature of the female experience is outside of the colonized situation, and this can never be known until patriarchy ends. But, what we can attempt to understand is what body of

knowledge has been created out of the female experience, and leave it to later scholars to sort out.

I keep having to leave this work to do other things.
For instance, it is hard for me to sit and write for long
periods of time. I notice dust on the floor and have to get
out the vacuum cleaner and clean it up because it makes
me nervous to work if the room isn't clean. My desk is a
wreck since my little girl likes to scribble on my equally
important notes to myself. She comes home from nursery
school in a little while, so half my mind is on whether her
father or I will pick her up today, and so on. Now I can
hardly imagine what my writing would be like were these
things not on my mind. If I had a house slave, as most
male writers do, to do all these small services, I might be
able to pay attention to more lofty thoughts, and so my
work would be totally different, probably more rarefied.
But is that a work of true human nature, or just the work
of one group of humans who manages to so stultify
thought by having a slave class that they are out of touch
with the nitty gritty of life in their works. Who is to say
that that work is more valid?

In our cultural history research, art and literature that
is called great stems from a tradition that rests on a slave
class. Look at any book on your bookshelf. Most say,
"And last but not least, I am grateful to my wife who
protected me from any intrusions and suffered alone with
the incantations of this budding author." Now we all
know what that means! He stayed locked in his study
thinking, while she took care of the kids, made him
meals, shopped, kept his house and study cleaned, took
abuse from him when he felt unable to work, and perhaps
even did all his transcribing, typing and editing, as well as
mailed his manuscripts and corresponded with publishers.
Terrific of him to thank her! But this is just the surface.
How can such a situation not affect the work he produces?
He rarely ever experiences life, or if he does, he knows
only a narrow portion of it. So his reality is blinded by
his position. . . .

## What Do We Teach?

But this still leaves unanswered the question of what it is
we teach. When I think about my own education I can

hardly remember a single fact I learned, although I have
many blue books still at hand to affirm that I did indeed
know some, and even get high grades on them. They have
slipped away, along with my images of the lofty professors who told me them. But I have more vivid memories
of the less lofty professors who bothered to show me how
they were going about learning whatever they were doing;
these were the ones who taught me just a little about how
to think and about the importance of having a reason for
learning anything, a framework to fit whatever it is I
wanted to learn into. Usually the framework that
helped me learn most coherently was one that I was trying to act on. For instance, when I was working in a
community school some years back, I read everything I
could about welfare, educational theories and philosophies, poverty, inner-city sociology, and so on. I was trying to do something, and all I needed was someone to tell
me where to look to learn.

Most universities are not structured with this premise in
mind. Instead the working premise seems to be that it is
good (for inner peace of something) to know certain
bodies of knowledge. Therefore we find that most college
students learn by rote what they promptly forget, sometimes even before the ink dries on their B.A.'s. Maybe in
fact what university students learn is how to develop the
self-confidence and chutzpa to bluff through what they
don't know, i.e., to put on a good show. For it is this very
skill which allows them to function as a class above those
who have not been to college.

But as feminists it is not this skill, or the sterile body
of information we are trying to teach. I think all that we
teach should have intrinsic to it an understanding of the
power dynamic of patriarchy, and a purpose that is constantly up front about action against this dynamic. I mean
it's more how we look at whatever body of information
we have. Say we are studying history. We read many letters and diaries of women who have lived in different
times and places before us. What do we want to know
from this history? We want to ask what their objective
situation was, what were the cultural myths that bound
them there, what intersections were there between them
as individuals and the historical events and conditions surrounding their lives, how might they have changed their

situation (i.e. what were the dimensions they could have moved in and why didn't they?). We don't want to stop here.

To answer any of these questions a student would have to look more in depth at a time period of the life of one woman than just her own writings. She would have to learn the historian's craft of how to do research: what laws were passed to see what many women were doing that threatened male authorities, what did other observers think of the same historical moment, from what position were they speaking, what were the physical boundaries of life at that time, etc.

To make any of this research mean something to our struggle today, intrinsic to this course should be a personal autobiography or written statement about the student's own life. What are the intersections of the individual and the historical moment there, what are the mythologies that blind us, what are the boundaries of action. Asking these questions of history moves us further along in our struggle, gives us depth to look at our own condition, and gives us more of an idea how sisters long dead dealt with similar questions. History becomes a breathing body of our collective consciousness, and not a work of fact to be buried between the covers of some journal.

This is to say I don't particularly feel any body of knowledge is more or less relevant to feminist curricula, but it is how we look at that knowledge, what questions we ask of it, and how it is useful for an understanding of our own struggle that makes it relevant or not.

## How Do We Teach?

Historically the purpose of public education in the United States was to create a more sophisticated manner of rule by intellectual and psychological indoctrination. To this purpose today has been added the need for a technically knowledgeable working class. Education channels people in a class society. Because of this it has always been conducted in the style of hierarchical rule ("Teach the kids respect," they've called it.) Feminism, instead, is based on the elimination of all domination/submission relationships, and these are inherent in a class-based society. Therefore, we must look carefully at how we teach as intrinsic to what we teach.

It is true that some people have more skill or knowledge than others. They have this not by divine birth right, but because they have spent some time acquiring it. Those who become students want to learn this knowledge or skill, so the main question for every feminist teacher is how to teach without imposing authoritarian structures. Coupled with this is the need for building a consciousness of an alternative, e.g. collective learning and action. Unfortunately most students coming through our public-school systems have already developed a set of responses to those called teachers, so acting differently in one's role as teacher is not easy.

First off, students taking feminist courses in college are not apt to see this as you do. For the teacher feminism is a way of viewing everything else one is learning, doing, seeing. It is a philosophy, a politic and a life view, an analysis of the world. For the student it may be that, but it is usually just another course, on an equal par with pottery, dance technique, and French. Furthermore, feminism is quickly becoming a fad, so even the normal class expectation of seriousness may not apply. So the teacher is faced with a double job: helping people to understand the seriousness of a feminist philosophy and teaching so that students feel a strength of collective learning rather than hierarchal control.

Because there are set responses to things called schools, feminist classes should try to be as different as possible from such settings. They must try to include actual experiences of what we are talking about in our teaching so that real conclusions can be made (not unthought-out acceptance of ideas.)

For example, many schools now include in classes on mental illness days of work at mental hospitals. This is one example of a real setting to look at what is happening to women. Suppose a class were trying to understand the uses of mental illness in the oppression of women. Students might spend time interviewing female patients (most people in mental hospitals are female) to see what common case histories they have. Studies might be made of admission statistics that would include reason for admission and time of life large numbers of patients are ad-

mitted. For sure students would discover most women are
admitted in later adolescence when adult rules are supposed to develop, after childbirth, and during menopause.
Who could fail to understand that these are stress points
when the prevailing ideology might not take hold.

In addition, large portions of time could be arranged
away from school (see for example programs at Goddard,
Antioch, and Northeastern University where integral
to education are both resident and nonresident semesters.) In my experience, the most real learning occurs in
reflecting about what was happening in the real world as
opposed to the school world of pure ideas.

In most areas of our society, there is no room for taking any student work seriously. We have experts for that.
All is an exercise in thinking, so no wonder students
rarely put any more into papers than that. But we have a
rare opportunity in Feminist Studies. No real work has
been done by anyone in the history and lives of women
as an underclass. Only among socialists in the 1930s and
with the rise of Black Studies has any serious work been
done on studies of how the common people lived. Women
everywhere can begin to piece together oral histories of
grandmothers, diaries from antique stores, letters buried
in attics, and obscure family momentoes to develop a history of the people. Popular views of what happened in
specific time periods may be dispelled by such research.
For example, the usual response people give when asked
what they think about when you mention the 1920s is
flappers. But in fact, there were more Wobblies in the 20s
than flappers, although there were probably more flappers
in the upper classes. And most people were neither. So
there is ample opportunity for doing real research.

### Do People Learn in Schools?

Here we enter the foggy zone of the relation of a university to learning and to revolution. A decade ago the most
revolutionary segment of our society was in the universities. Now we know they are no longer there; whoever is
left there has been quieted either by the knowledge that
universities are not going to bend to student demands or
that even if they could, they have no power in the larger
society anyhow. So we are finding larger and larger num-

bers of young people not in schools anymore. But does this mean they aren't learning?

Just the opposite. I think they are learning more than their stay-in-school friends and that what they are learning is of more relevance to building the society we envision than what they would have learned in school. That's a pretty sweeping statement. For the last two years until coming to Goddard, I was part of a woman's collective. We published a newspaper called *Off Our Backs*, and then later some of us began to build a living collective as well. Women in the collective ranged in age from 17 to 32, but hierarchies were not defined by age. In publishing a newspaper, one must of necessity think about what is being printed, particularly since we were attempting to create a feminist philosophy in the content of what we printed. At its best time the collective functioned by printing nothing that had not had a thorough group discussion that at least clarified differences, if it did not reach a consensus on framework and theoretical content. To do this each member had to learn about those issues up for discussion: current news, the legal system, the history of the family, the role of romance in western civilization, etc. As collective members pushed themselves further intellectually, by necessity they challenged the foundations of their own lives, forcing change on many levels. This led to lesbian relationships and so on.

Now I doubt that intellectual work done in the context of schools produced the profound intellectual and personal growth such a collective experience does. In my year of teaching at Goddard, I've found that students learn the most through personal relationships with each other (either as couples or in the small, collective type cooking dorms we have), and not in classes. Every teacher knows this.

The common threads through the times when one learns seem to be (1) when one wants to, and (2) when one's whole being is called into question and one is challenged to face the operating assumptions of daily life. So if learning occurs through being together, why not have collectives while in school: living and learning/together. A woman would have to choose to spend one semester at a minimum in a collective that planned its work together.

As a group they all might study some basic theoretical works, but then they could split off and do separate work depending on interest, maybe in teams, but with constant discussion of what they are doing.

If exposure to the realities of women's lives outside the more equalitarian, but entirely mythological setting of school means a greater understanding, then much time should be planned in settings with other women: e.g., mental hospitals, prisons, around welfare offices, at Planned Parenthood, at health clinics, at employment agencies, looking at where women work. This time could be incorporated into classes, but it might be better to spend extended periods of time, so maybe it's important to encourage women to leave school for a while to work in a factory or at the telephone company, or interviewing other women—old and young. Goddard has a work period and so this is easier. Women who are still in the confines of school have less of the anger that women who are out in the real world feel. If it could be felt before graduation, maybe as teachers we could help each woman discover some inner core of herself that will tide her through a life-long struggle against patriarchal odds.

## How Does the Campus Relate to the Community?

Part of the American mobility mythology is that via education all who work hard can gain access to the upper classes, and therefore, to power. This is one of the reasons why most reform movements in this country have begun by agitating for education first (see women, blacks, and immigrants). The basic assumption of those making this struggle is that either there are merits in the class system or that it is immutable. But as feminists, one of our primary struggles is against the existence of a class system, no matter who is on top.

So what does higher education for women mean in this regard? That some women are being trained as a separate class, a class above those women who are not being trained. Furthermore, intellectual acrobatics and the mystification of knowledge are just the tools used to make those who have not been given a higher education feel they are inferior and therefore deserve to be ruled.

Because higher education is a double-edged sword, we

must be particularly careful to use our knowledge to help, not oppress other women. Programs, beginning at the freshman level, of campus women working with community women in areas of learning which teach real skills are a step in the right direction. Aside from medical skills, knowledge of women's history, the struggles of blacks and workers, communication skills such as writing or graphics all seem vital.

## And What is the Point of Feminist Studies in Schools?

This is the most difficult question to deal with. Consciousness of our shaky position is hardly enough. We need models, and there are some from the past-workers schools of the 1930s. Many of these schools were set up by socialists involved in labor organizing. They spoke both to the needs of workers' intellectual and artistic development as people with a cultural identity to share, as well as to the need for organizing a working-class opposition to a capitalist economy. Such schools contained both courses in writing children's stories and in printing posters and leaflets. Of course there were many theory and history courses as well.

These schools were rarely part of established universities, at first, although there were some. Where they were, they were noticeably different. Those run by colleges (Bryn Mawr had one) taught facts and skills. But they left out any analysis of a system that depended on wage laborers for profits for those who owned the corporations, and they excluded any consciousness of a worker identity or solidarity. Those that included these aspects as central to their curricula were separate from universities, were constantly in financial difficulties, and most finally closed. And so the whole worker education movement was soon coopted by universities anxious to cash in on the struggle but not to challenge the system that fed its scholars.

This same cooptation could happen with the women's movement. We are part of a revolutionary movement whose goal is to end patriarchal rule, and included in that, class divisions in society. Our intellectual work is to understand our collective history, to join us closer in solidarity with all women, and to create a new order out of the depth of understanding from our studies. I think this still is possible within universities, but only if we don't lose sight of what we're about.

Lastly, I like to think that the point of Feminist Studies is to build strong women five healthy ways: in body, in skills, in depth of collective history, in need of each other to grow, and in practicality and energy to struggle against great odds. We will succeed as teachers if we teach only some of that.

# EQUAL OPPORTUNITY FOR WOMEN: HOW POSSIBLE AND HOW QUICKLY

*FLORENCE HOWE*

I want to begin this morning by describing a Women's Studies course I taught with Anne Driver at Old Westbury this past year. I do so for several reasons which will become clear as I go along. Mainly I want to give you some idea of where women are coming from and how long it takes for them to learn where they want to go. And then I shall glance toward the future. In short, I shall assume that you know the facts, you are aware that the current educational system discriminates against women and deprives them of basic needs. I assume also that you need no persuasion about the guidelines established in April by The Regents. They are just: Indeed, with one or two omissions I shall get to later on, they may be regarded as Utopian. Since those guidelines acknowledge the limitations of the past and the present, I shall not dwell on either, but rather, on the questions, how do we get from here to there? and when?

To move from the Guidelines and to change the education of women in New York State is the responsibility of most of the people in this room. To do so, we need to understand not only the facts of women's lower salaries and lesser status, but the experience of their lives. And not the singular experience of some token professors like me, or the hardly existent token deans, or the not-yet-existent

*FLORENCE HOWE teaches English and Women's Studies at SUNY-Old Westbury. She is a founder of the Feminist Press and President of the Modern Language Association.*
Copyright © 1974 by Florence Howe.

token presidents, but the experiences of the masses of women in and out of school, whose lives and educational futures depend on people in this room.

First, then, the class at Old Westbury. The students were, by any standards of higher education, an unusual group: all females, their ages ranged from twenty to past fifty: they were religiously, racially, and ethnically diverse: a few were unmarried and several had five to eight children and a couple were heads of households: they included the affluent as well as the lower middle class and even a representative of the working poor. Not the usual college class, though I dare say we could fill colleges with such students if we wished. But this group is also a representative one—if we are looking for women who have been educated in our elementary and secondary schools during the past several decades. This group is useful for our purposes today also because many of them want to become teachers.

Anne Driver (an historian and former elementary-school teacher) and I (a teacher of literature and writing with some experience in teacher education) were interested in exploring the history of women's education in the U.S.—a much-ignored subject. We could find no texts (the last book on the subject was written in the year of my birth—1929). Instead, we used fiction, autobiography, and biography, planning to turn our students into researchers with us. On opening night—our class met Thursday evenings from seven P.M. on—we wanted to engage our students in the task at hand. We looked for a process that would sensitize them to the problems involved in the education of women.

And we did not offer them a lecture.

Since the group was small enough—under twenty—we asked the students to write briefly (fifteen minutes) and then report orally on the following question: What was the single most crucial experience in your educational life? We defined "crucial" to mean establishing the direction for or changing the course of a life. What educational experience changed your life or at least made you understand (or now makes you understand) something significant about yourself and your relation to the world? Once someone began to speak, we moved around the table clockwise, until all present, including the two teachers, had spoken.

(This, you may be interested in knowing, is a technique borrowed from consciousness-raising groups.)

The person who began was the oldest woman in the class. Sophie Zimmerman's story went back in time about thirty-five years, to when she was seventeen. That year, her mother had told her of a small sum of money in a bank account that she meant to use to send her to college. Sophie was her youngest, and she, at least, would have this special advantage. But then suddenly, Sophie's mother died, without telling anyone else of her plan for the money. Sophie was sent to live first with married sisters and finally to keep house for two bachelor brothers. There was the perfect solution: it was the thirties, when money and jobs were scarce; the brothers had jobs and needed a housekeeper. No one asked the young woman what she wanted to do; no one guessed that she wanted to go to college, and she herself assumed that no one would believe her if she mentioned her mother's plan. She spent four years housekeeping for her brothers and then escaped into her own domesticity by marrying. She bore and raised a number of children and now that they were grown and educated, she was, more than thirty years later, finally at college.

The second person to speak was one of the young ones in the class. At the age of twenty-two, Alice Grunfeld had already been a dropout and was now returning to college as a married student. Her older brother had dropped out of college several months before she had. Her family had greeted her brother's dropping out with alarm, and when he chose to return a year later, had given a huge party to celebrate the event. When Alice had dropped out, the action, she said, made hardly a ripple in the family's life, and when she had decided to return, there were discussions about whether she really ought to. After all, she had a good job now and could save money for a house and furnishings—she had married and would soon have children. Why go to college—it would be a waste of money. Alice concluded her story to the class by reporting that she was now pregnant and that, for the first time in her life, she knew what it was to be valued by her family. "I don't need to do another thing ever," Alice said, "I have had all the glory I ever thought it was possible for me, *a mere girl*, to have. I have never felt so loved by my family as now that I am about to have a baby. But as for my going to college, most everyone considers it a waste of time."

Had nothing changed in thirty years? That question did not need an explicit answer as diverse stories reported a consistent theme. The education of women was relatively unimportant compared to the education of men. And where it was considered at all, it was relegated the status of a diversion; when it became other than a diversion, it was considered a threat.

Thus, one woman reported that her husband had at first approved the idea of her returning to college, after an interruption of some twenty years. But when she began to refuse social engagements because she had to write a paper or study for an exam, he was not pleased. Other women acknowledged that their husbands felt threatened by the prospect of a wife with a college degree. Even if their salaries could not match their husbands', the women might become teachers or guidance counselors, "professionals," and thus a social cut above salesmen or owners of small businesses.

An observer that evening might have drawn several other conclusions from the stories that were told. With two exceptions,[1] these stories about a "crucial educational experience" focused not on educational institutions and personnel, but on the attitudes of family members or husbands toward a daughter's or wife's education. And in all instances, whatever the story, the woman's attitude was never aggressive about her own desires or needs. In every case, women accepted passively (in one case, actively) the role assigned to them or deferred to a more convenient time—albeit twenty or thirty years hence—their own interests or futures. Indeed, to some of these women, the idea of having their own interests or futures was still a novelty.

Let me add at once also that these anecdotes were not told with pathos, acrimony, or anger. Given their content, they were told with remarkable good humor. Whatever pain lay beneath the surface was dispersed by the comic gift with which each woman delivered her narrative. When Sophie was asked, toward the end of the evening, whether she felt angry—then or now—with her brothers,

---

[1] The two exceptions were my own story and one of race prejudice that involved a teacher.

she replied, "No, and I've never told them this story—even to this day. Why should I? What's done is done. It wasn't their fault—that was the way things were."

*That was the way things were.*

I have raised these matters for a particular purpose: to make clear that the education of women is not simply an educational problem but a social one, some would say a political problem. Now I don't believe that schools are to blame for social problems; nor do I believe that schools can solve social problems. Indeed, that has not been their function historically. But schools have contributed to the perpetuation of this particular social problem, mainly by reflecting as passively as those women in my class current social expectations regarding women.

One of the first purposes of the class I have described was to establish the education of women as a social problem, not a question of individual laziness or an individual's lack of motivation or drive. Two ingredients were essential to that purpose. First, sharing personal experiences established the presence of social patterns rather than individual hang-ups. We needed no sociological report to tell us that we had all accepted passively the notion of female inferiority, male superiority—in education and in everyday life. That was obvious. But the more difficult question was why had we done so, and was it inevitable that we should? Could the social pattern be altered?

The second ingredient—history—helped with those questions. As we read the lives of eighteenth- and nineteenth-century women, we searched especially for their significant educational experiences and for their views of education. What education had Elizabeth Cady Stanton or Harriet Tubman managed to get and to what use had she put it? The students learned that the social patterns of their contemporary lives had historical roots and that something could be learned from studying that history. Here are several items students began to generalize about: women like Stanton and Tubman struggled for what education they could get—and much of it was not formal schooling or even what we would call book-learning at all. They used their education, moreover, socially. In their daily lives, they taught others—either on the lecture platform or on the underground railroad. What emerged from discussions of women in the past was a sense not only of individual achievement, but more importantly, of commitment to social change.

At the last meeting, the class granted permission to a reporter (who had earlier in the term been a visitor) to ask several questions directly of them. She wanted to know what they thought of the course, what they felt they had accomplished in it. It wasn't a question of accomplishment, students agreed. They had learned a good deal about the subject they had studied—the education of women—but more importantly, the course had "changed their lives." The specific examples offered had several features in common: they were confident in tone and if not aggressive, at least assertive in quality ("I now take myself and my studies seriously."); they hearkened back to the beginning by their reference to family life ("I have begun to talk with my husband about our lives together and to explain to him how I feel about getting an interesting job and having him share household responsibilities."); most of all, they were future-oriented and socially committed ("I am going to be a lawyer—I don't care what my family or anyone else thinks about that. As a lawyer, I can be useful to the women's movement.")

This was the most interesting result of the course; that studying history—their own history, of course—made women future-oriented and socially committed. They were saying, "Here I am, beginning to understand how I got into this state of mind and material circumstance, and even how whole generations of women got here from the nineteenth century and before; but now I can also, and on the basis of that new awareness and understanding, think about the future and about changing the way things are." The pattern is very simple. Until you have a history, you have no future. Perhaps it is not at all surprising to you. But for women it is a new experience, partly because our history has been totally obscure to us; partly also because we have tended, in the manner of *man*kind, to internalize social problems as personal ones and so imagine them accessible only of individual rather than social solutions.

While schools cannot solve social problems, they can illuminate them. Indeed, one of their prime functions is precisely that: to enlighten students about their present and their past. Or to facilitate students' enlightening each other, as in the class I have described. But I would add to the curriculum the future; not simply to learn about the past for its own sake or to understand the present, but to imagine and even plot paths to the future. Many Women's Studies courses are organized in this way and for obvious reasons. To study the past and to understand the present are only the first half of women's educational needs. As Kenneth Clark has said in another context, why study a slum except to change it, or a disease, except to eliminate it.

Curriculum in general ought to include attempts at outlining a series of alternative routes along which we may move toward change. Whatever those paths, they would suggest to students a fundamental notion that seems now excluded from education at all levels. Despite the fact that we have witnessed massive technological change in our lifetimes, most of us have been taught that human nature —however defined—does not change, indeed cannot change. Men are men, and women, women. Social institutions like marriage and the family are allegedly unalterable. People have always been prejudiced and will always be. And so forth. If we believe that things are as they are, then indeed there is no hope for change. Or if we have no energy for change, there is no hope.

For change is slow, difficult, and costly, at least of time and energy. There are few, if any, short-cuts. One must have either an appetite for change or a stake in it. Change is not pleasant for those content with the status quo or for those who covet stability.

The class I described met for seventeen evenings, some of them stormy sessions, confused and exhausting for all. The students read ten novels, a volume of history, six or seven essays, and sufficient autobiography or biographical material to produce two papers each on the education of particular women. Most of the students, moreover, had also attended a previous introductory Women's Studies course that had met for ten evenings. The period of "change" for those women, therefore, had been a year. And while I am sanguine about the process having begun, it is a process and it was only a beginning.

What I am getting at is this. I believe that it is possible to effect equal opportunity for women, or I would not have

wrenched my life into its present course. I believe also that
guidelines are essential first steps and that feminists in
decision-making jobs will be helpful, but ultimately change
depends on two factors:

First, the energy with which feminists can teach others
—masses of others, who will then teach still others, in colleges and public schools; and second, the willingness of
men (and women) in power to facilitate the process of
change.

(A word about feminists. I use the term to mean energetic "advocates" of equal opportunity for women. The
statements that preface your guidelines are feminist statements. They do not ask *whether* women have been ill
treated by the educational system; they state the fact
categorically and *advocate* change. Let me state also
parenthetically that men may be "feminists" and women
"antifeminists," under the terms of my definition.)

Nineteenth-century feminists like Emma Willard, the
founder in 1821 of Troy Seminary, the first secondary
school for women in the country, and Mary Lyon, the
founder, a decade later, of Mt. Holyoke, the first woman's
college, knew what they were doing when they set goals
for themselves; I will not be content, one of them said,
until I have sent two hundred teachers into the world.
They knew that in their day only women teachers would
care about and feel responsible for the education of other
female students. And they were, in their day, and for some
time afterwards, correct. But something interfered with
that process late in the nineteenth century, as more and
more women became teachers. Feminist energies were concentrated increasingly on the issue of suffrage. Women
were trained as teachers not because of their commitment
to the education of women, but because they could be
hired more cheaply than men. Whatever the factors, the
result is clear; women teachers at some point in time no
longer were feminists. The schools feminists had founded
endured and women passed through them—but the institutions were drained of their feminist content and their
commitment to change. It is hardly surprising that once
feminists lost control of the education of women, women
were educated to believe in their own limited capacities
and in the unlimited capacities of males.

Our chief goal now is obvious; to restore a feminist

perspective to education. The guidelines—perhaps I can by now call them *feminist* guidelines—provide us with a major institutional step forward. The length and duration of that step will depend on the two factors I listed earlier: the energy of feminist educators and the willingness of those in power to facilitate change. Of all the guidelines, I would place priority upon the reeducation and education of teachers in the system. These are, in my opinion, the significant people, the crucial agents for change, since most of them are both women and teachers.

I want here to put forward several practical suggestions, not because I imagine them to be exhaustive, but because by next year at this time, we should be reporting successes and problems in implementing the Guidelines.

There are at least two ways to educate or reeducate teachers. First, the Women's Studies route, illustrated sufficiently by the description of the class at Old Westbury. At last count, nearly a thousand Women's Studies courses are being offered this fall at colleges and universities across the country. Up to now, these have owed their existence chiefly to the energies of the Women's Movement. But I do not mind admitting that these energies have not extended themselves adequately or rapidly enough into schools of education, and that they are just beginning to turn round corners into high schools and elementary schools. Your guideline, whether it take the form of in-service courses for public-school teachers, or whether, as I would have it extended, reach broadly into colleges and schools of education, your guideline opens the door for such compensatory education, and obviously for male teachers as well as for females.

If we were interested in moving relatively swiftly to reeducate teachers, we might think in terms of summer institutes for that purpose. Or we might be more ambitious still and spend summers training teams of feminists to work with the staffs of whole elementary schools through a school year, both on teacher reeducation and on curricular reform. At the very least, the system will need to recruit feminists to teach in-service courses for teachers— and these in a number of areas apart from the history of women; stereotypes in literature, including children's literature; child development; psychology and sociology of sex roles—just to name a few obvious examples.

A second approach might be to turn to the textbook and curriculum specialists in the system, first assuming that they are themselves informed feminists. We might put into teachers' hands, a year from now, say, a new curriculum outline, materials, and a group of experimental texts with which to try teaching courses in sexual stereotyping to a high-school class in behavioral science. And we might provide elementary-school teachers with social-science texts in which working mothers, and fathers who share household responsibilities, are prominent features. This is probably the route that, in the end, will reach more teachers, and hence students, most quickly. And I do not disparage that route, though as a teacher and a teacher of teachers, I prefer another.

The route I prefer is one that combines teacher education and curriculum and textbook reform. Partly it is a question of general philosophy about education; I believe that a teacher is at her best when she organizes, and hence controls, her own curriculum. Our best teachers do that—they work within prescribed guidelines, but they make choices in line with the needs of their students. At the same time, I believe that curriculum is soundest when it is formed out of the experience in the classroom, even through making errors, and especially with the cooperation of students who, if they are mature enough to understand the process, may gain special incentive from knowing that they are helping to produce curriculum that may be useful for other students to come.

In-service courses that will be offered this fall in New York City by The Feminist Press, an organization with which I am associated, will be run on that model; they will combine compensatory education for teachers of history and literature with curriculum workshops. Teachers will study with the aim in mind of organizing usable units for their own students; they will, in the course of the year, try such units in their classrooms, perhaps helpful observers present. They will learn to find, develop, and share new materials and methods in women's history and literature with other teachers in the group. In short, they will learn in a Women's Studies course, how to create curriculum and methodology for future classrooms.

One final note on curriculum and curriculum-planning in the next decade. Social problems, as we all know, do not simply fade away. They tend to persist and worsen, especially if they are ignored, even with the best of intentions. To substitute in textbooks children colored brown or women at gas pumps is not to deal with the continued existence of racism or sexism. Instead of declaring sexism illegal or immoral and vowing never to look that way again, I would rather we work directly with its presence among us. I would like to see the subject of sex-role stereotyping become openly part of the curriculum at whatever level of a student's education—at least for the next decade. I think that where we have made strides against bigotry we have done so through its presence as a subject for analysis and discussion—even anger and confrontation—in the classroom. The feelings are there—among all of us. We live in a society that is both racist and sexist—and it is now permissible to say so, even at some of the highest levels of government. But to say so is not enough; even official statements are not enough. Nor is the consciousness of feminists enough. We need what someone once called "the entering wedge"—the crucial place in the system likely to respond significantly and productively to change.

I think that wedge is teacher education. Feminists can work with the worst texts or with none. They can produce their own, with the help of their students and other resources in the community. More important even than texts, they can begin to stimulate the dialogue in the classroom that will allow both male and female students to imagine and plan for their futures. The questions are complex enough to keep many classrooms busy; here are a small sampling. If all women prepare themselves for work, who will care for children and who will take responsibility for housekeeping chores? How will men's lives be affected by the changes in the status and education of women? And if women are treated precisely as men are, and if sexism were eliminated, on what terms will women and men live together? Will sexual distinctiveness take new forms? Or should we rather plan for a social order without sexual hierarchy, one symbolized, perhaps by our similarly blue-jeaned sons and daughters?

And there are other kinds of questions, perhaps more immediate for the schools at large. Are the needs for physical activity of boys and girls identical? Should and could athletics become coeducational on all levels? Or should girls demand and be granted separate and equal funds for the development of physical-education programs? And in general, is it wise to homogenize the education of girls and boys? Is that not, like the establishment of coeducation in the nineteenth century, likely to keep us where we are? What if we were to cultivate as well a measure of self-consciousness at least about the separate social histories of women and men?

No, I am not beginning a new lecture here, nor shall I cease because I have exhausted the possible list of questions. But I shall stop in the belief that I have made my point; it is time to begin what is, after all, a task to which many of us will commit lifetimes.

# APPENDIX A

Suggestions for further reading—an annotated bibliography

*Chapter One:* "No Woman Geniuses?"

BEM, SANDRA L. and DARYL J., "Training the Woman to Know Her Place: The Power Of a Nonconscious Ideology," in D. J. Bem (ed.), *Beliefs, Attitudes, and Human Affairs.* Belmont, California: Brooks-Cole, 1970.
  Feminist critique of the often unconscious sexism pervading society and its effect in limiting women's aspiration and opportunities.

BERNARD, JESSE, "Sex Differences: An Overview," paper presented at American Association for the Advancement of Science, Washington, D.C., December 1972.
  An analysis of the objectives and methodology of sex-differences research as well as the pitfalls in the typical critical postures which attack this body of research.

BROVERMAN, INGE K., et al., "Sex Role Stereotypes and Clinical Judgments of Mental Health," *Journal of Clinical Psychology*, vol. 34, February 1971.
  A survey of clinical psychiatrists, psychologists, and psychiatric social workers found characteristics considered appropriate for a healthy adult (sex-unspecified) to be the same as those for a healthy male, whereas the traits of a healthy female were incompatible with those of a healthy adult. The characteristics selected parallel those of traditional sex-role stereotypes.

BROVERMAN, INGE, et al., "Sex-Role Stereotypes: A Current Appraisal," in *Journal of Social Issues*, December 1972.
  A comprehensive review of sex-role stereotype research.

FREEMAN, JO, "Growing Up Girlish," *Transaction*, Vol. 8, no. 1/2 November/December, 1970, pp. 36–43.

A perceptive analysis of the sex-role stereotyping of girls' behavior with a discussion of some current literature.

FRIEDAN, BETTY, *The Feminine Mystique*. New York: Dell, 1963.

In this best-seller which marked the beginning of the current women's liberation movement in the United States, author Friedan documents the "Back-to-the-home" trend among American women in the postwar period (1945–1960). An increasing proportion of the total college population, college women included, accepted marriage and family-oriented outlook—with a resulting decrease in the academic involvement and career goals of women. See particularly Chapter 7, "The Sex-Directed Educators."

HORNER, MATINA, "The Motive to Avoid Success and Changing Aspirations of College Women," in *Readings on the Psychology of Women*, Judith Bardwick (ed.). New York: Harper and Row, 1972.

An overview of Horner's work on the motive to avoid success.

KAGAN, JEROME, "The Emergence of Sex Differences," *School Review*, February 1972, pp. 217–227.

A discussion of sex differences in behavior apparent in infants under two years. The author discusses the possible biological bases for these early differences.

MILLMAN, MARCIA, "Observations on Sex Role Research," *Journal of Marriage and the Family*, vol. 33, no. 4, November 1971.

A feminist analysis of sex role research. The sexism in sex role research.

SHERMAN, JULIA A., "Socializing for Female Competence." Paper presented at conference of American Association for the Advancement of Science, Washington, D.C., December 29, 1972.

The author believes goals of femininity and competence are not the same, and little is known about how to raise competent females.

WEISSTEIN, NAOMI, "Kinder, Kuche, Kirche as Scientific Law: Psychology Constructs the Female," *Motive*, vol.

29, nos. 6 and 7, 1969. Also in Morgan (ed.), *Sisterhood Is Powerful*.

> Charging that the clinical experience has proven unreliable and inconsistent, a professor of psychology argues that psychology has failed to understand people, particularly women. She cites experimental evidence for the crucial role of social expectations in determining behavior. A provocative and incisive article highlighting the need for a re-examination of the nature of women.

WESTON, PETER, and MARTHA MEDRICK, "Race, Social Class, and the Motive to Avoid Success in Women," in *Readings on the Psychology of Women*, Judith Bardwick (ed.). New York: Harper & Row, 1972.

> The Matina Horner type research conducted on a black college-women population.

*Chapter Two:* "Pink and Blue: the Color Line"

BREITBART, VICKI, "Day Care Who Cares?" New England Free Press, 791 Tremont St., Boston, Massachusetts 02118.

> The author analyzes the factors contributing to the need for day care. She suggests ways by which women can have nonsexist day care which they control.

HOIT, JO ANN, "Speaking of Spock," *Up From Under*, vol. I, no. 2, August/September 1970.

> A feminist critique of Dr. Spock's mother-centered child-care doctrine.

LYNN, DAVID B., "Determinants of Intellectual Growth in Women," *School Review*, February 1972, pp. 241–260.

> The author suggests that sex differences in the early learning tasks of sex-role identity may underlie perceived sex differences in cognitive style. The thesis, while provocative, is poorly documented and easily challenged.

JACKLIN, CAROL NAGY, and ELEANOR E. MACCOBY, "Sex Differences in Intellectual Abilities: A Reassessment and a look at Some Explanations," paper presented at AERA convention, April 1972.

> A review of recent literature on sex differences and

some hypotheses by the authors, who believe sex differences do exist but have been overstated.

MAC EWAN, PHYLISS and LOUISE GROSS, "On Day Care," *Women: A Journal of Liberation*, Winter 1970.

An argument for universal day-care opportunities and a discussion of the potential problems of sex role reinforcement.

MEADE, MARION, "Penelope Pitstop Isn't Enough," *New York Times*, September 13, 1970, Section 2.

In a survey of children's T.V. programs the author finds the few female characters presented to be passive and inept. One exception is a cartoon character Penelope Pitstop, a race-car driver.

MUSSEN, PAUL H., "Early Sex-Role Development," in *Handbook of Socialization Theory and Research*, David A. Goslin (ed.). Chicago: Rand McNally, 1969. pp. 707–729.

Although the author assumes that sex-role development is necessary and desirable, his review of current theories of sex-role development is comprehensive and quite good.

ROSS, DOROTHEA M., and S. A. ROSS, "Resistance by Preschool Boys to Sex-Inappropriate Behavior," *Journal of Educational Psychology*, vol. 63, no. 4, pp. 342–346.

Although the same number of girls and boys resisted suggestions to select "sex-inappropriate" toys, the boys showed more anxiety and exhibited more resistance behavior.

SELCER, BOBBI, "How Liberated are 'Liberated' Children?" *Radical Therapist*, February 1972, pp. 14–15.

A comparison of sex-role attitudes of Orthodox Jewish children and non-Jewish children whose mothers are involved in Women's Liberation; the latter group exhibited far less sex-stereotyped behavior in play.

WEITZMAN, LENORE J., DEBORAH EIFLER, ELIZABETH HOKADA, and CATHERINE ROSS, "Sex Role Socialization in Picture Books for Preschool Children." Paper read at the meeting of American Sociological Association, Denver, September 2, 1971. Institute of Governmental Affairs, University of California, Davis, California 95616.

A feminist, comprehensive, and detailed analysis of Caldecott Winners, with emphasis on last five years.

*Chapter Three:* "Down with Dick and Jane"

BARRY, KATHLEEN, "View from the Doll Corner," *Women: A Journal of Liberation,* vol. 1, no. 1, Fall 1969.

> While Gesell's developmental levels are believed by many educators to apply to all children, boys and girls receive differentiated treatment; discussion of some ways the treatment of girls limits their potential.

BETTELHEIM, BRUNO, "How Can Elementary Schools Help Boys Learn to Become Men?" *The Instructor,* March 1969, pp. 61–62.

> In this interview, Bettelheim argues for increased opportunities of experience and greater responsibility for boys; refuses to discuss whether girls' needs are being met in schools.

DAVIS, O. L., and J. SLOBODIAN, "Teacher Behavior Toward Boys and Girls During First Grade Reading Instruction," *American Educational Research Journal,* May 1967, pp. 261–269.

> Observations of ten first-grade teachers and their pupils during the spring of 1965 did not support the hypothesis that female first-grade teachers discriminate against boys and favor girls. The authors conclude that additional studies of classroom teachers' behavior, nonverbal as well as verbal, would be valuable.

*Dick and Jane as Victims: Sex-Role Stereotyping in Children's Readers,* Women on Words and Images, P.O. Box 2163, Princeton, New Jersey 08540 (1970).

> This pamphlet discusses both subtle and blatant forms of stereotyping found in texts and illustrations of fifteen widely used series of readers.

"Feminists Look at the 100 Books: The Portrayal of Women in Children's Books on Puerto Rican Themes," *Interracial Books for Children; quarterly bulletin of Council on Interracial Books for Children,* 29 West 15th Street, New York, New York 10011. Spring 1972.

> Analyzes themes of books by age group. The books overwhelmingly portrayed women in sharply stereotyped, limiting roles and men in broad, active, and varied roles.

Feminists on Children's Media, "A Feminist Look at Children's Books," *Notes From the Third Year,* 1970.

FRISOF, JAMIE KELEM, "Textbooks and Channeling," *Women: A Journal of Liberation*, Fall, 1969.

>An analysis of selected social-studies texts used in grades 1-5. Pictures of males are prevalent and women are shown as dull and unimportant.

HOWE, FLORENCE, "Liberated Chinese Primers," *Women: A Journal of Liberation*, Fall, 1970, pp. 33-34.

>A discussion of four nonsexist children's books showing positive images for females and males.

IGLITZIN, LYNNE B., "A Child's-Eye View of Sex-Roles," *Today's Education*, December, 1972.

LEVY, BETTY, "The School's Role in the Sex-Role Stereotyping of Girls: A Feminist Review of the Literature," *Feminist Studies*, vol. 1, no. 1. Summer, 1972, pp. 5-23.

MEYER, W. J., and G. THOMPSON, "Sex Differences in the Distribution of Teacher Approval and Disapproval among Sixth-grade Children," *Journal of Educational Psychology*, vol. 47, no. 7, November 1956, pp. 385-396.

>The articles argue that girls are not favored by teachers in the elementary schools, which some researchers claim are "feminine" institutions.

MINUCHIN, PATRICIA, "The Schooling of Tomorrow's Women," *School Review*, vol. 80, no. 2. February 1972, pp. 199-207.

MINUCHIN, PATRICIA, "Sex Differences in an Educational Context," *National Elementary Principal*, November, 1966.

NILSEN, ALLEEN PACE, "Women in Children's Literature," *College English*, May 1971, pp. 918-926.

>A survey of the winners and runners-up for the Caldecott Award for picture books reveals that an unreasonable proportion of stories are about males, few about females. The author also discusses the male-biased "Why Johnny Can't Read" campaign.

PELTIER, GARY L., "Sex Differences in the School: Problem and Proposed Solution," *Phi Delta Kappan*, November 1968, pp. 182-185.

>Young boys are discriminated against in school. A poorly reasoned, documented, and sexist argument. The author suggests higher salaries for male teachers.

TORRANCE, E. PAUL, "Changing Reactions of Preadolescent Girls to Tasks Requiring Creative Scientific Thinking,"

*The Journal of Genetic Psychology*, 1963, pp. 102, 217–223.

*Chapter Four:* "Sexism in High School"

ASTIN, HELEN, "Sex Differences on Mathematical and Scientific Precocity," paper delivered at AAAS Symposium, December 1972.

> Empirical study of sex differences among junior-high-school science and math-contest winners. The girls are dramatically behind in achievement and interest.

DWORKIN, CONNIE, "High-School Women: The Suburban Scene," in Robin Morgan (ed.), *Sisterhood is Powerful*. New York: Vintage, 1970.

> Personal account of an eighth-grader's introduction to Women's Liberation and her action to liberate herself and her school.

ENTWISLE, DORIS R., and ELLEN GREENBERGER, *A Survey of Cognitive Styles in Maryland Ninth Graders IV Views of Women's Roles*, Johns Hopkins University, Report No. 89, November 1970.

> A study showing the disparity between what girls and boys perceive as women's role. Girls imagined more opportunity of choice for women than the boys did.

GRANT (WEST) ANN, "Women's Liberation, or Exploding the Fairy Princess Myth," *Scholastic Teacher*, November 1971.

HENRY, JULES, "A Day at Rome High," in *Culture Against Man*. New York: Vintage, 1963.

> Although the styles are distinctly 50s, this description of high-school culture offers still relevant insights into the peer group and high-school pressures which reinforce rigid sex roles.

MOWSESIAN, RICHARD, "Educational and Career Aspirations of High-School Females," *Journal of National Assn. of Women Deans and Counselors*, Winter 1972.

> Women's educational and career aspirations decrease as they progress through high school.

"Should Girls Play on Boys' Teams?" *Good Housekeeping*, October 1969.

> A noncommittal review of the 1969 status of co-ed athletic competition.

STINCHCOMBE, ARTHUR L., *Rebellion in a High School*, Chicago: Quadrangle Books, 1964.

All data are analyzed according to sex in this question-naire-based study of the student population of a small-town California high school. The author finds less alienation and therefore less rebellion among girls than boys for two main reasons: (1) unsuccessful girls reorient toward marriage without loss of self-respect, (2) vocational courses for girls—commercial, secretarial, etc.—are more generally accepted as useful job preparation than are those for boys.


Chapter Five: "Are Colleges Fit for Women?"

BERNARD, JESSIE, *Academic Women*. University Park, Pennsylvania State University Press, 1964.

A wide-ranging study of the female college teacher. Though the author concludes from the evidence that there is not widespread sex discrimination, the data presented suggest otherwise. Dr. Bernard herself has since changed her mind about this.

EHRLICH, CAROL, "The Male Sociologist's Burden: The Place of Women in Marriage and Family Texts," *Journal of Marriage and the Family*, August 1971, pp. 427–487.

An analysis of six representative college texts pub-lished in 1964 or later revealed an abundance of value judgments and myth often presented as fact in dis-cussion of the female role.

EPSTEIN, GILDA, and ARLINE BRONZAFT, "Female Freshmen View Their Roles as Women," *Journal of Marriage and the Family*, vol. 34, no. 4, November 1972.

A survey of public university freshmen women from lower-middle-class and working-class backgrounds. A plurality foresaw a future which combined marriage, motherhood, and career.

GERBER, ELLEN, "The Changing Female Image: A Brief Commentary on Sport Competition for Women," *Jour-nal of Health, Physical Education, Recreation*. October 1971.

GRAHAM, PATRICIA A., "Women in Academe," *Science*, vol. 169, September 25, 1970, pp. 1284–1290.

In a concise, well-written article the author discusses the discrimination which results in women Ph.D's often holding positions which are not commensurate with their ability. She discusses outright discrimination, internal ambivalence, the suburban syndrome, and nepotism rules. Suggested remedies include increased appointments of women to senior faculty and administrative positions, delayed tenure decisions, and day care centers for the children of university personnel.

HOWE, FLORENCE, "Identity and Expression: A Course for Women," *College English*, vol. 33, no. 8, May 1971.

A description of effective methods for increasing consciousness, along with writing ability, in the classroom. Useful bibliography.

*How Harvard Rules Women.* The New University Conference. Chicago, 1970.

A comprehensive description of the minority status of the women at Harvard.

HUSBANDS, SANDRA ACKER, "Women's Place in Higher Education," *School Review*, vol. 80, no. 2, February 1972, pp. 261–273.

An analysis of factors which pressure college women into passive roles and "feminine" areas of study. Women's colleges often provide inferior education while coeducational institutions are male dominated. Author suggests Women's Studies programs may provide needed compensatory experiences for women.

LAFEVRE, CAROL, "The Mature Woman as Graduate Student," *School Review*, vol. 80, no. 2, February 1972, pp. 281–297.

This study of Ph.D. candidates with children indicates that women can successfully return to school even though sex-role training for women does not encourage this.

LAWS, JUDITH LONG, "A Feminist Review of Marital Adjustment Literature," *Journal of Marriage and the Family*. August 1971.

The author finds literature in this field is biased to support the institution of the nuclear family and the maintenance of traditional rigid sex roles.

OLTMAN, RUTH M., *Campus 1970: Where Do Women Stand?* Washington, D.C.: American Association of University Women, December 1970.

A survey to evaluate the activities of women and the

extent of their participation at all levels of involvement—as students, administrators, faculty, and trustees. Analysis of questionnaires completed by the presidents of 450 colleges and universities illustrates the sex inequities on American campuses and points up discrepancies between stated policy and actual fact.

PULLEN, DORIS L., "The Educational Establishment: Wasted Women," in Mary Low Thompson (ed.). *Voices of the New Feminism*, Boston: Beacon Press, 1970.

A overview of the deteriorating position of women in the hierarchy of higher education. The author believes that women's colleges should lead the way as models of educational opportunities for women based on the needs and life styles of this day.

ROSSI, ALICE S., "Women in Science: Why So Few?" *Science Magazine*, vol. 148, May 28, 1965, p. 1196.

A concise discussion of the institutional, psychological, and social factors which deter women from entering the field of science.

SANDLER, BERNICE, "A Feminist Approach to the Women's College," *Ms. Magazine*, 1973.

SCOTT, ANN, "The Half-Eaten Apple: A Look at Sex Discrimination in the University," *Reporter*, May 14, 1970.

In her study of her own university, a professor of English finds evidence of many discriminatory practices. She demands that the university initiate a strong program of reform to counteract and eventually change cultural biases against women.

TWIFEL, MINNA, and ELLEN BIRDSEYE, "The Secretary in Academia," *Women: A Journal of Liberation*.

## Chapter Six: "A View from the Desk"

BAYER, ALAN E., and HELEN S. ASTIN, "Sex Differences in Academic Rank and Salary Among Science Doctorates in Teaching," *Journal of Human Resources*, Spring, 1968, pp. 191–200.

The authors find that discrimination against women more often exists in regard to salary than to tenure or promotion. Women in the natural sciences receive promotion on a par with men; however, women in the social sciences lag behind.

"Discriminating Against the Pregnant Teacher," NEA

DuShane Emergency Fund. *Today's Education*. December 1971, pp. 33–35.

Discussion of some forms such discrimination may take including firing, loss of tenure, leave without pay, forced leave; suggestions for affirmative action.

DIVOKY, DIANE, "Sexism, Yes." *Learning*, November 1972.

The feminist half of a debate with Sheila Johnson (see "Sexism, No" in same issue) over whether schools practice sexism.

ENGSTRAND, SOPHIE, *Miss Munday* (New York: Dial Press, 1940).

A fictional portrayal of a young teacher in the 1930s.

FENNER, MILDRED, "Women in Educational Journalism," *Contemporary Education*, vol. XLIII, no. 4, February 1972.

The female apologist view of women's second-class place in educational journalism.

FOFF, ARTHUR, "Scholars and Scapegoats," *The English Journal*, vol. 47, 1958.

An analysis of fictional portrayals of teacher stereotypes and their social implications.

GOLDMAN, JANE, "Women at the Bottom: Teaching in Elementary School," *No More Teachers' Dirty Looks*, Bay Area Radical Teachers' Organization, 1972.

PARRISH, JOHN B., "Women in Top Level Teaching and Research," *American Association of University Women Journal*, January 1962.

A statistical study of the percentage of women at various levels of the academic hierarchy. Women held only twenty-three percent of all teaching and research positions in higher education nationally, and only 9.9 percent in eighteen leading endowment and enrollment universities. The author also documents a definite sex-typing of academic fields.

STICHELL, JOHN, "Paired Teaching—Why Not?" *Today's Education*, May 1972.

"Teachers: Seven Women: A Panel Discussion by 7 Teachers," *Women: A Journal of Liberation*, vol. 2, no. 3.

THURBER, JAMES, "Here Lies Miss Groby" in *My World and Welcome to It*. New York: Harcourt and Brace, 1937.

Scathing character sketch of the stereotypic female English teacher.

*Chapter Seven:* "The Feminist Response"

AHLUM, CAROL, and JACKIE FRALLEY, "The High School Classroom: Feminist Studies," *Today's Education*, December 1972.

A brief survey of recent attempts by high-school teachers to incorporate women's studies into the high-school curriculum.

*An Action Proposal to Eliminate Sex Discrimination in the Ann Arbor Public Schools.* The Committee to Eliminate Sex Discrimination in the Public Schools, and The Discrimination in Education Committee of NOW (Ann Arbor Chapter). March 1972. Available from: Marcia Federbush, 1000 Cedar Bend Drive, Ann Arbor, Michigan, 48105.

Useful as a model for local affirmative action groups. See also Federbush, *Let Them Aspire.*

FEDERBUSH, MARCIA, *Let Them Aspire: A Plea and Proposal for Equality of Opportunity for Males and Females in the Ann Arbor Public Schools.* May 1971. Available from: Marcia Federbush, 1000 Cedar Bend Drive, Ann Arbor, Michigan 48105.

This report includes a detailed analysis of sex discrimination in the Ann Arbor Public School System. A useful model for local task force efforts.

HEYN, LEAH, "For Boys Only: Diary of an Intrusion into Male Territory," *Up From Under*, vol. I, no. 1. January/February 1971.

A female student's battle to enroll in woodworking class rather than the traditional girl's class, home economics.

HOWE, FLORENCE, et. al. (eds.), *Female Studies V.* 1972. KNOW, Inc., Box 10197, Pittsburgh, Pennsylvania 15221.

A collection of essays on women's education; Does not overlap with *Female Studies IV.*

HOWE, FLORENCE, and SHIELA TOBIAS (eds.), *"Female Studies IV.* 1971. KNOW, Inc., Box 10197, Pittsburgh, Pennsylvania 15221.

A collection of articles on teaching women's studies by women involved in some of the first courses and programs in the United States.

HOFFMAN, NANCY, et al. (eds.), *Female Studies VI.: Closer*

*to the Ground*, Clearinghouse on Women's Studies, Box 334, Old Westbury, New York 11568.

Women's classes, criticism, and programs, 1972.

KOONTZ, ELIZABETH D., *Plans For Widening Women's Educational Opportunities*, United States Department of Labor. Employment Standards Administration, Women's Bureau, Washington, D.C. 20210.

A paper on psychological and institutional discrimination and some new approaches for women.

MACCLEAN, VIRGINIA, "Thoughts on Sex Education for Our Daughters," *Women: A Journal of Liberation.*

ROSSI, ALICE, "Job Discrimination and What Women Can Do About It." *The Atlantic Monthly*, March 1970.

Personal anecdotes of antifemale prejudice and profeminist court decisions concerning job discrimination.

SALPER, ROBERTA, "Women's Studies," *Ramparts*, December 1971.

SCHUMACKER, DORIN, "Changing the School Environment," *Women, A Journal of Liberation*, vol. 2, no. 4.

One woman's attempt to raise the consciousness of parents, teachers, and administrators of her daughter's university elementary school.

SANDLER, BERNICE, "Uncle Sam Wants to Help Women: Ending Sex Discrimination On the Campus," Association of American Colleges, October 1972.

Discussion of campus sex discrimination and of the relevant legislation and court decisions available to combat it.

# WORKS OF GENERAL INTEREST

Books

ANDERSON, SCARVIA, *Sex Differences and Discrimination in Education*. Worthington, Ohio: Charles A. Jones, 1973.

BARDWICK, JUDITH, *Readings on the Psychology of Women*. New York: Harper & Row, 1972.

CROSS, BARBARA (ed.), *Educated Women in America*. New York: Thomas Crowell, 1965.

EPSTEIN, CYNTHIA, *Woman's Place: Options and Limits in Professional Careers*. Berkeley: University of California Press, 1970.

FLEXNOR, ELEANOR, *A Century of Struggle*. Cambridge: Harvard University Press, 1959.

> In Chapters 2 and 9 the author outlines the beginnings of higher education for women in nineteenth-century America, including the heroic struggles of pioneers like Dr. Elizabeth Blackwell and astronomer Maria Mitchell to obtain an education in their professions.

FRAZIER, NANCY, and MYRA SADKER, *Sexism in School and Society*. New York: Harper and Row, 1973.

HARRISON, BARBARA, *Unlearning the Lie*. New York: Random House, 1973.

LIFTON, ROBERT (ed.), *The Woman in America*, Boston: Beacon Press, 1965.

> A collection of essays on women which first appeared in *Daedalus*, Spring 1964.

MACCOBY, ELEANOR E. (ed.), *The Development of Sex*

*Differences*, Stanford, California: Stanford University Press, 1966.

MERRIAM, EVE, *Growing Up Female In America: Ten Lives*. New York: Doubleday, 1971.

> A well-edited collection of the diaries, journals, and letters of ten women of diverse economic, social, and ethnic backgrounds.

*Report on Sex Bias in the Public Schools*, National Organization of Women, New York City Chapter, 47 East 19th Street, New York, N.Y. 10003.

> The original edition was read verbatim into the Congressional Record in 1971. It is now available in a Third Edition.

SCOTT, ANN, *The American Woman: Who Was She?* Englewood Cliffs, New Jersey: Prentice-Hall, 1971.

> A documentary history of American women which includes a chapter on education.

SULLEROT, EVELYNE, *Woman, Society and Change*. New York: McGraw-Hill, 1971.

> A cross-cultural discussion of the changing role of women in society.

TOBIAS, SHIELA, E. KUSNETZ, and D. SPITZ (eds.), *Proceedings of the Cornell Conference on Woman, Jan. 22–25, 1969.* Pittsburgh, Pennsylvania: Know, Inc., 1969.

## Major Anthologies

ADAMS, ELSIE, and MARY LOUISE BRISCOE (eds.), *Up Against the Wall Mother . . .* Beverly Hills: Glencoe Press, 1971.

BABCOX, DEBORAH, and MADELINE BELKIN (eds.), *Liberation Now*. (New York: Dell, 1971).

> Most articles in this collection were written by activists in the current Women's Liberation movement. Topics include problems of black and Third World Women, psychology, housework, education, and politics.

GORNICK, VIVIAN, and BARBARA MORAN (eds.), *Women in Sexist Society: Studies in Power and Powerlessness*, (New York: Signet, 1971).

KRADITOR, AILEEN S. (ed.), *Up from the Pedestal: Selected Writings in the History of American Feminism.* Chicago: Quadrangle, 1968.

MORGAN, ROBIN (ed.), *Sisterhood Is Powerful: An anthology of Writings from the Women's Liberation Movement.* New York: Vintage, 1970.

*Notes from the (First) (Second) (Third) Year.* Box A. A. Old Chelsea Station, New York, N. Y. 10011.

REEVES, NANCY, *Womankind: Beyond the Stereotypes.* Chicago: Aldine–Atherton, 1971.

## Special Journal Issues on Women

*Atlantic*, March 1970.

*Daedalus*, Spring 1964.

*Edcentric*, December 1971.

National Student Association, Inc., Center for Educational Reform, 2115 S. Street, Washington, D.C. 20008.

Articles dealing with educational reform, women, and alternatives to the traditional educational system.

*Journal of Marriage and the Family*, August 1971.

*The National Elementary Principal*, vol. 46, no. 2. November 1966.

Special issue: "Sex differences and the Schools."

*Scholastic Teacher/Elementary Edition*, November 1971.

Special issue: Women's Liberation and Schools.

*Scholastic Teacher/Secondary Edition*, November 1971.

Special issue: Women's Liberation and Schools.

*School Review*, February 1972.

Special issue: "Women and Education."

*Today's Education*, December 1972.

Special issue: "The Schools and Sex Role Stereotyping."

*Transaction*, vol. 8, nos. 1 and 2.

Special issue, "The American Woman."

## Periodicals and Newsletters

*Feminist Studies:* Edited by Ann Calderwood. 606 W. 116th St., New York, New York 10027.

An interdisciplinary journal for feminist scholarship.

*KNOW News Service*, Know, Inc. P. O. Box 10197, Pittsburgh, Pennsylvania 15221.

News of KNOW Press activities and the Women's Movement.

*Ms. magazine,* 370 Lexington Ave., New York, New York 10019.

> The commercial magazine for Women's Movement writings. It often includes articles and features on sexism in education, and prints nonsexist "stories for free children."

*Off Our Backs,* Box 4859, Cleveland Park Station, Washington, D.C., 20008.

> A journal written by a Washington collective for working women, with many articles on education.

*The Spokeswoman,* Urban Research Corp., 5465 South Shore Drive, Chicago, Illinois 60615.

> A monthly feminist newsletter containing information about major events across the country of special interest to women. Includes legislation, conferences, legal actions, lists, books, and other materials newly available, current research.

*The New Feminist,* P.O. Box 597, Station "A". Toronto 116, Ontario, Canada.

> A Canadian feminist newsletter which often lists books and educational resources available in the U.S.

*Women: A Journal of Liberation,* 3028 Greenmont Ave., Baltimore, Maryland.

> A journal published by a Baltimore Women's liberation group. Includes articles on a wide variety of feminist issues. Frequent analysis and critique of public education.

*Women in Action: Newsletter of the Federal Woman's Program,* Helene Markoff, Director, FWP, Civil Service Commission, 1900 E. St., N.W., Room 7530, Washington, D.C.

> Carries news of programs, new films, and publications.

*Women's Studies Abstracts,* Edited by Sara Stauffer Whales. Women's Studies Abstracts, P.O. Box 1, Rush, New York 14543.

> A quarterly journal containing abstracts of current writings and research concerning women, lists of additional references, and feature essays.

*Women's Studies: An Interdisciplinary Journal.* Edited by: Wendy Martin, Dept. of English, Queens College, University of New York.

Articles of scholarship, criticism, and feminist analysis about women.

*Women's Studies Newsletter*, Clearing House on Women's Studies, Box 334, Old Westbury, New York 11568.

News of Women's Studies Programs across the country. Serves as a clearing house for feminist educators of all school levels, includes teaching suggestions.

*This Magazine Is About Schools*, P.O. Box 876, Terminal A Toronto 1, Ontario, Canada.

Many feature articles on women, alternatives to traditional education and critical analysis of schools.

*Up From Under: By For and About Women*. Up From Under, 339 Lafayette St., New York, New York 10012.

Articles and graphics relating to a broad variety of women's issues. This journal is intended for working-class women: frequent articles on education, day care, and women's personal accounts of schooling.

# APPENDIX B
**Materials and Resources**

## BIBLIOGRAPHIES

"A List of Literature on Sexism in Education," Feminists on Children's Media, P.O. Box 4315, Grand Central Station, New York, New York 10017.

AHLUM, CAROL, and JACQUELINE FRALLEY, *Feminist Resources on Elementary and Secondary Schools*, The Feminist Press, SUNY College at Old Westbury, Box 334, Old Westbury, New York 11568. Includes an annotated bibliography, lists of audio-visual material, other bibliographies. Very helpful for parents, students, teachers, and librarians.

ASTIN, HELEN, NANCY SUNIEWICH, and SUSAN DIRECK, *Women: A Bibliography on Their Education and Careers*, Washington, D.C.: Human Services Press. 1971.

*Bibliography on Sexism in Children's Books*. Feminists on Children's Media, P.O. Box 4315, Grand Central Station, New York 10017. An annotated bibliography.

*Bibliography on the Treatment of Girls in School*, The Feminist Press, SUNY College at Old Westbury, P.O. Box 334, Old Westbury, New York 11568.

Cambridge-Goddard Feminist Studies Program, 1878 Massachusetts Ave., Cambridge, Massachusetts 02140. Annotated bibliographies on women.

*Children are People, Too*. Up Haste, 2506 B Haste Street, Berkeley, California 94704. An annotated bibliography of nonsexist books compiled by Up Haste Bookstore.

HARMON, LINDA A., *Status of Women in Higher Education, 1963–1972: A Selective Bibliography*, Series in Bibliography No. 2, Iowa State University, The Library. Attn:

Photo-duplication Center, Ames, Iowa 50010. Includes books, periodicals, legislation, government publications, dissertations.

KNOW, Inc., P.O. Box 10197, Pittsburgh, Pennsylvania 15221. List of books by, for, and about feminists; includes children's books; reprints of articles available at inexpensive prices.

LEWIS, SUSAN, "Exploding the Fairy Princess and Other Myths," *Scholastic Teacher/Elementary Teachers' Edition*, November 1971, an annotated list of nonsexist children's books. Updating *Little Miss Muffet Fights Back*.

*Little Miss Muffet Fights Back*, Feminists on Children's Media, P.O. Box 4315, Grand Central Station, New York 10017. An annotated bibliography of books the group recommends as nonsexist.

SELLS, LUCY, "Current Research on Sex Roles," 1181 Euclid Ave., Berkeley California 94708. Annotated bibliography on current research; additional lists of action organizations, other bibliographies.

STAVN, DIANE G., *Reducing the Miss Muffet Syndrome; an Annotated Bibliography*. *Library Journal*, January 15, 1972. Nonsexist children's books recommended for consideration by librarians.

*Womanpower: A Selected Bibliography on Educated Women in the Labor Force*. Radcliffe Institute, 3 James St., Cambridge, Massachusetts 02138.

## Resources for Action and Information

American Association of University Women, 2401 Virginia Ave., N.W., Washington, D.C. 20037. Information on the status and problems of university women.

Association of American Colleges, 1818 R St., N.W., Washington, D.C. 20009. A useful list of women's caucuses, committees, and professional organizations. Project on the status of women of AAC has publications and data on women in higher education and women and law.

Business and Professional Women's Foundation, 2012 Massachusetts Ave., N.W., Washington, D.C. 20036. Lists of bibliographies, tapes on sex role concepts, 1969.

CHMAJ, BETTY, *American Women and American Studies*. American Studies Association Commission on the status of women, 1971. Available from KNOW press, Box 10197, Pittsburgh, Pennsylvania 15232. Report on the status of women in university American studies programs. Includes detailed course syllabi.

Children's Liberation Workshop, P.O. Box 207, Toronto, 116, Ontario, Canada. This group is working on writing nonsexist children's books. Write for list.

Clearing House for Feminist Media, P.O. Box 207, Anacaster, Ontario, Canada. Resource list will be sent quarterly to anyone supplying stamped, self-addressed envelopes; while emphasis is on research and publications in Canada, most material available in U.S.; useful to parents, teachers, and others involved in education.

Clearing House on Women's Studies, an education project of the Feminist Press, SUNY College at Old Westbury, Box 334, Old Westbury, New York 11568. This is an education committee involved in a variety of educational projects. *Women's Studies Newsletter*; news of programs, activities, and conferences across the country. Letters are published to help women to communicate with others involved in similar projects. *Female Studies, VI: Closer to the Ground*. Nancy Hoffman, Cynthia Secor, and Andrian Kinsley, editors. Women's Programs criticisms and Programs. *Guide to Current Female Studies II*. Carol Ahlum and Florence Howe, editors. October 1972. Listing of college, high school, and continuing education programs. See Feminist Press for earlier guide. Fact Sheet—Female Studies #2. Notes on degree programs, resource information. Free on request.

*Continuing Education Programs and Services for Women*, Women's Bureau of the U.S. Labor Dept. Available from Superintendent of Documents, Government Printing Office, Washington, D.C.

*Fact Sheet on Sex Bias in Elementary Schoolbooks*, Prepared by Alma Graham, Associate Editor, American Heritage Dictionary, 551 Fifth Ave., New York, New York. A brief and informative review of sexist language used in dictionaries and schoolbooks.

FEDERBUSH, MARSHA, *Let Them Aspire*, Available from author: 1000 Cedar Bend, Ann Arbor, Michigan. Comprehensive task-force report on sexism in Ann Arbor Public Schools. Excellent model for local feminist education task forces.

*Female Studies I*. Shiela Tobias, editor. Available from KNOW, Inc., P.O. Box 10197, Pittsburgh, Pennsylvania 15232. 17 Course descriptions and bibliographies.

*Female Studies II*. Florence Howe, editor, for the MLA Commission on Women. December 1970. Available from KNOW, Inc., 66 course descriptions, bibliographies. 5 essays.

*Female Studies III*. Florence Howe and Carol Ahlum, editors. For the MLA Commission on Women, December 1971. Available from KNOW, Inc. Includes the New Guide to Current Female Studies, 54 new course descriptions and bibliographies, and descriptions of 17 Women's Studies programs. December 1971.

*Female Studies, IV: Teaching About Women; Essays on Teaching Women's Studies*. Carol Ohmann and Elaine Showalter, editors. For the MLA Commission on the Status of Women. December 1971. Available from KNOW, Inc. Seven essays by teachers of women's studies, bibliographical reports, anthologies reviewed.

*Female Studies, V*. Available from KNOW, Inc. P.O. Box 10197. Pittsburgh, Pennsylvania 15221. Reprints of fifteen essays from the Conference on Women in Education, held in Pittsburgh, November 1971.

*Female Studies, VI: Closer to the Ground. Women's classes, criticisms, programs*, Nancy Hoffman, Cynthia Secor, and Andrian Kinsley, editors. Available from: Clearing House on Women's Studies, SUNY, Old Westbury, Box 334, Old Westbury, New York 11568.

Feminists on Children's Media. *A List of Literature on Sexism in Children's Books*. P.O. Box 4315, Grand Central Station, New York 10017. List describing material by Feminists on Children's Media and other sources. Send stamped, self-addressed envelope. *Little Miss Muffet Fights Back*, an Annotated bibliography of children's books.

The Feminist Press, SUNY College at Old Westbury, Box 334, Old Westbury, New York 11568. A nonprofit feminist corporation involved in publishing nonsexist children's books and adult biographies. Other activities include consulting for school systems attempting to eliminate sexism in education. *Bibliography on the Treatment of Women in Schools*. See also: Clearinghouse on Women's Studies.

Feminist Speakers Bureau, New Talent Feminist Association, 250 West 57th St., New York 10019. Feminists available, some nationally known, to speak on broad range of topics, including women in education. Brochure available.

*The Guide to Current Female Studies II.* Carol Ahlum and Florence Howe, editors. October 1972. Clearinghouse on Women's Studies, the Feminist Press, SUNY College at Old Westbury, New York 11568. College, high school, and community courses; continuing education programs listed alphabetically by school. This guide does not include items listed in the New Guide to Female Studies.

"Improving the Image of Women in Textbooks," Women at Scott, Foresman, 1900 E. Lake Ave., Glenview, Illinois 60025. Guidelines for writers and editors to improve female images by a group at a major publisher of children's readers.

International Institute of Women's Studies, 1615 Myrtle St., N.W., Washington, D.C. 20012. Information on Women's studies, irregular newsletter of seminars and activities of the Institute.

The Joyful World Press, Shirley Boccaccio, 486 Belvedere St., San Francisco, California 94117. Feminist children's books and posters.

KNOW, Inc., P.O. Box 10197, Pittsburgh, Pennsylvania 15232. This feminist press is a nonprofit corporation publishing feminist articles and article reprints, bibliographies, and other materials. Lists available. Books By, For, and About Women. A free bibliography: KNOW NEWS SERVICE; an informative monthly news bulletin of the press on the women's movement. Publisher of Female Studies I, IV—collections of articles, syllabi, and bibliographies. See Feminist Press.

KNOW also distributes materials from other feminist groups. Send a stamped, self-addressed envelope for a complete listing.

Lollipop Power, Inc., P.O. Box 1171, Chapel Hill, North Carolina 27541. This press publishes nonsexist children's books.

National Foundation for the Improvement of Education, Resource Center, 1507 M. St., Washington, D.C. 20036. Attn: Shirley McCune. Center will assist groups or in-

dividual teachers working to eliminate sex role stereotyping in schools. Also funds program for curriculum
development. Contact: Florence Howe, The Feminist
Press, Box 334, Old Westbury, New York 11568.

National Lesbian Information Service, Box 15368, San
Francisco, California 94115. Group will provide resource information to educators, parents and concerned
individuals. Newsletter.

New England Free Press, Rm. 401, 791 Tremont St., Boston, Massachusetts 02118. Inexpensive reprints of feminist articles, on a wide variety of topics.

*The New Guide to Current Female Studies.* Carol Ahlum
and Florence Howe, editors, for the MLA Commission.
October 15, 1971. Available from: KNOW, Inc., P.O.
Box 10197, Pittsburgh, Pennsylvania 15221. A directory
listing 610 courses and institutional addresses.

*Resources for Day Care: A List of Publications.* Day Care
and Child Development Council of America, Inc., 1401
K St., N.W., Washington, D.C. 20005. Government publications and other resources.

Sourcebook Press, 185 Madison Ave., New York 10016.
Reprints of 40 articles on the history of women's rights.

*Trends in Educational Attainments of Women.* Women's
Bureau, U.S. Dept. of Labor, Washington, D.C. 1969.
A useful compilation of statistics.

U.S. Department of Labor, Women's Bureau, Washington,
D.C. 20210. Lists of publications on women, articles,
and statistics, including information on education.

Woman's Archives, Radcliffe College, Cambridge, Massachusetts. An excellent collection of material on women
in history.

Women's History Research Center, 2325 Oak St., Berkeley,
California 94708. Supporting members receive regular
publications. Archive of historical and current material
by and about the Women's Movement. Includes topical
indices on women, directories of women's periodicals,
tapes, research. Brochure on request. Complete catalog
and partial indices are for sale. Open to public by appointment only.

*Women's Organizations and Leaders, 1973 Directory,* To
be published October 1973. Ms. Myra Barrer, Today
Publications, National Press Building, Washington, D.C.

**Audio-Visual Resources**

*Feminists on Children's Media,* P.O. Box 4315, Grand
Central Station, New York 10017. Multimedia program
of slides, tapes, and readings, examines the influence of
sexism in picture books, award-winning fiction for older
children, and school readers.

Festival of Women's Films, 1582 York Ave., New York
10023. Festival included many fine films by and about
women. Complete program notes, including description,
prices, and distribution of films available.

*Films Available By, About, and For Women,* Janice K.
Mendelhall, Federal Women's Program Coordinator,
General Services Administration, Washington, D.C. A
three-page annotated list of films.

*Free to Be You and Me, Ms.* magazine, Dept. R, 370 Lexington Ave., New York 10017. A record of nonsexist
songs for children of preschool and early elementary
school age.

*The International Women's History Periodical Archive,*
Bell and Howell, Worcester, Ohio. This publishing project
of Women's History Research Center makes available a
small library collection.

N.E.T., Indiana University, Bloomington, Indiana 47401.
Write for list of films on women. Note especially:
"Modern Women: The Uneasy Life," concerned with
the feelings of educated women toward roles as career
women and housewives.

Newday Films, 267 W. 25th St., New York, New York
10001. Write for a list of films from this five-member
women's film-making collective. Films include: "Growing Up Female: As Six Become One."

Newsreel, 332 7th Ave., New York 10001. Send for their
free rental catalog of films. Includes "Woman's Film."

Radio Free People, 133 Mercer St., New York 10012.
Write for a free catalog of tapes.

San Francisco Women's Media Group, 905 Diamond, San
Francisco, California 94114. Tapes on many topics, including sex-role socialization.

*The Silenced Majority: A Women's Liberation Multimedia
Kit,* Media Plus, Inc., 60 Riverside Drive, Suite 11D,
New York, New York 10024. A five-part program of

color-sound filmstrips, discussion materials. Part 3: Women in Education.

Source No. 1: Communications, Ed Centric, Center for Educational Reform, 2115 S St., N.W., Washington, D.C. 20008. Listing of anti-racist-sexist broadcasting, radical librarians, video groups, and other media resources.

W.B.A.I., 359 E 62 St., New York 10021. Frequent programs on women, education. Tapes available for purchase. See especially Folio of October 1972, featuring Women. Folio subscription.

Women's Film Cooperative, 84 Lyon St., New Haven, Connecticut 06511. Write for a list of films.

Women's History Research Center. Write for a list of tapes and prices. 2325 Oak Street, Berkeley, California 94708.

## Legislation and Governmental Resources

"Discrimination Against Women: Hearings Before the Special Subcommittee on Education of the Committee on Education and Labor, House of Representatives, Ninety-first Congress, Second Session, on Section 805 of H.R. 16098. Testimony, statements, and statistical data concerning socialization and discrimination. Available free from your congressperson.

"Federal Laws and Regulations Concerning Sex Discrimination in Educational Institutions, October 1972" Association of American Colleges in *The Spokeswoman*, December 1, 1972. A comprehensive chart on laws, their meanings, enforcement. Resources for further information.

"Goals and Timetables vs. Quotas: Legal Background Concerning Numerical Goals for Women and Minorities." From Project on the Status of Women, Association of American Colleges, 1818 R Street, N.W., Washington, D.C. 20009.

H.R. 14451. Bill in the House of Representatives on Education of Women. Patsy T. Mink, Representative from Hawaii, House of Representatives, Washington, D.C. 20515.

DuShane Fund Reports, NEA DuShane Emergency Fund, 1201 Sixteenth St., NW, Washington, D.C. 20036.

Special Memorandum: Equal rights for Women Educators Promised with New Legislation, August 25, 1972. Need for Studies of Sex Discrimination in Public Schools." Citizens Advisory Council on the Status of Women, Department of Labor Building, Room 1336, Washington, D.C. 20210. Appendix on Judicial Opinions.

1971 Catalog of Federal Domestic Assistance. Executive Office of the President, Office of Management and Budget, Washington, D.C. Available from: Superintendent of Documents, U.S. Government Printing Office, Washington, D.C. An extensive catalog of programs which are possible sources of funds in higher education.

*W.E.A.L. Washington Report*. Women's Equity Action League, Washington Report, 1253 4th St., S.W., Washington, D.C. 20024. A concise monthly legislative summary of congressional and court action of interest to women.

*Womanpower:* A monthly report on fair employment practices for women. Womanpower, c/o Betsy Hagan Associates, 222 Rawson Road, Brookline, Massachusetts 02146.

Women's Rights Law Reporter, 119 F Avenue, New York, New York 10003.

# FOR THOSE
# CONCERNED ABOUT EDUCATION

☐ **FREEDOM AND BEYOND**
*John Holt* 3378-08

A provocative book which takes education out of the class-room and provides a critique of American society and the place of schools within it. Holt discusses education in terms of the job market and the alienation of workers and shows that the prime function of schools is at cross purposes with our system of universal compulsory education. Schools that serve to keep children off the streets, out of the way, that channel kids into streams of winners and losers, that indoctrinate rather than stimulate cannot serve children. He envisions a deschooled society—one in which people learn what they need and want to know. "Holt has what so many writers on education lack, an easy and most readable style. It is a splendid book about fifty years ahead of its time."— A. S. Neill, author of *Summerhill*. "John Holt . . . is a major spokesman for the reform movement in American education."—*Time* $1.75

*Also by John Holt*

☐ **WHAT DO I DO MONDAY?**  $1.75  9584-21

☐ **THE UNDERACHIEVING SCHOOL**  $1.25  9160-07

☐ **HOW CHILDREN FAIL**  $1.50  3869-04

☐ **HOW CHILDREN LEARN**  $1.25  3871-00

At your local bookstore or use this handy coupon for ordering:

| | |
|---|---|
| **Dell** | **DELL BOOKS**<br>**P.O. BOX 1000, PINEBROOK, N.J. 07058** |

Please send me the books I have checked above. I am enclosing $_____ (please add 35¢ per copy to cover postage and handling). Send check or money order—no cash or C.O.D.'s. Please allow up to 8 weeks for shipment.

Mr/Mrs/Miss_____

Address_____

City_____State/Zip_____

*An invaluable resource!*

# DICTIONARY OF PSYCHOLOGY

## by J.P. Chaplin

This clear reference details the many techniques and varieties of psychological thought. It includes:

- Definitions of terms
- Descriptions of movements
- Discussions of leaders in the field
- Extended articles for special names and topics
- Illustrations
- Appendices
- Symbols, formulas, and combining forms

and more! A must for anyone with an interest in psychology!

## A LAUREL EDITION $1.95

At your local bookstore or use this handy coupon for ordering:

**Dell** | **DELL BOOKS**  Dict. of Psych. $1.95 (31926-9)
**P.O. BOX 1000, PINEBROOK, N.J. 07058**

Please send me the above title. I am enclosing $_____
(please add 35¢ per copy to cover postage and handling). Send check or money order—no cash or C.O.D.'s. Please allow up to 8 weeks for shipment.

Mr/Mrs/Miss_____

Address_____

City_____ State/Zip_____

# IN 1918 AMERICA FACED AN ENERGY CRISIS

**UNCLE SAM NEEDS THAT EXTRA SHOVELFUL**

Help Uncle Sam o Win the War
by following these Directions

UNITED STATES FUEL ADMINISTRATION

An icy winter gripped the nation. Frozen harbors blocked the movement of coal. Businesses and factories closed. Homes went without heat Prices skyrocketed. It was America's first energy crisis now long since forgotten, like the winter of '76-'77 and the oil embargo of '73-'74. Unfortunately, forgetting a crisis doesn't solve the problems that cause it. Today, the country is relying too heavily on foreign oil. That reliance is costing us over $40 billion dollars a year Unless we conserve, the world will soon run out of oil, if we don't run out of money first. So the crises of the past may be forgotten, but the energy problems of today and tomorrow remain to be solved. The best solution is the simplest conservation. It's something every American can do.

## ENERGY CONSERVATION -
## IT'S YOUR CHANCE TO SAVE, AMERICA

Department of Energy, Washington, D.C

A PUBLIC SERVICE MESSAGE FROM DELL PUBLISHING CO., INC.